Johnson and
Boswell

HESKETH PEARSON

Johnson and Boswell

THE STORY OF THEIR LIVES

HARPER & BROTHERS, PUBLISHERS, NEW YORK

Pearson, Hesketh, 1887–
     Johnson and Boswell; the story of their lives. New
York, Harper ₁1959, ᶜ1958₎
     390 p.   illus.   22 cm.
     Includes bibliography.

     1. Johnson, Samuel, 1709–1784. 2. Boswell, James, 1740–1795.

                    Full name: Edward Hesketh Gibbons Pearson.

PR3533.P34   928.2   58–8862 ‡
Library of Congress

Contents

CONTENTS

Illustrations

Johnson and Boswell

CHAPTER I

The Depression of Poverty

"POOR PEOPLE'S CHILDREN never respect them," said Samuel Johnson towards the end of his life: "I did not respect my own mother, though I loved her; and one day, when in anger she called me a puppy, I asked her if she knew what they called a puppy's mother."

From which it is clear that the child possessed four of the main characteristics afterwards noticeable in the man: a passion for truth, an affectionate disposition, a ready wit, and a love of power mostly manifested by scoring the last point in a debate.

Michael Johnson, his father, was about fifty years of age, Sarah, his mother, thirty-seven, when they married. Michael's parents had belonged to the poorest class of labourers, and a local charity had enabled him to serve as an apprentice to a stationer in London. In 1681 he started business as a book-seller at Lichfield. His trade prospered. Soon he had branches or bookstalls at Uttoxeter, Ashby-de-la-Zouch, Birmingham and elsewhere, while the literate gentlemen of the neighbour-hood depended on him for their books and sometimes for his advice about their purchases. At the time of his marriage in 1706 he was a substantial member of the community, and two years later he began to build himself a house in the market place, becoming a sheriff of the city in 1709. He was then a tall, stout man, pious and melancholy by temperament, positive in opinion, active, industrious and obstinate. His wife Sarah came from a different social class. Her father Cornelius Ford was a farmer, and some of her relations belonged to such

respectable professions as medicine and the law. Their dissimilar family connections caused much friction in the home of
Michael and Sarah, for the wife did not allow the husband to
forget that she came from superior stock. But his business in
other towns always gave him an excuse for mounting his horse
and taking the road when feeling depressed by his genealogical
inferiority. Apart from this fretful trait in her character, Sarah
seems to have been a good-natured soul, honest, charitable, a
careful housekeeper, a considerate mother.

She was forty years old when their first son Samuel was born
on 7th September (Old Style), 1709.[1] Being a short, slight
woman, her labours were arduous and perilous, and when at
last Samuel appeared he was more dead than alive. Since his
survival was considered unlikely, his christening took place
within a few hours. The baby was sent to a wet-nurse in the
parish of St. Chad's, and it is possible that the scrofula from
which he suffered thereafter, as well as the blindness in one eye
and the deafness in one ear, were due to what his godfather
called "the bad humours of the nurse", though his mother
believed that they were inherited from her family. She visited
him every day, going there and coming back by different routes
to avoid the ridicule of her neighbours, and she would often
reappear unexpectedly at the nurse's cottage to make sure her
baby was not being neglected the moment her back was turned,
making the excuse that she had forgotten her glove or her fan.
He was taken home in ten weeks, his appearance being such
that his aunt declared she would not have picked up such a
poor creature in the street.

He suffered the usual medical attention of the time and was
subjected to the usual superstitions. The disease of the glands
called scrofula was then known as 'the King's Evil', and many
infants were taken to London to be 'touched' by the monarch,

---

[1] This became 18th September after the New Style had been introduced
into England on 3rd September 1752, which day was called the 14th of
that month.

whose divine right of succession was supposed to include curative powers of a miraculous nature. The ceremony had lapsed since the reign of William III, whose right to rule had been determined by Parliament instead of God, but it was revived by Queen Anne to stress her Stuart ancestry at a time when many Jacobites favoured the direct male line and claimed James the Second's son as their rightful King. A number of scrofulous children were said to have been cured by this means, and the excitement of the occasion may have helped nature to produce the desired effect; but at least the parents enjoyed the trip to town and a sight of Majesty.

Sam and his mother made the three-day journey to London from Lichfield by coach when he was two and a half years old. On the way he became sick, which revolted one woman passenger but caused another to comfort and croon over him. They stayed with a bookseller in Little Britain, and Sam's mother, severely economical by nature and necessity, burgeoned into luxury, buying for the child a speckled linen frock and a small silver cup and spoon, with two teaspoons for herself. In the company of some two hundred other infants Sam was duly 'touched' at St. James's Palace by Queen Anne, who also placed around his neck a white ribbon attached to a thin gold medal, a decoration he never ceased to wear as a charm. In after years he retained a vague and solemn memory of the Queen as "a lady in diamonds and a long black hood". To make up for her burst of luxury in London, Sam's mother took him back to Lichfield in a stage wagon. She was pregnant at the time, and her second son Nathaniel was born a few months after their return home.

In the summer of 1712, Michael Johnson became a magistrate and Brother of the Lichfield Corporation, a body which controlled the city's affairs. But Michael, however efficient as a magistrate, could not control his own affairs. He never troubled to keep accounts, never knew what profits he was making, never considered his living expenses. He had contracted debts in the early years and failed to pay them off because all his money went to the support of his establishment. He refused to discuss the state of his finances with his wife, who, unable to talk about books, did not want to discuss anything else. As a consequence, she was full of complaints and suspicions, while he was usually resentful and morose. It was not a congenial domestic atmosphere for the children.

Sam loved his mother, who gave him coffee when she could ill afford it, taught him how to read and write, and explained the difference between heaven and hell. She also introduced him to fairy tales, which delighted him so much that when, many years later, they were discarded in nurseries for moral tales like 'Goody Two Shoes', he exclaimed: "Babies do not want to hear about babies; they like to be told of giants and castles, and of somewhat which can stretch and stimulate their little minds." When told that the edifying stories sold well, he remained unimpressed: "Remember always that the parents *buy* the books, and that the children never read them."

He had little love for his father, whose preoccupation with trade and debts and household expenses left scarcely any time for the instruction or entertainment of his children. Indeed the boy's real objection to his father was that the child had to entertain the parent. Sam was a precocious youngster with a phenomenal memory, and his father enjoyed exhibiting his accomplishments to the neighbours. After a certain amount of petting and kissing, Sam was expected to show off on social occasions; and at last he came to loathe his father's caresses because they preluded a display of his mental alertness in one form or another. Many times on the arrival of visitors he escaped these dreaded displays by climbing a tree and remaining out of sight until the danger was over. "That is the great misery of late marriages," he once declared; "the unhappy produce of them becomes the plaything of dotage: an old man's child leads much such a life as a little boy's dog, teased with

4

awkward fondness and forced to sit up and beg to divert a company, who at last go away complaining of their disagreeable entertainment." He never forgot the discomfort to which he had been subjected, and many years after, when a proud father proposed that his two boys should repeat the verses in Gray's *Elegy* alternately so that their individual diction could be compared, Johnson demurred: "No, pray, sir, let the dears both speak it at once; more noise will by that means be made, and the noise will be sooner over."

Like every intelligent boy with a marked individuality, he hated enforced instruction, and he did well at school not because he liked learning lessons but because he disliked punishment, while his remarkable memory made learning easy. He once admitted that he had never worked willingly in his life, as man or boy, nor had he ever made a real effort to do his best, except three times whilst at school when fear of the rod or a desire to excel drove him to make it. He grew up with the firm conviction that children resented being taught what they did not want to know and that such teaching was valueless. Nothing could be learnt, he declared, unless the interest of the pupil were engaged, and "no attention can be obtained from children without the infliction of pain". This was his own experience, for he was naturally indolent and seldom worked without compulsion.

His formal education began in a dame's school; then he received instruction from an ex-shoemaker who had published a spelling-book and dedicated it to 'the Universe', which failed to appreciate the honour, no copy having survived. After that, Sam went to Lichfield Grammar School in his eighth year. At first he was taught by the under-master, Humphrey Hawkins, who ran the lower school for over fifty years at an annual salary of ten pounds, and somehow managed to support a wife and family on his master's pay and what he received for a few odd jobs such as keeping church accounts and washing clerical linen. He must have recognised that Sam was an exceptional pupil, for he "indulged and caressed" the boy, who painlessly picked up his knowledge of Latin. Over two years were spent with Hawkins, and then Sam moved to the upper school, where he came under the eye of the headmaster, John Hunter, a thorough scholar and a sound flagellator. In those days the beating of boys was almost a routine occupation, and the victims did not hesitate to continue the treatment when they had to control their own offspring or pupils. But Hunter overdid it, abandoning himself to the enjoyment of corporal punishment and thrashing his boys without bothering to find out whether they were ignorant or negligent. If a lad failed to answer any question whatever, he received a whipping, though it was obvious that if he had known all the answers he would not have needed a master to teach him. While engaged in the pastime of flogging, Hunter would sometimes say "This I do to save you from the gallows." Perhaps it is unnecessary to add that he was in holy orders and generally regarded as an excellent headmaster, though Johnson called him "so brutal that no man who had been educated by him ever sent his son to the same school." He has, however, the credit of being the only person who ever managed to frighten Sam, for his granddaughter Anna Seward resembled him in appearance, and the mere sight of her sometimes made the ageing Johnson quake.

Though inattentive to his lessons, Sam did well enough at school on account of his memory. He would lazily leave his tasks to the last moment and then accomplish them in the time most boys took to commence the process of cerebration. Whatever he attempted he did easily, impressing his schoolfellows so much with what appeared to them uncanny powers that they tried to obtain his assistance in their own labours, three of them going to the length of calling for him in the mornings and taking it in turns to carry him on their shoulders to school. Partly owing to shortsightedness he never joined in their sports, except during a hard winter when he allowed them, barefooted, to draw him along the ice; but his talk in school diverted them

6

from their lessons and he received the envious admiration usually aroused by mental superiority. For getting himself or those he favoured out of any scholastic difficulty he relied entirely on his memory, which was so exceptional that after a single reading or hearing he could repeat verbatim whole pages of prose and poetry, both English and Latin. Throughout life his reading of a thing was tantamount to memorising it. During the holidays, when other boys were playing games or enjoying some form of collective amusement, he preferred the company of a select friend, with whom he wandered in the fields, some-times conversing with his companion but usually talking to himself.

One of his friends was Edmund Hector, who eventually be-came a surgeon in Birmingham and for whom Johnson main-tained an affection to the end of his life. Another was John Taylor, who became a clergyman and lived comfortably at Ashbourne in Derbyshire on the endowments of several bene-fices, but displayed more interest in the breeding of cattle than in the cure of souls. With him too Johnson remained on terms of friendship, visiting him several times in later years. Sam never managed to become friendly with his younger brother Nathaniel, but in youth the difference of three years is con-siderable. There was rivalry between them for the attention and affection of their mother, and no doubt the elder boy took advantage of his seniority and size, because Nathaniel once complained that Sam had scarcely ever shown him common civility. Nathaniel did not suffer from his brother's fits of melancholia or physical disabilities, but was apparently a hearty and convivial fellow who could stand any amount of discomfort without noticing it, for when he had been working a few years in his father's business he heard some people speaking of the badness of the roads and remarked that though he had travelled about the country more than most folk he had never seen a bad road in his life. As a young man he must have done something to upset his mother, because in a letter to her he referred to his 'crimes' which had given both her and himself so much trouble, and implied that he would shortly emigrate to Georgia. The 'crimes' probably consisted of spending sums he had collected from his father's customers. He never left England, but died at about the age of twenty-five. Over forty years after his death Sam applied to a female acquaintance at Frome in Somerset for personal details of Nathaniel, who had resided there for less than a year in 1736–7: "He was likely enough to attract notice while he stayed as a lively noisy man that loved company. His memory might probably continue for some time in some favourite alehouse." With characteristic reserve, Sam did not describe Nathaniel in this letter as his brother, but as a near relative.

The feeling of antipathy between the brothers contributed to the disharmony of home life. "The poor and the busy have no leisure for sentimental sorrow," Johnson said, and he might have added that his parents had neither the time nor the inclination to indulge his affectionate nature. There must have been a lot of nagging in the household, Sarah scolding her boys for their behaviour without telling them how to behave, Michael complaining of his debts without making a serious effort to live within his means, yet discouraging his wife from receiving neighbours or paying them visits because he could not afford the price of tea. His early experience of domesticity left an indelible impression on Sam, who never ceased to inveigh against parental authority, always sympathised with sons and daughters in their conflicts with fathers and mothers, and ridiculed the notion that young people should obey their parents over such questions as marriage or even respect their opinions when opposed to their own. It is doubtful whether the religious instruction he received from his mother or father had much effect on such a strongly marked individuality as his; though it happened that the inherent gloom of his disposition reflected the Calvinistic teaching of Sarah, while the romantic side of his nature responded to the High Church and Tory

8

Jacobitism of Michael. Being much fonder of his mother than of his father, he believed that the most deplorable element in his constitution, the hypochondria, was attributable to the latter.

CHAPTER 2

Self-Education

SAM'S NATIVE DEPRESSION was temporarily dissipated at the age of sixteen when his cousin Cornelius Ford came to stay with them in order to settle some question of Sarah's dowry. Cornelius was a mundane parson of thirty-one, who had been the companion of light wits and heavy drinkers. Like Justice Shallow, he had "heard the chimes at midnight", had known "where the bona robas were", and no doubt had "had the best of them all at commandment." Having lived with aristocrats as well as poets, he could talk the language of one class and repeat the verses of the other. He belonged to a world far removed from the humdrum life of a provincial bookshop and was just the type of man to appeal to an ambitious youngster yearning for something that did not distantly remind him of beatings at school, bickerings at home, and beggary at both. It so happened that Cornelius was passing through a respectable phase. Having run through his money in London, he had recently married a woman thirteen years his senior, had paid off his pressing debts with part of her fortune, had taken holy orders, and was living a quiet life at Pedmore, near Stourbridge in Worcestershire. He was therefore in a mood to talk of life and literature to an intelligent and appreciative youth, to show off his stores of learning and knowledge of the world, and he asked Sam to pay him a visit at Pedmore. Sam went, and his eyes were opened to a new earth, if not a new heaven. He met all sorts of interesting people, including the Lytteltons of Hagley Park near-by, and learnt, or tried to learn, how to comport himself in elegant society. His own conversational faculty was disclosed and developed in these novel and stimulating surroundings, and the period he spent in the home of Cornelius was one of the happiest and most inspiriting he ever experienced. When term-time came round he refused to leave, and six months elapsed before he presented himself at Lichfield Grammar School. To his intense relief Hunter rejected the truant, and with the help of Cornelius he obtained admission to Stourbridge School, where he spent about half a year, writing a certain amount of poetry, bothering little about his lessons, and making no attempt to placate his master. A renewal of pupillage must have been excessively tedious after his relatively Capuan life with Cornelius, who, by the way, returned in due course to his drinking and drabbing companions in London, being portrayed by Hogarth in 'A Midnight Modern Conversation' as the parson officiating at the punch-bowl.

Leaving Stourbridge School at the close of 1726, Sam returned home. Though his father was now senior bailiff of the city, debts were more pressing than ever and there was no money for the elder boy to prepare for a profession at one of the universities. But he prepared himself for the life he was to lead far more effectively than he could have done at Oxford or Cambridge. Apparently he helped in the shop, and even in the parchment factory which his father owned near Stowe Pool, for he learnt a good deal about book-binding and tanning; but most of his time was spent in reading whatever he fancied, both ancient and modern, especially the Latin authors. He cannot have been a good salesman of books, once confessing that he was never able "to supersede the pleasures of reading by the attentions of traffic". It is more than probable that customers were discouraged from buying such works as he wished to reserve for his own perusal, and his father frequently complained of his neglect of valued patrons. But as a consequence of the two years he spent at home apparently idling he acquired an extensive knowledge of literature, which with the help of his prodigious memory was of immeasurable value for the work he was destined to do.

His recent familiarity with social circles in the Stourbridge neighbourhood had fitted him to mix with Lichfield society, and his ability as a talker made him a welcome guest at the house of Gilbert Walmesley, who lived at the Bishop's Palace in the Cathedral Close and was some thirty years his senior. Like Cornelius Ford, this new acquaintance "had mingled with the gay world without exemption from its vices or its follies". Like Ford, too, he had become respectable in his habits and pious in his opinions; but unlike Ford he never reverted to the laxness of his youth. His erudition was profound, his conversation copious, and so greatly did the youngster benefit from his kindness and company that over half a century later Johnson wrote: "It may be doubted whether a day now passes in which I have not some advantage from his friendship." Walmesley's benevolent behaviour and acute recognition of Sam's worth were especially commendable because the former was a keen Whig in politics and yet could patiently endure from a youth those assertions of Jacobitical Toryism that would have enraged him from a man of his own age and class. Another budding genius later to be found at Walmesley's table was David Garrick, some seven years junior to Johnson. Though Garrick's parents lived at Lichfield, they belonged to a different social stratum from the Johnsons', and it is fairly certain that the friendship between Sam and David started at the Bishop's Palace two or three years after the commencement of Walmesley's hospitality to the bookseller's boy.

His dinners and talks at Walmesley's and his meetings with the more literate and prosperous members of the community deepened his disgust with the penury and pettiness of home life, alienating him still more from his father, and it was about this period that he behaved in a manner later to be repented. On market days Michael Johnson visited Uttoxeter to sell books at a stall, and during an illness he asked his son to go instead. "My pride prevented me from doing my duty and I gave my father a refusal," Sam confessed. To expiate his act he visited Uttoxeter on market day fifty years later and stood with bared head for an hour before the same stall, exposed to the derision of the bystanders. He hoped by this penance to propitiate heaven for a single instance of filial disobedience. Fortunately heaven was in a baptismal mood, and it rained steadily during his hour of atonement.

There is a story that an old schoolfellow supplied Sam with the funds to continue his education at Oxford University, but as he remained there for only just over a year it is probable that he maintained himself on a forty-pounds legacy of his mother's, which enabled him to enter Pembroke College as a commoner at the age of nineteen. He started badly with his Tutor, William Jorden, a kindly man but apparently a bore, one of whose lectures on logic was enough to secure Sam's absence from the next four; and when Jorden demanded an explanation, Sam coolly replied that he had been sliding in Christ Church meadow. But Jorden had a forgiving nature and soon they were on good terms. The main subject that engaged Sam's attention at Oxford was Greek, chiefly Homer and Euripides, but as usual his studies and the performance of his tasks were of a desultory nature. He scarcely ever read a book right through from cover to cover in his life, but he had the faculty of seizing the essence of any work of literature by judicious skipping.

His wit and knowledge impressed his contemporaries, who often abandoned their labours to enjoy his conversation, and he joined in their frolics. By order of the Master one of the servitors used to go round the rooms at a certain hour and knock at the doors, reporting the absence of those who did not answer. Sam disliked the habit and sometimes would not acknowledge his presence when summoned to do so. He revenged what he thought an ignominy by joining others in the sport of hunting the servitor, to the accompaniment of yells and songs and the banging of pots and pans, not seldom endangering the life and limbs of the victim, who turned and doubled like a hare being coursed. As time went on, and Sam's means of subsistence fell off, poverty became apparent in his footwear and apparel; and it did not please him when he found a new pair of shoes outside his chamber one morning, placed there by a well-meaning though tactless gentleman-commoner. He flung them away in a rage.

His circumstances at Oxford induced a rebellious mood in Sam for the only time in his life. Hearing in after years that a junior Fellow of his time had described him as gay, frolicsome and happy while at Oxford, he exclaimed: "I was rude and violent. It was bitterness which they mistook for frolic. I was miserably poor, and I thought to fight my way by my literature and my wit; so I disregarded all power and all authority." His defiance and discontent took the usual forms: he treated reprimands with contempt, informing Jorden that he had been paid twopence "for non-attendance at a lecture not worth a penny"; and he went out of his way to annoy the Tutors and Fellows. But sometimes his combativeness, his desire to astonish, took a more scholarly turn. At a hint from his Tutor he translated Pope's *Messiah* into Latin verse, knocking off one hundred and nineteen lines in a day. Everyone was amazed and Sam must have been sufficiently elated to send a copy home, because Michael published it without obtaining permission from his son, whose excessive anger revealed a long-felt resentment at his parent's endeavours to make him exhibit his cleverness in company. If anyone but his father had done such a thing, Sam exploded, he would have cut his throat. This sentiment was hardly in accord with the pious views he had encountered in William Law's *Serious Call to a Devout and Holy Life*, a book he came across at Oxford and which is supposed to have turned his thoughts seriously to religion. But his was not the kind of nature to be greatly influenced by reading. What he found in books he brought to them. Law's *Serious Call* came to a mind ready to hear it.

At the end of a year he had not paid his fees for a term and was practically penniless. He determined to go home, no doubt to see if he could raise enough money to prolong his stay at the university. Certainly he hoped to return, because he left his books with an old schoolfellow, John Taylor, then at Christ Church. One morning early in December 1729, after a total residence of thirteen months at Oxford, he left for Lichfield, accompanied by Taylor as far as Banbury. He hoped to be back at the end of the vacation, but it was nearly twenty-five years before he saw Pembroke College again.

CHAPTER 3

Morbidity and Marriage

BY HIS OWN CONFESSION Johnson suffered continuous ill-health from his twentieth year onwards, and he seldom enjoyed "a single day of ease" from the time he left Oxford at the age of twenty to the end of his life. This chronic condition of mind and body must be remembered whenever his behaviour appears intemperate; especially the state of his mind, which at times seemed to be deranged. He had inherited melancholia, doubtless from innumerable depressed ancestors, and his belief that his fits of something like insanity came solely from his father was curiously naïve. Indeed the illustration he gave of his father's madness displays his own mental aberration. When Michael's factory at Stowe Pool had become partly ruined for want of money to repair it, he locked the front door every night on leaving it, though there was nothing to prevent anyone from gaining entrance through the dilapidated back. "This was madness," said his son. But it was simply habit, established by preoccupation, or absence, not confusion, of mind. If everybody who acted in a thoughtless manner and did unnecessary things were to be adjudged mad, the large majority of the world's population could be certified as mentally unfit.

Johnson's own peculiarities were far more pronounced than his father's, being intensified by a vivid imagination.

> Great wits are sure to madness near allied
> And thin partitions do their bounds divide

wrote Dryden, and the partitions were thinner in Johnson's case because the activity of his fancy, operating upon his innate gloom, opened up all sorts of dreadful ideas, creating in him a terror of the unknown and a recurrent apprehension of mental breakdown, while the Calvinistic strain in his religion sometimes made him feel predestined to lunacy in this world and hell in the next.

The disorder first became acute on leaving Oxford and he tried to check it by violent exercise, walking to and from Birmingham and elsewhere, sometimes covering more than thirty miles in a day. The virulence of his disease at this time was no doubt partly due to poverty, his inability to return to the university and pursue the studies necessary to a profession and a degree, the pessimism caused by a hopeless outlook. Conscious of his gifts, he yet saw no chance of earning a living by their exercise. He wrote a full account of his mental case in Latin and gave it to his godfather, Dr. Swinfen, who was so much struck by the cogency of the performance that he showed it to several friends. Johnson got to hear that his extremely confidential statement had been seen by others, and after a heated expostulation his relationship with Swinfen cooled.

For some eighteen months he exercised his body with walking and at intervals his mind with verses, though when asked by a benevolently-disposed friend for a short poem he replied that "versifying against one's inclination is the most disagreeable thing in the world". He occasionally helped his father, whose business was going from bad to worse and could not have been improved by the dejected demeanour and desultory habits of his son. In the summer of 1731 the young man made an effort to obtain a position as master at Stourbridge Grammar School, but having no degree he was rejected. In December of that year his father died, his mother and brother keeping on the business. Some months later he received £20 from his father's estate, which he said was all he could hope for until the death of his mother, "which I pray may be late." It was now vitally necessary that he should secure employment, and through the influence of friends he was given the job of assistant master, or 'usher' as it was called, at the Grammar School of Market Bosworth in Leicestershire. He was compelled to live at Bosworth Hall, the house of the school's patron, Sir Wolstan Dixie, where he acted the part of domestic chaplain, saying grace at the meals of the household. Dixie was an ignorant bully who made life so intolerable for the wretched usher that Johnson always spoke of the months there with horror. At the school one day was the same as another, he told his friend Hector, and he did not know whether it was more disagreeable for him to teach, or the boys to learn, the nonsensical rules of Greek and Latin grammar. Four months of it were four months too many, and he returned to Lichfield in July 1731. After attempting but failing to get a mastership at Ashbourne School, he resigned himself to the shop, to study, and to despondency.

There were brighter moments during these years of mental gloom, such alleviations being due to women. His appearance was not attractive; the scars of scrofula and the pittings of small-pox disfigured his face; mental preoccupation made him clumsy in movement, negligent in manner, spasmodic in gesture; while poverty showed in his dress. But when he spoke, such exterior things were forgotten, his manner and voice being especially ingratiating when he wished to please a woman whose looks or conversation pleased him. The order and periods are uncertain, but perhaps the first girl to excite his tender feelings was his friend Hector's sister. The next may have been Lucy Porter, whose aunt had married Johnson's schoolmaster, Hunter, and who was on a visit to Lichfield from her native Birmingham, where her father was a mercer. But Sam's deepest emotion was aroused by Molly Aston, whose sister was married to Gilbert Walmesley and who frequently stayed at the Bishop's Palace. Molly echoed the Whiggish views of her family, but her vivacity more than compensated for her opinions and the young Tory was enraptured by her company. Many

years later he said: "I wonder when anybody ever experiences measureless delight. *I* never did, I'm sure, except the first evening I spent tête-à-tête with Molly Aston." Another woman who engaged his more platonic affection at a rather later date was Miss Hill Boothby, of Ashbourne. She was an intensely religious person, of a Methodistical turn of mind, who could read the scriptures in Hebrew. Johnson admired her intelligence and her virtue, and for a long time kept up a correspondence with her; but when, some twenty years after their early friendship, she hoped to convert him to her way of thinking in spiritual matters and sent him a book to that end, he replied: "My Sweet Angel. . . . In all things that terminate here I shall be much guided by your influence, and should take or leave by your direction, but I cannot receive my religion from any human hand."

Edmund Hector, now a surgeon in Birmingham, asked Johnson to pay him a visit in the autumn of 1732, and what may have been envisaged as a fortnight's holiday was expanded to a stay of six months in Hector's lodgings, which were in the house of a bookseller, Thomas Warren, near the Swan Inn. Hector knew a lot of people in the neighbourhood, and his guest enjoyed the social round. Among others, he was introduced to the mercer, Henry Porter, and his wife Elizabeth, whose daughter Lucy had attracted Sam at Lichfield. Mrs. Porter expressed herself as charmed by the visitor's conversation and thought him the most sensible man she had ever met. She was a plump, blonde, lively woman, some twenty years his senior; and though her manners were arch and she affected elegance her cheerfulness and common sense appealed to Johnson. Apart from some pieces which he wrote for Warren's local newspaper, *The Birmingham Journal,* he led an idle life, and Hector felt that unless his friend had something to occupy his mind he would go melancholy-mad. Discontent made him quarrelsome and after spending six months at Hector's expense he went into lodgings by himself. Here he began to work on a

French translation of a Portuguese Jesuit's *Voyage to Abyssinia,* which he had read at Oxford. Both Warren and Hector urged him to produce an English version; but indolence overcame him and he stopped work after the first part had gone to the printer. If Hector had not assured him that the poor printer's family would suffer as a consequence of his neglect, he would not have finished the job. As it was, Hector wrote the remainder, Johnson dictating from his bed. The proofs were corrected by his amanuensis; the book came out in 1735; and Warren paid five guineas for his reluctant labour.

He returned to Lichfield in February 1734, still unsettled in mind and prospects. In August he issued a printed prospectus appealing for subscribers to a cheap edition of the Latin poems of Politian; but so few people seemed anxious to read them that he abandoned the scheme. His outlook at the age of twenty-five was bleak, but it brightened after the death of Henry Porter that autumn. Where sex is concerned the attraction of youth to middle-age is almost as common as that of middle-age to youth. Elizabeth Porter was not the sort of person to pine for her dead husband. Sufficiently juvenile at the age of forty-five to enjoy life, and flattered by the attentions of a clever, entertaining fellow young enough to be her son, she was easily persuaded to join hands with Johnson; while he, potent but chaste, saw in her the satisfaction of his physical needs as well as one who could share his thoughts and sympathise with his condition. But, apart from such mutual benefits, they had probably fallen in love with one another before the death of her husband. The fact that she possessed over six hundred pounds contributed to the speediness of the present engagement, but did not influence their decision. Johnson is one of the few people in history whose word may be taken on such a point. "Sir, it was a love marriage on both sides," he told a friend long afterwards, and that he appreciated the full meaning of the term is shown in his remark that "those who never were in love never were happy".

We may assume that on hearing of her widowhood Johnson at once found an excuse to revisit Birmingham, whence, not three months after Porter's death, he made a serious attempt to live by his pen, explaining in a letter to Edward Cave, founder and editor of *The Gentleman's Magazine*, exactly how the periodical could be improved, suggesting himself as the man to do it, and giving his name as 'S. Smith', hoping no doubt that Cave would guess someone of note behind the pseudonym. But Cave did not need the advice of Smith, and Johnson turned his thoughts once more to teaching, getting a job as private tutor in a family near Lichfield. Neither his mother nor Mrs. Porter's relations favoured the match. One of her sons never saw her again, the other remained hostile for many years, but her daughter Lucy took a friendly view of the project and in time became deeply attached to her stepfather. Johnson's mother expressed amazement when he asked for the maternal blessing: "No, Sam, my willing consent you will never have to so preposterous a union. You are not twenty-five and she is turned fifty. If she had any prudence, this request had never been made to me. Where are your means of subsistence? Porter has died poor, in consequence of his wife's expensive habits. You have great talents, but as yet have turned them into no profitable channel." Sam retorted: "Mother, I have not deceived Mrs. Porter; I have told her the worst of me: that I am of mean extraction; that I have no money; and that I have had an uncle hanged. She replied that she valued no one more or less for his descent; that she had no more money than myself; and that, though she had not had a relation hanged, she had fifty who deserved hanging." Which explains at least part of the lady's attraction for a man who enjoyed a well-turned phrase.

While tutoring, Johnson was busy making arrangements for opening a school of his own, though he had not altogether relinquished the hope of obtaining a position elsewhere. Hearing that the headmaster of Solihull School would shortly be leaving, he asked Gilbert Walmesley to put his name forward as a successor. But the governors of the school made full enquiries, and though they heard that he was an excellent scholar they also learned that he had "the character of being a very haughty, ill-natured gent" with "such a way of distorting his face" that the boys under his control might be affected thereby. This refusal confirmed Johnson's decision to start a school where his nature and mannerisms would not be subjected to the criticism of employers. Helped by Walmesley, he took a large house at Edial, near Lichfield, which was duly furnished and adapted to the needs of a boarding-school.

During the preliminary stages of these arrangements Johnson's marriage with Elizabeth Porter (henceforth to be known by Sam's pet name of 'Tetty') took place at St. Werburgh's Church, Derby, on 9th July 1735, some ten months after the death of her first husband. Obviously they decided not to be married at Birmingham or Lichfield because of antagonism in the home-town of the bride and ridicule in that of the bridegroom. They went on horseback to Derby, and Johnson's account of the journey would have seemed curious to Romeo, if commonplace to Petruchio:

"Sir, she had read the old romances, and had got into her head the fantastical notion that a woman of spirit should use her lover like a dog. So, sir, at first she told me that I rode too fast and she could not keep up with me, and when I rode a little slower she passed me and complained that I lagged behind. I was not to be made the slave of caprice, and I resolved to begin as I meant to end. I therefore pushed on briskly till I was fairly out of her sight. The road lay between two hedges, so I was sure she could not miss it, and I contrived that she should soon come up with me. When she did, I observed her to be in tears."

The boarding-school at Edial was ready that autumn, but there were very few boarders. Three are known to have resorted to Johnson for instruction: David Garrick (aged eighteen), his brother George, and a fellow called Offely. There may have been two or three more; but had there been twenty, Johnson's time and that of his pupils were wasted. He was much too intelligent to be a schoolmaster or routineer of any description, and his oddities aroused risibility instead of reverence in the boys. In the years ahead David Garrick reduced many drinking parties to helpless laughter with imitations of Johnson making ponderous and awkward love to Tetty, founded on observations through the bedroom keyhole, and exhibitions of Johnson reciting from a play while absent-mindedly mistaking the bed-clothes for his shirt and tucking them into his breeches, to the accompaniment of Tetty's frantic attempts to retrieve them and cover herself up. Garrick's pleasant fancies were perhaps founded on the fact that Johnson's affection for his wife was occasionally noticeable and his ungainly mannerisms were frequently in evidence. But the master was too frightening a figure to be ragged by the boys, and David himself was aware of an occasion when Johnson had summarily dealt with im-pertinence at the Lichfield Guildhall. Sitting in the wings during the performance of a play, Johnson had temporarily vacated his chair, to find it occupied on his return by an inn-keeper who refused to relinquish it when politely asked to do so; whereupon Johnson picked up man and chair and flung them both into the pit. David had no desire to share the innkeeper's experience and behaved himself at Edial, though his inattention to the classics and his love of writing comic scenes evoked a prophecy from his master. "Pray, sir, what is your opinion of my son David?" asked Mrs. Garrick. "Why, madam, David will either be hanged or become a great man," replied Johnson.

The Edial venture lasted scarcely eighteen months. Johnson again applied for an assistant-mastership at a grammar school but was again refused. Tetty's money had vanished in the speculation, and all that they had to show for it was the better part of a blank-verse tragedy, *Irene*, written in his spare time. He decided to try his luck in London; and as David Garrick was to continue his training for the Bar at Rochester, they made the journey together. Tetty and her daughter remained behind while Johnson explored the possibilities of the metropolis. Sam and David set forth on the great adventure that would end in so much fame for both of them on 2nd March 1737, possibly taking it in turns to ride a single horse. Many years later, at a large dinner-party, Johnson happened to refer to the time when he came to London with twopence halfpenny in his pocket. Garrick expostulated: "Eh? what do you say? With twopence halfpenny in your pocket?" "Why, yes," answered Johnson, "when I came with twopence halfpenny in *my* pocket, and thou, Davy, with three halfpence in thine."

CHAPTER 4

The Tide of Life

THE LONDON of Johnson's early years was a foul and lawless place. It was as full of garbage as of thieves. Henry Fielding had not yet tackled the gangster element within the city; Dick Turpin was still at large on the outskirts; and murderers lurked in obscene alleys. Filth of every kind was flung into the gutters and lay rotting there; the kennels that were supposed to drain off the refuse were constantly choked with offal; and foot passengers had to dodge the excremental and other waste matter discharged indiscriminately from windows by heedless housewives. The whole city reeked and stank, and it took some time for the nostrils of a newcomer to become habituated to the effluvia. Mad dogs and frantic cows not infrequently added to the risks of pedestrians, whose lives were further imperilled by the lack of pavements and the onset of vehicles which almost touched the houses as they careered along the street.

It does not appear that Johnson was greatly perturbed by the dangers and odours of the place, or by witnessing the pillory, the gallows, the decapitated heads on Temple Bar, or the vile behaviour of mobs; but he was distressed by the prevalent poverty, the more so because he shared it. He certainly had above twopence halfpenny in his pocket on arrival, but he cannot have had enough to feel the pleasure of idleness, for he soon borrowed some money from a bookseller, who, on hearing that he intended to earn his living as an author, eyed his massive physique and suggested that he would do better as a porter. At first he might have done better as a porter; he could scarcely have done worse. Taking a lodging in Exeter Street, Strand, he dined at a tavern near-by: "I had a cut of meat for sixpence, and bread for a penny, and gave the waiter a penny, so that I was quite well served, nay, better than the rest, for they gave the waiter nothing." The company at the tavern was good but anonymous, no one knowing the name of anyone else but most of them knowing the others by sight, and Johnson heard much talk about travel. It happened that Gilbert Walmesley's brother-in-law, Henry Hervey, who had known Johnson while stationed with his regiment at Lichfield, was now living in London and often invited Johnson to his house, where the company was genteel but rakish. The wine flowed liberally and the talk was unrestrained. Johnson enjoyed himself in such surroundings and remembered his entertainment with gratitude. Harry Hervey, said he, "was a vicious man, but very kind to me. If you call a dog 'Hervey' I shall love him."

After four months of wandering about the streets and watching the people and sitting in taverns and dining with the dissolute, Johnson decided to finish his tragedy, and in July 1737 he retired to lodgings in Church Street, Greenwich, near the Golden Hart. He tried to assist composition by walking in the Park, but inspiration flagged and he made another attempt to arouse the interest of Edward Cave, this time signing his own name to a letter wherein he suggested that he should translate the History of the Council of Trent. Probably Cave's reply was friendly enough for Johnson to call at St. John's Gate, Clerkenwell, whence Cave issued *The Gentleman's Magazine*; and their conversation must have encouraged him to anticipate employment on the periodical, for he left London to arrange affairs at Lichfield before settling down with his wife in the capital. He spent three months at Lichfield, where he completed *Irene*, got rid of the house at Edial, and persuaded his step-daughter Lucy Porter to help his mother in the bookshop, his brother Nathaniel having died within a day or two of his departure for London in March. Lucy became very fond of

Sarah Johnson; and though her humour, honesty and shrewd-
ness made her welcome at the houses of the best society in
Lichfield, she would never accept invitations on market-days,
lest 'Granny' should catch cold by serving in the shop. On
such occasions Lucy herself stood behind the counter, friendly
with the customers and not too proud to thank the poorest for
buying a penny battledore.

Somehow, perhaps from the Edial sale, Johnson scraped up
enough money to take Tetty with him to London in October
1737 and to hire lodgings first in Woodstock Street, Hanover
Square, and then in Castle Street, Cavendish Square, a district
which in those days was a health-resort compared with the
purlieus of Fleet Street and the Strand. One of the first things
he did was to read his play in a Strand tavern to Peter Garrick
(David's elder brother), who knew the manager of Drury Lane
Theatre. Peter was impressed, but the manager was not, and
Johnson had to shelve his tragedy for twelve years. Work of
some sort being absolutely necessary, he got into touch with
Cave and started his professional career as a hack journalist.

The son of a Rugby working-man, Cave was expelled from
the local grammar school, became a printer's apprentice,
eventually bought a printing business at St. John's Gate,
Clerkenwell, and in 1731 started the first good monthly magazine to be published in England. Himself not over-gifted with
brains, he had the intelligence to perceive their possession by
others, and gathered around him a motley crew of clever and
needy poets, translators and talkers. His magazine became the
sole interest and object of his life. He "never looked out of the
window", said Johnson, "but with a view to *The Gentleman's
Magazine*." Fat in body, slow in mind, stubborn in purpose,
stingy in payment, industrious as a mole, Cave was the first
man to make a reputable success of a monthly review, and he
managed somehow to retain the liking of his contributors without ever becoming popular with them.

He did not take long to discern the ability of Johnson, whose first considerable poem, *London*, impressed him so much that he agreed to print it if the publisher Robert Dodsley would bring it out. The poem was an imitation of Juvenal's third Satire, which dealt with the evils of Roman life, easily adapted by Johnson to those of London. At first Johnson did not own the authorship, but Cave and Dodsley were not left long in doubt, and the latter paid ten guineas for the copyright. In his first letter to Cave on the subject Johnson said that the author "lies at present under very disadvantageous circumstances of fortune", and the printer at once sent him a donation. *London* was issued in May 1738 and a second edition was soon on sale, but Johnson's condition was not ameliorated and for many years he could have echoed two lines in his poem:

This mournful truth is ev'rywhere confess'd:
SLOW RISES WORTH BY POVERTY DEPRESS'D

Like the first works of so many imaginative men, *London* was extremely critical of the ruling powers, and Alexander Pope admired it so much that when, a year later, Johnson made his last effort to obtain a headmastership (at Appleby in Leicestershire), the great poet of the hour influenced an application to Dean Swift that Johnson should be granted a degree by Dublin University. Nothing came of it; but before wholly abandoning the hope of earning a steady income from a reputable profession, he tried to find out whether he could practise as an advocate in the courts without a doctorate in civil law. "I am a total stranger to these studies," he admitted, "but whatever is a profession, and maintains numbers, must be within the reach of common abilities and some degree of industry." Here again he discovered that a degree was indispensable; and though he was to regret not having made a profession of the law, he was spared many awkward collisions with the judiciary. Thereafter he tried to reconcile himself to the semi-starvation wages of a literary drudge.

One of his jobs in the early forties of the century was to write the reports of parliamentary debates. In those days the House of Commons jealously guarded the secrets of their sessions, and such accounts as appeared in the papers were made up of rough notes taken by reporters on the spot or descriptions from memory by less scrupulous politicians. To avoid legal action, *The Gentleman's Magazine* made slight changes in the names of the speakers and called Parliament 'The Senate of Lilliput'. Johnson never attended debates and was simply supplied with the names of the various debaters and the attitudes they had adopted. His reports were therefore forms of self-expression; and the words he put into the mouths of speakers were so much superior to any that came out of them that there were no protestations. Many years later he heard someone describe a certain speech by William Pitt (afterwards Earl of Chatham) as better than anything by Demosthenes. "That speech I wrote in a garret in Exeter Street," said Johnson, who lived to regret having dealt with the debates, saying that at the time he did not realise that people were taking his fiction for fact. That his fancies are still preferred to truth is proved by a passage in *The Oxford Dictionary of Quotations* ascribed to Pitt the Elder, who answered a parliamentary veteran in Johnson's words:

"Sir, the atrocious crime of being a young man, which the honourable gentleman has with such spirit and decency charged upon me, I shall neither attempt to palliate nor deny, but content myself with wishing that I may be one of those whose follies may cease with their youth, and not of that number who are ignorant in spite of experience."

Other jobs undertaken by Johnson for *The Gentleman's Magazine* were sub-editing, translating, poetising, selecting contributions, judging awards, answering correspondents, and defending the periodical from the attacks of competitors. He was constantly in arrears with the work he had undertaken, and as constantly Cave tried to keep him up to the scratch. He wrote innumerable essays, Greek and Latin epigrams, and several short biographies, those of Sir Francis Drake and

Admiral Blake being noteworthy. In fact he turned his hand to every sort of composition and gradually became the chief factotum of the undertaking. Always in need of money, sometimes in need of a meal, he accepted whatever work was offered; and when the publisher Thomas Osborne, who had just bought the Earl of Oxford's library, asked him to catalogue it, he spent many months on the labour. Osborne was an insolent, vulgar fellow who treated his employees as inferiors and judged people by the amount of money they had. One day he took advantage of Johnson's poverty and insulted him. Whereupon Johnson knocked him down and advised him not to get up in a hurry unless he wished to be kicked downstairs, after which their business relationship ceased.

/ One of Johnson's early acquaintances in journalism was a curious character with whom he formed a close friendship. He was always attracted to the kind of gay, mundane, wanton fellow who knew all about the world, the flesh and the devil, and had an air of good breeding, especially if, having had his fling, he showed some sign of turning over a new leaf. We have already seen how much Johnson liked Ford, Walmesley and Hervey. His new friend, Richard Savage, possessed all these attributes, with something else that never failed to engage Johnson's sympathy: misfortune.

Savage claimed to be the bastard son of Earl Rivers and the Countess of Macclesfield. His putative mother, having got rid of him, pursued him with a vindictive hatred that makes Lady Macbeth by comparison appear a model of female virtue. Divorced by her husband, she had a fortune of her own at her disposal and she married again. Earl Rivers, before dying, wished to provide for his illegitimate children, but was informed by the ex-Countess that Richard was dead. She then did her best to justify the truth of her statement by trying to get the boy sent to the American plantations, but in this scheme she was foiled. Brought up in poverty, he eventually discovered the name of his mother and applied to her for assistance, which was refused. He wrote a play at the age of eighteen, and a second play two years later, though without profit, except that he became known to Sir Richard Steele, who publicised his misfortune and helped him in other ways, but ceased to do so on hearing that his protégé had made fun of him. Constant attendance at the theatre brought Savage into touch with a famous actress, Nance Oldfield, who allowed him £50 a year until her death in 1730. After that he wrote another play and several poems, but fame was withheld from him until he was accused of killing a man in a brothel that traded as a coffee-house. Though it was clear that he had only acted in self-defence, and the chief witness against him was a prostitute, he was condemned to death. An appeal was made by his friends to Queen Caroline, but his mother managed to blacken his character in that quarter, and he would certainly have been hanged if the Countess of Hertford had not exposed the mother's cruelty to the Queen and obtained the royal pardon.

Later, he threatened to expose his mother in a written account of her behaviour; upon which one of her relations, Lord Tyrconnel, bought his silence by receiving him as one of the family and giving him a pension of £200. This prosperous period was abbreviated by Savage, who treated Tyrconnel's house as his own, pawned the books in his library, and ordered the butler to bring the best wines in the cellar for his companions, who "forgot the respect due to the house in which they were entertained, indulged themselves in the utmost extravagance of merriment, practised the most licentious frolics, and committed all the outrages of drunkenness". Savage's own explanation of his expulsion from the house and the annulment of his pension was that Tyrconnel objected to his spending all his nights in taverns, demanded more of his company than he felt inclined to give, and resented his independent conduct. Accusations and counter-charges between the two went on for some time; and being now at liberty to attack his mother, Savage wrote a poem, *The Bastard*, inscribed with "due reverence" to that parent, who was subjected to so much un-favourable comment on its account that she had to quit Bath for London. The poem contains the only phrase by Savage that has become a familiar quotation:

> He lives to build, not boast, a generous race;
> No tenth transmitter of a foolish face.

The rest of his life was passed in poverty, though he managed to get £50 out of the Queen by writing a poem on her virtues, with the promise of more to come if he continued to sing her praises annually; which he did, styling himself 'Volunteer Laureate', to the annoyance of the official one, Colley Cibber. With the death of the Queen late in 1737 his means of sub-sistence dried up and he became wholly dependent on friends for food and shelter.

At this point in his fortunes he became acquainted with Johnson, who sympathised with his predicament and helped him whenever possible. Johnson took notice of all his faults: his high opinion of himself, his assumption that he should be supported by others, his resentment against those who refused to support him, his propensity to cadge from all his friends, his readiness to take offence, his carelessness with money whether earned or borrowed. But his unconquerable gaiety of nature, his fortitude in distress, his adaptability and charm of manners, his knowledge of life, the vivacity and intelligence of his con-versation, and the essential kindliness of his disposition more than atoned for the depravity of his tastes and the instability of his character, and Johnson took so much pleasure in his company that they often wandered about the streets together deep in talk, oblivious of the passing hours and even forgetful of hunger. They passed the whole of one night walking round and round St. James's Square, neither of them at that time having a lodging, both in the highest spirits, full of patriotism, critical of their rulers, setting all the affairs of the nation to rights, and then finding that they had scarcely fourpence between them to buy breakfast.

Like all men of generous nature, Johnson in his early life was against the Government of his time and in favour of any Opposition that seemed to promise better conditions for the people. He thoroughly disliked George II and the materialistic Whig Minister, Sir Robert Walpole, and no doubt would have favoured the restoration of a Stuart monarchy. Indeed he went so far as to write what an opponent called a "bloody Jacobitical pamphlet", which brought him into some danger. But, as with all men of intelligence, his ardour cooled with the years and he stood simply for a stable and patriotic Government; so it may be said that he started life as a Jacobitical Tory idealist and ended it as a Hanoverian Tory realist.

To return to Savage, his condition became so acute that a few friends subscribed enough money to send him into the country, with a promise that they would provide more at intervals to keep him there. He parted from Johnson with tears in his eyes and took a coach to Bristol, whence he was supposed to sail for Swansea. But he started a round of pleasure at Bristol, being invited to dine at many houses, and wrote letters to his friends complaining of their conduct in not sending him enough money, which caused them to cancel further contributions. Only the poet Pope continued the £20 a year which he had promised. At last Savage left for Swansea. He had looked forward to a delightful rural existence, listening to the song of nightingales in all seasons from every tree. But a year of it, with no winter nightingales, was more than enough and he returned to Bristol, borrowed £30 for his fare to London, spent it, and ultimately found himself in prison for debt. Here apparently he made himself quite comfortable, being treated well by the keeper, and here he died at the age of forty-five, after an incarceration of six months.

Some six months later Johnson published *The Life of Richard Savage* (February 1744), which remains the best short biography in the English language. In less than forty thousand words he gives us the life and character of his strange subject with an honesty and charity not previously brought to the art of biography and not often to be found in the work of his successors. He could write of Savage that "an irregular and dissipated manner of life had made him the slave of every passion that happened to be excited by the presence of its object", while issuing the warning that "those are no proper judges of his conduct who have slumbered away their time on the down of plenty". Stranger even than his theme is the fact that at the age of thirty-five Johnson knew as much about life as he was to know at the age of seventy. His comments are as profound as his story is powerful. It was probably the only book he wrote that derived from some inner compulsion, not from a religious motive or the mere desire for fame or money, and as a consequence it is the most readable and the most valuable of all his works.

CHAPTER 5

Intimacies

THERE MUST HAVE BEEN, if not a serious quarrel, at least a break in the relationship between Johnson and his wife during the year 1739. He, as we know, was sometimes without a lodging, wandering in the streets and possibly sleeping in sheds with scarcely the money to pay for a meal. She, it appears, was staying with a friend for a while near the Tower of London; and it must have been at this period that they had to sell the inconsiderable property in their possession, including the small silver cup Sam's mother had bought for him when they visited London in his third year, "one of the last pieces of plate which dear Tetty sold in our distress," he afterwards related. In the autumn of 1739 he stayed at Lichfield with his mother and Lucy Porter, and at Ashbourne with his old schoolmate Taylor. There may have been a little money coming in from *The Gentleman's Magazine,* because Tetty moved back to their address in Castle Street, Cavendish Square, and he was able to promise her £20 on hearing that she had accidentally hurt her leg. "I shall be very uneasy till I know you are recovered," he wrote from Lichfield on 31st January 1740, "and beg that you will omit nothing that can contribute to it, nor deny yourself anything that may make confinement less melancholy. You have already suffered more than I can bear to reflect upon, and I hope more than either of us shall suffer again. One part at least I have often flattered myself we shall avoid for the future, our troubles will surely never separate us more . . . I beg therefore that you will more regard my happiness than to expose yourself to any hazards. I still promise myself many happy years from your tenderness and affection, which I sometimes hope our misfortunes have not yet deprived me of. . . . Of the time which I have spent from thee, and of my dear Lucy and other affairs, my heart will be at ease on Monday to give thee a particular account, especially if a letter should inform me that thy leg is better, for I hope you do not think so unkindly of me as to imagine that I can be at rest while I believe my dear Tetty in pain. Be assured, my dear Girl, that I have seen nobody in these rambles upon which I have been forced that has not contributed to confirm my esteem and affection for thee, though that esteem and affection only contributed to increase my unhappiness when I reflected that the most amiable woman in the world was exposed by my means to miseries which I could not relieve. I am, my charming Love, yours Sam: Johnson."

Sarah Johnson's shop at Lichfield was doing badly, and on the same day that the above letter was written a sum of £80 was advanced to Sam and his mother by Theophilus Levett, the town clerk and coroner, who charged 4½% interest, with the house as security. Johnson undertook to pay the interest and to repay the principal, and though he was not always able to deal promptly with the former when due he begged Levett on such occasions not to mention the matter to his mother and eventually managed to clear the debt.

Returning to London, he was hopeful that his tragedy *Irene* would at last be seen at Drury Lane, but his manners were not to the taste of the tricky manager and again he had to exercise patience. David Garrick, who had dropped the law and joined his brother in the wine trade, was solely interested in the stage and did his best for Johnson's play, a skit of his own being produced at Drury Lane early in 1740. Johnson had already done what he could for Garrick. Although Edward Cave had no great relish for mirth, yet he could bear it; and when Johnson asked him to see David in a comic role, he agreed.

The room over the arch of St. John's Gate was prepared, several of the printers were asked to read parts, and Garrick displayed his capabilities in the chief character of Fielding's farce *The Mock-Doctor*.

There was nothing that Johnson would not do for a friend, his own melancholy making companionship, especially that of lively natures, the mainstay of existence. He favourably compared the calm of friendship with the storm of love in a short ode for *The Gentleman's Magazine*, two verses of which express his feeling:

> Friendship, peculiar boon of heaven,
>   The noble mind's delight and pride,
> To men and angels only given
>   To all the lower world denied . . .

> Thy gentle flows of guiltless joys
>   On fools and villains ne'er descend;
> In vain for thee the tyrant sighs,
>   And hugs a flatterer for a friend.

Another quality besides high spirits attracted him in those he liked, for he was easily imposed upon by men whose religious opinions accorded with and fortified his own. One of these was a man whose real name was unknown but who is remembered as George Psalmanazar. He made a reputation as the author of a book about Formosa, which largely derived from his own fancy. Some eight years after its publication he became pious, repented of the deception, confessed his fault, and began to earn a precarious livelihood as a literary hack. Johnson frequently went to see him at a public-house in Old Street, where he was usually to be found surrounded by admirers, and was deeply impressed by his virtuous conversation, asserting in the years ahead that Psalmanazar was the best man he had ever known, one whose virtues would have excited wonder in a saint. No

37

one ever dreamt of referring to Formosa in the good man's company, and Johnson was afraid even to mention China, his reverence being such that he never disputed anything said by Psalmanazar. "I should as soon think of contradicting a bishop," he declared.

Probity, cheerfulness and a love of liquor were combined in another acquaintance of these days: William Collins, the poet, whose head was always full of ideas but whose pocket was usually empty of money. He planned many works, but seldom went further than the plan. "A man doubtful of his dinner, or trembling at a creditor, is not much disposed to abstract meditation or remote enquiries," said Johnson, who once delivered Collins from legal duress by arranging terms with a bookseller, raising enough money on a future translation to set the poet at liberty. At last Collins inherited £2,000 from an uncle, but when freed from the fear of poverty he became insane, which gave rise to gloomy reflections in the mind of Johnson, who wrote to a friend: "How little can we venture to exult in any intellectual powers or literary attainments when we consider the condition of poor Collins. I knew him a few years ago full of projects, versed in many languages, high in fancy and strong in intention. This busy and forcible mind is now under the government of those who lately would not have been able to comprehend the least and most narrow of its designs." Long afterwards Johnson provided a short biography of Collins for his *Lives of the Poets*.

Of the two great literary figures in the 1740s Johnson got to know Samuel Richardson, but there is no evidence that he ever met Henry Fielding. The first had invented a new kind of sentimental romance in which he played variations on such themes as chastity, passion, virtue and vice, the whole pervaded by a high moral tone and conducted by letters from one character to another. *Pamela* and *Clarissa Harlowe* can be described as the godmothers of all the domestic, maudlin, goody-goody novels and dramas that have deluged the bookstalls and the stage since their time. French writers, in especial, raved and wept over them, and they influenced the course of fiction in Germany as well as France, Goethe being as much affected as Rousseau. Nowadays the average intelligent reader will read *Clarissa* just long enough to know that he does not wish to read it any longer, and will turn with relief to Fielding, who may be regarded as the true parent of the English novel at its best. Whatever is most natural in our fiction derives from him. *Tom Jones* was the first, and is perhaps still the only, novel in the language wherein all the characters, their circumstances and behaviour, are described with absolute fidelity, reality and impartiality.

Johnson's attitude to the two men was dictated by his religion. He had been bitten early by the bug of puritanism, and the copybook morality of Richardson appealed to him, while the ruthless truth-to-nature of Fielding offended him. Honesty compelled him to admit that he had read Fielding's feeblest work *Amelia* through without stopping, but in conversation he called the author of *Joseph Andrews* "a blockhead", amending the description to "a barren rascal", and adding that there was more knowledge of the heart in one of Richardson's letters than in the whole of *Tom Jones*, which was merely his way of saying that Fielding did not write with the object of preaching virtue but was solely concerned with the faithful portrayal of human nature. Johnson's fear that readers would be contaminated by the sight of mankind in the raw led to a burst of indignation many years later when a pious female, Hannah More, referred to a passage in *Tom Jones*: "I am shocked" said he, "to hear you quote from so vicious a book. I am sorry to hear you have read it, a confession which no modest lady should ever make. I scarcely know a more corrupt work." He then denied that Fielding had genius and broke into a panegyric on Richardson.

On several occasions during his early struggles Richardson came to his rescue. "I am obliged to entreat your assistance,"

Johnson wrote in March 1756. "I am now under arrest for five pounds eighteen shillings . . . If you will be so good as to send me this sum, I will gratefully repay you, and add it to all former obligations." Richardson sent the money; but his kindness did not shut Johnson's eyes to his weakness, to his love of being surrounded by female sycophants and his inability to discuss anything except his own works. His death, according to Johnson, was due to a want of variety among his flatterers, "like a man obliged to breathe the same air till it is exhausted." Johnson would have found a more open-handed generosity and infinitely better company in the author of that corrupt and vicious work, *Tom Jones*.

The friends he made were sufficiently varied in character, ranging from a stiff-necked unimaginative lawyer, John Hawkins, to a genial sympathetic doctor, Richard Bathurst. These two provide the best examples of Johnson's catholicity of taste in social intercourse. Hawkins, who lived to be the executor of Johnson's will and to write his life, was a cold-hearted, ill-natured fellow, a perfect pattern of the industrious apprentice, rising early, working hard, and amassing information. He was fond of music and wrote lyrics, fond of money and married it. The articles he wrote for *The Gentleman's Magazine* brought him into touch with Johnson, who appreciated his veracity but little else about him, and after an acquaintanceship of thirty years summed him up in conversation as "an honest man at the bottom, but, to be sure, he is penurious and he is mean, and it must be owned he has a degree of brutality and a tendency to savageness that cannot easily be defended". In fact Hawkins had so many faults that he thought the rest of the world entirely wicked, mistaking his criticism of others for virtue in himself. His outward piety deceived Johnson, who always preferred the man who made a pretence of religion to the man who honestly flouted it.

As different from Hawkins as Fielding was from Richardson, a surgeon named Richard Bathurst became Johnson's most intimate friend. "My dear Bathurst whom I loved better than ever I loved any human creature!" he once exclaimed. They had much in common, both being interested in medicine and neither caring for fools, rogues and Whigs. Bathurst was downright in his opinions and too honest to obtain the influence necessary to rise in his profession. How seldom, said he, on coming into the company of any new person, one felt any wish or inclination to see him again—an attitude of mind that tends to retard progress in a world where good jobs are often at the disposal of unpleasant people. At one point in his career he was greatly helped by Johnson, who spoke of him as "a man to my very heart's content". A periodical called *The Adventurer* was started in 1752, and Bathurst was paid for several essays which were dictated to him by Johnson. At length the doctor threw up a job at the Middlesex Hospital and went to the West Indies as a surgeon. Havana was captured by British troops in 1762 after a long siege, though it was handed back to Spain with the restoration of peace a year later. Johnson described it as "a conquest too dearly obtained, for Bathurst died before it". As a rule Johnson's prayers for the clemency of the Almighty were confined to his family, but Bathurst was 'recommended' with his mother, father and brother on Easter Day, 1764.

It is possible that Johnson would have spent less time with friends in taverns if his home-life had been more comfortable. He was constantly having disagreements with Tetty, and they frequently changed their lodgings, though they seldom lived far from Fleet Street. Like so many women, she loved neatness and cleanliness. Like so many men, he was careless and absentminded. She chafed at the condition of the parlour floor when he was at home. "A clean floor is *so* comfortable," was her refrain, until he told her that there had been enough talk about the floor and they might now turn their attention to the ceiling. His complaints were reserved for the food, for it was his opinion that "a man seldom thinks with more earnestness of anything than he does of his dinner", and so his wife was able to deliver a shrewd thrust when he was on the point of saying grace one day: "Nay, hold, Mr. Johnson, and do not make a farce of thanking God for a dinner which you will presently protest not eatable."

Occasionally they read plays to one another, and he thought that she read comedy better than he had ever heard it read, but in tragedy "I did better, she always mouthed too much". He considered that the main fault in her character was a propensity to make people dissatisfied with their lot. She would lament the sorrows of celibacy to an old maid, the dependence of pupillage to a young heir, and once she remarked to a waterman who was rowing her on the Thames that he was no happier than a galley-slave, one being chained to the oar by authority, the other by want. Garrick told a friend that Tetty was "a little painted poppet, full of affectation and rural airs of elegance", and a doctor who knew her well said that, when not drunk or under the influence of opium, she spent her time in bed reading romances. All of which may be true; but her husband cherished her, and that he felt remorse for whatever acrimony had subsisted between them became clear when a lady mentioned what she believed to be Shenstone's idea that quarrels between friends and lovers contributed to happiness because of the reconciliations which followed. "Why, what a pernicious maxim is this now!" Johnson cried. "*All* quarrels ought to be avoided studiously, particularly conjugal ones, as no one can possibly tell where they may end; besides that lasting dislike is often the consequence of occasional disgust, and that the cup of life is surely bitter enough without squeezing in the hateful rind of resentment."

In the last few years of Tetty's life her husband managed to pay for lodgings in Hampstead, the doctor having said that she must have good air. He often joined her there for week-ends, but had to remain in the city the rest of the time. His solitude caused him to help in the founding of a club which met from 1749 onwards at the King's Head Tavern in Ivy Lane, near St.

Paul's. Both Bathurst and Hawkins were members, though the latter begged to be excused from paying his share of the supper, as he did not eat it. "No man is angry at another for being inferior to himself," said Johnson. "We all scorned him and admitted his plea. For my part I was such a fool as to pay my share for wine, though I never tasted any. But Hawkins was a most unclubable man!" Johnson was at his best at these weekly meetings, disputing, joking, telling stories, arguing that black was white and yellow was red, and giving full vent to his sense of fun by comical imitations of people. Once he decided to celebrate the birth of the first book by Mrs. Charlotte Lennox, whose intelligence he rated above that of any other female writer. At eight in the evening about twenty people assembled at the Devil Tavern, including members of the club, the authoress and her husband. Johnson had ordered a huge apple-pie, which he decorated with bay-leaves, and during the proceedings he invoked the Muses ceremoniously, encircling the lady's brows with a crown of laurel. Refreshments came and went, conversation flowed, and at five in the morning, wrote Hawkins, "Johnson's face shone with meridian splendour, though his drink had been only lemonade," while the others had imbibed freely of bacchic products. With the arrival of dawn the waiters were unconscious, and two hours passed before they were capable of adding up the reckoning. At eight o'clock the party broke up, and the grave Hawkins experienced a sensation of shame at the thought that the entertainment had resembled a debauch.

CHAPTER 6

The Dictionary

By 1745 Johnson was writing about half of every number of *The Gentleman's Magazine* and, together with other jobs, earning enough to consider some project of his own. By nature indolent, it occurred to him that the easiest way to make money as well as reputation was to edit Shakespeare's plays; so he issued a pamphlet containing observations on *Macbeth*, comments on the work of previous editors, and proposals for a new edition; but the proposition was nipped in the bud by another publisher, who claimed copyright of the plays and threatened Cave with an action in the Court of Chancery. What Johnson would have liked to write at this period was a Life of Alfred the Great, his patriotic feelings having been stirred by the attempt of Charles Edward Stuart in 1745 to regain the English throne. But he probably felt that the sifting of truth from legend would cause too much conjecture, and he dismissed Alfred from his mind.

Having abandoned Shakespeare for the time being, he was still faced with the necessity of winning a place in the world by the execution of some considerable enterprise, and at last, having cogitated on the scheme in past years, he determined to compile a dictionary of the English language that could favourably compare with similar works produced by French and Italian academices. Such an undertaking had been long in the air, Addison and Pope having considered it. Nathan Bailey's Dictionary had been issued in 1721, but his word-definitions lacked exactitude. A famous publisher named Robert Dodsley (known in those days as a bookseller) proposed that Johnson should do the job. First of all he declined it, but, indigence getting the better of inclination, he bent up "each corporal agent to this terrible feat" and wrote out a plan for its accomplishment. It was too big an affair for one publisher to handle, and Dodsley got half-a-dozen others to help him finance the venture. For the sum of £1,575 Johnson undertook to finish the work in a matter of three years. When an old Oxford friend, William Adams, staggered by this optimistic forecast, reminded him that the forty members of the French Academy had taken forty years to compile their dictionary, Johnson replied: "Sir, thus it is. This is the proportion. Let me see: forty times forty is sixteen hundred. As three to sixteen hundred, so is the proportion of an Englishman to a French-man." The contract was signed on 18th June 1746, when the publishers breakfasted with Johnson—at least, he asked them to breakfast, and the chance of their feeding at an author's expense must have been so novel that they were not likely to have missed it.

It would have been impossible to prepare such a work in the restricted area of lodgings, and Johnson took a roomy house in Gough Square, where he lived for the next twelve years. He engaged half-a-dozen amanuenses, five of whom were Scots, and after they had finished the work for which they were engaged he continued to help them, writing a preface for one, getting a job for another, giving money to a third, paying for the burial of a fourth's wife, and so on. All of them worked on the dictionary in the good-sized attic of the Gough Square house. Johnson neglected to write the 'Plan' of the dictionary by a certain date, and Dodsley's suggestion that it should be addressed to the Earl of Chesterfield gave him an excuse for further delay. Chesterfield was a Secretary of State and a patron of letters, and, having reluctantly fallen in with Dodsley's suggestion, Johnson occasionally called to see him. For a while it seemed as if the Earl's patronage would help the great design, but in the event it only helped Johnson to write a memorable letter. In the first glow of pleasure caused by his connection with a notable literary undertaking, Chesterfield gave Johnson £10 and received him courteously. But their temperaments were radically dissimilar, Chesterfield priding himself on never laughing aloud, Johnson believing that "the size of a man's understanding might always be justly measured by his mirth." Probably the laughter of Johnson made Chesterfield limp. At any rate there was something about the lexicographer's manners and appearance that did not harmonise with the peer's social requirements, and Johnson must have entertained the suspicion of Polixenes in *The Winter's Tale*: "Methinks my favour here begins to warp." He was not the man to waste his time waiting on a nobleman who showed no desire for his company, and he ceased to wait.

His attention was not wholly devoted to the dictionary. In 1747 David Garrick, whose performance as Richard III had drawn playgoing London to Goodman's Fields Theatre in the city, became manager of Drury Lane Theatre, and Johnson wrote a Prologue for the opening of his season there, in which a sonorous tribute was paid to Shakespeare, whose language had made a dictionary necessary:

> Each change of many-coloured life he drew,
> Exhausted worlds, and then imagined new:
> Existence saw him spurn her bounded reign,
> And panting Time toiled after him in vain.

But recalling that Garrick could hardly be expected to emulate Shakespeare, our poet descended to earth:

> The drama's laws the drama's patrons give,
> For we that live to please, must please to live.

The following year he wrote his most famous poem, an imitation of Juvenal's tenth Satire, which he entitled *The Vanity of Human Wishes*, the main theme appearing in the statement "That life protracted is protracted woe". It reveals his gloomy, pessimistic nature more markedly than anything else he wrote. There is no happiness to be gained in this world, he says; fame, wealth, genius, power and glory are fleeting and ultimately valueless:

> From Marlborough's eyes the streams of dotage flow,
> And Swift expires a driveller and a show.

The consolations for human beings are a trust in God, an assurance of a future state, and the acquisition by prayer of virtue, resignation, love, patience and faith—

> With these celestial Wisdom calms the mind,
> And makes the happiness she does not find.

It is worthy of remark that Sir Walter Scott, who had enjoyed the combination of fame, wealth, genius, power and glory to a greater extent than any other writer in history, and who was familiar with the whole body of British verse from Spenser and Shakespeare to Byron and Burns, preferred Johnson's *London* and *The Vanity of Human Wishes* to anything else in poetry.

The greater part of the second poem was written at Hampstead during a visit to Tetty, some seventy lines being composed one day while he walked about before a word of them was committed to paper. Dodsley gave him fifteen guineas for the copyright in November and brought it out early in January 1749. A month later David Garrick produced at Drury Lane Theatre the blank verse tragedy *Irene* which Johnson had written some twelve years earlier. After all his disappointments over the play it might have been expected that he would raise no obstacles to its presentation by Garrick; but their disagreement over certain matters became so fierce that the manager asked their friend Taylor to intervene. "Sir," Johnson expostulated, "the fellow wants me to make Mahomet run mad, that he may have an opportunity of tossing his hands and kicking his heels!" After much argument he gave way on certain points and Garrick gave way on others.

The occasion being important, or at least unusual, he dressed for the part of author, and during rehearsals the performers were favoured by his appearance in a scarlet waistcoat richly laced with gold and a gold-laced hat, in which attire he was observed in a side-box during one or more of the performances. Before the rise of the curtain on the first night the audience amused themselves with cat-calls and the usual noises of people who like to hear themselves before hearing anyone else, but they were hushed by Johnson's admonitory prologue with its closing line: "Ye fops be silent, and ye critics just!" and listened with close attention until the heroine was about to be strangled with a bowstring, when they drowned her lines with shouts of "Murder!" For the remainder of the run she was despatched off-stage. The play was given nine performances, from which the author received the profits of three, together with £100 from Dodsley for the publishing rights. But Johnson had enjoyed chatting with the fellows in the Green Room, thereafter taking a more lenient view of their profession, and he was so much attracted to the ladies that he had to deny himself the pleasure of their company, saying to Garrick: "I'll come no more behind your scenes, David, for the silk stockings and white bosoms of your actresses excite my amorous propensities."[1]

His amorous propensities were easily excited and he had difficulty in restraining them. While his wife showed an increasing desire for drink and drugs, there was a proportionate decrease in her desire for sexual relationship, and for some years before her death she refused intercourse with him, sleeping in a separate bed and pleading ill-health. She even told him that he might lie with as many women as he pleased, so long as he loved her only. But his principles prevented him from taking advantage of this, no doubt to the detriment of his mental and physical being. While she was living in Hampstead a widowed friend of hers, Mrs. Elizabeth Desmoulins, daughter of Johnson's god-

[1] In David Hume's account of what Garrick told him, Johnson used the word 'bubbies' for 'bosoms' and 'genitals' for 'amorous propensities'.

father, Dr. Samuel Swinfen, often stayed at the same house to keep her company. When Johnson spent week-ends at Hampstead he would sometimes remain talking till two or three in the morning with his friend Bathurst, who was in lodgings near-by. Elizabeth Desmoulins sat up on such occasions to let him in and to put a warming-pan between his sheets. But that did not complete her duties for the night. The moment Johnson was in bed he called to her to come for a talk. This sometimes developed into a pillow-talk, accompanied by cuddling and kissing, until his feelings became too strong and he thrust her from him with an agonised appeal that she should go. About ten years his junior, she declared that she respected him so highly that it would have been impossible to repulse him if he had gone further than fondling.

Though Tetty's unresponsiveness to the lover doubtless caused those sensual thoughts to which he so often referred in his written prayers and meditations, she was still able to appreciate the writer, and it gave him extreme pleasure when she said of his essays in *The Rambler*: "I thought very well of you before, but I did not imagine you could have written anything to equal this." His main object in writing, apart from earning money, was to instruct his readers and if possible improve their minds. To augment his income and to enlarge the mental outlook of his subscribers he started a brief bi-weekly periodical which, for want of a better name, he called *The Rambler*. With very little assistance from others, he wrote the whole paper while still busy on his dictionary, keeping it up for two years, from March 1750 to March 1752. Often he had to produce a number at the last moment, having no time to read what he had written or to correct proofs. Occasionally he left it almost too late. "I do not remember," he noted in 1753, "that since I left Oxford I ever rose early by mere choice, but once or twice at Edial, and two or three times for *The Rambler*." His excellent memory for words and careless method of reading were revealed in one number wherein he criticised a speech of Lady Macbeth's, attributing it to her husband. Cave paid him four guineas a week for the work, but as the sale of each twopenny issue scarcely reached five hundred copies the publisher must have been out of pocket.

It is hardly worth dwelling upon what no one is now likely to read, and all that need be said is that most of his essays repeat in prose the despondent philosophy already expressed in poetry. A man's reflections on life are, as a rule, influenced by his state of health: if his digestive organs are in good working order, he finds the mere act of living a pleasure; if not, a pain. In his manhood Johnson never enjoyed good health, and his outlook was conditioned thereby; though it must be added that the suffering he witnessed around him would, in a man of his sensitiveness, give a doleful tendency to his views of human existence. In the ponderous periods of *The Rambler* he moralised on the infelicity of life, asserting that "the cure for the greatest part of human miseries is not radical, but palliative", and preaching the necessity of fortitude and faith. Among other things he provided a text for future biographers: "There are many who think it an act of piety to hide the faults or failings of their friends, even when they can no longer suffer by their detection; we therefore see whole ranks of characters adorned with uniform panegyrick, and not to be known from one another but by extrinsick and casual circumstances. . . . If we owe regard to the memory of the dead, there is yet more respect to be paid to knowledge, to virtue and to truth." Occasionally Johnson attempted to enliven his papers with humour; but though as a talker he could exhibit that quality with ease, the high spirits of the Rambler may be likened to the attempts of an elephant to dance. Johnson's jocularity as an essayist is no joke.

But there was not much cause for fun in the circumstances of his life just then. The sorrow with which he witnessed his wife's decline, and the difficulty he experienced in providing for her comfort, left him little time for social amusement. On her last removal to Hampstead she complained that the staircase of the house was in a very bad condition, the plaster having fallen from the walls in many places. "Oh, that's nothing," said the landlord; "it's only the knocks against it of the coffins of the poor souls that have died in the lodging." In March 1752 she followed the poor souls, leaving her husband in deep distress. His friend Taylor, for whom he sent, found him in tears and extreme agitation. He never ceased to pray and mourn for her, and nearly three years after her death he wrote to a friend about the loss he had suffered: "I have ever since seemed to myself broken off from mankind, a kind of solitary wanderer in the wild of life, without any certain direction or fixed point of view: a gloomy gazer on a world to which I have little relation."

Just over a year from the death of his wife he decided to marry again. He even visited the church at Bromley where Tetty lay buried, received the sacrament, prayed for her soul, and as it were took leave of her before proceeding with his "design of a new wife". As we hear nothing further of plan, person or proposal, we may surmise that his desire for a suitable spouse weakened the more he looked for her, or that with the dictionary still on his hands he could neither support her nor attend to her wants until it was published, when he abandoned the search from indolence.

The committee of publishers sometimes proved obstructive, doling out money in a niggardly manner, perhaps because they did not believe he was giving the whole of his mind to the job. The fact that their belief was justified displeased Johnson, who on at least one occasion threatened to suspend work unless they sent something on account. At length the seven years' labour drew towards a close, and it became known that the dictionary was nearing completion. On the eve of publication Johnson seemed more concerned over the insanity of William Collins than the effects of his great work, writing to ask a friend whether it would give the poet pleasure to receive a letter: "I have often been near his state, and therefore have it in great commiseration." Lord Chesterfield, on the other hand, was chiefly solicitous about the dedication of the dictionary, and to make certain of having his name prominently displayed in that connection he wrote two articles in a periodical elaborately complimenting Johnson as one who would "bring this as near to perfection as any man could do", acclaiming him as the infallible Pope of etymology, and declaring that "I make a total surrender of all my rights and privileges in the English language, as a free-born British subject, to the said Mr. Johnson, during the term of his dictatorship." When Johnson read these articles he observed to David Garrick: "I have sailed a long and painful voyage round the world of the English language, and does he now send out two cockboats to tow me into harbour?"

Guessing that the newspaper puff would not be sufficient to achieve his purpose, Chesterfield asked a poet and a painter to call on Johnson, to apologise for his seeming neglect and to tender his future friendship and patronage. The poet's name was Sir Thomas Robinson, who later became Governor of Barbados, was recalled "on some complaints", and in time helped to deface the interior of Westminster Abbey by having the largest monument in the Poet's Corner erected in his honour. On the occasion of his visit to Gough Square he flattered Johnson in a nauseating manner and went so far as to assert that if he could afford it he would settle £500 a year on the lexicographer. "And who are you that talk thus liberally?" enquired Johnson. "I am Sir Thomas Robinson, a Yorkshire baronet." Johnson's reception of this information surprised the baronet: "Sir, if the first peer of the realm were to make me such an offer, I would show him the way downstairs." It then seemed necessary that Chesterfield should be apprised of Johnson's feelings in a less abrupt fashion, and the famous letter written to that peer contains two sentences that explain why the word 'garret' in the first edition of *The Vanity of Human Wishes* was changed to 'patron' in subsequent editions:

There mark what ills the scholar's life assail,
Toil, envy, want, the patron, and the jail.

"Seven years, my Lord, have now past since I waited in your outward rooms, or was repulsed from your door; during which time I have been pushing on my work through difficulties of which it is useless to complain, and have brought it at last to the verge of publication without one act of assistance, one word of encouragement, or one smile of favour. Such treatment I did not expect, for I never had a Patron before. . . .

"Is not a Patron, my Lord, one who looks with unconcern on a man struggling for life in the water, and, when he has reached ground, encumbers him with help? The notice which you have been pleased to take of my labours, had it been early, had been kind; but it has been delayed till I am indifferent and cannot enjoy it, till I am solitary and cannot impart it, till I am known and do not want it. . . ."

In his preface to the dictionary Johnson said that he had received little assistance from the learned and no patronage from the great, and that the work had been done "not in the soft obscurities of retirement, or under the shelter of academic bowers, but amidst inconvenience and distraction, in sickness and in sorrow . . . I have protracted my work till most of those whom I wished to please have sunk into the grave, and success and miscarriage are empty sounds: I therefore dismiss it with frigid tranquillity, having little to fear or hope from censure or from praise". Nevertheless he knew that adverse criticism might upset his tranquillity, confiding in a friend: "I hope however the critics will let me be at peace; for though I do not much fear their strength or skill, I am a little afraid of myself, and would not willingly feel so much ill-will in my bosom as literary quarrels are apt to excite." Another friend received portions of his dictionary before publication with an appeal: "The favour which I beg is that if you do not like them you will say nothing."

The final sheets of the dictionary were despatched by messenger to one of the publishers, Andrew Millar, early in 1755. "Well, what did he say?" asked Johnson of the messenger, who answered: "Sir, he said 'Thank God I have done with him'." Johnson smiled. "I am glad that he thanks God for anything."

Before the work was issued Johnson stayed at Oxford to visit the libraries and to consult with Thomas Warton, a Fellow of Trinity College, about the granting of a degree which could give an air of authority to the labours of the lexicographer. It was twenty-five years since he had last seen the place, and it gave him pleasure when the servants he had known at Pembroke College recognised him, a pleasure that was somewhat mitigated by the cool reception of Radcliffe, the Master, who neither asked him to dinner nor ordered a copy of the dictionary, which provoked Johnson to call him "a man who lives by the revenues of literature and will not move a finger to support it". Warton however was very hospitable, and they did much visiting and country-walking together. Soon to become Professor of Poetry, and in time Poet Laureate, Thomas Warton was unconventional in dress, appearance and habits, preferring the society of drunks in a tavern to that of dons in a college. In talking he "gobbled like a turkey", said Johnson, and he was too much absorbed in his own pursuits to keep his friendships "in constant repair", which may have been why Johnson thought him cold-hearted; but on this occasion his friendly efforts to obtain the coveted degree were successful, and Johnson was able to add the letters M.A. to his name on the title-page of the dictionary, publication of which had been delayed for that purpose.

April 1755 saw the first appearance of the *magnum opus*, containing rather over 41,000 entries, in two folio volumes, the price being £4 10s. It was in any true sense the first dictionary of the English language, on which all future dictionaries were to be founded, and, as the achievement of one man, unique in the annals of literature. It is also the only dictionary ever produced that reveals the character of its compiler, and is therefore the sole work of its kind that can be opened for amusement as well as instruction. Johnson's own comicalities being apparent:

"*Pension.* An allowance made to anyone without an equivalent. In England it is generally understood to mean pay given to a state hireling for treason to his country."

"*Oats.* A grain which in England is generally given to horses, but in Scotland supports the people."

"*Grub Street.* The name of a street in London, much inhabited by writers of small histories, dictionaries, and temporary poems; whence any mean production is called Grub Street."

"*Lexicographer.* A writer of dictionaries, a harmless drudge."

"*Excise.* A hateful tax levied upon commodities, and adjudged not by the common judges of property, but wretches hired by those to whom Excise is paid."

This last observation offended the Commissioners of Excise, and the Attorney-General was asked whether they could obtain legal redress, but he advised them that it would be more prudent to abstain from action. In an essay he afterwards wrote, Johnson pushed the point home by referring to "the two lowest of all human beings, a Scribbler for a party and a Commissioner of Excise."

He displayed another peculiarity by carefully refraining from quoting any ungodly writer's authority for a word, "lest it should send people to look in a book that might injure them for ever," he naïvely explained. Two young women complimented him on the fact that he had excluded all naughty words. "What, my dears!" he cried: "then you have been looking for them." They seemed confused. Occasionally his definitions were criticised. On asking how he had come to describe 'pastern' as the knee of a horse, a lady was unprepared for his answer: "Ignorance, madam, pure ignorance." Not the accuracy but the phraseology of his definition of 'network' provoked comment: "Anything reticulated or decussated, at

55

equal distances, with interstices between the intersections." He did not think very highly of his work, saying that he could have finished it easily in two years if he had been blessed with diligence and good health; and when someone remarked that there were four or five faults in it, he confessed: "Alas, sir! there are four or five hundred." On its appearance nearly everyone he knew depressed him with threats of censure from the public and critics; but one man, Charles Burney, an organist at King's Lynn who was to become a great friend, wrote appreciatively of his labours. "Yours is the only letter of good will that I have yet received," Johnson acknowledged in December 1757, "though indeed I am promised something of that sort from Sweden."

CHAPTER 7

Friends and Dependants

THE MONEY HE RECEIVED for the dictionary covered Johnson's running expenses and enabled him, together with his earnings as a journalist, to live in some comfort during its progress; but there cannot have been a balance in his favour at the end of seven years, and instead of being able to sit back in ease for a while to enjoy his achievement he had to work as hard as ever to keep a roof over his head. He wanted to see his mother again, spending a few days at Oxford on the way, but his labours chained him to London. He prepared a shorter dictionary for the press, edited a monthly publication called *The Literary Magazine*, for which he also wrote essays, and, having suffered arrest for debt, supplemented his income by obtaining subscriptions for the annotated edition of Shakespeare which he had previously designed. In 1756 he was offered a good living in Lincolnshire if he felt disposed to take holy orders. But he could not see himself as a pastor instructing peasants, and the London inns were more to his taste than the eastern fens. The offer was made by the father of a new friend, Bennet Langton, whose admiration for the essays in *The Rambler* had made him seek an introduction to their author.

Langton was a tall, thin, solemn young man when Johnson first met him, and he grew more gaunt and solemn with the years. He came of an ancient family that had settled at Langton, near Spilsby in Lincolnshire. Expecting to see a neat, well-dressed and eminently respectable personage, he was taken aback when he first beheld the vast, ungainly figure of Johnson descending from his bedroom at midday in a wig that did not fit his head and clothes that seemed to be falling off his body. But as usual the Rambler's conversation soon made his visitor oblivious of his appearance, and a friendship began that lasted a lifetime. Johnson soon formed a high opinion of Langton, saying that "his mind is as exalted as his stature. I am half afraid of him, but he is no less amiable than formidable". In after years Johnson went further: "The earth does not bear a worthier man than Langton." And further still: "I know not who will go to Heaven if Langton does not."

Not long after they became acquainted Langton went to Oxford and struck up another friendship with a fellow who in most respects was utterly unlike himself. This was Topham Beauclerk, a direct descendant of Charles II and Nell Gwynne; and as that also means that he was a direct descendant of Charles I, the differences in those monarchs were reflected in himself. He was an odd combination of satirist, bibliophile, logician, joker, debauchee and thinker. At one moment he would be discussing some momentous question with the utmost gravity, at the next he would be soaring on the wings of folly. He was a man of high principles and low practices, but as he was also excellent company no one bothered about his opinions or behaviour. Shortly after Langton and Beauclerk had formed an intimacy Johnson went to stay at Oxford and was introduced to the latter. He was amazed that the serious Langton should be so friendly with the frivolous Beauclerk; but, as we have seen, he was quickly drawn to intelligent men whose conduct he could not approve, and he was soon on familiar terms with 'Beau', as he called him. Indeed it became apparent in time that the young man could take liberties with him that other friends would not dare to take, and Beauclerk was one of the original members of The Club, later to be known as The Literary Club, which was founded in 1764 on a proposition by Sir Joshua Reynolds, seconded by Johnson. Other members included Edmund Burke, Bennet Langton, John Hawkins and Oliver Goldsmith.

Though Beauclerk became a sort of licensed jester at Johnson's court, he was frequently subjected to reproof. "You never open your mouth but with intention to give pain," Johnson admonished him; "and you have often given me pain, not from the power of what you said but from seeing your intention." Beauclerk learnt from the same source that his body was all vice, his mind all virtue. All the same, Johnson found his company irresistible, and when, about three o'clock one morning, Beauclerk and Langton having supped late, the two decided to knock Johnson up, they were not reprimanded. The noise they made at his door gave him the notion that he was the victim of ruffians, and he appeared at his window in shirt and wig, holding a poker. On recognising them he cried, "What, is it you, you dogs! I'll have a frisk with you." He quickly dressed and they made for Covent Garden, where Johnson tried to assist the fruit and vegetable merchants with their hampers. Finding that his help was not valued, they went to a tavern for a bowl of spiced and sugared red wine with bitter oranges, and spouted verse to one another. Then they took a boat from the Temple to Billingsgate, where they enjoyed themselves so much that Johnson and Beauclerk decided to finish the day in dissipation, Langton having promised to breakfast with some young female friends and being reproached by Johnson for leaving them "to go and sit with a set of wretched un-idea'd girls." David Garrick, on being told of their excursion, said to Johnson: "I heard of your frolic t'other night. You'll be in the Chronicle!" but Johnson was unrepentant and in reporting the actor's warning added: "*He* durst not do such a thing. His *wife* would not *let* him." It is doubtful whether Johnson when past fifty would have done such a thing with anyone else, and no surprise was felt when he said, on hearing that his frolicsome friend was seriously ill, "I would walk to the extent of the diameter of the earth to save Beauclerk," or when, the illness proving mortal, he wrote: "Such another will not easily be found among mankind."

Langton and Beauclerk belonged to the generation that followed Johnson's, the first being twenty-eight, the second thirty, years younger than he. But it is an interesting fact that all his friends were considerably his junior. The earliest of all, David Garrick, was nearly eight years younger, Oliver Goldsmith nineteen, Edmund Burke twenty, John Hawkins ten. Bathurst apart, the first of his London friends, Joshua Reynolds, was his junior by fourteen years. They had met in the days when Johnson and his wife lodged in Castle Street, Cavendish Square. Opposite the Johnsons lived the two daughters of Admiral Cotterell, with whom they were on visiting terms, and in their house Reynolds was introduced to the author of the *Life of Savage*, which he had greatly admired. In those days, and indeed for many years, Johnson's clothes were extremely shabby, and one evening a new housemaid tried to stop him from entering the Cotterells' home, thinking that he had mistaken the front door for the tradesmen's entrance. This annoyed him, his annoyance deepening when the Duchess of Argyll called and he was not introduced to her with sufficient ceremony. He was not pacified by the greater attention paid to the Duchess than to himself, and at last he made his presence felt by confirming the housemaid's view that he should have gone to the kitchen. Turning to Reynolds, he said in a loud voice: "I wonder which of us could get most money by his trade in one week, were we to work hard at it from morning till night?" The assertion of his presence caused the absence of the Duchess, who left almost at once.

Though Reynolds rose rapidly in the world's esteem, becoming the greatest portrait painter of his age and the first President of the Royal Academy, he never failed in his friendship and admiration for Johnson, whom he regarded as his preceptor. On his side the writer did justice to the painter's character, if not to his art, calling him the most invulnerable man he knew, "with whom, if you should quarrel, you would find the most difficulty how to abuse." Perhaps, with his many virtues, Reynolds was rather inclined to sacrifice honesty for popularity. "Everybody in the world speaks well of him," says Sir Peter Teazle in *The School for Scandal.* "Then he has bowed as low to knaves and fools as to the honest dignity of genius and virtue," replies Sir Oliver Surface. "What! do you blame him for not making enemies?" "Yes, if he has merit enough to deserve them." Everybody spoke well of Reynolds, who had no enemies. He was just a little too good to be true, and there may have been an implied criticism in Johnson's comment: "Sir Joshua Reynolds possesses the largest share of inoffensiveness of any man that I know."

Passing to the other extreme, as we so often do with Johnson, we come to a very different kind of person whom most of his friends would have thought offensive. Always interested in medicine, Johnson had probably run across Robert Levett in a tavern round about 1746, got into conversation with him, and found his advice helpful. When Johnson tenanted a house of his own Levett occupied a room in it. Born near Hull in 1705, he was the only man senior to himself with whom Johnson maintained a close friendship during the last half of his life. He had been a waiter in a Paris coffee-house, where he had picked up a certain amount of medical knowledge from the doctors who patronised it and whose influence enabled him to attend lectures on physic and surgery. Eventually settling in London, he developed a pretty considerable practice among the poor, travelling most days on foot from Houndsditch in the east to Marylebone in the west. He was a thin fellow, sour-looking, deeply-lined, dark-visaged, grotesquely rigid in manner and dumb in company. He drank too much, but that was not entirely his fault, because many of his patients could only pay for his services in drink and he felt morally bound to accept fees even when rendered in kind. "Levett," said Johnson, "is a brutal fellow, but I have a good regard for him, for his brutality is in his manners, not his mind." Midday callers on Johnson would usually find him in dishabille having breakfast with Levett, who kept their teacups replenished and never opened his mouth except to fill it with the beverage. There was mutual esteem between them, Johnson declaring that he would not be satisfied with the ministrations of the entire Royal College of Physicians unless Levett were present, permitting no one to treat him with disrespect, and assuring his friends that Levett was no dependant, being indebted to him for nothing more than bed and breakfast and an occasional Sunday dinner. Actually he had a permanent home with Johnson and attended to the inmates when they were ill.

Hardly a romantic figure, Levett once yielded to the softer emotions. When close upon sixty he allowed a patient to persuade him that she was related to a rich man who had dispossessed her of a considerable fortune. As she was inhabiting a small coal-shed in Fetter Lane at the time, he took pity on her; and as she believed that he had a lucrative practice, she took advantage of his pity. They were married, and four months later a writ was issued against him on account of her debts. Johnson came to the rescue and Levett remained in hiding for a while. The appearance shortly afterwards of Mrs. Levett at the Old Bailey on a charge of pocket-picking pleased her husband, who had by now discovered that she was a prostitute, and he was prevented with difficulty from attending her trial in the fond hope that she would be hanged. But she was acquitted, and the romance ended with their separation.

Another dependant of Johnson's whom he treated with the utmost regard and consideration was Anna Williams. She was the daughter of a Welsh physician, had been a near friend of Tetty's, and had lost her sight, being almost totally blind when Johnson offered her a home. All his friends considered it an honour to be invited to take tea with her, and she was generally regarded as the mistress of his house. Early in their acquaintance he said that he had never known "a being more pure from anything vicious". Though inclined like other people to be peevish when matters were not adjusted to her satisfaction, she possessed much sense, conversed on a wide variety of subjects, and showed remarkable fortitude and cheerfulness in her affliction. Johnson was unfailingly kind to her, obtaining subscriptions for her *Essays in Verse and Prose*, influencing Garrick to give her a benefit performance at Drury Lane, which brought her £200, and making her feel that she was doing him a favour by residing under his roof. After her death, fifteen months before his own, he wrote: "Had she had good humour and prompt elocution, her universal curiosity and comprehensive knowledge would have made her the delight of all that knew her." But, as with most people, her humour became less good with advancing years.

Apart from his innate benevolence, Johnson invited people to live at his expense because their constant presence gave him a sense of patriarchal power. Having no family of his own, he liked to be surrounded by his adopted children, as he practically regarded them, and it probably made him feel like a sultan when attended by a black servant. No one ever needed a servant less than he, and no one ever made fewer demands on one. The condition of his clothes, the state of his wig, showed plainly that the first were rarely brushed, the second was seldom combed. He employed, or rather adopted, Francis Barber, a young native of Jamaica, about a fortnight after the death of Tetty. Colonel Bathurst, father of his intimate friend, brought Francis to England, and died, leaving the lad his freedom. The Colonel's son suggested that Frank (as he was called) should become Johnson's servant, and his future welfare was assured. In spite of Anna Williams's opinion that it was a waste of money, Johnson sent him to Bishop's Stortford Grammar School. Twice he had a disagreement with Johnson and ran away, once to serve in an apothecary's shop and once to join the Navy, from which his master extracted him with difficulty. "No man will be a sailor who has contrivance enough to get himself into a jail," said Johnson, "for being in a ship is being in a jail with the chance of being drowned." That being his opinion, he assumed that Frank was yearning for release and begged Tobias Smollett to use what influence he could to set the poor fellow free on the ground that a malady in the throat made him unfit for service. While disclosing that he and Johnson "were never cater-cousins", Smollett did as he was asked, and Frank, much to his chagrin, was discharged.

Johnson always treated the youth like a son. In time he married a pretty white girl and displayed jealousy at a dance because of the attentions paid to her by other men. Leaving the party in a rage, he started to walk home, but was overtaken by Johnson in a carriage. "What is the matter, child? Art sick?" asked Johnson. On learning the true reason he exploded: "Are you jealous of your wife, you stupid blockhead?" "To be sure, sir, I don't quite approve." "Why, what do they *do* to her, man? Do the footmen kiss her?" "No, sir, no! Kiss my *wife*, sir! I *hope not*, sir!" "Why, what *do* they do to her, my lad?" "Why, nothing, sir, I'm sure, sir." "Why, then, go back directly and dance, you dog, do; and let's hear no more of such empty lamentations." Frank, like so many men of his colour, aroused strong feelings in women of the opposite complexion, and when he accompanied his master to Lincolnshire a female haymaker there became so infatuated that she followed him back to London. After Frank's nautical adventure he remained with his master to the end.

CHAPTER 8

From Ireland

So CONSIDERABLE was the reputation won by his dictionary that the state of Johnson's health had become a matter of public interest by the end of the year in which it appeared. In December 1755 he had a cough so violent that he once fainted under its convulsions, and a report of his death appeared in the papers. He had peculiar ideas about the treatment of illness and probably owed his recovery from some of his cures to the toughness of his constitution. At about this period he suffered a severe attack of gout in the ankle, plunged his leg into a pail of cold water when the paroxysm was at its worst, and exulted in the fact that the gout disappeared.

Though working as hard as most journalists he yet regarded himself as slothful, and in April 1758 he started to contribute a weekly essay called 'The Idler' to a publication known as *The Universal Chronicle*. This he continued for two years. The essays are a little lighter in tone than those in *The Rambler*, but the sadness underlying the satire makes his humour heavy. He did not waste much time on them. While visiting Oxford he asked Bennet Langton one evening when the post went off. In half-an-hour, he was informed. "Then we shall do very well," said he, and sat down to write his weekly essay. Langton asked if he might read it. "You shall not do more than I have done myself," replied Johnson as he folded and posted it. In view of his strong leanings towards monarchy, he certainly cannot have read, before despatching it, the essay which described a courtier as one "whose business is to watch the looks of a being, weak and foolish as himself".

While he was writing his essays, and collecting subscriptions for his edition of Shakespeare, and possibly doing a little work on it, his mother died in January 1759 at the age of ninety. He had not seen her for about twenty years and his neglect of her made him feel remorseful. On hearing of her illness he wrote several short letters both to her and to Lucy Porter, enclosing money and promising more. "Pray send me your blessing and forgive all that I have done amiss to you," he implored his mother, whom he also advised to "eat as much as you can". He assured Lucy that he would travel to Lichfield if possible, but that she must not tell his mother, lest he should disappoint her. His last note began: "Dear Honoured Mother: Neither your condition nor your character make it fit for me to say much. You have been the best mother, and I believe the best woman, in the world." On hearing of her death he wrote to Lucy that if his mother were to live again "surely I should behave better to her". There was no point in his visiting Lichfield now, he said, "nor can I bear the place." He entrusted her with all the arrangements that had to be made, leaving herself and Catherine Chambers, his mother's old maidservant, in possession of the house, the latter to receive whatever stock was left for the continuance of the business. But money was needed to pay for his mother's funeral and debts, and he arranged with a publisher to write a story for £100. He knocked it off in the evenings of a single week, and then dismissed it from his mind until, twenty-two years later, a friend produced a copy as they were travelling in a carriage and he re-read it with intense interest. A second edition had quickly followed the first, and he received a final payment of £25.

The tale, entitled *Rasselas, Prince of Abyssinia*, contains his ultimate reflections on the sorry business of human life, and has for many years been the favourite reading of those who suffer from a dyspeptic view of the universe. Imaginatively, and looking at life as a whole, his picture is true. But people do not live imaginatively; for the most part they seize the moment, looking neither before nor after, and extract what pleasure they can from the fleeting hours, which, when all is said, is the sensible thing to do. Johnson himself did the same; but while writing he was engulfed in silence, sorrow and solitude, with an ever-present sense while in that condition of the woe, futility and frustration of the sentient world. Perhaps the most sensible and satisfying philosophy of life would comprise a recognition of three essential elements: the sheer joy of existence, a constant sense of the miraculous, and a perception of the impossibility of fulfilment in a temporary state that should never detract from present obtainable happiness. Johnson's somewhat lop-sided view of this world was transmuted by his belief in another, the effect issuing in words of sombre majesty:

"Praise is to an old man an empty sound. . . . Nothing is now of much importance, for I cannot extend my interest beyond myself . . . to me, who am now declining to decrepitude, there is little to be feared from the malevolence of men, and yet less to be hoped from their affection or esteem. Something they may yet take away, but they can give me nothing. Riches would now be useless, and high employment would be pain. My retrospect of life recalls to my view many opportunities of good neglected, much time squandered upon trifles, and more lost in idleness and vacancy. I leave many great designs un-attempted, and many great attempts unfinished. My mind is burdened with no heavy crime, and therefore I compose myself to tranquillity; endeavour to abstract my thoughts from hopes and cares which, though reason knows them to be vain, still try to keep their old possession of the heart; expect, with serene humility, that hour which nature cannot long delay, and hope to possess in a better state that happiness which here I could not find, and that virtue which here I have not attained."

Johnson seems to have regarded himself as old at an age when most men are in the prime of life, and the above passage, written in his fiftieth year, might have been composed in his thirties. It would not have surprised the reader of his *Life of*

Savage to find therein any of the comments in *Rasselas*, such as "Human life is everywhere a state in which much is to be endured and little to be enjoyed", or "I live in the crowd of jollity, not so much to enjoy company as to shun myself", or "Integrity without knowledge is weak and useless, and knowledge without integrity is dangerous and dreadful".

After his mother's death, Johnson abandoned his house at Gough Square and occupied chambers in Staple Inn, whence he moved to Gray's Inn. He then visited Oxford, where he wore his new gown, had several swims in the river, saw a lot of Langton and Beauclerk, challenged a Fellow to climb a wall, and drank three bottles of port at a sitting with no deleterious effects. Returning to London he continued to do odd jobs, prefaces or dedications for other people's works, essays of his own, and, when in the mood, notes on Shakespeare's plays. He moved to chambers two doors down Inner Temple Lane, where he remained for some years. Anna Williams went into lodgings, Levett continued to attend him, and Frank was always at hand. During this period he was extremely poor and more than usually idle; but people were constantly calling on him for advice, passing through three very dirty rooms to a small one that resembled a counting-house and contained a large deal writing-desk, a battered walnut-wood table, and five ragged chairs of different sets. Here they might find him taking breakfast in an absent-minded way, rolling his body and making curious gesticulations which suggested to one visitor that he was mentally defective, and dressed in a dirty brown coat and waistcoat, with breeches that had once been crimson but were now brown, an old black wig on his head and stockings slipping down to his feet, which were thrust into an ancient pair of shoes instead of slippers.

The queerest folk regarded him as an oracle and placed their problems before him. One man came to confess that he had taken paper and packthread belonging to his employer. On being questioned he admitted that his employer had told him to take as much as he liked. Johnson decided that he was mad and advised him to study algebra, for by doing so "your mind would get less *muddy*, and you will leave off tormenting your neighbours about paper and packthread, while we all live together in a world that is bursting with sin and sorrow." Johnson was often teased by such frivolous complaints. A young fellow who had inherited a fortune wished to qualify for genteel society by picking up some knowledge of literature. On finding that he was weak in Latin, Johnson advised a study of natural history and began to speak of the animal world, in which some creatures were oviparous, others viviparous. "And the cat here, sir, pray in which class is she?" asked the youth, eager for information. Johnson felt that further conversation at his visitor's present mental level would be wasted. "You would do well," said he, "to look for some person to be always about you, sir, who is capable of explaining such matters, and not come to me to know whether the cat lays eggs or not. Get a discreet man to keep you company; there are many who would be glad of your table and fifty pounds a year."

In addition to half-wits Johnson came into touch while living in the Temple with two men whose reputations have survived to the present day: Oliver Goldsmith and Edmund Burke. With both he formed a firm and lasting friendship, their affection and admiration for him being as strong as his for them. Oliver Goldsmith lived within a few hundred yards of Johnson's chambers; they saw much of one another, and in these years Goldsmith knew Johnson with a more intuitive intimacy than any of his other friends were to experience. Each of them was poor, each was a journalist, and the early struggles of both had been severe, though of a different nature. Goldsmith had wandered penniless about Europe, visiting and debating at the leading universities and keeping himself in food and shelter on the road by playing the flute. Finding that the English people were not so fond of dances and simple tunes as the French and Italian, he tried schoolmastering, acting, and doctoring in

London, failed at everything he attempted, and turned to journalism as a last resort. After a year or two of hackwork he proved himself a delightful essayist in a series of papers contributed to a periodical and later published as *The Citizen of the World*. Like so many Irishmen, he was generous, improvident, and variable in temperament, one day eating, drinking and merry-making, the next morose, penniless and disillusioned; now charming, now savage. The success of his essays enabled him to move to lodgings at the pleasant suburb of Canonbury, where his behaviour on an occasion described by Johnson was typical:

"I received one morning a message from poor Goldsmith that he was in great distress, and as it was not in his power to come to me, begging that I would come to him as soon as possible. I sent him a guinea and promised to come to him directly. I accordingly went as soon as I was dressed and found that his landlady had arrested him for his rent, at which he was in a violent passion. I perceived that he had already changed my guinea, and had got a bottle of Madeira and a glass before him. I put the cork into the bottle, desired he would be calm, and began to talk to him of the means by which he might be extricated. He then told me that he had a novel ready for the press, which he produced to me. I looked into it and saw its merit, told the landlady I should soon return, and having gone to a bookseller sold it for sixty pounds. I brought Goldsmith the money, and he discharged his rent, not without rating his landlady in a high tone for having used him so ill."

The novel was *The Vicar of Wakefield*, of which Johnson once remarked: "It is very faulty; there is nothing of real life in it, and very little of nature. It is a mere fanciful performance." The bookseller concerned was wise enough not to publish it until the author had made a reputation with his poem *The Traveller*, to which Johnson contributed his wisest lines in verse:

How small, of all that human hearts endure,
That part which laws or kings can cause or cure.
Still to ourselves in every place consigned
Our own felicity we make or find;
With secret course, which no loud storms annoy,
Glides the smooth current of domestic joy.

Johnson also added four lines to Goldsmith's poem *The Deserted Village*, the truth of which we are better able to estimate than were his contemporaries:

. . . trade's proud empire hastes to swift decay,
As ocean sweeps the labour'd mole away:
While self-dependent power can time defy,
As rocks resist the billows and the sky.

Goldsmith loved Johnson for his great-hearted sympathy, and said of Levett: "He is poor and honest, which is recommendation enough for Johnson," and of a man who had earned a bad reputation: "He is now become miserable, and that ensures the protection of Johnson." Many people thought Goldsmith absurdly vain and jealous, but his exhibitions of irritation and bursts of petulance were due to an excessive touchiness. He was neither vainer nor more jealous than other men, but he was so sensitive to neglect or ridicule that he reacted instantaneously to things that most people would have had the prudence to ignore or to suffer without apparent resentment. He was like a shy child who longs to show off yet cries over fancied slights, and he aroused Johnson's protective instinct. But he revealed his real self and his true feeling about his benefactor in the dedication of that most charming of comedies, *She Stoops to Conquer*, to Johnson: "By inscribing this slight performance to you, I do not mean so much to compliment you as myself. It may do me some honour to inform the public that I have lived many years in intimacy with you. It may serve the interests of mankind also to inform them that the greatest wit may be found in a character without impairing the most unaffected piety." When Goldsmith died heavily in debt, Johnson said of him: "Let not his frailties be remembered; he was a very great man," a sentiment so wholly out of tune with his views on biography that it explains why his friend was not among the poets whose lives he was one day to record, though he admired Goldsmith more than any other writer of his age. "I think I have had no hero a great while," he admitted towards the close of his life; "Dr. Goldsmith was my last."

Another Irishman, Edmund Burke, was of a contrary nature, arousing Johnson's combativeness along with his admiration. Burke being a Whig and Johnson a Tory, they were careful to keep off politics, and the regard they had for one another was so considerable that their strongly held and conflicting opinions on public affairs were suppressed whenever they met. Johnson had a very poor opinion of Burke's attempts at wit and humour, but praised his variety of knowledge, fluency of language, fertility of ideas. "I never heard Burke make a good joke in my life," said he, while admitting that he had never known Burke at a loss for conversation at any moment on any subject: "His stream of mind is perpetual." Rather too much so, for "So desirous is he to talk that, if one is speaking at this end of the table, he'll speak to somebody at the other end." When Johnson was feeling below par he remarked: "That fellow calls forth all my powers. Were I to see Burke now it would kill me." Each fought for victory in front of others, and Johnson treated these social skirmishes as gladiatorial displays, sometimes refusing to let Burke utter a word, for fear that once started there would be no stopping him. When Johnson had held the floor, or rather the table, for a whole evening, Burke made the best of a bad job by owning to a friend: "It is enough for me to have rung the bell to him." To illustrate the nature of Burke's personality, Johnson said: "If a man were to go by chance at the same time with Burke under a shed to shun a shower, he would say 'This is an extraordinary man'. If Burke should go into a stable to see his horse dressed, the ostler would say 'We have had an extraordinary man here'." But this merely shows that Burke was a born politician, the sort of man who made a business of impressing anyone who might have a vote or a voice to be enlisted. He also had the politician's love of information for its own sake, addiction to rhetoric, bursts of righteous indignation, spasms of moral fervour, and flair for collecting money from mysterious sources.

It is strange how much Johnson, the essential Englishman, owed to Irishmen. It was largely due to the efforts of two fellow-countrymen of Goldsmith and Burke that he was enabled to spend the last twenty-two years of his life free from financial care. One of them, Arthur Murphy, was a genial soul who had picked up a living as a journalist, an actor and a playwright. Popular in social circles for his agreeable talk and amusing stories, he was quick-tempered but good-hearted. Johnson liked him so much that on two occasions Murphy was able to perform services of singular value that a less acceptable person might have failed to discharge. The other Irishman, who assisted in the first of these services, was Thomas Sheridan, whose son was to write *The School for Scandal*. Thomas was a much-mannered actor, intensely conceited, and scornful of anyone who appeared to compete with himself. Such was his self-esteem that he solemnly presented John Home, author of *Douglas*, with a gold medal as an award of merit from himself. Not receiving all the appreciation which he felt to be his due as an actor, he started to teach elocution and to lecture on oratory. Johnson thought him honest and enjoyed the society of his wife, but had something else to say: "Why, sir, Sherry is dull, naturally dull, but it must have taken him a great deal of pains to become what we now see him. Such an excess of stupidity, sir, is not in Nature."

However, dullness demands attention, and Sheridan, who was teaching elocution to a young Scottish barrister named

Alexander Wedderburn, dwelt on the claims of his friend Samuel Johnson to a Government pension. Wedderburn mentioned the matter to his patron, Lord Bute, then chief Minister, who in July 1762 obtained the King's consent to grant Johnson a pension of £300 a year. Johnson's extreme independence of mind being well-known, it was felt that he should be sounded before the offer was made, and Arthur Murphy was empowered to take the soundings. "By slow and studied approaches the message was disclosed," wrote Murphy. "Johnson made a long pause: he asked if it was seriously intended: he fell into a profound meditation, and his own definition of a pensioner occurred to him. He was told that he at least did not come within the definition." Nevertheless his description of a pension as "generally understood to mean pay given to a state hireling for treason to his country" was, he felt, a little strong for a prospective pensioner, and he consulted his friends as to the propriety of his acceptance. They assured him that it was simply a reward for literary merit and that his dictionary definition in no way applied to him. Having ruminated on the offer, he called on Wedderburn, who took him to see Bute. Expressing his satisfaction that the favour was not conferred on him for having dipped his pen in faction, he was relieved to hear from Bute: "No, sir, it is not offered to you for having dipped your pen in faction, nor with a design that you ever should." The Minister assured him that the pension "is not given you for anything you are to do, but for what you have done". To leave Johnson in no doubt on the point, this remark was repeated.

Unfortunately, before the year 1762 was out the granting of another pension cost him a friend. Thomas Sheridan's attempts to correct Wedderburn's Scottish accent and make him talk like a civilised Sassenach were achieving success, and, though another reason might be given, his efforts in that direction were no doubt sufficient to earn him a place on the Civil List. When Johnson heard that £200 a year had been bestowed on Thomas Sheridan, he exclaimed: "What! have they given *him* a pension? Then it is time for me to give up mine." It was of course a joke, and after a pause he added: "However, I am glad that Mr. Sheridan has a pension, for he is a very good man." The joke, not the afterthought, was duly reported to Thomas, who did not think it funny and never again spoke to Johnson.

CHAPTER 9

The Man

HIS TWO COMMENTS on Sheridan's pension reveal two outstanding aspects of Johnson's character: his truth and his
tenderness. He did not think the pension was deserved and
said so, but he thought well of the man and was pleased on his
account. No man was ever more careful than Johnson to speak
and write the truth, though he often took up a point of view
for the sake of victory in a dispute and often spoke carelessly in
the company of friends who were not likely to misunderstand
him. He scorned anything in the nature of pretence. When
people criticised him for taking a pension from a Hanoverian
monarch though his sympathies were known to be with the
House of Stuart, he remarked that he remained the same man
that he had always been, adding: "It is true that I cannot now
curse the House of Hanover, nor would it be decent for me to
drink King James's health in the wine that King George gives
me the money to pay for. But, sir, I think that the pleasure of
cursing the House of Hanover and drinking King James's
health are amply overbalanced by £300 a year." When these
critics were again mentioned, he said with a smile: "I wish my
pension were twice as large, that they might make twice as
much noise." So strong was his attachment to truth that he
would not excuse the general indulgence in social lying, the
sort of thing that everyone says to spare the feelings of others;
and when Goldsmith claimed that he only told white lies, light
as feathers, which he threw up in the air and which hurt
nobody, Johnson growled: "I wish, sir, you would take the
trouble of moulting your feathers."

Johnson's reputation for rudeness was largely due to his steady refusal to tell lies of convenience, though some of his brusquerie was caused by the fact that, with his defective sight and hearing, he could not always see the expression on people's faces nor catch the intonation of their voices. But occasionally his rudeness was wholly gratuitous. When Dr. Barnard, Dean of Derry, happened to say in a large mixed company that men never improved after the age of forty-five, Johnson pulled him up smartly: "That is not true, sir. You, who perhaps are forty-eight, may still improve if you will try; I wish you would set about it; and I am afraid there is great room for it." Though Johnson did his utmost to soothe the insulted clergyman later in the evening, it is not surprising that his victim decided "He is not a gentleman." Oddly enough another Dr. Barnard, Provost of Eton, took a different view. "He was the only man that did justice to my good breeding," said Johnson to a few friends; "and you may observe that I am well-bred to a degree of needless scrupulosity." Not noticing the amazement on the faces of his hearers, he then enumerated his accomplishments in this respect, particularising his care never to interrupt the conversation of others, his close attention to what they were saying, and his refusal to push himself forward. Had his friends said what was in their minds, there would have been a good deal of interruption from him, very little attention to their opinions, and not much attempt to hold himself backward.

All the same, he believed that he had good manners because, when not excited by opposition, he conscientiously displayed them, and so kindly were his instincts that he told his friend Taylor: "When I am musing alone, I feel a pang for every moment that any human being has by my peevishness or obstinacy spent in uneasiness." He was doubtless unaware of the uneasiness he caused in verbal combat with his loud imperious tone of voice and intimidating aspect. He fought to win, bringing all his mental powers to the fray, and when he felt that he was losing ground in an argument he became abusive: "There is no arguing with Johnson," said Goldsmith, "for when his pistol misses fire he knocks you down with the butt end of it." But Goldsmith also knew the duellist who held the pistol: "Johnson, to be sure, has a roughness in his manner, but no man alive has a more tender heart. He has nothing of the bear but his skin." Johnson was well aware that his nature embraced opposites. Once, when he had been fasting, his hostess remarked that he could do nothing in moderation, and he explained: "Did you never hear nor read, madam, that every man has his genius, and that the great rule by which all excellence is attained and all success procured is to follow genius? And have you not observed that my genius is always in extremes, that I am very noisy or very silent, very gloomy or very merry, very sour or very kind? And would you have me cross my genius when it leads me sometimes to voracity and sometimes to abstinence?"

These extremes were nowhere so marked as in his religion, which at one moment uplifted him, at another cast him down. The explanation of many contradictions in his nature, and of his arrogant self-assertion, is that his religion sat uncomfortably upon him. He was an exceptionally rational man dealing with an essentially irrational emotion, and the two states of mind did not cohere. As a symbol of the mystery of the universe institutional religion may be satisfying; as an explanation of that mystery it is inadequate, because reason rebels against anything short of personal revelation, which is granted to few and incommunicable to the rest. Johnson distrusted personal revelation: "If a man pretends to a principle of action of which I can know nothing, nay, not so much as that he has it but only that he pretends to it, how can I tell what that person may be prompted to do?" And he considered the inward light professed by Methodists to be incompatible with social security. Having to depend on his rational faculty for everything he heard or saw, he was thrown back upon unreasoning faith for his religion; but such was his honesty that he often experienced internal discomfort, and he dreaded attacks on his belief as no true believer could. The really religious man is able to dismiss as irrelevant any form of criticism, hostility or ridicule, but a remark of Johnson's reveals the permanent condition of his mind on a subject he regarded as all-important: "Being angry with one who controverts an opinion which you value, is a necessary consequence of the uneasiness which you feel. Every man who attacks my belief diminishes in some degree my confidence in it, and therefore makes me uneasy; and I am angry with him who makes me uneasy."

As with so many highly intelligent men before and since his time, a spiritual anchorage of some sort appeared to be necessary to save his sanity, and his nature craved for the peace and certainty of absolute truth. A religion was therefore indispensable to his temperament, and he doggedly accepted that which he had received from his mother, with its stern emphasis on a sense of sin. "A fallible being will fail somewhere," he once said, and he would have been extremely angry if someone had reminded him that the articles of his faith had been drawn up by fallible beings. He accepted what he wished to accept, rejected what he wished to reject. He could swallow the Thirty-nine Articles, but the Mass stuck in his throat. It may be said that he shut one eye to preserve his sight; and he adopted the motto of the egotist: "He that is not with me is against me." This led him into all sorts of absurd positions, as when he said of an acquaintance: "Sir, if it were not for the notion of immortality, he would cut a throat to fill his pockets." Because of his anxiety that people should agree with him he had little suspicion of hypocrisy in religion, and humbugs whose pretensions he would have quickly ridiculed in the ordinary affairs of life could easily impose on him over questions of faith.

In effect he believed in a God who, having created human beings with passions, exposed them to temptation, and then tortured them for doing what he had given them the faculty and inclination to do. Johnson's reason would have repudiated such a concept; but his need for guidance and a supreme authority forced him to believe the superstition. "Men will submit to any rule by which they may be exempted from the tyranny of caprice and of chance," he admitted, and his own submission was complete.

There is something equally moving and obtuse in the prayers and meditations which he privately composed. He asked God to "look down with mercy upon me depraved with vain imaginations, and entangled in long habits of sin". He constantly referred to his slothfulness, his unmethodical life, his negligence of church-going. He often arrived late for the church service, sometimes fell asleep during the sermon, and on weekdays found it difficult to leave bed before two in the afternoon. "Almighty God," he commenced one prayer, "who seest that I have no power of myself to help myself . . ." and he constantly made resolutions which he invariably broke. One of his entries may be quoted as typical of the rest:

"April 21, 1764. My indolence, since my last reception of the Sacrament, has sunk into grosser sluggishness, and my dissipation spread into wilder negligence. My thoughts have been clouded with sensuality, and, except that from the beginning of this year I have in some measure forborne excess of strong drink, my appetites have predominated over my reason. A kind of strange oblivion has overspread me, so that I know not what has become of the last year, and perceive that incidents and intelligence pass over me without leaving any impression. This is not the life to which Heaven is promised."

Desirous to atone for so many shortcomings, he invited a fellow-worshipper whose pious behaviour in church had impressed him to accompany him home. He had intended to give the man dinner, but found him so foolish that he "talked to him with temper" and suffered him to go empty away. At the age of sixty-two Johnson determined to read within a year the whole Bible, "a very great part of which I had never looked upon." He carried through the heroic resolution and hoped to repeat the achievement every year for the rest of his life; but his nature warred against such a proceeding and even two hours in church were a penance. "I hope in time to take pleasure in public worship," he wrote despairingly in April 1773.

With bad health, poor eyesight, defective hearing, a belief in hell, a fear of eternal damnation, an awe inspired by an avenging deity, a ceaseless sense of his own unworthiness, and constant attacks of hypochondria, we need not wonder that Johnson hated solitude and refused to believe in earthly happiness. It is the weakness of human nature to generalise from its own condition, and because Johnson was subject to depression and constitutionally wretched he believed that other people were the same. He dreaded being alone and would rather have the company of a fool than none at all, which was one of the reasons why he kept a houseful of dependants when he could afford it. He went to the theatre to escape from himself and loved taverns because there was plenty of company: a tavern chair, he said, was the throne of human felicity. Though aware that no man could get away from himself, he embraced every means of eluding his private thoughts. "That the mind is its own peace," said he, "is the boast of a fallen angel that had learned to lie," and he harped on the dangers of solitude to human beings.

While recognising that melancholy was merely deepened by drink, and frequently abstaining from strong liquor on that account, he once remarked that a man was never happy except when drunk. Such an opinion derived from his own spiritual and physical state, for he told a friend that he had never passed a week in his life which he would wish to repeat, "were an angel to make the proposal to him." When Anna Williams, disgusted by drunkenness, said "I wonder what pleasure men can take in making beasts of themselves", Johnson replied: "I wonder, madam, that you have not penetration enough to see the strong inducement to this excess, for he who makes a *beast* of himself gets rid of the pain of being a man." He could argue on the opposite side when it suited him, but what he then said truthfully expressed his belief in drink as the only alleviation of life's misery. Nothing aroused his ire more quickly than the assertion of happiness in another, whether male or female, and his wrath was considerable when a friend described his wife's sister as really happy, calling upon her to confirm the fact, which she did in good set terms. Now here was a somewhat feeble specimen of humanity daring to claim an experience wholly beyond Johnson's own capability. His pride was hurt; his whole being revolted against such a monstrosity; and he bellowed at his friend: "If your sister-in-law is really the contented being she professes herself, her life gives the lie to every research of humanity; for she is happy without health, without beauty, without money, and without understanding." The lady did not pursue the subject, and when he reported the incident elsewhere another lady expressed consternation, which drew this from the unrepentant Johnson: "The same stupidity which prompted her to extol felicity she never felt, hindered her from feeling what shocks you on repetition. I tell you the woman is ugly and sickly and foolish and poor, and would it not make a man hang himself to hear such a creature say it was happy?"

His mind, darkened by superstition, was not enlightened by the arts of music and painting. Deafness interfered with his appreciation of one, shortsightedness of the other. But he seems to have been born without an ear for music. "All animated nature loves music—except myself," he confessed, and at a dinner-party he made the best of his deprivation, saying: "No man of talent, or whose mind was capable of better things, ever would or could devote his time and attention to so idle and frivolous a pursuit" as music. A young woman whispered to her neighbour: "I wonder what Dr. Johnson thinks of King David?" He overheard it and handsomely recanted: "Madam, I thank you; I stand rebuked before you and promise that, on one subject at least, you shall never hear me talk nonsense again." As one of his most intimate friends, Joshua Reynolds, was the leading painter of the day, Johnson did his best to take an interest in the art, but his true feeling emerged in a letter reporting the second annual exhibition of modern paintings, the first of which had taken place in 1760, at the Society of Arts in the Strand: "This exhibition has filled the heads of the artists and lovers of art," he wrote. "Surely life, if it be not long, is tedious, since we are forced to call in the assistance of so many trifles to rid us of our time, of that time which never can return."

To one art however he was susceptible, the art of literature, and to literature in its highest form, manifest in the plays of Shakespeare, he was so sensitive that as a boy the Ghost scene in *Hamlet* frightened him out of the kitchen, in which he was reading it, up to the street door, where he could compose his mind by the sight of real people. While studying *Macbeth* his eyes left the page and he looked around in alarm, startled to find himself alone. Later in life he was so shaken by the final scenes of *King Lear* and *Othello* that he could not endure to read them again. What he enjoyed without qualification was Shakespeare's comedy. He became almost lyrical over Falstaff —"No man but Shakespeare could have drawn Sir John," he declared—and he surrendered unconditionally to *Henry IV*, of which he wrote: "Perhaps no author has ever in two plays afforded so much delight . . . the incidents are multiplied with wonderful fertility of invention, and the characters diversified with the utmost nicety of discernment and the profoundest skill in the nature of man." Though he severely criticised Shakespeare's addiction to verbal quibbles, he recognised that the poet stood head and shoulders above all other writers in knowledge of human nature, in felicity and magnificence of language. A love of disputation once led him to say that Edward Young had suggested night more poetically than Shakespeare, and another time that William Congreve's description of a temple was better than anything of the kind in Shakespeare; but he quickly pulled himself together, saying of the first: "Young froths and foams and bubbles sometimes very vigorously, but we must not compare the noise made by your tea-kettle here with the roaring of the ocean," and of the second that he only had one ten-guinea piece whereas Shakespeare had ten thousand pounds. A famous French poet was also given his quietus: "Corneille is to Shakespeare as a clipped hedge is to a forest." Johnson's main complaint, as we should expect, was that Shakespeare "seems to write without any moral purpose . . . he makes no just distribution of good or evil, nor is always careful to shew in the virtuous a disapprobation of the wicked . . . it is always a writer's duty to make the world better . . ." But the natural puritan can never enter into the mind of the instinctive artist, who sees life not as a moral battle, but as a conflict of personalities.

Johnson tinkered with his edition of Shakespeare's plays for nine years. He collected many subscriptions soon after publishing his proposals for it in 1756, and they continued to trickle in during the years that followed. But his friends became anxious for his reputation as time went by and nothing further was heard of it, and in 1762 Charles Churchill made an acid comment on the delay in his satire *The Ghost*:

> He for subscribers baits his hook,
> And takes your cash; but where's the book?
> No matter where; wise fear, you know,
> Forbids the robbing of a foe;
> But what, to serve our private ends,
> Forbids the cheating of our friends?

A year after that a young bookseller called on Johnson with a subscription and asked that the name of the subscriber should be included in the printed list. "I shall print no list of subscribers," said Johnson. The bookseller must have looked astonished. "Sir," explained Johnson, "I have two very cogent reasons for not printing any list of subscribers: one that I have lost all the names, the other that I have spent all the money."

When at last, in October 1765, the edition was published, all those who claimed that they had subscribed received their copies, and the editor's friends breathed a sigh of relief. Johnson's Preface to the plays was assailed by many who considered criticism of Shakespeare a form of blasphemy, but it remains one of the great critical essays in the language, a remarkable example of wisdom and uncommon sense, usually miscalled common sense. Most of his strictures are just, and his praise is as stately as it is veracious: "The stream of time, which is continually washing the dissoluble fabrics of other poets, passes without injury by the adamant of Shakespeare." As usual, he thought little of his labours, writing to a friend: "To tell the truth, as I felt no solicitude about this work, I receive no great comfort from its conclusion; but yet am well enough pleased that the public has no further claim upon me." He had started the job in order to earn money, but before finishing it he received his pension, and he had no intention of undertaking another editorial work nor indeed of writing another book. Slothful by nature, he could not understand anyone wanting to write when it was so much more pleasant to talk. "No man but a blockhead ever wrote except for money," he said, and the remark has been repeated with fatuous relish by every blockhead since his time. It would be truer to say that only a blockhead ever wrote for money, which can be made much more easily and in larger sums by a dozen other forms of activity. Apart from the fact that work, like idleness, becomes a habit, the best authors write because of some inner compulsion to express themselves; and though they may hope that their efforts will enable them to live, those who feel the compulsion will go on writing in spite of failure and earn a living by some other means. Johnson, who admitted that he often spoke loosely and talked nonsense, never said a sillier thing than this, as he must have been aware from personal experience, since he supplied countless dedications to other men's books and prologues to other men's plays for nothing, and produced all his most durable work for much less money than he could have got for it.

Having finished his labours on Shakespeare, he had to occupy himself somehow to keep his mind from brooding and to kill time. "Life must be filled up," he said, "and the man who is not capable of intellectual pleasures must content himself with such as his senses can afford"—girls and gambling in the case that provoked this comment. One of his remarks has often been quoted: "There are few ways in which a man can be more innocently employed than in getting money." But another of his sayings should be set against it: "Why, a fellow must do something, and what so easy *to a narrow mind* as hoarding halfpence till they turn into sixpences?" He would have agreed with Hannah More that "trifles make the sum of human things", for there was nothing, said he, "too little for so little a creature as man. It is by studying little things that we attain the great art of having as little misery and as much happiness as possible."

His interests were very wide and he could talk on any subject. He loved making chemical experiments and he studied medicine as well as the law. People noticed that he collected orange peel, but they dared not ask him why. The reason appears in a letter to an old friend: he dried it, powdered it, put a quantity into a glass of hot port, and drank it as a remedy for indigestion. With such trifles, useful or not, did he pass away the time, a good deal of which was spent in bed. He slept badly at night and often felt drowsy in the morning. Though constantly resolving to get up at 9 a.m., he may have soothed his conscience with the words of the psalmist: "It is but lost labour that ye haste to rise up early." He read a great deal, but fitfully, in bed and out of it. "A man ought to read just as inclination leads him," he observed, "for what he reads as a task will do him little good." He usually carried a book about with him, and when bored, either alone or in company, he would turn over the leaves and become oblivious of his surroundings. Though he wrote with ease, he disliked the labour of writing and was a bad correspondent. "I know not how it happens," he informed John Taylor, "but I fancy that I write letters with more difficulty than some other people who write nothing but letters, at least I find myself very unwilling to take up a pen only to tell my friends that I am well . . ."

One very pleasurable way of filling in the time was the filling of his belly. He would emerge from his house at about four in the afternoon and visit friends or meet them in taverns, seldom returning home till the early hours of the following morning. Dining, supping and drinking were lengthy operations in those days, and Johnson thoroughly enjoyed the process of eating. "I mind my belly very studiously and very carefully," he admitted, "for I look upon it that he who does not mind his belly will hardly mind anything else." His table-companions can have had little doubt on the point, for he fell upon the food voraciously, the effort of mastication making the veins swell and the perspiration appear on his forehead. His appetite was so ravenous, his indulgence so abandoned, that he scarcely attended to the conversation or the needs of others, and ignored the remarks addressed to him. In eating fish he used his fingers because he was short-sighted and afraid of bones. He considered himself a first-rate judge of cooking and good food, and criticised meals that were not to his taste. When an intimate friend invited him to a plain dinner, he remarked: "This was a good dinner enough, to be sure, but it was not a dinner to *ask* a man to." Having gorged himself to repletion, he did not like being pressed to another helping, and once startled his fellow-guests by rising from his chair, knife in hand, and loudly proclaiming: "I vow to God I cannot eat a bit more!"

His drinking habits were more temperate. He could abstain from wine and spirits for years together because he found that heavy drinking increased his melancholia and interfered with digestion. But in his days of indulgence he seldom got fuddled. Joshua Reynolds said that he had only once seen Johnson intoxicated. This was when they went on a trip to Devonshire in the summer of 1762, spending most of their time at Plymouth. After supper one night, Johnson, having drunk three bottles of wine, found it difficult to articulate a long word. He made several attempts and at length managed to pronounce it accurately. Success made him decisive: "Well, Sir Joshua, I think it is now time to go to bed." During his long periods as a total abstainer his chief liquid gratification was tea, which he could drink at all times and in great quantities. People disagreed about the number of cups, smallish then, that he could down at a sitting. Fifteen was the more moderate estimate, but those who were as immoderate in calculation as he was in absorption put it at twenty-five.

While the cups or glasses were emptied and replenished the stream of conversation never ceased to flow, and Johnson talked for as long as the company remained together, sitting up to all hours and resenting the fact that his companions sometimes felt sleepy and wanted to go to bed. His manner could be charming or alarming; it depended on the company and the cooking. With his large body, strong features, and a face scarred with early scrofula, he had a heavy look, but when he was speaking his countenance glowed with animation. His utterance was deliberate, loud and impressive, which made everything he said seem more remarkable that it sometimes was. He never got rid of his Staffordshire accent, pronouncing 'punch' *poonsh*, 'once' *woonse*, 'superior' *shuperior*, 'supreme' *shupreme*, and 'there' to rhyme with *fear*. He used many long and resonant words, imposing like his speech. Goldsmith was once dilating on a fable of little fishes and saying that the skill consisted in making them talk as such. Noticing that Johnson was silently laughing at such an absurdity, Goldsmith neatly turned the laugh: "Why, Dr. Johnson, this is not so easy as you seem to think, for if you were to make little fishes talk they would talk like whales." Johnson's laugh was as striking as his talk. It was gargantuan, and so infectious that it made other people laugh too. When retailing anecdotes he was excessively amusing, keeping the company in fits of merriment, though there was something of the playfulness of a lion in his jocularity: one kept clear of his paws. It was noticed that he seldom began a subject, though once it was started he soon became the leading contributor. He had the art of drawing people out, of making them talk on their favourite subjects; and as they talked best on what interested them most, their conversation pleased him the more. But he did not like the sycophantic appreciation of those who thought they would please him by laughing heartily at whatever he said, checking one of them with: "What provokes your risibility, sir? Have I said anything that you understand? Then I ask pardon of the rest of the company." He did not talk for effect except when engaged in an argument, his sole object being to win. "I never considered whether I should be a grave man or a merry man," he said, "but just let inclination, for the time, have its course." Most of all he enjoyed an intimate talk with his friends, when his affectionate disposition, not his combative powers, had full play. "That is the happiest conversation," he observed, "where there is no competition, no vanity, but a calm quiet interchange of sentiments." He rarely resorted to irony, but now and again the lion's claws were discernible beneath the velvet paws. When a man left the party in a tavern, someone asked Johnson who he was. "I cannot exactly tell you, sir, and I would be loth to speak ill of any person who I do not know deserves it, but I am afraid he is an attorney." Asked by an actor named Henderson for his opinion of Joseph Reed's *Dido*, Johnson replied: "Sir, I never did the man an injury, yet he would read his tragedy to me."

On the whole his general conversation may be described as informative and instructive rather than entertaining and fanciful. It was unlike that of Sydney Smith, out of whom wit and fun and fancy oozed and bubbled and spouted as from a human geyser, and who might be said to have been witty in his sleep. What was best in Johnson's talk was the intermittent concentration of solid sense into pithy axioms. Two comments in his letters illustrate this quality in his table-talk: "Success always produces either love or hatred," and "What is nearest us touches us most. The passions rise higher at domestic than at imperial tragedies". He could always bring his intelligence to bear on the most trivial topic. For example, a man who had a high appreciation of rank as well as intellect said that if he were asked to dine with England's leading duke, and on the same day with Britain's leading genius, he would not know which invitation to accept. Johnson told him: "To be sure, sir, if you were to dine only once, and it were never to be known where you dined, you would choose rather to dine with the first man for genius; but to gain most respect, you should dine with the first duke in England. For nine people in ten that you meet with would have a higher opinion of you for having dined with a duke; and the great genius himself would receive you better because you had been with the great duke."

Johnson had certain favourite themes on which he liked to enlarge. They mostly came under the heading of what he called 'cant'. The weather was one. The English being chary of conversation with strangers, or having nothing interesting to say, usually fall back on the weather as a subject not only safe but devoid of interest. It therefore begins to assume importance in their lives, making them believe that it gravely affects their condition of mind and body, and in casual talk the state of their health usually follows the state of the weather. Johnson thought the whole thing silly. "What is climate to happiness?" he asked; and when a friend complained of a rainy day but admitted it was good for the vegetables, he agreed: "Why, yes, sir, it is good for vegetables, and for the animals who eat those vegetables, and for the animals who eat those animals." Another complaint of the disagreeable effects of bad weather brought this from him: "Sir, this is all imagination, which physicians encourage, for man lives in air as a fish lives in water, so that if the atmosphere press heavy from above, there is an equal resistance from below." He admitted that bad weather was hard upon people who were obliged to work in the open air, but ridiculed those who were not necessarily exposed to it, yet grumbled. Driving along the Surrey lanes, a lady expressed a wish for rain to lay the dust, but quickly regretted the expression. "I cannot bear," said Johnson, "when I know how many families will perish next winter for want of that bread which the present drought will bring them, to hear ladies sighing for rain, only that their complexions may not suffer from the heat, or their clothes be incommoded by the dust. For shame! Leave off such foppish lamentations, and study to relieve those whose distresses are real." His own indifference to such external discomforts made him a good travelling companion, for the rain, the sun, the night, the day, were all the same to him, and people who bothered about such things were in his opinion empty-headed.

Another form of humbug that provoked his derision was the distress people affected to feel over the misfortunes of others. "Everyone in this world," said he, "has as much as they can do in caring for themselves, and few have leisure really to *think* of their neighbours' distresses, however they may delight their tongues with *talking* of them." And when a female friend exhibited grief at the loss of a cousin who had been killed in America, he did not sympathise: "Prithee, my dear, have done with canting. How would the world be worse for it, I may ask, if all your relations were at once spitted like larks, and roasted for Presto's supper?" (Presto was her dog.) When told that someone had felt extremely sorry at the report of a friend's death, he tried to gauge the depth of feeling: "Not sorrier, I suppose, than the horse is when the cow miscarries?" Though he felt the death of his friends keenly, he would not allow others to indulge in the outward display of protracted grief: "We must either outlive our friends, you know, or our friends must outlive us, and I see no man that would hesitate about the choice."

The theory of equality was a further theme for satire. He believed in rank, and felt that the classes of society then existing represented as rational an order as human nature at the time allowed. Perhaps he perceived the possibilities of class evolution, but he was wholly opposed to any sudden means of changing the social structure. He respected the nobility so long as the nobility deserved respect; and in any case they had been created by the Crown, they had historical associations, they were the responsible chiefs of the community, and they created no jealousy because their rank was accidental and unrelated to merit. When therefore the social equality of man was discussed he left no one in any doubt of his feelings, and once gave a practical demonstration of the theory being popularised by Rousseau. He was dining with Catherine Macaulay, of whom he said "to make *her* ridiculous is like blacking the chimney." For some time she dwelt on the natural equality of man, until Johnson rose from the table and gravely addressed her: "Madam, I am now become a convert to your way of thinking. I am convinced that all mankind are upon an equal footing; and to give you an unquestionable proof that I am in earnest, here is a very sensible civil, well-behaved fellow-citizen, your footman," turning to whom he continued: "Mr. John, pray be seated in my place and permit me to wait upon you in my turn; your mistress says, you hear, that we are all equal." In telling the story Johnson reported the singular circumstance that Catherine Macaulay had never liked him since.

CHAPTER 10

The Meeting

JOHNSON had the bravery of great physical strength and the hardihood of one who feared God more than he feared man. What were the temporal pains inflicted by human beings compared with the eternal agony of hell-fire? We have seen how he dealt with a tough customer who refused to yield his seat at a play, and his method was equally effective with recalcitrant dogs. It was reported that at Beauclerk's country-house two large mastiffs had quarrelled so fiercely that no one dared approach them except Johnson, who seized each by the scruff of the neck and tore them apart, putting one out of the door, the other out of the window. Beauclerk having described the incident, Johnson was asked if it were true. "The dogs have been somewhat magnified, I believe, sir," he answered; "they were, as I remember, two stout young pointers, but the story has gained but little." The mere sight of him must have frightened anyone who thought of molesting him, but one night four footpads put their courage in eight hands and set upon him. They should have added to their number, for single-handed he kept them off until the watch arrived, and all of them were marched into custody. Occasionally he acted in a dare-devil manner. While bathing at Oxford he was warned that a certain pool was dangerous; he promptly swam into it. While handling a gun he was told that it would burst if over-loaded; he charged it with six or seven balls and fired it at a wall. Such exhibitions were childish enough, but they showed that he was careless of physical danger, and it would have been a David of no ordinary courage to tackle this Goliath.

Such a one was not Samuel Foote, the playwright and actor. Foote was an extremely amusing mimic, very popular with the aristocracy because he made them laugh and asked to dine at all the great houses to entertain the guests. At the cost of meeting an actor socially, peers of the realm obtained a free and hilarious performance. Foote lost a leg in a riding accident, and to recompense him the Duke of York allowed him to build a small theatre in the Haymarket, where he was soon making audiences shout with joy at his outrageous imitations of eminent men. Garrick was one of his victims, none of whom dared to take legal proceedings for fear of universal ridicule. Johnson did not care for this cruel form of humour, and when he met Foote at dinner he determined not to be amused: "I went on eating my dinner pretty sullenly, affecting not to mind him. But the dog was so very comical that I was obliged to lay down my knife and fork, throw myself back upon my chair, and fairly laugh it out. No, sir, he was irresistible." However, Johnson had no wish to hear audiences laugh at a parody of himself on the stage, however irresistible, and when he heard that Foote was about to add him to the gallery of grotesques at the Haymarket he asked the bookseller Tom Davies, with whom he was dining, what was the price of an oak stick. Sixpence, he was informed. "Why, then, sir, give me leave to send your servant to purchase me a shilling one. I'll have a double quantity, for I am told that Foote means to *take me off*, as he calls it, and I am determined the fellow shall not do it with impunity." On hearing from Davies of Johnson's intention, Foote changed his mind. "Sir, fear restrained him," was Johnson's comment; "he knew I would have broken his bones. I would have saved him the trouble of cutting off a leg; I would not have left him a leg to cut off."

Foote's caricature would have been an extraordinary exhibition, guaranteed to bring down the house; for Johnson's oddities were notorious, and even those who had never seen him had heard of his queer mannerisms and strange appearance.

He was six feet tall in his shoes, but as his habitual stoop rounded his shoulders he gave the impression of bulk more than height. In the street he walked heavily at a good rate, his legs well apart, his left arm across his breast so that the hand came under the chin. But his tendency was to walk zigzag fashion, and some quaint superstition of numbers often made him count his steps from one point to another and even to go back and re-count them if the first numeration were unsatisfactory. There were times too when he felt it necessary to start off with the right or left foot and return to re-start if he had begun with the wrong one. He was walking one day with the sister of Joshua Reynolds in the meadows at Twickenham, and she noticed that his hands and feet were performing the strangest motions. He seemed to be holding the reins of a horse with his hands, like a jockey going at full speed, while his feet were made to touch either at the heels or at the toes, as if they were forming triangles. Passers-by stopped to stare and laugh at his antics. She had also observed his arrival with Anna Williams at her brother's house, when he whirled his blind companion about on the steps as he performed an involuntary gyration, and then gave a sudden spring over the threshold, leaving Anna to grope her way into the house or to be guided by the servant who opened the door.

His physical actions indoors were also curious. As he sat meditating in a chair he moved his body to and fro, see-sawing, the palm of his hand keeping pace on his knee, his head inclining towards his right shoulder and usually in a state of tremor. He made singular ruminative noises with his mouth, chewing, clucking, sibilating, blowing; and sometimes he seemed to be the victim of St. Vitus's dance, his legs and arms jerking convulsively as if at the mercy of a nerve. Joshua Reynolds declared that these antic gestures were only apparent when he was lost in reverie or reading a book, and that while his attention was engaged in conversation his vocal mannerisms were silenced, his limbs stilled. But as he was fairly often

95

abstracted from the general conversation on account of deafness, his physical eccentricities were noticeable in every gathering; and when a girl asked him why he made such queer sounds and motions, he replied: "From habit. Do *you*, my dear, take care to guard against bad habits."

Another of his idiosyncrasies was audible soliloquy. Whether musing alone or in company, whether standing or walking, he quoted prayers and poetry or uttered stray thoughts to himself. But this habit is more common than is generally supposed. Muttering to themselves, people walk the streets with bits and pieces of tragedy, as it were, hanging about them like so many mental tatters. Johnson's gesticulations and rumblings were reinforced by the fierce and piercing quality of his light grey eyes, the effect produced by his appearance being more fearsome than funny, while the ill-health which, he wrote, "has crusted me into inactivity" had made him alarmingly corpulent at the age of sixty, of which he was well aware, making a private note in September 1769: "I have grown fat too fast. My lungs seem encumbered, and my breath fails me if my strength is in any unusual degree exerted or my motion accelerated."

Nevertheless he ceased to be a stationary figure in London after the granting of his pension; and though his appetite increased with the means of gratifying it, he began to tour the country at regular intervals, paying visits to distant friends whom otherwise he could have seen only in the metropolis. He went to Devonshire with Joshua Reynolds, to Lincolnshire for a holiday with Bennet Langton's family, to Lichfield and Ashbourne, to Oxford and Cambridge, and to Easton Mauditt in Northamptonshire, where he stayed with the vicar, Thomas Percy, who edited the *Reliques of Ancient Poetry* and afterwards became the Bishop of Dromore in Ireland. But he always returned to London with the relief of one who had been exiled from home, and in 1764 he helped to found The Club, which dined weekly at the Turk's Head in Gerrard Street, Soho, the sessions lasting from seven in the evening till midnight or after.

When David Garrick got to hear of The Club, he said to Reynolds "I like it much; I think I shall be of you." His remark was passed on to Johnson, who promptly put his one-time pupil in his place: "*He'll be of us!* How does he know we will *permit* him? The first duke in England has no right to hold such language." Johnson was very fond of David, but recognised his principal defect as a clubman: "Garrick never enters a room but he regards himself as the object of general attention, from whom the entertainment of the company is expected; and true it is that he seldom disappoints them, for he has infinite humour, a very just proportion of wit, and more convivial pleasantry than almost any man. But then *off* as well as *on* the stage he is always an actor, for he thinks it so incumbent upon him to be sportive that his gaiety becomes mechanical from being habitual, and he can exert his spirits at all times alike, without consulting his real disposition to hilarity." All the same, with Johnson's support, Garrick became a member of The Club after sufficient time had elapsed to make him repent his early presumption.

Johnson's relationship to Garrick was a little like that of father to son, for he took upon himself the duties of reproval but was jealous of his rights and allowed no one else the satisfaction of censure. As already remarked, he liked the company of men junior to himself, and invariably championed the young against the old. There was, he knew, a ceaseless struggle between a father who aims at power and a son who yearns for independence, but he sympathised with the desire of youth. "A man commonly grows wickeder as he grows older," he said; "at least he but changes the vices of youth, headstrong passion and wild temerity for treacherous caution and desire to circumvent. I am always on the young people's side when there is a dispute between them and the old ones, for you have at least a chance for virtue till age has withered its very root." True, he was liable to suppress the ill-manners or over-familiarity of youth, as when a young fellow asked abruptly: "Mr. Johnson, would you advise me to marry?" and he replied angrily: "I would advise no man to marry, sir, who is not likely to propagate understanding." Having stunned the youngster, he left the room, but soon returned to put the lad at his ease. His advice to young men who had married against the wish of their parents always displayed a fellow-feeling. "If you married imprudently," he told one of them, "you married at your own hazard at an age when you had a right of choice. It would be hard if the man might not choose his own wife who has a right to plead before the judges of his country."

Although he longed to retain the affection of his school-friends, writing to Hector "Your letters are always so welcome that you need not increase their value by making them scarce", and begging Taylor not to let their early friendship languish, yet he preferred the society of those whose freshness of outlook and natural high spirits helped to keep his own melancholy at bay: "Sir, I love the acquaintance of young people; because in the first place I don't like to think myself growing old. In the next place, young acquaintances must last longest, if they do last . . . I love the young dogs of this age: they have more wit and humour and knowledge of life than we had; but then the dogs are not so good scholars." It was well for one of the young dogs that he favoured the breed, and well for himself that this particular puppy could suffer his snarling without taking offence.

On the evening of 16th May 1763, Johnson entered the book-shop of Thomas Davies, at No. 8 Russell Street, Covent Garden. Tom had been an actor and had married a very pretty actress. He gave himself airs, which made him disliked by some who thought a bookseller should be humble. Johnson considered that he had a good heart, and forgave him when he published two volumes of essays "by the Author of the Rambler" without permission. He was friendly, hospitable, rather self-important, inclined to dramatise himself, to create theatrical situations, and to mimic his acquaintances. When Johnson walked into his shop on the present occasion he was sitting in the back-parlour with his wife and a young Scot who had already called several times on the chance of an introduction to Johnson. It was well-known that Johnson entertained unfavourable views of Scotland and its inhabitants. His attitude was largely owing to the fact that the natives of that country who settled in England formed a sort of clique, employing Scotch servants, patronising Scotch tradesmen, applauding Scottish plays and books without regard to merit; while the chief Minister of the time, Bute, was a Scot who favoured his race in the bestowal of jobs; and Johnson felt that this exclusive spirit of nationalism should be opposed. Once a Scot was so ill-advised as to praise his country's scenery, saying that Scotland had a great many noble wild prospects. "I believe, sir, you have a great many," agreed Johnson. "Norway, too, has noble wild prospects; and Lapland is remarkable for prodigious noble wild prospects. But, sir, let me tell you, the noblest prospect which a Scotchman ever sees is the high road that leads him to England." The Scot collapsed, and Johnson puffed with pleasure.

Aware of this antipathy, the young Scot in Davies's back-parlour was nervous about his reception, and it did not make him less apprehensive when Tom announced Johnson's arrival in the style of Horatio's horrific exclamation to Hamlet that the Ghost has appeared on the scene: "Look, my lord! it comes." While Davies was introducing his young friend, James Boswell, to Samuel Johnson, he was begged by the former in an agitated undertone not to mention the country of his birth. Naturally Tom at once added "from Scotland". Upon which Boswell dithered "I do indeed come from Scotland, but I cannot help it", and was paralysed by Johnson's answer: "That, sir, I find is what a great many of your countrymen cannot help." They all sat down, Boswell quaking. Johnson then complained to Davies that Garrick had refused him a free seat for Anna Williams because the house would be full and the seat worth three shillings. Here was an opening for a little ameliorative flattery, and Boswell took it: "Oh, sir, I cannot think Garrick would grudge such a trifle to you!" But he quickly regretted the presumption. "Sir, I have known David Garrick longer than you have done, and I know no right you have to talk to me on the subject." Anyone but Boswell would have thrown in his hand at this point; but the young Scot was made of sterner stuff and, instead of retiring hurt, consoled himself by taking notes of Johnson's conversation. Later in the evening he was left alone with the great man, who treated him with civility, and when he left Davies cheered him up with "Don't be uneasy; I can see he likes you well."

To make sure of this, Boswell called at Johnson's chambers in the Temple eight days after that first disheartening meeting, was courteously received, and even told to remain when the other visitors left. "I am afraid that I intrude upon you," said Boswell. "It is benevolent to allow me to sit and hear you." Johnson answered that he was obliged to any man who visited him; and when Boswell rose to go for the second time he was again requested to stay. At their third meeting three weeks later Johnson asked why he did not call more frequently. Boswell adverted to the discouragement he had received when introduced by Davies. "Poh, poh!" said Johnson with a pleasant smile, "never mind these things. Come to me as often as you can. I shall be glad to see you."

But Boswell was too busy tasting the delights of London to seek moral instruction from Johnson, and their next serious talk took place at the Mitre Tavern in Fleet Street on 25th June, when Boswell gave Johnson a good supper and they sat together four or five hours over two bottles of port. Taking advantage of his guest's amiable mood, Boswell gave a sketch of his life, at the conclusion of which Johnson was moved to say: "Give me your hand, I have taken a liking to you."

We can fill in the sketch with some details which Boswell would have thought it prudent to omit.

CHAPTER 11

From Scotland

VARIOUS LAKES in Scotland have been credited for centuries past with harbouring a species of icthyosaurus, but the country has never produced so queer a fish as James Boswell, who first emerged into daylight at Edinburgh on 29th October 1740, when Johnson was thirty-one years old. The Boswells had been lairds of Auchinleck in Ayrshire since 1504, when James IV gave the barony to Thomas Boswell, who perished with his benefactor nine years later on Flodden field. The family had married into the nobility, our James being very proud of his descent from Robert Bruce, the Earls of Lennox, Mar, and other grandees. In later times the Boswells had become Whiggish and respectable, the father and grandfather of James having entered the legal profession. His father, Alexander, rose to be one of the judges of the Court of Session, and then a judge of the High Court with the honorary title of Lord Auchinleck. A stern disciplinarian, with strong prejudices, high principles, a caustic tongue and a magisterial manner, Alexander put the fear of the Lord, backed by fear of the laird, into his three sons: James the eldest, John some three years younger, and David about eight years younger. The greater part of his first nine years was spent by James at his father's house in Blair's Land, Parliament Close, Edinburgh, after which Alexander inherited the Auchinleck estate and the children saw a lot of the ancestral seat. Their mother is for us a shadowy simulacrum of a woman. She was unselfish, pious and kindly, but the wife of Alexander Boswell would have had few chances to develop her personality and none to assert it.

In his early twenties James wrote that omens of his future greatness had appeared at his nativity. It could be replied, in Hotspur's words to Glendower, that the same omens would have appeared if his mother's cat had but kittened and himself had never been born. But James has a better claim to astronomical disturbance at his birth than most people. He was a prodigy of a very peculiar kind, though no one at first could have guessed that he was at all exceptional. The reaction of an unusual boy against the conditions of his youth is often as violent as his upbringing is strict, and some of Boswell's later licentiousness may be attributed to the austerity of his early life. Instead of his going to the High School at Edinburgh and roughing it with all sorts and conditions of lads, his father sent him to a carefully picked private institution and engaged a tutor for domestic coaching. James was a nervous child, frightened of the dark, of ghosts, and of God. The Presbyterian form of worship at that time was not calculated to inspire confidence in the young, and it took James many years to shake off the doleful ideas he had imbibed from it. He was tormented with visions of hell, the pastors and parents of those days being firmly convinced that discipline could only be maintained and character formed by immediate fear of the rod and dread of the wrath to come; and if he had been as mentally robust as some of his later and less reputable companions, his early religious training would have turned him into a convinced atheist. But mental robustness was never to be among his characteristics, and the youngster's spiritual condition was such that at the age of twelve he suffered from nervous dyspepsia, together with some sort of skin disease, and was packed off to Moffat for hydropathic treatment. There, under threat of chastisement, he was compelled to remain for half an hour at a time in a disagreeable receptacle filled with warm water. Whether boredom or first-love cured his scurviness we cannot tell, but he was greatly attracted to a girl called Mackay, who remained unconscious of the feeling she had inspired, possibly because the sarcasm of his tutor prevented him from declaring it.

A year later he went to Edinburgh University, where he became attached to two fellow-students, the first a Scot named John Johnston, the second an English boy from Berwick-on-Tweed, William Johnson Temple, who was to become a lifelong intimate, and incidentally the forebear of two Archbishops of Canterbury. The usual amount of Greek and Latin was pumped into James at the University, the religious treatment being continued at home, and it was doubtless an overdose of the Hebrew scriptures, not the classic authors, that caused a breakdown in his health at the age of seventeen. He was ill for several months, and his recovery was in the nature of a miracle. He seemed to be re-born. A new James Boswell left his bed, strong, energetic, sleek, ready for a round with his father. Never an impressive figure, he now carried his five and a half feet with as much dignity as he could manage, and made up for his lack of inches with self-assertion. His black hair and eyes to match were at least noticeable, and having lost his bashfulness along with his theological terrors he suddenly became socially adaptable. Amorous by nature, he started to hang about the theatre, to flirt with actresses, to write poems, and to dally with the ladies of the town. He frequented taverns and talked with actors. He wanted a commission in the Army, and above all he longed for London, the charms of which were painted in many colours by all his acquaintances who knew it. He developed a passion for an heiress named Martha White, or for her fortune, and decided that she would make him a good wife, a decision which seems to have been at variance with hers, for she eventually married the Earl of Elgin. He disclosed an ambition to be on friendly terms with men of intellect, and obtained an introduction to the famous historian David Hume, whose sceptical mind appealed to the young man, whose rebirth had coincided with a strong opposition to his father's faith. More important for us than all these excitements, an actor named Love, manager of the Edinburgh theatre, advised him to keep a journal of everyday happenings, which he began soon afterwards, continuing the practice fairly regularly for the rest of his life, a habit to which we are indebted for the *Life of Samuel Johnson*, and much else.

While his head was buzzing with the thoughts and his heart fluttering with the emotions of this new life, his father's eye kept him closely and steadily at his studies, and his days in term-time were fully occupied with legal and cognate themes. Having determined that he should follow the law, his father prevented his mind from straying to more genial subjects by taking him on the Northern Circuit for the first three weeks of September 1758. Lord Auchinleck judged criminal cases at Perth, Inverness and Aberdeen, and Sir David Dalrymple, who accompanied them, acted as deputy-advocate or Crown Prosecutor. James enjoyed the trip because he travelled in the same chaise all the way with Dalrymple, who did his best to ease the relationship between father and son. Here was a man whom the youngster could admire wholeheartedly, for Dalrymple had been educated at Eton and Utrecht, knew London well, corresponded with wits and men of fashion like Horace Walpole, and loved literature. He carried his learning lightly and was successful in his profession, being raised to the Bench in 1766, thereafter to be known as Lord Hailes.

But their northern journey did not allay the differences between the judge and his son. The pleasures of Edinburgh were becoming too seductive for a serious student, and James was despatched to Glasgow, where he laboured on civil law at the University with no enticements to self-indulgence. The lectures of Adam Smith on literature and philosophy relieved the monotony, but they were not exciting enough to keep his mind from brooding on paternal tyranny. The healthy rebelliousness of youth against unimaginative authority was strengthened in his case by a growing repugnance to Presbyterianism, and in a moment of gloomy despair he broke loose.

What followed was largely due to his father's lack of understanding. Early in 1760 he dashed off to London, riding from Carlisle to the capital, day and night, in two and a half days. On arrival he put up at a Roman Catholic wig-maker's, which suggests that he had been in close touch with actors of that faith in the two Scottish cities, witnessed the celebration of Mass at the Bavarian Chapel, and promptly went what Sydney Smith called "the whole lamb" by joining the Roman Church. This was a somewhat extreme form of breaking the Fifth Commandment. Apart from dishonouring his father and mother, it then meant that he abandoned all hope of obtaining a commission in the Army or Navy, of being a barrister or Member of Parliament, of having a vote for the latter, of getting any kind of Government job, and of inheriting the property of Auchinleck. In short it did not pay to be a Roman Catholic in those days, and James was not of the stuff from which martyrs are made. Though he toyed with the idea of entering a French monastery, he quickly realised that he was not a born ascetic and that the pleasures of life were more in his line than the pains.

He was careful to keep his father in ignorance of his sudden conviction that the Pope's view of God was clearer than Calvin's though he wrote to say that London was preferable to Glasgow. His father at once asked the Earl of Eglinton, an Ayrshire acquaintance who was living in Mayfair, to see what could be done with James. It soon transpired that James was quite capable of looking after himself, and that his conversion to Roman Catholicism had been speedily followed by his conversion to paganism. A letter of introduction to Samuel Derrick from one of his theatrical friends in the north had done the trick. Derrick was a dapper little fellow who had failed as an actor, was now busily failing as an author, but would shortly follow Beau Nash as Master of Ceremonies at Bath and monarch thereof. It pleased him to act as Boswell's cicerone, and they saw London together. It was not exactly the city to which Johnson had been introduced twenty odd years before; at least they viewed a greater variety of its aspects than he had done, such as the public executions at Tyburn, the public floggings anywhere, the brothels and gambling-dens and drinking-cellars of Covent Garden, the gardens of Vauxhall and Ranelagh, where the nobility took their pleasure unashamed, and those of Marylebone, where many were to be seen in disguise. It was a noisy, bawdy, brutal and smelly city, but to a young man like Boswell it was stimulating, thrilling and fulfilling. Garrick's appearances at Drury Lane Theatre were the chief feature of the entertainment world, and the famous actor was marked down by the young playgoer as a man to be met. His high spirits were manifested during an interval at one performance, when he amused the audience by imitating the bellow of a cow. The gallery shouted "Encore the cow!" and the laughter aroused by his mimicry incited him to try the neighing and braying of other animals; but these were not so successful and he was advised by a clerical friend to stick to the cow.

From his experiences of the seamy side of London life he was delivered by Eglinton, who invited him to stay in more elegant quarters and introduced him to the fashionable world. He met the popular author of the hour, Laurence Sterne; he was introduced to peers and peeresses, Members of Parliament and leading social lights; he amused the debauched and hare-brained Duke of York, whom he entertained with his antics at the Jockey Club during a race-meeting at Newmarket, an occurrence that went to his head and resulted two years later in a piece of published doggerel called *The Cub at Newmarket*, which he dedicated to the Duke without permission, causing that prince to curse Eglinton, who naturally cooled towards Boswell. But such annoyances were in the future, and for about three months the young man surrendered to the joys of London, revelled in his day-to-day existence, coveted a commission in the Guards so that he could strut with pride in the choicest circles, and enjoyed his first serious love-affair with a lady in Southampton Street, Strand, his second with a lady in Berwick Street, Soho, and so on with several others in various parts of the town; for what Boswell called his love-affairs were nothing more than lust-affairs.

His father was sensible enough to perceive that he must sow his wild oats and left him alone for a while; but when it became clear that the quantity of oats was unlimited and that epistolary requests would be ignored, the judge suddenly journeyed south and reduced James to trembling acquiescence. After the gaieties of London, returning to Edinburgh was like returning to prison, and home life seemed more dismal and restricted than ever. He was again set to the study of law and severely examined if he arrived home at a time when all respectable people were abed, a form of subjection so nerve-fraying that after he had left home and was living alone in London he was apprehensive lest the landlord of his lodgings should reprove him for staying out late at night. But he was no longer docile, and the inevitable war between father and son made him at first despondent and at last openly rebellious. Likening himself to a race-horse yoked to a dung-cart, he insisted that all his inclinations were towards the Army; but the most he could get out of his father was a grudging half-promise to pay for a commission in a line regiment. This was not at all what James wanted; he had no desire to spend his days marching and fighting; he wished to look fine and be a gentleman, and in that respect the Guards alone filled the bill. However, as he could not get his way, he determined to make the best of his legal boredom by writing prose and poetry, by forming a society of jovial companions who could forget their tribulations in mirth, and by having affairs with divers women who did not mistake his attentions for love, from one of whom, in his expressive idiom, he "catch'd a Tartar, too, with a vengeance".

His friend Temple had gone to Cambridge, but he saw much of John Johnston, and he made friends with a young Army officer of literary pretensions, the Hon. Andrew Erskine, with whom he also commenced an artificial correspondence, which was published in due course. Wherever he went James could not help bragging of his talks with the Duke of York, and his vanity was much tickled when rumours got abroad that he and the King's brother had led a riotous night-life together, like Poins and Prince Hal in the play, and had called one another by their christian names. Not content with dedicating his doggerel to the Duke, he wrote *An Ode to Tragedy* "by a Gentleman of Scotland" and dedicated it to himself. He was determined to become famous somehow, and if he could not do so by genius he would manage it by impudence. His dissipations and poems, though they helped to pass away the time, did not interfere with his labours. He worked hard at civil law; his father coached him in Roman law; and he improved his knowledge of Greek. It may have been to brace himself for conflict with his father that he plunged into a cold bath every morning all the year round, and as a further sign of antagonism to his father's will he became an active Freemason. Nothing that the older man could say had the least effect on his dislike of law, his wish to become an officer in the Guards. His parent's assurance that he would never be able to obtain a commission, with the further declaration that even if he succeeded he would never achieve a higher rank than that of ensign, failed to cool his enthusiasm. His real aims were freedom, independence, a life in London, and a smart uniform.

He was encouraged in his attitude by the arrival in Edinburgh of the Irishman Thomas Sheridan, who made a religion of elocution and hoped to teach the Scots how to pronounce English. James, who was always on the outlook for a man with settled convictions, only drawing the line at his father, soon made the acquaintance of Sheridan and became a disciple, calling him "My Mentor! My Socrates!" Sheridan not only lent him money but, seeing that he was more anxious to live in London than to be a soldier, suggested that he should study for the bar in England. James snatched at the proposition; but as his father rejected it, he dismissed it from his mind and announced his unalterable loyalty to the Guards.

In 1761 he came of age, and as he could no longer be bullied as a boy his father threatened to disinherit him. This however was impossible, the estate being entailed. Instead the judge bribed his son with an allowance of £100 a year to sign a deed appointing trustees of the estate in the event of James's succession to it, the trustees to be chosen by himself. The allowance enabled James to live independently of the family. His father also agreed to let him go to London in search of a commission in the Guards on condition that he first passed his examination in civil law. This he managed to do in July 1762. His father then settled the young man's debts, arranged to pay him £200 a year, and bade him a portentous farewell. It would not have pleased Lord Auchinleck to know that, just before leaving Edinburgh, his son attended a service in a Church of England chapel; and it might have distressed him to know that, just after leaving Edinburgh, James heard that he too had a son, in his case illegitimate.

CHAPTER 12

At Large

BEFORE LEAVING for the south Boswell promised to send his friend Johnston regular instalments of his journal, and this he did every week until he left London. Johnston was also entrusted with the superintendence of Boswell's baby, whose mother's name was Peggy Doig, and arrangements were made for the child's baptism and material welfare. Boswell professed to be proud of his son and pictured himself as a fond parent, though when he met Peggy in London some months after her delivery he reproved her for what he had done and exhorted her not to be caught napping again. The boy died when just over a year old, and Boswell, who had never set eyes on him, was much upset and thought of going into mourning, but thought better of it.

This curious changeableness, not merely of mood but of temperament, was the distinguishing mark of Boswell's nature, and explains not a little of his genius. Most intelligent human beings contain within themselves contradictory characteristics, but as a rule one of these is preponderant, influences the whole character, and gives the possessor a core which colours the rest. Thus we can usually foretell how a particular man will behave under certain circumstances, and the phrase "How like him!" sums up our recognition of his main peculiarity. But Boswell's singularity was that he had no prime characteristic, that he changed continually from one person to another as mood or circumstance altered. He was a human chameleon, varying his colour with his company, his nature with his notions. He said that it was possible to become a character merely by wishing it, and though he frequently failed to achieve this he could not help becoming someone else in the process. Like an actor he was always trying to get into the skin of a part, but the attempt usually resulted in the performance of a different part. Wishing to play Ariel, he dropped into Caliban. Essaying Prospero, he became Trinculo. Lacking a centre, he could not direct his course to any particular point on the circumference, his life being spent drifting about on the periphery Dryden's verses on Buckingham could be adapted to our subject:

> A man so various that he seemed to be
> Not one, but all mankind's epitome.
> Loose in opinions, very seldom strong,
> Was everything by starts, and nothing long:
> But, in the course of one revolving moon,
> Was drunkard, lecher, genius and buffoon.

A nature of this kind provoked a good deal of distrust and derision, but it enabled Boswell to gain the friendships of utterly dissimilar types of men, to each of whom he adapted himself with triumphant ease, becoming pious with one, impious with another, and so on. No hard work was involved, because his personality changed with the atmosphere of his surroundings and he was not acting but living a part on all occasions. The histrionic, purposeful Boswell usually failed, the protean, haphazard Boswell nearly always succeeded. This lack of a cardinal characteristic was his chief asset both as companion and writer. It enabled him to take a keen interest in all sorts of things outside himself, and it gave an exceptional detachment to his power of observation. Moreover it saved him from preoccupation, thereby freeing his natural high spirits and helping him to live fully in the passing hour. Burke said that Boswell had no more merit in being cheerful and good-natured than a man could claim for having a sound constitution.

For such a fellow the constant company of others was vitally necessary, and it was noticed that his whole countenance brightened at the sight of a human face. Johnson called him "a very *clubable* man", and the phrase summed him up well, for he could talk to a serious person on his right hand about immortality, to a frivolous one on his left about a minuet, and leave each with the impression that he was solely interested in the subject under discussion, as indeed he was for the moment. Johnson loved social life because it made him less miserable, Boswell because it made him more happy; and now for the first time he was about to be happy without any care of parental disapproval.

One of the many James Boswells we are about to meet revealed himself on leaving Edinburgh by alighting from the chaise at Holyrood Palace and performing mystical rites thereat. He bowed to the Palace, to the stone replica of the Scottish crown over the entrance, and to the chapel. Then, from the court in front of the Palace, he bowed three times to Arthur's Seat, the hill whereon he had spent many pleasant holidays in his youth; and in this way he satisfied his superstitious, poetic and patriotic soul. The chaise journeyed on, and he spent four nights on the road, at Berwick, Durham, Doncaster and Biggleswade, experiencing much trepidation on account of highwaymen as he drove through the dark to the latter. The view of London from Highgate Hill transported him, and induced thoughts on the immortality of the soul, making him spout poetry, and on the delights of sex, making him sing bawdy songs. He put up at the Black Lion in Water Lane, Whitefriars, which had been recommended by one of his actor friends. He was twenty-two years of age, full of fire and enthusiasm, and the cold November weather on the day he arrived did not freeze his spirits. At once he plunged into the life of the metropolis, keeping a diary of his doings which enabled him to capture and fix his moods on paper. Its peculiar excellence is due to what we have called his lack of a central characteristic. Had he possessed a marked personality, his entries would have been far more restrained. But since his mind radiated in all directions from no discernible base, revealing what Hamlet calls "a pipe for fortune's finger to sound what stop she please", and as he had in an eminent degree the gift of dramatic reporting, he was fitted to produce the most candid and the most vivid journal ever written.

We cannot here pursue his countless divagations, but we must use his disclosures to illuminate his nature; and the first thing to be noticed is that he was capable of entering fully into any social occasion, at the same time watching keenly his own behaviour, acting as participant and spectator in equal degree. The highly-bred, dignified self-assurance of the English nobility made a deep impression on him, and he longed to be like them, even shunning his own countrymen on account of their vulgar talk, coarse accent and common manners. The fellows whose society he had once enjoyed irritated him, and he recalled with remorse his own behaviour in their company, his cheap jokes, horseplay and buffoonery. The trouble was, he decided, that the moment he had taken a glass of punch he began to sing songs and behave in an unseemly manner, joking with his inferiors, slapping backs, poking ribs, indulging in mimicry, bawling with laughter, and making himself altogether ridiculous. He noted again and again that he must set a guard on his native high spirits, particularly on their licentious expression, and cultivate the decorum, the polish, the unhurried speech, the nonchalance of an English gentleman. He noticed his chameleon-like quality, how his nature changed with his company, how he became boorish or refined, religious or profane, chivalrous or mean-spirited, intelligent or vulgar, in accordance with his social surroundings, and he was constantly telling himself to maintain a composed and genteel manner under all circumstances. As such a metamorphosis was not natural to him, all that he could do, when he remembered to do it, was to become rather pompous in bearing, to achieve a consequential style of conversation, and to strut about in an unconsciously comical fashion.

He probably amused the people he was trying to copy as much as those in whose company he could forget his self-imposed manners, and as he had an amiable and entertaining personality he was welcomed wherever he went. The Duke of Queensberry promised to use his influence to obtain a commission in the Guards for the young Scot, while Lady Northumberland asked him to her receptions, said that he could call whenever he liked, and assured him that she would do all in her power to further his ambition. After a brief period of misunderstanding, partly caused by the dedication of *The Cub at Newmarket* to the Duke of York, whose displeasure had been forcibly expressed, the Earl of Eglinton resumed his friendship with the author and offered to do everything possible on his behalf. Altogether Boswell's reception in London was flattering, the only drawback being that as time went on the commission seemed further off than ever. The publication of the *Letters* between himself and Erskine did nothing to forward his immediate desire, but he experienced the pride of the author who sees his name for the first time on a title-page, and he read with satisfaction a most eulogistic review of the collection in *The London Chronicle*, which described it as "a book of true genius", though his gratification would have been more complete if he had not written the review himself.

By the end of November 1762 he had taken comfortable lodgings in Downing Street, Westminster, where he could feed with his landlord or entertain his friends. His changeable temperament caused trouble here. At first he was very friendly with the landlord, but in his belief that he was letting himself down he became more aloof, and was surprised when the landlord created a scene on account of a rowdy party in his sitting-room. He left Downing Street soon afterwards and occupied the chambers of his friend Temple in Farrar's Buildings, Inner Temple Lane. Wherever he was he managed to enjoy himself.

He went to theatres, taverns, pleasure gardens, parties. He even witnessed a cock-fight, but felt sorry for the cocks and failed to understand how the onlookers could enjoy such a gory show with indifference to the mutilation of the birds. Sometimes he played the violin in the privacy of his lodgings; and when he felt in the mood he called on Thomas Sheridan, who explained at great length how words should be pronounced and speeches delivered. Sheridan was jealous of Garrick and had many criticisms to pass on his performances. But Boswell shared the world's admiration for the great actor, and when at last they met he found that Garrick was as charming off the stage as he was startling on it.

One day Eglinton got him an invitation to the Beefsteak Club, where he made the acquaintance of three strange men: Lord Sandwich, a jovial rake, John Wilkes, a facetious rake, and Charles Churchill, a satirical rake. They were the leading spirits of a queer clique known as the Hell-Fire Club; they took part in bacchanalian and libidinous orgies at the ancient Cistercian Abbey of Medmenham in Buckinghamshire, being known as "the Monks of Medmenham". Prayers to Satan were offered up, the Black Mass was celebrated, and various priapean and venereous rites were performed with becoming mystery or unbecoming monstrosity. Apart from their notion of fun and games, each of these men made a mark on his time.

Sandwich was a leading politician at different periods of his life, and like most members of his tribe utterly untrustworthy. As First Lord of the Admiralty he let down the Navy, as a clubman he let down his fellow-members. When Boswell met them Sandwich and Wilkes were hand and glove, but the moment that the actions of Wilkes made him unpopular with the governing class it was Sandwich who impeached him in the House of Lords for obscene and seditious libel, an action that made the Earl known as Jemmy Twitcher, a character in *The Beggar's Opera* who rounds on his old ally Macheath. But in the case of Sandwich the common doom of man was reversed, the evil he did being interred with his bones, the good living after him in the shape of two slices of bread divided by meat, a form of nourishment that enabled him to remain at the gaming-table when inconvenienced by hunger.

John Wilkes was the most redoubtable figure in the politics of his period. Becoming, through the influence of Pitt, Member of Parliament for Aylesbury, he soon showed that he had no use for Pitt's successor, Lord Bute, who stupidly chose a Scot, Tobias Smollett, to defend his Government in a paper called *The Briton*. Bute being unpopular largely on account of his favouritism of the Scots, Wilkes started a periodical, *The North Briton*, the policy of which was decidedly anti-Scottish. His chief collaborator was Charles Churchill, an atheistical clergyman whose satirical poem *The Rosciad*, ridiculing the stage, made his reputation while blasting that of several actors. The famous Number 45 of their paper, which by implication accused the King in his speech to Parliament of approving a lie, gave the Government an excuse to proceed against Wilkes. A general warrant was issued, its main object being to catch the chief delinquent. Wilkes was arrested, imprisoned in the Tower, released by order of the Chief Justice on a point of parliamentary privilege, and became the hero of the mob, who shouted themselves hoarse with the cry of "Wilkes and Liberty!" All this occurred in the year after Boswell met him, but another introduction took place after these excitements in May 1763, when Boswell found the combination of profanity and profligacy in Wilkes and Churchill very much to his taste, though he quickly transformed himself into a sedate and reverent disciple on calling to see Johnson immediately afterwards. Wilkes's next performance caused a temporary disappearance from public life. He privately printed an obscenely libellous work entitled *An Essay on Woman*, in which it was pretended that his own notes had been written by the Bishop of Gloucester. For this he would have been sent by the House of Lords to Newgate Prison if he had not escaped to the continent. Later he was expelled from the House of Commons, and later still outlawed. He returned to England in 1768, was elected M.P. for Middlesex, imprisoned, and expelled three more times from the House. He became a popular idol and was chosen as Lord Mayor of London in 1774, when the Government abandoned the unequal struggle and admitted him to Parliament. Ugly, cross-eyed, malicious, blasphemous, and quite shameless, he boasted that he could beat the handsomest man in the kingdom at the art of seducing women. Generous, courageous and honest in his dealings with men, he was also a stimulating companion and a pleasing wit, as when Sandwich told him that he would die either of the pox or on the gallows, and he replied: "That depends, my Lord, on whether I embrace your mistress or your principles." His friend Churchill, being an apostate priest, was even more ruthless in repartee. Having left his wife, he persuaded a girl of fifteen to run away with him, and when her wrathful father wanted to know when he could expect her back Churchill replied that he would probably "have done with her" in about ten days. However, the barks of these gay dogs were far worse than their bites. Wilkes was more considerate than most people in his personal relationships, and Churchill did not desert his youthful mistress, but before his death, a year after their elopement, did his best to provide both for her and for his wife.

If Johnson had not entered his life at the moment when he was finding so much pleasure in the society of Wilkes, it is difficult to say what would have happened to Boswell, whose uncertainty of direction made him extremely susceptible to the influence of any strong character. Perhaps the highest tribute that can be paid to the strength of Johnson is that he was able to give Boswell a purpose in life and hold him to it. With many a longing and lingering look at the glittering, fascinating, and extremely carnal world typified by Wilkes and company, Boswell henceforth recognised the superior quality of Johnson's life and conversation, and tried hard, if not always with success, to live up to his example and maxims, as well as his belief in churchgoing. The ritual and precepts of orthodox religion appealed to the imagination of Boswell, who continually attended services in the Church of England, but even when in a devout mood he could not prevent his mind from straying to attractive women, either in the congregation or in his fancy, and he tried to find consistency in this by linking up gratitude to the Almighty with love of God's creatures, especially feminine. Having determined, for the sake of his health, to keep clear of prostitutes, he lived in hopes that some fashionable woman would show an inclination to please him. But there were no offers from that quarter, and eventually he consoled himself with an actress who, if not a fine lady herself, had at least played aristocratic parts, and even on one occasion the Queen in *Hamlet*.

Somehow Boswell made the acquaintance of Louisa Lewis, who had recently appeared at Covent Garden Theatre, and marked her down as a possible bedfellow. In their preliminary skirmishes he took the precaution to warn her that she could expect little cash and to hint that her favours would have to be granted for love. This of course protracted the engagement, but after much fencing she agreed to spend a night with him. Naturally he blurted out the whole story to his friends, and instantly regretted having done so. He chose the Black Lion in Water Lane for the assignation, and their raptures were accompanied by the bells of St. Bride's near-by. She complimented him on his vigour as a lover, which made him feel that if it were generally known every woman he met would covet his embraces. He was pleased to note that the adventure had been conducted on a prudent scale of expenditure, eighteen shillings covering the cost of supper, wine, bed and breakfast. But his pleasure was abated when he had to face a further charge, and he taxed Louisa with giving him venereal disease, which she denied. He had previously experienced two 'visitations' of a similar kind, the first lasting ten weeks, the second

Dr. Johnson in his travelling dress "as described
in Boswell's Tour" *from an engraving by T. Trotter*
(The Trustees of the British Museum)

SAMUEL JOHNSON *after Sir Joshua Reynolds*
(The National Portrait Gallery, London)

JAMES BOSWELL *by Sir Joshua Reynolds,* 1786
(The National Portrait Gallery, London)

MRS. SAMUEL JOHNSON
(The Hulton Picture Library)

TOPHAM BEAUCLERK
by G. P. Harding
(The Hulton Picture Library)

SIR JOSHUA REYNOLDS *a self-portrait*
(The National Portrait Gallery, London)

BENNET LANGTON
by George Dance, 1798
(The Trustees of the British Museum)

HESTER PIOZZI (Mrs. Thrale)
by George Dance, 1793
(The National Portrait Gallery, London)

DAVID GARRICK *by Robert Edge Pine*
(The National Portrait Gallery, London)

FRANCIS D'ARBLAY (Fanny Burney)
by Edward Francis Burney
(The National Portrait Gallery, London)

OLIVER GOLDSMITH
by Sir Joshua Reynolds
(The National Portrait Gallery, London)

ANNA WILLIAMS
by Frances Reynolds
(The Trustees of Johnson's House)

PASCAL PAOLI *from the portrait*
by Henry Bembridge, 1768
(The Trustees of the British Museum)

ANNA SEWARD *by T. Kettle,* 1762
(The National Portrait Gallery, London)

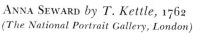

EDMUND BURKE *from the studio*
of Sir Joshua Reynolds, 1771
(The National Portrait Gallery, London)

DR. JOHNSON in old age
*from the portrait by
Sir Joshua Reynolds*
(*The Trustees of
the British Museum*)

JAMES BOSWELL
by George Dance, 1793
(*The National Portrait
Gallery, London*)

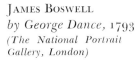

four months. This one kept him indoors for about five weeks, and he wrote sternly to Louisa saying that his surgeon's bill came to five guineas and demanding the return of two guineas which she had borrowed from him, his letter containing all the accusations customary on such occasions. To his surprise she sent the two guineas without a word, and he relented towards her, but kept the money.

Normally the mere act of walking or driving about London thrilled him to an extraordinary degree, his joy rising to ecstasy. Now he regarded the place with distaste and began to think tolerantly of home-life with father. But with the cure came new vigour and old carelessness. The comparatively idyllic episode with Louisa was followed by a number of prosaic affairs with prostitutes or females in search of a shilling. He paid his devotions to Venus in strange places. It was not the habit of English gentlemen in the eighteenth century to lead girls up dark alleys for the purpose of coition, but in this respect Boswell did not model himself on the Lovelaces of the time. St. James's Park, hard by his rooms in Downing Street, was mostly the scene of his performances, but the murky courts off the Strand sometimes concealed his ardours. Once he chose Westminster Bridge, enjoying the fancy that the river was flowing beneath them; another time he walked about London disguised as a low ruffian, and nearly got himself into trouble when, in his attempt to ravish a girl who had decided that sixpence was not enough, her screams brought a crowd, whom he appeased on the ground that an officer on half-pay could not afford more; and there was an occasion when his frail companion stole a handkerchief from his pocket while his attention was engaged in a more pressing matter. He suffered spasms of disgust with himself after each of these sordid affairs, and at length Johnson's friendship and improving conversation decided him to abandon promiscuity.

Gradually it became clear that the Duke of Queensberry and Lady Northumberland were not going out of their way to get him a commission, and he began to vacillate between a return to the law and a further attempt to become an officer in the Guards. Sometimes he felt that his uncertain state of mind argued a condition of idiocy, and his sympathy went out to his brother John, who suffered from bouts of insanity all his life. John called to see him in London and received much kindness. Distance and freedom had lent enchantment to his view of their father, though he was much annoyed by the discovery that Lord Auchinleck had opened some of his private papers that should have been sent to Johnston, and he despatched a strongly worded letter to his parent, who retaliated by threatening to sell the estate rather than let his firstborn inherit it. In a long letter, commencing with the single word 'James', he reproved the young man for his unfilial conduct, for the publication of his childish correspondence with Erskine, for his exhibitions of mimicry while in Scotland, and for keeping a journal, which would prevent anyone who knew of it from wishing to know its author.

Boswell was now frightened that all his schemes were petering out. Queensberry wrote to say that he had better dismiss the thought of becoming a Guards officer; Lady Northumberland let him down lightly; and Eglinton failed to obtain the interest of Lord Bute. Living on a see-saw of hope and despair, Boswell at one moment thought he would return to Scotland and behave as his father wished, at the next determined that nothing should induce him to set foot in the country. The delight he took in the spectacle of life could change his mood in an instant from misery to joy, when he was able to perceive that happiness was not to be found in any particular thing but that it was interfused with everything. Merely to hear Pitt speak in Parliament inspired him with an ambition to win a great reputation.

At last he adopted a middle course: he would not join the Army and he would not return at once to Edinburgh; but if his father would allow him to study law in France and spend some time travelling on the continent, he promised obedience to the parental will by becoming an advocate at the Scottish Bar. He begged Sir David Dalrymple to intercede with his father and to smooth things over. Dalrymple did so, diplomatically suggesting Utrecht instead of France for legal study, and Auchinleck consented to the plan, with permission that his son should visit Paris and a few of the German Courts.

What with wine, women and Wilkes, Boswell did not see as much of Johnson after their first meeting as his higher self judged proper, nor did he think it wise to mention his friendship with Wilkes, who had been described by Johnson as "an abusive scoundrel, and instead of applying to my Lord Chief Justice to punish him, I would send half a dozen footmen and have him well ducked." When the hour of his leaving England approached Boswell felt that he must make up for lost time by seeing a lot of Johnson, whose advice concerning a mode of legal study would be valuable, and he opened the campaign for the moral regeneration of Boswell at the Mitre on 25th June 1763, when, as we have seen, he gave a sketch of his life which pleased his guest. They met again at the Mitre on 1st July in company with Oliver Goldsmith, who was too much like Boswell in character to inspire anything but disapproval in the biographer, who with unconscious comedy portrayed himself in writing of Goldsmith: "He, I am afraid, had no settled system of any sort, so that his conduct must not be strictly scrutinised." Boswell was also envious of Goldsmith's standing with Johnson, especially when left out of an invitation, after their supper together, to take tea with Anna Williams. However, this final favour was bestowed upon him before he left London. On 5th July he visited Johnson, who promised to attend a supper-party the following evening at his Downing Street lodgings. But on the night of the 5th the quarrel between himself and his landlord took place, and he had to call on Johnson the following morning to relate his distress. "Consider, sir, how insignificant this will appear a twelvemonth hence," said Johnson. Instead of making the obvious retort that the present moment was not a year ahead, Boswell took comfort and held his party at the Mitre. They met fairly regularly during the month, and when Boswell asked for advice on his future studies Johnson suggested that they should make a day of it at Greenwich. That same evening they were walking down the Strand arm-in-arm when a prostitute accosted them. "No, no, my girl, it won't do," said Johnson in a kindly manner, and as they continued on their way they agreed that illicit copulation produced more misery than happiness in the world, a point on which Boswell could speak with authority.

On Saturday 30th July they travelled down the Thames by boat, getting out just short of London Bridge and taking another boat just beyond it because the tide swirled through the arches at a dangerous rate and there were many accidents on that account. When they reached Greenwich, Boswell pulled Johnson's poem *London* out of his pocket and declaimed the uninspired verses on "the seat which gave Eliza birth". He had read and greatly admired nearly all Johnson's works during his student days in Scotland, and could usually produce an apt quotation from them. Then they entered upon what both of them conceived to be the business of the day: Johnson's advice as to Boswell's course of study. But it is plain that Boswell was not in the least interested in his course of study, his explanation of how he failed to recall a word of Johnson's lecture being charmingly disingenuous: "I recollect with admiration an animating blaze of eloquence, which roused every intellectual power in me to the highest pitch, but must have dazzled me so much that my memory could not preserve the substance of his discourse." Boswell was far more interested in the smallest details of human character than in the whole realm of classical learning. He remembered for example that as they walked in Greenwich Park that evening Johnson said: "Is not this very fine?" "Yes, sir, but not equal to Fleet Street." "You are right, sir." They finished the day pleasantly at the Turk's Head coffee-house, where over supper Johnson decided to visit

Boswell's ancestral home and promised to accompany him to Harwich when he left England in a few days' time, a mark of affection that bereft the young man of speech.

They were constantly together during Boswell's last week in London. On Sunday 31st July, the day after their trip to Greenwich, Boswell attended a meeting of Quakers in Lombard Street and heard a woman preach. "Sir," said Johnson when told of it, "a woman's preaching is like a dog's walking on his hinder legs. It is not done well, but you are surprised to find it done at all." That afternoon Boswell attended afternoon service at St. Paul's, and then stood in the centre of the cathedral to repeat the odd ritual he had performed at Holyrood, bowing to north, south, east and west as a mark of veneration. Without the steadying influence of Johnson on Monday 1st August, he was not in a condition to withstand temptation, and being cajoled in the Strand by the daughter of an officer he yielded, arguing with himself that his fault was the less because the woman's was greater. On Tuesday the 2nd Johnson spent some time in the chambers of Boswell, who was privileged in the evening to take tea with Anna Williams. On Wednesday the 3rd they supped at the Turk's Head. As he dared not mention the subject to Johnson, Boswell asked Sir David Dalrymple whether he ought to maintain a correspondence with Wilkes. If known, would it hurt him? He hoped Sir David would think it right. Apparently Sir David did not think it wrong.

On Friday 5th August, Johnson and Boswell set forth in the Harwich stage coach. Boswell was depressed at leaving London. Lord Auchinleck was allowing him £240 a year, on which he could live in comfort, and he had every intention of drawing on his father for any further sums required; but even so he hated the thought of quitting a place where he had first known true happiness. They stopped for dinner at an inn, where a female passenger said that she had educated her children and had never allowed them to be idle. "I wish, madam, you would educate me too," remarked Johnson, "for I have been an idle fellow all my life . . . and that gentleman there" (pointing to Boswell) "has been idle. He was idle at Edinburgh. His father sent him to Glasgow, where he continued to be idle. He then came to London, where he has been very idle; and now he is going to Utrecht, where he will be as idle as ever". Boswell, travelling in the character of a gentleman, privately complained of such an exposure. "Poh, poh! they know nothing about you, and will think of it no more," said Johnson. When the journey continued, the same passenger spoke against the Roman Catholics and the horrors of the Inquisition. Being terrified by opposition to his own faith, Johnson accepted torture as a means of arriving at the truth and defended the Inquisition, saying that "the civil power should unite with the Church in punishing those who dared to attack the established religion", an opinion he shared with every barbarous bigot in history. At one stage on the road to Colchester, where they stopped the night, Boswell ostentatiously tipped the coachman a shilling, most passengers only giving sixpence, and it appealed to his normally prudent nature when Johnson took him to task for making the coachman dissatisfied with all the other passengers, including Johnson. At Harwich they entered the church, where Johnson made Boswell kneel down and pray for himself, and coming out of it they stood for a while discussing Bishop Berkeley's theory of the non-existence of matter. Boswell said that, while convinced the doctrine was untrue, it was impossible to refute it. Johnson struck his foot violently against a large stone, saying "I refute it *thus*".

Johnson walked down to the beach to see Boswell off. They embraced and promised an exchange of letters. "I hope, sir, you will not forget me in my absence," said Boswell. "Nay, sir, it is more likely you should forget me than that I should forget you," said Johnson, who remained on the spot, rolling his great body from side to side, until the boat became indistinct, when he returned to the town.

CHAPTER 13

In Search of a Character

As HE REQUIRED the constant company of other people to stimulate him and to give him self-confidence, Boswell's arrival at Utrecht brought on a fit of acute depression. Like Johnson, he was subject to these fits at regular intervals throughout life. From the memoirs of the period it seems that melancholia was a popular disease in the eighteenth century. It was probably common enough in the nineteenth as well, but the novelty of discovery had worn off and it had become unfashionable. In the age with which we are dealing its regular recurrence was commonly due to over-eating and over-drinking, and the consequent condition of the sufferer's liver. We have noted a few other causes in the case of Johnson, but with Boswell the periods of gloom, sometimes due to over-eating and over-drinking, were prolonged by over-acting. Though solitude was the usual origin of his trouble, he seemed to enjoy the expression of his misery, writing to his friends Johnston and Temple about his symptoms in the manner of one who wallowed in despair, dwelling on his state as a dreadful experience only to be defeated by steadiness of purpose. He was prone to self-dramatisation, describing himself to others and addressing himself in his memoranda in the third person; which denoted his mercurial nature and objectivity of temperament, both due to the lack of a salient characteristic.

Utrecht and its inhabitants were depressing after London, Johnson, Wilkes and the rest. There was no variety, no colourful company; so he ran away to Rotterdam and elsewhere, his breast torn by conflicting emotions, wretchedness and self-pity uppermost. But after a while he picked up Johnson's *Rambler* essays and acquired fortitude. He learnt therein that he was merely suffering the ills common to mankind. The knowledge steadied him and he returned to Utrecht, where he began to study Greek, Latin and French, to pursue his journal, to attend lectures, and to keep company. He determined to be worthy of his father and of Johnson; he drew up a plan of life which he read with regularity; and he frequently reminded himself in his memoranda that he must be serious and self-assured and on the watch against a propensity to act the fool. He now wished to think of women solely in terms of marriage, writing at length to Temple about one who seemed adequate for the purpose, and he decided to remain chaste with the object of reserving his potency for a wife.

Finding it impossible to be like himself, because unaware of what himself was like, he longed to resemble someone else, such as Johnson or the poet Thomas Gray, of whom he heard from Temple, or Temple himself, or even his own father, all of whom appeared to him consistent personalities; but he failed to maintain their firmness of purpose and behaviour, for he was a creature of moods and could not make up his mind without the help of someone to make it up for him. For example, he wondered whether the Almighty was against the practice of whoring, and he discussed with companions the question of whether fornication was a sin. Wavering in opinion but anxious not to condemn himself, he concluded that it was a venial offence, but that over-indulgence might be regarded as sinful. In spite of the fact that vice made him happier than virtue, he adopted a moral attitude to everything, possibly in the belief that propriety of sentiment more than counterbalanced impropriety of behaviour. But while in Holland he maintained a strict standard of conduct. He exercised his French and Dutch by writing 'Themes' or essays in those languages; he wrote ten lines of verse a day in the belief that practice would make him a poet;

he rose early as part of his discipline to cure low spirits; he read Voltaire, took fencing lessons, smoked a pipe, fell in love with a widow, dressed carefully, and gave consideration to the state of his bowels. Though he never ceased to tell himself to be reserved, the whole story of his life was laid bare to a friend under the influence of a glass too much. He visited the Hague, made the acquaintance of several Dutch relations, and received the sacrament at a Church of England service in the Ambassador's chapel. Ritual of any kind appealed to his sense of the dramatic, and once he went out into the fields near Utrecht, drew his sword, and in view of the cathedral tower called God to witness that, assuming his will were free, he would endure his attacks of melancholy without complaint. He soon discovered Utrecht to be an agreeable place. Introduced by the Countess of Nassau to all the leading social lights, he attended the assemblies regularly, received innumerable invitations to private parties, and the chief cause of his dejection was removed without the assistance of vows.

People who are intensely interested in themselves are seldom much interested in others. Boswell was an exception, and history affords no more remarkable one. Though absorbed in himself and desirous above all things to discover and stabilise the core of his character, his lack of a basic quality made him more concerned with other personalities, more anxious to hear their opinions and note their peculiarities, than anyone else of whom we have record. It happened that at Utrecht his two main passions, an interest in human nature and an interest of a different sort in women, were provoked and stimulated by a girl he met at a party. Isabella van Tuyll, also known as Belle de Zuylen, addressed by Boswell as Zélide, belonged to an ancient Dutch family. Her father owned a large estate near Utrecht, and she was brought up in strictly orthodox style in extremely conventional surroundings. But like Boswell she broke the shackles of her upbringing and adopted unorthodox views which she expressed in an unconventional manner. Her conversation, a perpetual surprise, scandalised the majority of her respectable acquaintances, though her physical attractiveness, her wit and her family's position made her a welcome guest at every social gathering. At a later date she would have been described as an "advanced woman", at a still later date as a "highbrow". She read Voltaire and Rousseau, questioned the religion of her country, and indulged in philosophical speculations. Boswell was fascinated by her, but criticised everything in her which he sensed in himself. She had a habit of blurting out her inmost thoughts; so had he, but he thought it undignified in a woman. A creature of moods, she admitted that what she felt one day she did not feel the next; it was the same with him, but he thought her mind unbalanced and her nature insufficiently feminine. He strongly disapproved of her clandestine correspondence with the opposite sex; he disliked her freedom from all social formalities; and he censured her vanity. Her attitude towards love too closely resembled his own to please him, for she demanded liberty to do as she liked, while he insisted on liberty only to do as he liked. In other words, what was right for a man was wrong for a woman. Naturally she thought him funny and ridiculous, but all the same rather lovable. She laughed at him, which both intrigued and irritated him. He could not help admiring her quickness and independence of mind, but when he was being serious her vivacity and gaiety jarred upon him. His lectures on her levity, and his admonitions on her study of metaphysics, amused her; and when he gravely announced that "whatever men may do, a woman without virtue is terrible", she could hardly contain herself. He fell in love with her, but was so much annoyed with himself for having done so that he told her frankly that nothing could induce him to marry her. He hoped by this to produce a favourable reaction, but her attitude remained frivolous and disappointing: she really did not seem to mind.

He left Utrecht with a clear understanding that their friendship was firmly established and that they would write to one another. But his vanity had been severely punctured, and he sent her a long letter recapitulating all her faults, informing her that she had really been in love with him, and asking: "Would you not have gone with me to the world's end?" Even if he had been disinherited by his father, it pleased him to believe that she would have said: "Sir, here is my portion. It is yours. We may live genteelly upon it!" She replied that he had the childish vanity of an imbecile. Yet he could not keep her out of his thoughts, wondering whether she would tone down her more exhilarating qualities and become domesticated as a wife; and he wrote to her father saying that, if her present engagement fell through, he would like to marry her, adding however that, if she was disposed to marry him, she would have to sign an oath of fidelity, to give an undertaking never to write to anyone of whom he disapproved, never to publish anything without his consent, and never to criticise the religion and customs of the country in which she was residing, meaning England or Scotland. He even renewed his proposal four years later, again demanding assurances from her of the conduct he desired. But on this occasion his father's opposition made him drop the design, which was fortunate, Boswell having assured her on an earlier occasion: "I am very certain that if we were married together, it would not be long before we should be both very miserable." No doubt Zélide, cooped up in Scotland with all the marital restrictions outlined in Boswell's letters, would have cordially agreed.

Having spent ten months in Utrecht, Boswell obtained his father's permission to tour the principalities of Germany. It happened that the Earl Marischal of Scotland, George Keith, was returning to Potsdam at the request of Frederick the Great, and to oblige Lord Auchinleck he allowed Boswell a seat in his coach. Keith had been an adherent of the Stuarts, had fought for the Old Pretender at Sheriffmuir in 1715, and had been outlawed; but the behaviour of the Young Pretender had aroused his contempt, and he refused to take part in the rising of 1745.

Thenceforward he became the trusted adviser of the King of Prussia and was made Governor of Neuchâtel, where he befriended Rousseau. In a diplomatic capacity he was able to help the British Government, for which he received a pardon and enough money to recover his confiscated estates. But his loyalty was now devoted to the man who had treated him well at the nadir of his fortunes, and he was on his way to rejoin Frederick, with whom he remained until his own death some fourteen years after giving Boswell a lift to Berlin.

It was part of Boswell's charm that he retained throughout life the unconcealed egotism of a child, seldom damped by the disillusionment of manhood. When he witnessed rural activities he wished to be a farmer. When he was shown a library he wanted to possess one. Before leaving his servant behind in Holland he asked the man to write a character-sketch of himself as a master. Braced by a favourable testimonial, he engaged another servant and did his best to live up to the former's good opinion of him.

Germany in those days was a collection of more or less independent principalities, with Prussia in a commanding position at the conclusion of the Seven Years War (1763), during which Frederick had defeated a coalition of half-a-dozen Powers. But the forces against him were so considerable that he might have been vanquished if Russia had not withdrawn from the conflict in the nick of time. At the moment of Boswell's visit Prussia was recognised as a first-class Power and Frederick as the greatest soldier of the age; which meant of course that the primary object of Boswell's journey to the capital was an interview with the monarch. A first sight of him on the parade-ground at Potsdam inspired Boswell with countless thoughts, one of them being that all the terrors and discomforts of campaigning could be undergone for the sake of achieving such greatness. Making up his mind to have conference with the hero, who should be made to realise that his interviewer was no ordinary person, Boswell did his utmost to bring it about. Once the mere sight of the King walking in a garden almost incited him to fling himself at the conqueror's feet. He asked the Earl Marischal to arrange an introduction; he petitioned the British Minister, Andrew Mitchell, to contrive it; and finally he addressed a letter to Henri de Catt, reader to the King and a personal friend, begging for a presentation. But Frederick remained distant and unapproachable, and even Boswell's attempt to attract his attention at a parade by sporting the blue bonnet of a Scottish gentleman was a complete failure. A few weeks later our traveller was at Dresden, where he was able to solace himself with the reflection that Frederick's bombardment of the city in 1760 had been the action of a detestable barbarian.

His reception elsewhere was more satisfactory. The Duke of Brunswick's friendliness went to his head and kept him awake at night. At Dessau a coach was sent to fetch him to the Court, where he was presented to three princesses and a prince. Considering that he had as good a claim to a title as the majority of those in attendance, he called himself Baron Boswell and maintained the rank throughout his travels. At Dresden the Court was in mourning, and he had no black suit, but he overcame the difficulty by donning a red coat resembling that of a British officer and wearing a strip of crape round his arm. Apart from such occasions, his wardrobe was well supplied, and at Gotha he appeared in a velvet suit of many colours. Wherever he went he was welcomed. People liked him because he was easy with them, taking his tone from theirs and quickly getting on terms of familiarity. Most Britons do not speak until they are spoken to, and even then are liable to be monosyllabic. Boswell broke through this restraint, addressing whomsoever he met and chatting away till the other joined in. He also enjoyed the sound of his own voice and would talk nonsense rather than not talk at all. He had no conversational inhibitions and found that it was easy to make friends if he did not mind appearing foolish. One Court official at Karlsruhe was exceptionally silent. Discovering that he was keen on horses, Boswell promptly discussed a subject of which he was entirely ignorant, and the fellow became eloquent.

Altogether our young Scot enjoyed himself in Germany. He often drove about in a Court coach, at the sight of which the average pedestrian bowed to the ground, which delighted him. He suffered little from hypochondria, and apart from the disappointment of not speaking to Frederick the Great his sole mortification was sustained at Mannheim, where the Elector Palatine did not invite him to dinner. He tried hard not to be impressed by the outward shows of royalty, but without success, and he could not help feeling important when dancing with a princess or receiving the attention of a duke.

As usual, his mental attitude fluctuated. At one moment he made up his mind not to copy anyone else but to be himself. At another he decided to be Johnson or Temple or Gray or Lord Auchinleck. He saw the tombs of the great religious reformers Luther and Melanchthon at Wittenberg, and a solemn mood overcame him, Obtaining pen, ink and paper, he lay on the ground, and resting the paper on the metal plate above the body of Melanchthon he wrote to Samuel Johnson vowing "an eternal attachment" and declaring: "It shall be my study to do what I can to render your life happy, and if you die before me, I shall endeavour to do honour to your memory, and, elevated by the remembrance of you, persist in noble piety." His posture and action struck the onlookers with amazement, and it occurred to him that there was something odd and superstitious about his behaviour, nearly thirteen years passing before he sent the letter to Johnson. Descending quickly from the level of the mood which inspired this communication, he wandered about Wittenberg with a military drummer, finishing up at an inn where they dined together on brandy, bread and cheese, an episode which he felt was beneath his dignity.

There were other incidents which did not accord with his noble sentiments. A soldier's wife, safely assailable because pregnant, entered his room to sell chocolate. His vow of chastity was broken, and though he regretted the circumstance he dismissed it from his mind. Later he entertained himself with less reputable females, and was sufficiently shocked by his coarse behaviour to think of the manly and decent example set by his father. In certain other respects he disclosed sensitivity. At a stag-hunt he sympathised with the wretched victim of the chase, while admitting that the excitement of the sport deadened the finer feelings. He was also shocked to observe, at a duck-decoy, that the keeper half-wrung the necks of the birds and left them to expire slowly on the ground.

The grossness of the people was matched by the crudeness of their inns, and in his excursions between the various capitals he slept on tables or floors and sometimes in stables where the proximity of horses, cows, hens and dogs made him feel like a soldier on active service. For ten days during one journey he did not take off his clothes. The method of travelling too was rudimentary. It was performed by post-wagon, a large jolting cart with boards for seats, unfavourable to meditation and adverse to rest. He made the best of these discomforts by thinking of the luxuries which awaited him at the next Court to be visited. There was an occasion when danger awaited him as well. The Court language throughout the principalities was French, and Frederick the Great had set the fashion of praising everything about that nation, from culture to cookery. At a large party near Berlin the company overdid the fashion. In a sullen mood Boswell did the opposite, to such effect that a French officer called him a scoundrel. Dinner was not yet over and Boswell had about half an hour in which to digest the insult along with his food. Timid by nature, the thought of a duel frightened him. Rising from the table he demanded conference of the officer in the garden, where he admitted that he had been wrong and begged the other to confess the same. The officer must have been equally anxious to avoid a fight, because he agreed at once to follow Boswell's public apology with one of his own. At the ensuing supper-party Boswell made it clear that the officer was a gentleman, the officer made it clear that Boswell was not a ruffian, and everything ended happily, with the assistance of hock. But despite the assurances of fellow-Scots that his honour had been vindicated, Boswell felt that he had behaved as a craven and resolved to be more careful in the future.

Like St. Paul, Boswell wanted to see Rome. But Lord Auchinleck did not think that his son wished to visit the city for the same reason as St. Paul, and was hostile to the project. At Boswell's request the Earl Marischal wrote to obtain the father's permission, adding that an extra allowance to cover the expenses of the trip would be advisable. Boswell further intended to interview Rousseau and Voltaire while in Switzerland, for which purpose he had prepared himself by studying their works. Ultimately his father gave a reluctant consent. Boswell's last visit of note before leaving Germany was to the Court of Baden-Durlach at Karlsruhe. He discussed all sorts of things with the Margrave and they got on famously together. So much so, indeed, that Boswell hoped the Margrave would make him a Knight of the Order of Fidelity. He even went so far as to ask for the honour, and the Margrave said that he would consider it. Boswell announced his kinship with the House of Stuart. The Margrave asked to see his pedigree. Boswell was radiant. Mystery surrounds their later correspondence. Boswell wrote from Turin to repeat his request for the Order, but it is not certain that the Margrave received his letter. Two further communications from Boswell may not have been read by the Prince, a letter from whom almost certainly did not reach Boswell. Possibly there was some interference by Court officials. Whatever the cause, Boswell was never able to adorn himself with the Order of Fidelity.

CHAPTER 14

A Biographer Abroad

"THERE IS some soul of goodness in things evil, would men observingly distil it out," says Shakespeare, and the converse is equally true. The possession of certain vices creates or stimulates certain virtues: for example, an excessive sensuality is often to be found in a person of exceptional benevolence. This seeming contradiction is especially noticeable in Boswell, whose folly has been stigmatised by unimaginative people, incapable of perceiving that it was an inevitable part of the peculiar faculty they eulogise. No one with a fairly balanced nature could have attained Boswell's reckless freedom and self-exposure as a diarist. We must therefore view his personal conduct as a necessary attribute of his artistic achievement. His love of titled people may be dismissed as the ordinary childish complaint of snobbery, a false sense of values too common to need comment, though he would have explained it as a romantic concept of recognised heritable right. But what throws light on his curiously precarious personality is his zeal for friendship with remarkable men of every kind. He never missed an opportunity to become acquainted with celebrities. This derived from his own sense of insecurity. He felt obscurely that contact with greatness would strengthen his own purpose, infect him with virtue, and consolidate what was too pliant in himself. In a way this feeling was justified, because contiguity with men of character gave him a sense of stability; but separation from them soon resulted in his usual state of fluctuation and exposed him to influences which in more elevated moments he deplored.

It was the same with his religion. He felt towards God roughly what he felt towards his monarch: a superstitious reverence. In his eyes God was a sort of preternatural Johnson; and just as he tried to see Johnson from different angles, so did he approach God from various points of view, enjoying the Roman Catholic Church for its ritual, approving the Church of England for the decorum and beauty of its service, esteeming the Quakers for their earnestness and simplicity, and only drawing the line at the Presbyterians because they were vindictive kill-joys and depressing bores. He loved to talk of God, laying special stress on the Almighty's infinite mercy to sinners, and he received much comfort from hearing others pronounce in favour of the soul's immortality, for it fortified his self-importance to believe in a divine Father who was super-intending his personal welfare and it flattered his egotism to think that Boswell would go on for ever, a sobering thought for those who shared his belief. In short he created a God with a marked tendency to favour his own weaknesses and on whom he could rely for support whatever the circumstances. This highly convenient and spiritually parasitic faith was due to the lack of a distinctive element in his composition, a foundation on which he could depend in spite of deviations.

One more aspect of his nature must be traced to its source in order to complete a portrait, each feature of which will be illustrated as the story unfolds. His sexual desires were not those of a normal man. They were feverish, hysterical, rash and indiscriminate. It scarcely seemed to matter whether the woman was a duchess or a drab, though the former would have delighted him as much as the latter repelled him. All that really signified was that he should feel either relieved or triumphant. Women were his natural prey, and if he could not have one he made the best of another. He used the same language in his letters to most of them: he was pining, he was afflicted, he was cruelly ill-treated, he suffered torments, he cried his heart out, he languished, his passion overwhelmed him, he lived solely to be transported to the realms of bliss, and so on and so forth. If much that he wrote had not been expressed so absurdly, his letters might have wrung the hearts of the women who received them; but he often spoilt an apparently sincere phrase by following it with a ludicrously naïf suggestion, and the recipients of his outpourings would have been pardoned for thinking them the ravings of an idiot. His peculiar form of mania was that of one who must break down a female's resistance to justify his manhood, or, in his less refined affairs, to vindicate his potency. It was the frenzy of one who had to conquer in order to gain confidence in himself, to demonstrate his personality. But by such exhibitions of physical strength he manifested the essential weakness of his mental constitution.

It is more than likely that the famous recluse whom he first visited appreciated the oddity of his make-up. Having seen Basle, Berne and Neuchâtel, he gave his Swiss servant Jacob Hänni a week's holiday and set forth to visit Rousseau at Môtiers, from the inn of which he sent a letter to the philosopher. The career of Jean-Jacques Rousseau is one of the strangest in the history of literature. A Genevan by birth, he started life as an engraver's apprentice. Quitting his native city at the age of sixteen, he took refuge in Savoy, where he was footman, adopted son, and possibly lover of his benefactress, Madame de Warens. Settling in Paris at the age of twenty-nine, he became fond of a seamstress, Thérèse Le Vasseur, who lived with him for the rest of his life and may have borne him five children; but as they were all sent to the Foundling Hospital in Paris and never heard of again, they may have been imaginary children. In Paris he wrote on music and other subjects for Diderot's Encyclopædia, becoming famous as the author of a prize essay on the question of whether morals had been corrupted or purified by the arts and sciences. He argued in favour of the simple primitive life, which naturally led to his being taken up and pampered by the aristocracy, who had no intention of living in the way he indicated. However, he determined to put his theories to the test and began a simple life in the country near Paris, where he produced a novel, *La Nouvelle Héloïse*, which became the chief influence in the French romantic movement. His next work, *Du Contrat Social*, was fated to be the bible of the Jacobins in the coming Revolution; while his third, *Émile*, by substituting natural religion for Church dogmas, caused his flight to Switzerland as an alternative to imprisonment. Geneva would not shelter him and made the State of Berne expel him; so, having set Europe by the ears, he retired to the canton of Neuchâtel, then a dependency of the Prussian King, and shut himself off from society, pleading illness when admirers appeared on the doorstep, a plea that had some basis, for he suffered from nervous debility as well as stricture. He was fifty-two, a figure of international renown, when Boswell arrived at Môtiers, and he must have read with some amusement the letter begging for an interview.

Boswell announced himself with his usual flourishes: he was a gentleman of an ancient Scottish family; he was a man of singular merit; he was different from the other visitors; his experiences had been various and astonishing; he wanted advice from the man who knew the human heart; and he must see Rousseau alone. While waiting for a reply he viewed the neighbouring mountains and meditated on the greatness of him who lived amongst them. The answer came. Rousseau was ill and not in a state to see anyone, but he would make an exception of Boswell on condition that the interview was brief. Boswell was not in a mood for brevity, but anything was better than nothing, and he presented himself at Rousseau's door dressed up to the nines, being received by Thérèse Le Vasseur.

No one could fail to like Boswell when he laid himself out to be liked, and Rousseau raised no objection when in a moment of enthusiasm his visitor grasped his hand and slapped him on the shoulder as they walked about. Rousseau spoke highly of the

Earl Marischal, who had protected him, criticised Catholic ecclesiastics, and confessed that mankind revolted him. Boswell managed to remain for an hour and a half and extracted a promise that Rousseau would see him again, health permitting. He went the next day, but after talking a short while Rousseau found him wearisome and dismissed him abruptly. At his third visit he faced Rousseau gravely, and fixing him with a steadfast eye asked whether he was a Christian. The answer was in the affirmative. Having advised Boswell not to be influenced by the opinions of others but to stand on his own feet, Rousseau suffered a spasm of pain and told him to go. Returning to the inn, Boswell wrote a sketch of his life, wherein he described an affair in Scotland with a married woman about which he desired Rousseau's advice. In a covering letter he said that he would return to Môtiers in order to benefit from the truths to be imbibed at the fount of knowledge there, which would enable him to behave like a man for the remainder of his life. Then he mounted his horse and set off for Neuchâtel, which he reached the following day and where he found a letter from his father granting him permission to make a stay of four months in Italy.

Nine days later he was back at Môtiers, where he heard from Thérèse that Rousseau was extremely ill. That did not deter him, and he found Rousseau bewailing his lot. But Boswell was chiefly concerned with himself and wanted to know what the other thought of the biographical sketch which he had written and left behind when last there. Rousseau acutely hinted that the young man thought and talked too much of himself, adding that if he returned in the afternoon he could remain for fifteen minutes. Boswell hoped that the visit might be extended to twenty, which made Rousseau laugh. At their next session Boswell said that he would like to keep a large number of women, supplying reasons for such a course. Rousseau treated his themes more sanely than they deserved, told him to do his duty in the social system to which he belonged, and said that the spiritual life was infinitely preferable to the sensual, that a man who was constantly shifting from one thing to another could accomplish nothing, and that the only way to atone for evil was to do good. Discovering that Boswell was not a glutton, Rousseau invited him to dinner the following day. During the intervening hours Boswell made a list of the questions he wished to ask, starting off with the request that Rousseau would write at intervals to such an admirable person as himself. He was already on friendly terms with Thérèse, and when he arrived for dinner he helped her to make the soup. They fed in the kitchen, Rousseau wearing a long garment with a nightcap on his head. They talked freely on a dozen topics. Rousseau had been asked to draw up a code of laws for Corsica, and they joked about the possibility of Boswell going there as his ambassador. Boswell having confessed that he would rather like to be a despot, Rousseau asked whether he liked cats. Boswell exhibited an aversion to cats. Whereupon Rousseau explained that a man's character was revealed by his attitude to cats, which were friendly but independent animals, refusing to do as they were told; and he implied that egotistical human beings who enjoyed imposing their wills on others naturally disliked creatures which totally ignored their commands. They discussed Johnson and Voltaire. The first, said Rousseau, would hate him; the second, he knew, disliked him. The thought of Voltaire rasped his nerves, and he told Boswell to go. But the visitor prolonged his stay with the aid of a little playfulness, and then amused his host with a description of his mimetic faculty. Rousseau thought him a queer character, and reminded him that the poor condition of the roads would delay him. But Boswell continued the conversation until Thérèse gave him a broad hint. The two men embraced and parted affectionately, Boswell stating that he was worthy of Rousseau's kindness, Rousseau admitting that he had enjoyed the young man's malice. Having promised to send Thérèse a garnet necklace, a promise he redeemed,

Boswell left for the inn, the landlady of which thought there were tears in his eyes.

After putting in a few days at Yverdon and Lausanne, our traveller arrived at Geneva and wasted no time in calling upon Voltaire, who lived at the village of Ferney some six miles out. Hiring a coach for the journey, he was received by several footmen at a palatial residence, the owner of which was clearly out of sympathy with Rousseau's notion of a simple life. François Marie Arouet, who took the name of Voltaire, was seventy years old at this time, and had made himself the most widely known man of letters in the civilised world. The son of a notary, he was educated by the Jesuits and studied law, which he did not like. He managed to live on an allowance while amusing himself with his pen, and soon made a reputation as a wit, which got him into the aristocratic society of Paris. But as his smart sayings were usually at the expense of important persons and established institutions, he sometimes found himself in the Bastille. He made a reputation as a dramatist, and his sayings became so notorious that one of his noble victims had him beaten by lackeys. He tried but failed to obtain redress; and when he began to take fencing-lessons preparatory to a duel, he was again sent to the Bastille. On his release he spent three years in England, where he met Swift, Pope and Gay, and recognised the superiority of the British Constitution to the French. He returned to Paris, made a fortune by cunning speculation, and began to lend money at a high rate of interest. His published *Letters on the English* annoyed the French Government, which ordered his arrest but left him alone when he retired to the country house of Madame du Châtelet. While living with her, Voltaire wrote plays and histories, being elected to the French Academy in 1746. After her death he went to stay at the Court of his admirer, Frederick the Great, who received him almost as a god. But nature had not cast him for the part, and three years of his society convinced the King that he more nearly resembled the devil. They parted in fury, though later correspondence between them lessened their hostility. Some years of wandering followed, but in 1758 Voltaire finally settled at Ferney, which, though in France, was near enough to Geneva for him to escape thither should danger threaten. In this way he was able to enjoy the social freedom of his native country within easy reach of the political freedom of a neighbouring State. By now he was the richest, most famous and most energetic author in the world, his reputation being sealed with the appearance of *Candide* in 1759. He made good use of his money, financing local industries, building houses, a church, a school, a hospital, a reservoir, lending money without interest to the surrounding community, draining the marshes, establishing fairs and markets, and relieving the poor during a famine. He also made full use of his freedom, attacking superstition, tyranny and intolerance in whatever form with a biting wit that made his opponents squirm. *Écrasez l'infâme!* was the motto of his campaign against the Roman Church, especially the Jesuits. His pamphleteering in support of the victims of oppression gave world-wide publicity to local examples of injustice. By his efforts the family of Jean Calas, a victim of popular Catholic frenzy, received handsome compensation, and the unfortunate man, though broken on the wheel, was pronounced innocent. Many cases were reconsidered and reversed at Voltaire's instigation.

But Voltaire himself was not free from some of the faults he censured in others. By disposition malicious, he violently resented attacks on himself, and in his younger days had tried to get a critic thrown into the Bastille, had demanded punitive measures against a hack writer for publishing a feeble poem under the name of 'Voltaire', and had even denounced a landlady for blasphemy; all of which suggests that a man must feel a certain tendency in himself in order to hate and expose it in others. His venom took a peculiarly unpleasant form about the time of Boswell's visit. Rousseau, believing that the drama was a corrupt influence, had attacked Voltaire for opposing the interdiction of theatrical performances by the law of Geneva, and in a personal letter had expressed his hatred of the wit. As a result, Voltaire pseudonymously made ribald fun of *La Nouvelle Héloïse* and probably influenced the Genevan authorities to ban *Émile*. But that did not satisfy his lust for revenge. He heard from a doctor about Rousseau's private life and issued a pamphlet, apparently written by a clergyman, wherein it was stated that Rousseau had abandoned his children, caused the death of Thérèse's mother by his brutal behaviour, and contracted venereal disease. This production shattered Rousseau, who was never again the man Boswell had met about a fortnight before its arrival. For the rest of his life he imagined enemies in every direction. People thought him mad, and at his sanest he was seldom far from the border-line. By an ironic coincidence, on the same day that he read Voltaire's pamphlet Boswell was penning him a letter in which, with a malice worthy of the theme, the writer described Voltaire's conversation as the most brilliant he had ever heard, and said that Rousseau, had he listened to it, would have loved the man.

Boswell, like Johnson at Lord Chesterfield's house, was practically repulsed from the door of Voltaire's. When he had entrusted a footman with a letter of introduction from a friend, the man returned with the message that Voltaire was in bed and excessively vexed by the intrusion. But Boswell had not hired a coach for the mere pleasure of enjoying the scenery between Geneva and Ferney. Voltaire kept open house and Boswell amused himself with the conversation of other callers. At last the great man entered in an elaborate dressing-gown, his lack of teeth giving him a slightly simian appearance, though the eyes were brilliant and the facial expression a strange combination of humour, benevolence and mockery. Boswell did not allow his admiration to interfere with his speech and was soon telling Voltaire that an academy of painting in Glasgow had not flourished. Voltaire remarked that it was difficult to paint with chilly feet. When Boswell said that he and Johnson intended to visit the Hebrides, Voltaire made it clear that he would stay where he was. Voltaire's house was run by his niece, Madame Denis, and when the company of twelve sat down to dinner Boswell made a point of being agreeable to her. Voltaire dined alone. As the gates of Geneva were closed at five, Boswell had to leave early and did not see his host again that day.

He was inspired the following morning, Christmas Day, to despatch a note to Voltaire's niece asking if he might spend a night in the sage's house. He received an invitation to do so. There was a crowd in the drawing-room when he arrived on 27th December, and he felt depressed by the similarity between this social gathering and every other he had attended. Presumably he expected all the acquaintances of a celebrated wit to be witty. In the evening Voltaire played chess with a Jesuit, Père Adam, who was one of his many dependants. Boswell stood by their table and talked, being told by Voltaire not to speak so fast. Voltaire disparaged Shakespeare because he had borrowed all his plots, praised Addison highly, and dismissed Johnson as superstitious on account of his orthodoxy. The Frenchman spoke English well, talked a good deal of nonsense, swore a lot, and occasionally hummed a tune. When supper was served Boswell forgot his hunger and remained alone with Voltaire. They had a violent argument on religion, with a Bible at hand. Voltaire's ridicule bewildered Boswell; and after a burst of eloquence the old man fell back in a faint, no doubt simulated in order to get rid of Boswell. But when he again opened his eyes the relentless Scot still stood before him and continued the discussion from where they had left off. Striking a lower key, Boswell spoke gravely, giving Voltaire no further opening for raillery, and insisted on an avowal of his true belief. Not wishing to prolong the interview, Voltaire confessed his reverence for the Creator, his submission to the Omniscient, and his aspiration towards virtue, though he would not declare his belief in a future state. Boswell tried to corner him by questioning his sincerity, but he remained unshaken. It is not clear whether his next remark, that he experienced no little anguish, was due to his failure to be convinced of immortality or his conviction of Boswell's existence. Boswell was proud of himself as a Christian champion and felt that he was now a man of mark: he had matched himself against the world's leading infidel and had held his own.

Neither of them felt sprightly the next morning, and Voltaire would probably have remained in bed if he had known that Boswell's first act on getting up was to delay his coach till the following day. Having decided to spend another night there, whether invited or not, he became cheerful, listened to a portion of the Mass in the church Voltaire had built in his grounds, surveyed the scenery and wrote some letters. Voltaire remained invisible until dinner-time. Clearly he was still suffering from a Boswellian hang-over; but in spite of his indisposition and despondency Boswell forced him to converse. On 29th December, Boswell had a heart-to-heart talk with Père Adam, who greatly admired Voltaire's benevolent nature but deeply regretted his antagonism to the Christian faith. Having inspected the library and donned his velvet suit, Boswell dined with the company and asked for a farewell interview with Voltaire, who had kept to himself all day, complaining of sickness.

Their final talk was in the drawing-room and lasted for about twenty minutes. Boswell started off by saying that he had changed his opinion since seeing Voltaire, who was a much better man than he had once fancied. Voltaire complimented his honesty. But Boswell wanted to get one thing clear: did Voltaire believe in the soul? Voltaire required a specific definition of the soul, implied that the mystery of life was impenetrable, and announced his belief in one God. Boswell hoped that Voltaire would write to him. Voltaire hoped so too. In order to keep him up to the scratch Boswell sent a letter from Turin, which, like most of his letters, was a quaint compound of self-praise, honesty and silliness. In his correspondence Boswell frequently commented on his good qualities in case those to whom he wrote had failed to notice them; and in his journal he kept on telling himself what a wonderful fellow he was in order to believe it. Voltaire's reply, dictated to his secretary, made fun of Boswell's concern over the soul and ironically insinuated that what was clear to clergymen and youthful students was concealed from an uninstructed person like himself. In a gust of oratory Boswell rejoined that Voltaire's works had come straight from the soul, and felt that he had scored a point.

CHAPTER 15

In Search of a Cause

HAVING BEARDED two lions in their dens, Boswell departed
for Italy with every intention of bearding a third before seeing
Scotland again. He travelled by chaise to Mont Cenis, over
which he was carried on a curious contraption of poles and
cords by four hefty fellows, a pair being relieved at intervals by
two others who trudged along behind. On arrival at Turin he
discovered that the outlaw Wilkes was there and sent him a
typical note in which a desire to see him was qualified by
strictures on his conduct. Wilkes was not in a particularly gay
mood, having recently lost his friend Churchill, who had died
at Boulogne. The sad news suggested to Boswell that they ought
to meet and discuss the immortality of the soul. But Wilkes had
no time for such deliberations, being in pursuit of his mistress,
who some months later ran away from him, hoping that he
would follow on discovering that she had pinched his spoons;
but to her mortification he abandoned his silver along with his
mistress and ran in the opposite direction.

Left to himself, Boswell spent his time at Turin in trying to
persuade certain ladies that he was a born lover. He had heard
that Italian women were notoriously free with their favours,
which argued that they were not morally responsible beings,
which of course enabled him to bamboozle himself that
he could not further debauch what was already corrupt. A
pleasing thought, upon which he proceeded to act. But the
ladies to whom he was introduced did not fall in with his view.
They might be as lewd as he thought them, but they were

sufficiently selective to choose their partners, and Boswell was not one of them. Indeed they treated him with contempt, and in self-defence he concluded that he was too good for them. As usual he made use of more compliant and less well-connected damsels, and as usual he suffered remorse for taking his pleasure in low company. But to say that he behaved like this is merely to say that he was Boswell. A record of his amorous affairs is no more interesting than a record of his daily evacuations. Though he was regularly shocked by his behaviour, there is no more significance in the remorse than in the action; and henceforth we may assume that, except for the periods when venereal disease intervened and put him in cold storage, his "deeds of darkness" were continuous and always followed by shame, until he was no longer able to perform the first or feel the second.

Having gravely discussed transubstantiation and the monastic life, when not engaged in chasing women, he left Turin towards the end of January 1765, feeling so humiliated by his latest rebuff that the sight of a criminal being half-hanged and half-strangled by the public executioner left him unperturbed, and to savour the contrast he entered a church, where he was able to become devout. At Rome he ran across Wilkes, and followed him to Naples, where they saw a lot of one another. Wilkes's perpetual gaiety was infectious, and whenever they were together Boswell's spirits rose. Wilkes said he had never been melancholy in his life, and told Boswell, who rather admired himself in the part of Hamlet, that there was enough pleasure to be got out of existence if one lived to an age that made Methuselah look like a chicken. They ascended Vesuvius together, but the suffocating smoke as they peered into the cavity at the top did not affect the cheerfulness of Wilkes. Back in Rome, Boswell reflected that as the trade of prostitution in the Holy City was licensed by the ecclesiastic in charge of such matters, his indulgence was almost sanctified, and he made the most of it, though the after-effects were distinctly unhallowed.

His other activities resembled those of the average tourist: he visited all the ruins, saw lots of pictures, studied antiquities, climbed the historic hills, inspected churches, and kissed the Pope's slippered foot. He also got to know several leading Jacobites, though he was careful not to risk his worldly prospects by meeting the Old Pretender. When one or two people were a little over-familiar with him, he did his best to copy the aloof manner of the Earl Marischal. He liked to think that he was different from other folk because at one moment he felt that nothing in life could give him pleasure, at another that he could enjoy everything, both moods probably being due to the state of his liver.

While at Rome he made the acquaintance of Lord Mountstuart, eldest son of the King's favourite, Lord Bute. There was every possibility that the young man would eventually be in a position to bestow important offices in the State, and in the hope of future eminence Boswell fastened on to him, being so agreeable that he received an invitation from Mountstuart to complete their Italian tour together. The party included Colonel James Edmonstone, a sort of bear-leader to Mountstuart, whose tutor Paul Henri Mallet accompanied them. They toured the Venetian States, quarrelling as they went. Owing to Boswell's incoherence of character he could never maintain either a natural or a predetermined form of behaviour, and his sense of independence was continually at war with his servility. For the sake of his future career he wanted to impress Mountstuart, to which end he became too submissive. Mountstuart noticed this and took advantage of it. At once Boswell's vanity was touched and he made it clear that Rousseau's friend and the descendant of Bruce was equal or superior to any lord in creation. He overdid that too and Mountstuart derided his oddity. Though his behaviour was silly, his spurt of self-assertion in this instance was creditable; but it led to much bickering during the early part of the trip. They tired of this in time and spent the rest of the journey either in sulks or in childish backchat. Mountstuart was fond of telling bawdy stories and both of them liked talking of their various sex-affairs. Boswell seems to have hoped that their friendship might result in his appointment as ambassador to a foreign Court, but his variations of temper were not favourable to his ambition. He resented being called 'Jamie' by Mountstuart, who was tartly informed that the Stuart family to which he belonged were prone to cheap jokes. At Venice they both enjoyed the same opera dancer, but they did not relish the consequence with its inevitable restrictions.

Boswell's other companions were not to his liking: Edmonstone treated him as a mere hanger-on, and Mallet despised him as an intellectual inferior. Altogether it was not an agreeable ramble. Even Venice palled on Boswell, who found the constant journeys by water tedious and the gondolas depressing. For that matter the approach to Rome had not excited him like his first view of London, and on the whole he was disappointed with Italy. The party separated at Milan, their farewells being more affectionate than their feelings had been. Separations usually engender warmth because they signify freedom. Boswell went on, via Parma and Florence, to Siena, where he recovered from his sexual disability, read Ariosto, sang and practised on the flute with the aid of an expert, was charmed by the social life of the place, paid his amorous addresses to one lady, whom he bombarded with sentimental appeals, and tried to make her jealous by pretending to fall in love with another. At last he did commence an intrigue with the second, called Moma, who was married and had a family of four children. It is impossible to diagnose the nature of his feelings for women, because his language was much the same to all of them and his chief desire was sexual satisfaction; but Moma certainly fell in love with him, and after their transports he seems to have felt a degree of sentimental fondness for her, founded partly on the memory of pleasure and partly on the gratification of his vanity by the emotions he had aroused in her.

Stern letters from Lord Auchinleck ordering his son to return home did not prevent the young man from lingering in Siena. All told, he spent nine months in Italy, five more than his father had allowed, and then, instead of leaving for Scotland, he sailed for Corsica, a trip he had contemplated when visiting Rousseau. In retrospect it appears almost inevitable that Boswell should have gone to Corsica, his nature being what it was. Frederick the Great having failed him, his desire to know a hero, a famous man of action, directed his eye to the Mediterranean, where a little nation was fighting for freedom under a great patriot. The visit to Corsica satisfied three aspects of his disjointed character: servility, independence and ambition. He could venerate a remarkable man, applaud a stand for liberty which symbolised his own gradual emancipation from his father, and gain a great deal of publicity by writing an account of a practically unknown place and people. Then, too, he needed a Cause. Many people who cannot stand firmly on their own feet require something that they can clutch to keep themselves upright; and so they become identified with a religious sect or a political party or an aesthetic group or an economic theory, with anything that can give them an object in life and focalise their uncertain aims. For reasons already stated, a Cause was more necessary for Boswell than for others of his kind, and he was irresistibly attracted to a country of which Rousseau had written "I have a presentiment that one day that little island will astonish Europe." Boswell might even have dreamt that he would write the saga whereby Europe would be astonished.

The Corsicans had been carrying on a kind of guerrilla war against their masters, the Genoan Republic, for some four centuries. In 1734 two of the Corsican leaders were Giafferi and Giacinto Paoli, who seem to have believed that a Westphalian baron named Theodore would save the island from Genoa if he were made King. They chanced it; the baron duly became a monarch and contrived the importation of certain munitions from foreign countries; but he took so long about it that the Genoese woke up and called the French to their aid. Theodore fled to England, where his tomb may be seen in St. Anne's churchyard, Soho. The French took nearly two years to subdue the refractory islanders, whose leaders found refuge in Naples, and then gradually evacuated the country; upon which the Corsicans again revolted, and in 1755 sent for the son of one of their old chiefs to come to their assistance. Pasquali Paoli, in his thirtieth year, was made their General and soon managed to organise an army, with which he drove the Genoese into several distant and almost impregnable coastal towns. He then gave his attention to the internal affairs of the country, but his activities were interrupted by the return of French troops, the Genoese having again asked for help and obtained it because France owed them money. But it was only a temporary alarm, for the French commander, Count de Marbeuf, contented himself with occupying such fortified ports as Bastia, Calvi and Ajaccio, leaving the rest of the island to its native inhabitants. Making themselves as snug as possible for a period of four years, at the conclusion of which the cash account with Genoa would be balanced, the French entered into a pact of non-aggression with the Corsicans, with whom they established a friendly understanding.

Paoli then got on with the job of civilising his countrymen by fostering trade and agriculture, planning a sound constitution, and stamping out vendettas. He was a man of energy and piety, incorruptible and humane. His ambition was to be known as the liberator and saviour of his country, and he believed himself to be the Almighty's agent in the work that had to be done. He had considerable organising ability and was a born soldier, but the influence he exercised was due to the devotion he inspired in his followers, who regarded him as an indulgent father, an upright judge, and a great leader. He had the right appearance for his position, being above middle-height and largely built, with well-proportioned limbs. He had a lofty carriage, a fair complexion, and penetrating blue eyes. Such was the man whom Boswell determined to see, the benevolent dictator of barbarous but obedient followers, in a warlike but temporarily peaceful country, its chief ports occupied by amicable aliens whose sole object was a quiet and agreeable life.

Obtaining a passport from the British naval commander in the Mediterranean as a safeguard in case of capture by pirates, and armed with letters of introduction from Rousseau and Count Rivarola, Consul for Sardinia at Leghorn, Boswell sailed from that port on 11th October 1765. He was to profit from the fact that his visit aroused suspicion among the politicians of Italy, who thought he was charged with the mission of arranging a treaty between Britain and Corsica. His denials were couched in such a form as to strengthen suspicion, and his movements in Corsica were watched and reported by the French, the Genoese and the Sardinians. The consequence was that papers would publish any bit of news about himself and his whereabouts that he cared to send them, and on leaving the island he started what amounted to a press campaign on the theme of Boswell and Paoli and the brave Corsicans and again Boswell. Having absorbed the information that if he made the least attempt to debauch any Corsican woman he could expect instant death, he decided in favour of chastity during his stay in the country, one of the few decisions that accorded with his subsequent behaviour. He received much hospitality as he travelled through the country. On leaving the town of Corte for a mountainous journey into the interior, he described an Arcadian scene:

My Corsican guides appeared so hearty that I often got down and walked along with them, doing just what I saw them do. When we grew hungry, we threw stones among the thick branches of the chestnut trees which overshadowed us, and in that manner we brought down a shower of chestnuts with which we filled our pockets, and went on eating them with great relish; and when this made us thirsty, we lay down by the side of the first brook, put our mouths to the stream and drank sufficiently.

At a small mountain village Boswell emerged with credit from an awkward duologue. On hearing from the guides that he was an Englishman, an intimidating native exclaimed:

"English! they are barbarians; they don't believe in the great God."

"Excuse me, sir," Boswell protested, "we do believe in God, and in Jesus Christ too."

"Hm. And in the Pope?"

"No."

"And why?"

"Because we are too far off."

"Too far off! Why, Sicily is as far off as England. Yet in Sicily they believe in the Pope."

"Oh, we are ten times farther off than Sicily."

"Aha!" said the comprehending Corsican.

At another place Boswell made a fluent speech to the inhabitants, exhorting them, with the firm conviction of one who had no intention of following his own advice, to remain in their present state of simplicity, which was far happier than a cultivated condition of refinement and vice. Rousseau would have applauded him.

At last he reached Sollacarò, where Paoli then resided, and the thought of meeting a man who appeared from all accounts to be superhuman made him nervous. The beginning of their interview failed to compose him. Having read his letters of introduction, Paoli walked him up and down the room for ten minutes, surveying him keenly in silence. The experience was, as Boswell said, "very severe upon me." Paoli afterwards confessed that at first he thought Boswell had come to spy on him, and the impression did not wear off when he observed his visitor making notes. But he must have guessed that no paid spy would be silly enough to record his conversation in his presence, and his frosty bearing began to thaw when Boswell complimented the Corsicans: "Sir, I am upon my travels, and have lately visited Rome. I am come from seeing the ruins of one brave people; I now see the rise of another." Boswell was invited to dinner and sat next to Paoli, feeling "some constraint in such a circle of heroes". But like most men of action Paoli talked a great deal and Boswell was soon at his ease. The lord of the local manor, Signor Colonna, was away from home, and Boswell was lent his house. Altogether he passed a week at Paoli's headquarters, though he liked to give the impression that he had remained there a good deal longer. He dined daily with the General, received visits from the nobles, and made excursions with a guard of honour. Once he was mounted on Paoli's own horse: "I allowed myself to indulge a momentary pride in this parade, as I was curious to experience what could really be the pleasure of state and distinction with which mankind are so strongly intoxicated." Apparently he was able to experience it vicariously.

Boswell noticed three things about Paoli that are common to most self-made rulers: he had an excellent memory; he was perpetually restless; and he hardly ever laughed. "Whether loud laughter in general society be a sign of weakness or rusticity I cannot say," wrote Boswell; "but I have remarked that real great men, and men of finished behaviour, seldom fall into it." It would have been interesting to hear that giant laugher Samuel Johnson's comments on this observation, which would have pleased Lord Chesterfield but which flatly contradicts Boswell's estimate of Johnson. However, the contradictions in Boswell's works are far more numerous than the confirmations. It cannot be said that Paoli's conversation, as recorded by Boswell, is more illuminating than that of other dictators. A fair specimen is his remark on the war against Genoa: "Sir, if the event prove happy, we shall be called great defenders of liberty. If the event shall prove unhappy, we shall be called unfortunate rebels," a thought that must have occurred to every fairly intelligent man who has taken part in a revolt. Paoli was, however, quick enough to spot the flaw in Boswell's suggestion that he should marry and have a son to succeed him: "Sir, what security can I have that my son will think and act as I do?" The General, who claimed to be gifted with second-sight, announced his belief that God had interposed to give freedom to Corsica, adding: "A people oppressed like the Corsicans are certainly worthy of divine assistance." Unhappily, a few years later God interposed to deprive them of freedom, but, as Paoli admitted, "His ways are unsearchable."

Though Boswell's ambitions wobbled and he was never quite certain whether he wanted to be an author or a soldier or a statesman, his admiration for Paoli steadily increased. Under the influence of Johnson he soared to be a writer. While listening to Pitt he longed to be an orator. In Paoli's company he would have been satisfied with nothing less than the leadership of a nation, though he did not strike such a high note in his account of the man: "From having known intimately so exalted a character, my sentiments of human nature were raised; while by a sort of contagion I felt an honest ardour to distinguish myself, and be useful as far as my situation and abilities would allow; and I was, for the rest of my life, set free from a slavish timidity in the presence of great men, for where shall I find a man greater than Paoli?" This passage was nicely attuned to the feelings of its subject, who would read it in due course.

The mansion in which Boswell lived at Sollacarò was in poor condition, his bedroom being damp and draughty. He caught a bad cold which developed into what he called "a tertian ague", probably a malarial complaint. Taking leave of Paoli, he set forth in the company of "a great swarthy priest" who entertained him with equine capers and comic songs. The General had provided him with two guards in case of accidents:

One of them called Ambrosio was a strange, iron-coloured, fearless creature. He had been much in war; careless of wounds, he was coolly intent on destroying the enemy. He told me, as a good anecdote, that, having been so lucky as to get a view of two Genoese exactly in a line, he took his aim and shot them both through the head at once. He talked of this just as one would talk of shooting a couple of crows. I was sure I needed be under no apprehension; but I don't know how, I desired Ambrosio to march before me that I might see him.

I was upon my guard how I treated him. But as sickness frets one's temper, I sometimes forgot myself and called him 'blockhead'; and once when he was at a loss which way to go, at a wild woody part of the country, I fell into a passion and called to him, "I am amazed that so brave a man can be so stupid." However, by afterwards calling him friend and speaking softly to him I soon made him forget my ill humour, and we proceeded as before.

Boswell's Swiss servant, Jacob Hänni, was tired of Corsica and said that, once back in his native land, nothing would ever prevail upon him to leave it again. Having reached Corte in safety, Boswell was laid low with the ague, but this did not prevent him from writing to Samuel Johnson from the palace of Paoli "sacred to wisdom and liberty", just as he had written from the tomb of Melanchthon "sacred to learning and piety". Johnson's reply, which he received at Paris some weeks later, promised him a hearty welcome home and contained a sentence that delighted him: "I long to see you and to hear you, and hope that we shall not be so long separated again." Paoli had given Boswell a letter of recommendation to the French commander at Bastia, the Count de Marbeuf, who behaved with the utmost generosity. Boswell was lodged comfortably in the Count's house and during his illness was looked after by servants, given the proper food, attended by a physician, and provided with books. When able to leave his room he was courteously entertained and treated with a consideration that won his gratitude.

He left Bastia for Genoa on 20th November 1765, having been absent from Italy just under six weeks. But he experienced some trying days before reaching the mainland. The winds were unfavourable and the boat had to put in at Capraja, a bleak island scarcely a score of miles from the Corsican coast, where to lessen his boredom he wrote a lot and wrangled with his Franciscan hosts. After being marooned for six days he exhibited his temper in a burst of indecent language to the master of a small vessel that would take him to Genoa, strode on board, and insisted on leaving at once; but an attack of sea-sickness drove him on shore again. However, the wind veered early the following morning, and they sailed, reaching Genoa on the 30th. He had been violently sea-sick all the way, and the letters from his father, which he read soon after landing, did not balance matters by making him homesick.

Lord Auchinleck reported that he had almost died of his urinary trouble, complained of James's neglect of duty in not writing, of his inexcusably long absence, and of his culpable extravagance. Three passionate love-letters from Moma were a pleasing contrast to the judge's strictures.

After a few days in Genoa, Boswell embarked for Marseilles; but the winds were unpropitious and he was compelled to travel most of the way on foot or horseback. Paoli had given him a large dog, called Jachone, and he tortured the poor brute. When the dog had an attack of sickness, he flung it into the sea, believing that it would reach land and keep abreast of the boat. But the dog had a different reasoning faculty and ran off to the nearest town. It was retrieved when Boswell went ashore, and pitilessly thrashed by its master. The wretched animal was then denied food, dragged along the road with a rope, twice strung up on a tree and half-strangled in the process, beaten repeatedly, once until the blood poured from its nose, and later forced to run after a chaise on icy roads until its feet were swollen and its cries of pain would have softened the heart of a hangman. At last, somewhere in France, Jachone ran away, possibly "to the woods, where he would find The unkindest beast more kinder than mankind". The narrator of these details seemed to think that he was merely trying to teach the dog discipline, and he has been half-excused on the ground that in the eighteenth century animals were not given the consideration accorded them in the twentieth. But the real explanation is that Boswell lacked imagination and loved to exercise power. He later benefited from the observation of Johnson's tenderness and felt so much shame at his treatment of Jachone that he erased the record of it from his journal. Example as well as experience teaches fools, but the naturally intelligent and imaginative man has no need of either to make him humane. Boswell was essentially foolish because of the absence of anything fundamental in his nature, and his behaviour to his dog, though it might have disgusted, would not have surprised those who knew him. The reason he disliked cats is now obvious, for those animals do not suffer fools gladly.

Jachone's agony may in part be ascribed to the shortcomings of Jacob, the servant whom Boswell would have liked to chastise. Boswell stupidly complained when the familiarity with which he treated Jacob was returned. Jacob upbraided Boswell for starving Jachone, and against instructions gave the dog food. Further, he said that his master was incapable of conducting himself properly with a servant, being sometimes jocular, sometimes severe, and he strongly advised Boswell against marriage, as he would not know how to live with a wife or how to bring up children. Jacob also accused Boswell of being mean over money. There was some truth in this charge, though Boswell could have claimed that he paid all his debts of dishonour, sometimes twice over. But he was stingy in certain respects, generous in others, like many people. The master and servant were relieved when they finally separated at Lyons.

Boswell was aware of his failure to be dignified and recognised that it was due to infirmity of purpose.

But on one point he was constant. He intended to tell the world all about Boswell, and while passing through France he commenced an elaborate publicity campaign. He had arranged with the editor of *The London Chronicle* to print paragraphs at regular intervals, the objects being to popularise the cause of Corsica, to arouse interest in the book he intended to write, above all to keep his own name well to the fore. These paragraphs, ostensibly from correspondents in Italy but all from the pen of Boswell, began to appear early in January 1766 and continued regularly until his arrival in England, after which the publication of the authentic facts in a volume by himself was puffed and breathlessly awaited.

Travelling in France was uncomfortable, because Boswell had worn the wrong sort of footwear for crossing the Corsican mountains and he now suffered agonies from ingrowing toenails. A surgeon performed the necessary operation in Paris, the effects being painful for some time. While in Paris he read in a paper that his mother had died. A little later he received a letter from his father announcing the fact and expecting his speedy return home. He wept profusely and was in great distress, receiving much comfort from Wilkes, who happened to be in Paris just then. He determined to go home and console his father. Learning that Thérèse Le Vasseur had arrived in the capital on her way to join Rousseau in England, he called at her hotel and they arranged to travel together. Rousseau's belief in one God had at length exasperated the Trinitarians of Môtiers, and a sermon against his infidelity by a local priest inspired the mob to stone his house. Unappreciative of this form of religious enthusiasm, he sought safety in a small island in the canton of Berne, but the State officials were unsympathetic and enforced his departure. David Hume having invited him to England, the two had journeyed thither from Paris, leaving Thérèse to follow them. While in Geneva a year before this, Boswell had finished a letter to Rousseau with the assurance that his occasional correspondence with Thérèse did not indicate any intention on his part to seduce her; for though he had often made romantic plans, he had never conceived an impossible one.

On the way from Paris to London he now proceeded to execute an impossible plan. Thérèse was willing, and after a feeble start Boswell justified himself in his own eyes as a lover. But Thérèse informed him that, though sturdy, he lacked skill, and offered to instruct him. Boswell was downcast, and so frightened at their next encounter that he fortified himself with wine. Her lessons in patience and gentleness were no doubt valuable, but they made him a little resentful, and he thought that he had erred in having an affair with her. Their last raptures occurred at Dover, and they were ready for a breakfast of beefsteaks by the time they arrived at Rochester. He handed her over to Rousseau at Chiswick, mentally comparing his own youthful vigour with the debilitated condition of the older man.

CHAPTER 16

From Wales

WHILE Boswell had been amusing himself on the continent, Johnson had made the acquaintance of two people whose hospitality and companionship were to give him greater comfort and pleasure nearly to the end of his life than he could receive from all his other friends put together. This was the second occasion on which Arthur Murphy was able to render him a service of incalculable value. For some years Murphy had been on friendly terms with a wealthy Southwark brewer named Henry Thrale, who had inherited the business from his father. One day in January 1765, Murphy, dining with the Thrales, said that they ought to know Johnson, whose character he described in such glowing terms that they tried hard to find a reason for inviting the paragon to dinner. They found an excuse in a shoemaker poet, James Woodhouse, whose verses had earned him invitations to several houses where literary lions were displayed. Murphy felt that Johnson would be interested to see the poet or the shoemaker and suggested that the Thrales should ask them to meet one another at dinner. The meeting took place, and the Thrales liked Johnson so much that he was asked to dine without the shoemaker the following week. The liking was mutual, and the Thrales were so sympathetic that Johnson soon spoke of his mental disorders, which he once described in such a heart-rending manner that Thrale told his wife to persuade their new friend to leave his stuffy home off Fleet Street and stay with them at their country residence in Streatham. From June to September 1766

Johnson was their guest at Streatham, and Mrs. Thrale's attentions helped to improve his physical health and to restore some degree of mental tranquillity. Thenceforward Thrale's houses at Southwark and Streatham were open to him whenever he liked, and a room at each was always reserved for him. "I long to come to that place which my dear friends allow me to call HOME," he once wrote to Mrs. Thrale. In fact he was adopted as one of the family and came to regard everything to do with the Thrales as a matter of grave importance and the object of his personal concern.

Henry Thrale and Johnson had little in common, and their attraction to one another was that of opposites. Educated at Eton and Oxford, Thrale had enjoyed a sufficiently large allowance from his father to make the Grand Tour, to hobnob with aristocrats, and to cultivate the society of actresses. His father's death made him a man of business at the age of thirty, and a few years later he made himself a man of affairs by entering Parliament as member for Southwark. He was nearly thirty-eight, about a dozen years older than his wife, when he met Johnson, who was perhaps chiefly struck by the brewer's politeness and unpretentiousness, by a composure seldom ruffled, by an unresentful disposition, by a speech free from oaths, ribaldry and profanity, and by a nature that appeared incapable of feeling hope or despair or anger or depression or excitement or happiness. Thrale was neither kind nor unkind, but indifferent. Being awakened one night and told that his sister's house was on fire, he ordered a servant to go to her assistance, turned over and slept to his usual hour. He was reserved, aloof and drowsy, making no attempt to become popular; and he was inscrutable, seeming to be incapable of giving a straightforward answer to a plain question. He treated catastrophes as trifles and conferred favours apathetically. He loved money but was generous with it, apparently not much caring whether he was giving or receiving it. He was large, lethargic, passionless and unimaginative. Johnson thought him scholarly, but that may have been because he lent a favourable ear to his friend's classical quotations; and the one taste they unquestionably shared was a love of guzzling.

His wife Hester differed from him in every respect. She was born in North Wales, the daughter of John Salusbury of Bachygraig, her ancestors being Welsh, but most of her girl-hood was passed on the borders of Hertfordshire and Bedford-shire. When Thrale arrived on the scene and proposed marriage, her father decided that she should not be exchanged for a barrel of porter; but John Salusbury died soon afterwards, and to please her mother she married Thrale, with whom she had never spent five minutes alone before their nuptials. At that time she was a lively little woman, just under five feet in height, with chestnut-coloured hair, marked eyebrows to match, a well-shaped nose, large light-grey eyes, and a good figure; not exactly pretty because of some defect in the mouth which looked like a scar, but attractive and vivacious. Her nature was affectionate, and as a friend she was both loyal and generous. Never in love with Thrale, she bore her marriage with good-temper and fortitude. She obeyed him in everything, calling him "my master", a description which Johnson adopted. She confessed that her husband was little tender of her person though partial to her understanding. She bore him many chil-dren and suffered not a few miscarriages, all of which she regarded as part of her duty, just as going to the office was part of his. Advised of one miscarriage, he refused to leave his office a minute before the usual time. Nothing could induce him to hurry. When she got to know Johnson well she spoke of her husband's "cold carriage" towards her, not with resentment, as it occasioned no dislike, but as a trait of character. Johnson administered cold comfort: "Why, how for heaven's sake, dearest madam, should any man delight in a wife that is to him neither use nor ornament? He cannot talk to you about his business, which you do not understand; nor about his pleasures, which you do not partake. If you have wit or beauty, you show them nowhere, so he has none of the reputation. If you have economy or understanding, you employ neither in attention to his property. You divide your time between your mamma and your babies, and wonder you do not by that means become agreeable to your husband." Her mother said that she was better employed in looking after her children than in becoming "My Lady Mashtub" of the brewery, so she remained domesticated until the children grew up, when she interested herself in her husband's trade.

From Johnson's remarks to her it will be seen that he was not always an ideal guest, and during his first extended visit to Streatham her tact as a hostess was severely tested by the dislike subsisting between him and her mother, whom she adored. The two lived in a state of perpetual bickering, because Mrs. Salusbury loved discussing the political situation as it appeared in the papers, and he detested such talk, distrusted newspaper reports, contradicted everything that appeared in print, and made it clear that he thought her agitations over foreign affairs ridiculous. To cure her credulity he actually went to the trouble of inventing campaigns and diplomatic intrigues, accounts of which he contrived to get published in several journals. The Russians and Turks being then at war, he concocted the story of a battle between them, but in order to make it absurd he laid the scene in an island at the conflux of the Borysthenes and the Danube, those rivers being a hundred leagues apart. Having believed the story implicitly because it was in print, Mrs. Salusbury at length discovered the deception and was furious, "the consequence of which," said Johnson, "was that I lost an agreeable companion and she was deprived of an innocent amusement." Her illness some six years later called forth all his tenderness, and they were completely reconciled.

Wherever Johnson went his friends were sure to go sooner or later, and in time the house of the Thrales, whether in Southwark or Streatham, became an intellectual centre, with Hester

Thrale as a fashionable hostess. Their guests included Goldsmith, Reynolds, Garrick, Burke and Burney, while not a few titled notabilities sought for invitations to meet the celebrated moralist and wit in such surroundings. Thrale commissioned Reynolds to paint the more famous members of the Johnson circle, hanging their portraits at Streatham, and he gave Johnson £100 to purchase books of his own choice for the library there. The Thrales recognised the social importance they had attained by Johnson's friendship, and eight years after their first meeting Hester wrote to him: "All the good we enjoy, all the flattery we receive, all the pleasure we bestow, comes ultimately if not immediately from you. Continue to us therefore your never-enough-valued friendship, and assure yourself of our most sincere and venerating affection." In another letter she asked: "Can we do anything without you? and can the earnestness of our friendship at all compensate for the trouble you have with us all?"

She was not averse to giving flattery, nor he to receiving it. "What signifies protesting so against flattery?" he asked. "When a person speaks well of one, it must be either true or false, you know. If true, let us rejoice in his good opinion; if he lies, it is a proof at least that he loves more to please me than to sit silent when he need say nothing." Hester certainly wished to please him, but she took care not to make her flattery fulsome, like that of Hannah More, who received a sharp rebuke from Johnson: "Madam, before you flatter a man so grossly to his face, you should consider whether or not your flattery is worth his having," to which his remark to Hester serves as commentary: "Madam, I am always sorry when I make bitter speeches, and I never do it but when I am insufferably vexed." Hester's chief weakness was a tendency to overpraise people and things, which offended his sense of truth: "Why, madam, you often provoke me to say severe things by unreasonable commendation. If you would not call for my praise, I would not give you my censure; but it constantly moves my indignation to be applied to, to speak well of a thing which I think contemptible." What he chiefly liked about the Thrales was that they were good-natured, extremely hospitable, and incapable of animosity. "Mrs. Thrale," he told someone, "is a sweet creature and never angry; she has a temper the most delightful of any woman I ever knew."

There were times when her cheerfulness must have been strained to the limit. Johnson hated going to bed. "I lie down that my acquaintance may sleep," he said; "but I lie down to endure oppressive misery, and soon rise again to pass the night in anxiety and pain." His pathetic appeals that she should sit up with him long after everyone else had retired for the night were never made in vain, and at length her health suffered from lack of sleep and the exertion to keep him entertained with conversation and cups of tea until three or four in the morning. It did not help her to endure these protracted sessions when he asserted that people never sacrificed themselves for the sake of pleasing others, and that she remained up with him for her own amusement. There was some truth in this vexatious statement because he could be excessively funny, keeping her in fits of laughter with his stories of people and engaging her interest with an affectionate intimacy and a fond confidence which he bestowed on no one else. Their deeper feeling for one another was clearly revealed when he spoke rather roughly to her before a large company at dinner. Everyone was surprised that she bore it so calmly, and when the ladies were alone one of them expressed amazement that he could speak in such a harsh manner to her. Her sole comment was: "Oh, dear good man!" Johnson got to hear of this, and a little later, when half-asleep in a chair, he was overheard saying softly to himself in a tone of great content: "Oh, dear good man!"

Hester Thrale kept a journal, like Boswell, recording therein many Johnsonian sayings and anecdotes. The picture that emerges is more familiar and lovable than that of the dominating character portrayed by Boswell; and to obtain a fair likeness of Johnson the modern biographer must make a synthesis from the memorials of four women as well as Boswell, who regarded Johnson as his personal property and made it his business to disparage any account not his own. In his analysis of Hester Thrale's record his jealousy made him disingenuous. He criticised her published *Anecdotes* on the ground that she depended too much on her memory, and it is true that she completed from memory remarks and incidents to which she had sketchily referred in her journal; but we now know that Boswell followed the same principle; and her memory, owing to a very much smaller intake of liquor, was more to be relied upon than his. Boswell did his utmost to make Fanny Burney let him see the Johnsonian excerpts from her diary, but she refused; and as she was sensible enough not to publish them in the biographer's lifetime, his references to her in his work were understandably reticent. She too gives a more human and charming view of her subject than Boswell could. Frances Reynolds, Sir Joshua's sister, also supplied some vivid sketches of Johnson's less ceremonious behaviour; while Anna Seward provided a more extended and lifelike account of a duologue between Johnson and another person than anything of the kind in Boswell, who naturally suppressed it, not only because he was envious of its superior merit but also because it shows Johnson in his least attractive mood. It will not be suppressed in this biography.

CHAPTER 17

Mainly Matrimonial

HAVING ARRIVED in London on 13th February 1766, and
deposited Thérèse Le Vasseur at Rousseau's lodgings in the
village of Chiswick, Boswell hastened to see Johnson, who had
now moved from his rooms in the Temple and taken a house off
Fleet Street in Johnson's Court, so named from an earlier
inhabitant. Anna Williams and Robert Levett were again
under his roof, and of course Francis Barber. In the previous
year Trinity College, Dublin, had made him a Doctor of Laws,
which had come as a welcome surprise, and thereafter he was
given the title of 'Doctor' by his friends, though he continued
to call himself 'Mister'. He warmly embraced Boswell, who
fell on his knees and begged a blessing. They supped at the
Mitre, Johnson drinking water while suffering from a severe
bout of abstinence. Boswell now felt himself a real man of the
world, and called on old acquaintances with an assured sense
of his own importance. His intimate friend William Temple
was in London, and on 15th February Boswell presented him
to Johnson at the Mitre. It was not in Boswell's nature to
maintain a discreet reserve, and before long it appeared from
his conversation that he had met Wilkes and Rousseau on the
continent. "It seems, sir, you have kept very good company
abroad—Rousseau and Wilkes!" said Johnson ironically. This
was just what Boswell wanted, and he asked whether Johnson
really thought Rousseau a bad man. "Sir, if you are talking
jestingly of this, I don't talk with you," replied Johnson, who
no doubt sensed that he was being drawn, though his indig-

nation made him continue: "If you mean to be serious, I think him one of the worst of men; a rascal who ought to be hunted out of society, as he has been. Three or four nations have expelled him, and it is a shame that he is protected in this country." Boswell missed the chance of a lifetime at this point by not inviting Johnson to dine with Rousseau at the Mitre. Instead he rather weakly said that though Rousseau's work might have done harm, he had meant well. Having easily disposed of that defence, Johnson vociferated: "Rousseau, sir, is a very bad man. I would sooner sign a sentence for his transportation than that of any felon who has gone from the Old Bailey these many years. Yes, I should like to have him work in the plantations." Here was an opportunity to kill two birds with one stone, and Boswell took it: "Sir, do you think him as bad a man as Voltaire?" His feelings of gratitude, affection and reverence, eloquently expressed to the two men both verbally and by letter, were obliterated in an atmosphere of orthodoxy, and he gave Johnson the last word: "Why, sir, it is difficult to settle the proportion of iniquity between them."

Malice is the child of vanity, and Boswell was subject to both. In his talks with Johnson we can frequently spot the malice, usually, as in the instance just quoted, at the expense of others who are absent. Although he loved to egg Johnson on with the object of making him reveal his feelings and opinions, there was sometimes malicious intent behind the plausibly innocent question, and occasionally Boswell's own folly produced the desired effect, as when he said that his head had ached as a consequence of drinking port with Johnson, who gave a different reason: "Nay, sir, it was not the wine that made your head ache but the sense that I put into it." Boswell's imbecile ejaculation "What, sir! will sense make the head ache?" was rewarded with "Yes, sir, when it is not used to it." Boswell's chief virtue was that he recorded such hits, if now and then his vanity made him describe the victim as "a gentleman present" or "one of the company".

He spent about a fortnight in London before going to Scotland, his father in the meantime writing to say that his allowance would be stopped if he did not return at once, though the letter failed to reach him until he was back in Edinburgh. Apart from seeing Johnson, his main purpose was to tackle William Pitt on the subject of Corsica. Though no longer in office, Pitt was a Privy Councillor and the leading figure in politics. Boswell wrote to ask for an interview. Pitt replied that he would be glad to see him but suggested that the Secretary of State was the right person to approach on behalf of Paoli. Boswell had no faith in Government officials, jumped at the chance of meeting Pitt, and became lyrical in his answer: "However you may by political circumstances be in one view a simple individual, yet, sir, Mr. Pitt will always be the Prime Minister of the brave, the Secretary of freedom and of spirit; and I hope that I may with propriety talk to him of the views of the illustrious Paoli." He did not wait for an appointment but called on Pitt in Bond Street one morning at nine o'clock, heard he was still in bed, and called again at eleven. Pitt received him graciously; and after saying that as a Privy Councillor he would have to pass on to the King and Council anything he heard from a foreign Power that concerned his own country, Pitt conducted the conversation in an atmosphere of friendliness and concluded it with an air of indecisiveness, though Boswell was able to close his book on Corsica with a sentence that must have equally pleased two eminent men: "I take the liberty to repeat an observation made to me by that illustrious minister, whom Paoli calls the Pericles of Great Britain—'It may be said of Paoli, as the Cardinal de Retz said of the great Montrose: He is one of those men who are no longer to be found but in the lives of Plutarch'."

Although Pitt was unable to do more than express his sympathy with the Corsicans, Boswell was anxious that he should show an interest in their Scottish champion, and a year later wrote from Auchinleck to Great Britain's Pericles, who had now become the Earl of Chatham: "I have the happiness of being capable to contemplate with supreme delight those distinguished spirits by whom God is sometimes pleased to honour humanity; and as I have no personal favour to ask of your Lordship, I will tell you, with the confidence of one who does not fear to be thought a flatterer, that your character, my Lord, has filled many of my best hours with that noble admiration which a disinterested soul can enjoy in the bower of philosophy." Having apprised the Earl of his forthcoming book on Corsica, he suddenly remembered that, despite his disavowal, he had a personal favour to ask: "Could your Lordship find time to honour me now and then with a letter? . . . To correspond with a Paoli and with a Chatham is enough to keep a young man ever ardent in the pursuit of virtuous fame." Apart from the joy of exhibiting to friends and acquaintances the letters he had received from famous persons, Boswell was an indefatigable autograph collector, and on at least two occasions asked Wilkes to sign his full name at the end of his letters.

After Eglinton had presented him at Court, where three words were bestowed upon him by the royal mouth, and after he had sampled the charms of a female wanderer in the strand and made up his mind to maintain the superiority of feeling and thought essential to a friend of Johnson, Boswell departed for Scotland, home and father. He reached Edinburgh early in March and was soon at Auchinleck, where he tried hard to comfort his parent and experienced no difficulty whatever in falling head over ears in love with the gardener's daughter, who of course aroused deeper feelings in him than he had ever known before and was inevitably followed by a woman who aroused still deeper feelings. The name of this last was Mrs. Dodds, whom he met at Moffat. She was separated from her husband, who had charge of their three children, and became Boswell's mistress. Eventually he took a house for her at Edinburgh, where he suffered pangs of jealousy on account of her early affairs but did his best to forget them by assessing her good qualities: "She is very handsome, very lively, and admirably formed for amorous dalliance," he told Temple. But Boswell's notions of amorous dalliance were fluid, and immediately after an ecstatic union with Mrs. Dodds he got drunk with some friends, visited a shady house in a mean wynd, spent the night with one of its inhabitants, and was horrified by the consequences. However, he was a cad who had the indecency to know it, and explained the situation to his mistress, who pardoned him and advised him to be temperate in future.

Temple, the recipient of these confessions, became a Church of England clergyman in 1766, when a cousin presented him with the Devonshire living of Mamhead, a few miles south of Exeter. He married in 1767 and remained to the end Boswell's greatest friend and only complete confidant, though they had few points of resemblance. Temple had wished to study law, but the family funds had dried up and he was forced to take holy orders. He was tolerant, humane and scholarly by nature, but very quiet, seldom opening his mouth in company. While at Cambridge he became friendly with Thomas Gray, his account of whom was used in Johnson's *Lives of the English Poets*. On the whole he was as good a parson as could be expected of one who would rather have been a barrister; and since two of his descendants have occupied the highest office in the English Church, it is clear that his legal aptitude was transmitted to succeeding generations.

What Temple would have enjoyed Boswell obtained but could not enjoy. The day of reckoning having arrived, James's promise to his father had to be redeemed. At the end of July 1766 he was admitted to the Faculty of Advocates and soon began to practise. His first important job was to defend a sheep-stealer named John Reid. This he did with so much zeal that he aroused antagonism in certain quarters which, for the sake of his career, he should have propitiated. With an imposing array of legal notabilities against him, including the Lord Advocate and the Solicitor-General, he and a lawyer named

Andrew Crosbie made such eloquent appeals that the jury returned a verdict of 'Not Proven' and Reid was set free, a result that irritated the law lords. Such acts of disinterestedness were typical of Boswell, whose nature compelled him to extremes which often harmed himself and sometimes benefited others. Reid however ended on the gallows some years later owing to his habit of mistaking other people's sheep for his own. Again Boswell defended him and supplied personal sympathy when the law was obdurate.

At the outset of his career as an advocate Boswell was fairly successful; he could speak easily and forcibly, and, as he admitted, "the absurdity of mankind makes nineteen out of twenty employ the son of the judge before whom their cause is heard." He took a keen interest in the great Douglas case which aroused all the popular frenzy usually reserved for religious and political causes. Lady Jane Douglas, childless by her first husband, married at the age of forty-eight an old colonel, John Stewart. The likelihood of issue being remote, the announcement that Lady Jane had produced twins in Paris caused a sensation, because, one of the twins having died, the survivor Archibald became heir to the Douglas estate if the Duke died without direct male issue. This did not please the guardians of the young Duke of Hamilton, who would inherit the estate but for Lady Jane's child; and when the Duke of Douglas died heirless in 1761, lawyers were employed to ferret out details. The evidence they collected seemed to prove that Lady Jane's twins were the offspring of a glass-manufacturer and a rope-dancer, and the case, first heard in 1762, was decided by the Court of Session in 1767, eight judges voting that Lady Jane's twins were not her own, seven in favour of legitimacy, the Lord President's casting vote for the Duke of Hamilton settling the matter. The lawyers representing Archibald Douglas then appealed to the House of Lords. Before the appeal was heard Boswell, who had enthusiastically embraced the cause of Archibald, behaved in a manner unbecoming to an advocate

174

and the son of a judge. He indited ballads on the subject and sang them at dinner-parties; he sent paragraphs and squibs to the papers; he published a fictional description of the affair under the title of *Dorando*; he wrote a pamphlet on *The Essence of the Douglas Cause*; and he issued a selection of Lady Jane Douglas's private letters, which did much to influence the attitude of the mob. In February 1769 the appeal to the House of Lords was successful, the verdict of the Court of Session was reversed, and Archibald Douglas was declared heir to the estate. The news caused hysteria in Edinburgh, and any judge who failed to light up his windows, whichever way he had voted, had his glass smashed. It was rumoured that Boswell actually led the crowd that attacked his father's house, and there is not much doubt that he was delirious with jubilation and potation, though he had probably taken the precaution to disguise himself as a "base mechanical". For the clearing-up process after the case was won, other claims being advanced, Archibald Douglas gave Boswell a regular job as counsel.

It is more than likely that hostility to his father at this time took the form of breaking his windows. Their mutual antipathy was deep, chiefly on account of their relationship. Had they been mere acquaintances, they might have liked one another. As it was, the son felt the father's personality to be oppressive and only endurable with the assistance of alcohol. Yet Boswell's feeling for his family was one of the props of his life. Like his religion, like Johnson, like Paoli, his ancestry provided a sense of security, giving him as much pride in himself as he was able to boast, and even at his most degraded moments enabling him to remember that he was born a gentlemen. When his brother David left home in October 1767 to take a business appointment in Spain, James made the lad swear a sort of feudal oath in the presence of witnesses, to the effect that he would be loyal to his lineage and dutiful to its present chief. There was something a little mad in this ceremony, but then, as Boswell perceived, there was a considerable streak of insanity in himself, which became apparent when his father determined to marry again. James felt that such an action was an insult to his mother and a disgrace to the family. There was also the possibility that if Lord Auchinleck had children by a second marriage they might inherit the estate. James suffered fits of rage and resentment. He could not keep it to himself, but talked and wrote of it in the wildest manner, even threatening to throw up his career, quit Scotland for ever, and take to the backwoods of America. But his mania subsided, and though he never liked his stepmother, who disliked him, his own marriage softened his attitude to his father's.

The procession of ladies who might have become Mrs. James Boswell was lengthy and various; and though the young man's deranged nature would have resulted in marriage with any one of them if circumstances had conduced to that end, his ultimate choice was determined more by accident than design. Dismissing several of his early selections, from a chambermaid to an heiress, we may note his prolonged attempt to capture a lady who would inherit an estate near Auchinleck. Her name was Catherine Blair, whom he thought sensible, well-bred, good-natured and religious. He soon worked himself up into the necessary condition of adoration and announced the fact to Temple, together with the information that his mistress Mrs. Dodds was about to bear him a child. Naturally he drank Catherine's health; infallibly he got drunk; and inevitably he spent the night with a girl he described as "a whore worthy of Boswell, if Boswell must have a whore". She soon proved her worth, the sequel being serious, and he infected his mistress, for which he expressed regret, his chief complaint being that the punishment for getting drunk was excessive.

In June 1767, Temple visited Edinburgh and Boswell asked him to call on Catherine Blair and report her feelings. In a letter detailing the course he should take, Boswell instructed Temple to mention his bad as well as his good qualities: his fickleness, his affairs with women, the possibility of insanity in

his family. Temple gave a favourable account of the lady and
Boswell decided, as soon as he had got rid of his disease, to
propose marriage. They met, quarrelled, and he resolved to
forget her. She wrote; he melted, and was again enraptured.
In December 1767 he examined her closely. She appeared to
be indifferent, which was hardly surprising in view of his confessions of inconstancy, though presumably she knew nothing
of his mistress or of the other amorous affairs upon which he
was engaged during his courtship of her. In February 1768 she
definitely turned him down, and he found relief in the thought
that he would marry an Englishwoman belonging to the nobility.
His daughter by Mrs. Dodds seems to have died young, and his
liaison with the mother finished in 1769, by which time he was
definitely engaged to be married.

But not before he had tried another heiress, this time Mary
Ann Boyd, a distant relation who stayed for a while with his
Ayrshire cousins, the Montgomeries, on a visit to whom he saw
Mary Ann and, needless to say, fell more entirely in love than
he had ever been before. In this condition he happened once
more to meet Catherine Blair, to whom he renewed his
protestations of passion, which were instantly transferred to
Mary Ann when it became clear that Catherine had no further
use for him. Having again fallen completely in love with
another girl, he left for northern Ireland in April 1769 to visit
the Boyds, Mary Ann's father owning property there. He was
accompanied by his and their cousin, Margaret Montgomerie,
whom he had known and flirted with at intervals for a large
part of his life, though her poverty had been a barrier to any
matrimonial designs he may have considered. His object now
was to arrange a marriage with Mary Ann, whose future estate
mainly concerned him. But during his journey, and while
staying in Ireland, his scheme was undermined by his affection.
He became uncomfortably conscious that he cared more for his
companion, cousin Margaret, than for the inheritance of Mary
Ann. That Margaret was two years his senior, possessed no

more than £1,000, and could hardly be termed a beauty were serious obstacles. Moreover she said that for his own sake he should marry Mary Ann; but this merely raised her in his esteem. Apparently his coolness to the Boyds, who at first favoured his suit, displeased them, and a good deal of his time in Ireland was spent in drunken orgies with the jovial spirits of Dublin and its neighbourhood. It would hardly have been in character if he had not disgusted himself with another sexual encounter when intoxicated, and another instalment of the familiar disease, at a moment when his emotions were being stirred by cousin Margaret.

Early in June they were home again, and Boswell had decided that his "dearest Peggie" was the love of his life. He wrote to test her feeling for him. Would she, conscious of all his short-comings, be his wife on £100 a year? He said that they would have to live abroad and that he could no longer regard himself as the inheritor of Auchinleck because of his father's decision to marry again. She accepted him on those terms, and the fact speaks loudly for him, since she was a very level-headed and good-hearted woman. Lord Auchinleck at first opposed the match but ultimately gave way, no doubt influenced thereto by his own domestic arrangements.

By this time Boswell was an author of distinction. His *Account of Corsica* was published in February 1768, and he continued to advocate the cause of the islanders in the newspapers, to raise sums for armaments in their defence, to get the subject debated in Parliament, and to bombard Chatham with letters, having totally ignored Johnson's advice: "I wish there were some cure, like the lover's leap, for all heads of which some single idea has obtained an unreasonable and irregular possession. Mind your own affairs, and leave the Corsicans to theirs." His book, well puffed in advance, was a considerable success, and its author, wishing to enjoy the fruits of fame, spent the spring of 1768 in London, his arrival at his lodgings in Half Moon Street, Piccadilly, being noticed in the papers by himself. In his book he had quoted without permission a letter from Johnson, and he thought that his friend had taken offence; so on hearing that Johnson was staying at Oxford he hurried thither, and was put at ease by a warm welcome. The next evening Johnson and one or two others supped with him at the Golden Cross inn, and the conversation turned on the question of whether animals would exist in a future state along with human beings. Johnson opposed the idea as unorthodox and was annoyed when Boswell pursued it. "But really, sir, when we see a very sensible dog, we don't know what to think of him," said Boswell. "No, sir, and when we see a very foolish *fellow*, we don't know what to think of *him*," returned Johnson, who was so much pleased by his repartee that he rose from the table, strode to the fireside, and stood for some time in mirthful exultation. But a little later he admitted that certain birds, if not immortal, were difficult to kill: "Swallows certainly sleep all the winter. A number of them conglobulate together by flying round and round, and then all in a heap throw themselves under water and lie in the bed of a river."

Boswell's recovery from the blow he had received was accelerated by Johnson's views on adultery, which echoed his own feelings and practically gave him the freedom of brothels. "Confusion of progeny constitutes the essence of the crime," pronounced Johnson, "and therefore a woman who breaks her marriage vows is much more criminal than a man who does it. A man, to be sure, is criminal in the eyes of God, but he does not do his wife a very material injury if he does not insult her; if for instance, from mere wantonness of appetite, he steals privately to her chambermaid. Sir, a wife ought not greatly to resent this. I would not receive home a daughter who had run away from her husband on that account. A wife should study to reclaim her husband by more attention to please him. Sir, a man will not, once in a hundred instances, leave his wife and go to a harlot, if his wife has not been negligent of pleasing."

With this certificate to the relative rectitude of males in

mind, Boswell returned to London, where his behaviour with street-walkers ran its normal course. While there he received a letter from Johnson, written before their meeting at Oxford and forwarded from Scotland, wherein he was reproved for printing a friend's letter without leave and advised to "empty your head of Corsica, which I think has filled it rather too long". To which he now replied: "My noble-minded friend . . . Empty my head of Corsica! Empty it of honour, empty it of humanity, empty it of friendship, empty it of piety. No! while I live, Corsica and the cause of the brave islanders shall ever employ much of my attention . . . " If Johnson had said "Empty your head of Boswell", it would have been sufficient. His book had made his reputation; henceforth he was to be known as "Corsica Boswell"; and he was feverishly writing and collecting *British Essays in favour of the Brave Corsicans*, which was issued in the autumn of 1769. Many notable people called at his lodgings to compliment him, among others General Oglethorpe, who for some years had been Governor of Georgia, organising a settlement of released debtors; the American, Benjamin Franklin; the actor David Garrick; and the historian David Hume, with whom Boswell was on familiar terms while regretting his anti-Christian views. These famous visitors helped him to forget the necessary confinement caused by his customary impurities. Johnson, too, back from Oxford, visited Half Moon Street, spoke highly of Boswell's Corsican journal, and roughly of popular liberty, with an eye on Wilkes: "They make a rout about *universal* liberty without considering that all that is to be valued, or indeed can be enjoyed, by individuals is *private* liberty. Political liberty is good only so far as it produces private liberty."

As soon as Boswell could leave his room he gave a supper to Johnson, two future bishops, Thomas Percy and John Douglas, the historian William Robertson, the Rev. Hugh Blair, Bennet Langton, and Tom Davies. In the course of the evening Johnson "tossed and gored several persons", and incidentally gave Boswell the chance to exhibit his malice by constantly taunting one of the victims with a repetition of Johnson's gibe, rather like a small schoolboy who thinks his joke becomes funnier the more often it is heard. Johnson happened to express displeasure with old Dr. Mounsey of Chelsea College because he "swore and talked bawdy". Percy contradicted this, saying that he had never heard Mounsey do so, though often in his company. Davies, after speaking quietly with Percy, loudly announced to Johnson: "O, sir, I have found out a very good reason why Dr. Percy never heard Mounsey swear or talk bawdy; for he tells me he never saw him but at the Duke of Northumberland's table." Johnson's displeasure was now directed to Percy: "And so, sir, you would shield this man from the charge of swearing and talking bawdy, because he did not do so at the Duke of Northumberland's table. Sir, you might as well tell us that you had seen him hold up his hand at the Old Bailey, and he neither swore nor talked bawdy; or that you had seen him in the cart at Tyburn, and he neither swore nor talked bawdy. And is it thus, sir, that you presume to controvert what I have related?" This angry reproof upset Percy, who shortly left the party to recuperate elsewhere. The conversation drifted to Dean Swift, the merit of whose *Conduct of the Allies* was disallowed by Johnson. The rest of the scene must be left to Boswell:

Then recollecting that Mr. Davies, by acting as an *informer*, had been the occasion of his talking somewhat too harshly to his friend Dr. Percy, for which, probably, when the first ebullition was over, he felt some compunction, he took an opportunity to give him a hit; so added, with a preparatory laugh, "Why, sir, Tom Davies might have written *The Conduct of the Allies*." Poor Tom being thus suddenly dragged into ludicrous notice in presence of the Scottish Doctors, to whom he was ambitious of appearing to advantage, was grievously mortified. Nor did his punishment rest here; for upon subsequent occasions, whenever he . . . assumed a strutting importance, I used to hail him—"the Author of *The Conduct of the Allies*."

Having registered an oath of chastity for six months in St. Paul's Cathedral, Boswell left for Scotland, where he received bad news of the Corsicans. The Genoan Government, weary of its failure to subdue the island, sold it to France in May 1768. On learning that the British Government had no intention of intervening merely because Boswell admired Paoli, the French sent reinforcements to the island with the object of a decisive conquest. Paoli put up a stout resistance, but was finally defeated in May 1769, just in time for Napoleon Bonaparte to be born a French citizen.

With the conclusion of the conflict Boswell decided to make a final appearance as a Corsican patriot. A great jubilee in honour of Shakespeare was organised by David Garrick at Stratford-on-Avon early in September 1769. It was a little belated, the bicentenary date of Shakespeare's birth having been more than five years earlier. But the year suited Garrick and the occasion suited Stratford so well that the name of the town might thenceforward have been changed to Mecca-on-Avon. One of the early pilgrims was Boswell, who saw no reason why Corsica should not be represented and every reason why the author of a book on Corsica should be seen. He also wanted to visit London before his marriage in order to place himself in the hands of a famous physician and be thoroughly dosed with medicines that would cleanse his body of much perilous matter. As usual the approach to London exalted his spirits, which were further cheered when he donned his Corsican outfit and surveyed himself in the glass; and he wrote to tell his fiancée that the mere sight of him in that garb would give her a higher esteem of herself as the object of his love. He met all sorts of celebrities at Stratford and was satisfied by the comments on his appearance, writing an account in *The London Magazine* of the striking effect he had made and illustrating it with an engraving of himself as "an armed Corsican Chief". (He was, by the way, making arrangements to become part-proprietor of *The London Magazine*.) Most of the jubilee celebrations were spoilt by persistent rain, but Boswell, having made his effect, left before the completion of the programme.

Paoli arrived in London on 22nd September, and Boswell called on him at once in Old Bond Street, being received with a shout of welcome and a Gallic embrace. Paoli had an interview with the King, was granted a pension, and remained an exile in England for the next twenty years. Of course Boswell had to show him Peggie Montgomerie's letter accepting his offer of marriage; and as soon as Johnson returned from Brighton, where the Thrales had a house, Boswell introduced him to Paoli. With both his heroes in London, and several doctors to be consulted, Boswell was kept fairly busy. The subject of his father's second marriage was much on his mind, and in order to draw Johnson he "censured a gentleman of my acquaintance for marrying a second time, as it shewed a disregard of his first wife." But Johnson thought otherwise: "Not at all, sir. On the contrary, were he not to marry again, it might be concluded that his first wife had given him a disgust to marriage; but by taking a second wife he pays the highest compliment to the first, by shewing that she made him so happy as a married man that he wishes to be so a second time." That this was his considered opinion is shown by his remark, on hearing of a man who had promptly married again after a wretched time with his first wife: "It was the triumph of hope over experience."

Boswell had been introduced to Mrs. Thrale the previous year, and now received an invitation to Streatham, where at one point the conversation turned on Garrick's light verse, which Mrs. Thrale praised, giving what she thought a particularly happy specimen: "I'd smile with the simple and feed with the poor." Johnson differed: "Nay, my dear lady, this will never do. Poor David! Smile with the simple! What folly is that? And who would feed with the poor that can help it? No, no; let me smile with the wise and feed with the rich." Boswell spitefully repeated this to Garrick and affected to be surprised by his irritation, yet knowing quite well that Garrick was extremely sensitive to Johnson's criticism and would rather have won his good opinion than the adulation of a crowd. It is quite likely that Boswell also reported Johnson's reply to a complaint that there was no mention of Garrick in his Preface to Shakespeare. Had Garrick not brought Shakespeare into notice? urged Boswell. "Sir, to allow that would be to lampoon the age" answered Johnson, who strongly objected to Garrick's stage alterations of Shakespeare's plays. But Johnson loved Garrick as a man, and their relationship was sketched in a charming scene when they dined in company with Goldsmith, Reynolds and others at Boswell's lodgings: "Garrick played round him with a fond vivacity, taking hold of the breasts of his coat, and, looking up in his face with a lively archness, complimented him on the good health which he seemed then to enjoy; while the sage, shaking his head, beheld him with a gentle complacency." After dinner they discussed Pope, and Johnson, having recited the concluding lines of *The Dunciad*, praised them highly. Boswell remarked that the lines were "too fine for such a poem—a poem on what"? The retort was irresistible and Johnson made it: "Why, on *dunces*. It was worth while being a dunce then. Ah, sir, hadst *thou* lived in those days!"

Boswell often diversified his amusements by watching the public execution of criminals, and in October of this year he was present at Tyburn for the ghoulish satisfaction of seeing six men die by strangulation, even sending a report of his presence to *The London Chronicle*, from which we learn that in order to be as near as possible he sat on the top of a hearse that was waiting to remove one of the bodies. His attraction to these unpleasant spectacles has been shared by many people with undeveloped minds and spiritually stunted natures, for what makes a mature human being vomit makes an immature creature gloat. Naturally he had a good reason for such morbid entertainments, and he told Johnson that none of the hanged men appeared to be concerned over their departure for another world, the implication being that he had hoped to witness an edifying exhibition of contrition. "Most of them, sir, have never thought at all," explained Johnson. "But is not the fear of death natural to man?" "So much so, sir, that the whole of life is but keeping away the thoughts of it." Boswell wondered why he had felt so little distress for the criminals, but Johnson said that distress for the misfortunes of others had been greatly exaggerated: "We have a certain degree of feeling to prompt us to do good; more than that Providence does not intend; it would be misery to no purpose." Boswell had an ulterior motive in his next question: "But suppose now, sir, that one of your intimate friends were apprehended for an offence for which he might be hanged?" "I should do what I could to bail him, and give him any other assistance; but if he were once fairly hanged, I should not suffer." "Would you eat your dinner that day, sir?" "Yes, sir, and eat it as if he were eating it with me. Why, there's Baretti, who is to be tried for his life tomorrow. Friends have risen up for him on every side; yet if he should be hanged, none of them will eat a slice of plum-pudding the less. Sir, that sympathetic feeling goes a very little way in depressing the mind." Yet Boswell expressed his regret that he could not feel for others as acutely as some people said they did. Johnson comforted him: "Sir, don't be duped by them any more. You will find these very feeling people are not very ready to do you good. They *pay* you by *feeling*."

Joseph Baretti, about whose possible execution Boswell wished to hear, had somehow won the affection of Johnson. The son of an Italian architect, he came to England in 1750, taught his native language, and published an English-Italian dictionary ten years after his arrival. He had a powerful physique, an unattractive face, a resonant voice, an impetuous manner and a trenchant speech. He took offence quickly and violently, but his conversation was entertaining, instructive and dramatic. People liked him very much or not at all. Johnson liked him, Boswell loathed him. Perhaps his command of English and conversational fluency irritated Boswell, the more so as Johnson listened with interest to the Italian's eloquence. When not enraged, Baretti was polite, but disagreement with his opinions made him angry and insolent. Johnson was the only person from whom he could bear contradiction. His present predicament was due to a combination of temper and terror. On Friday afternoon, 8th October 1769, he was walking up the Haymarket when, a few yards from Panton Street, he was addressed by a woman. He ignored her and she attacked him, receiving a blow in exchange. She yelled abuse at him and a crowd collected, the majority of whom were under the impression that he was a Frenchman and therefore a villain. He was seized, and was in the process of receiving rough usage from the mob when he managed to escape. Seeing enemies on every side, he dashed into a near-by shop in Oxendon Street, and in a panic stabbed the first person who impeded his course. The man died, and Baretti was committed for trial, appearing on 20th October in the Old Bailey dock accused of murder. Boswell would have enjoyed seeing him hanged, but the other members of the Johnson circle turned up in force to witness in favour of his character. Burke, Garrick, Beauclerk, Reynolds and Goldsmith spoke for his good-nature, active benevolence and humanity; but Johnson stuck to the essential points, recognising that the court chiefly wished to know whether Baretti was drunk when he knifed the man and whether he was of a bellicose nature. "I have no reason to think he was ever disordered with liquor in his life," testified Johnson, who further described him as "a very studious man, a man of great diligence, a man that I never knew to be otherwise than peaceable, and a man that I take to be rather timorous". It is possible that Baretti would rather have been executed for bravery than acquitted as a coward, but Johnson's description of him as "rather timorous" must have influenced the jury's verdict of 'Not Guilty'.

Unable to indulge himself with the pleasing vision of Baretti dangling at the end of a rope, Boswell did his best to make Johnson wriggle at their next meeting by arguing with him on the subject of religion and medicated baths, by fatuously asking what he would do if shut up in a castle alone with a new-born baby, and by exacerbating him with the views of two notorious infidels, David Hume and Samuel Foote, on the subject of death. Having reported Hume's remark that he was no more uneasy at the thought that he would not exist after this life than he was by the knowledge that he had not existed before it, Boswell continued: "Foote, sir, told me that when he was very ill he was not afraid to die." Johnson growled ominously: "It is not true, sir. Hold a pistol to Foote's breast, or to Hume's breast, and threaten to kill them, and you'll see how they behave." Undeterred by the signs of storm, Boswell proceeded: "But may we not fortify our minds for the approach of death?" There was a clap of thunder: "No, sir, let it alone. It matters not how a man dies, but how he lives." Boswell idiotically pursued the theme, and expressed himself as alarmed and distressed when Johnson angrily got rid of him with the words "Don't let us meet tomorrow." But Boswell knew how to deal with that. He sent a penitent, submissive letter, following it up with a personal call, and Johnson received him in a pleasant mood.

Before returning home Boswell spent a week-end with his friend Temple at Mamhead, and got Paoli and Johnson to witness his marriage contract with "Miss Peggie Montgomerie", with whom he had exchanged affectionate letters during his absence. The cousins were married at her home, Lainshaw in Ayrshire, on 25th November 1769, a few days after a similar ceremony at Edinburgh between Lord Auchinleck and his cousin Elizabeth Boswell. Paoli had hinted that he might be present at his friend's marriage, but he did not visit Scotland till the autumn of 1771, when Boswell reported the joy of his father on seeing the Corsican hero at Auchinleck, a joy that seems to have been confined to himself, for his father referred to Paoli as "a land-louping scoundrel of a Corsican". The deed being done, Boswell's hostility to his stepmother was perforce toned down and he behaved with prudence, his sole interest in her thenceforth being to watch for signs of approaching fecundity.

CHAPTER 18

Friendly Treatment

BY THE TIME of his marriage Boswell must have decided quite definitely that he would write a biography of Johnson. With his mediumistic faculty of absorbing incidents from real life, his keen eye for a good scene, his exceptional memory, and a wonderful subject, he knew that he could produce a work of unique quality. Besides it would deal with a remarkable circle, an extraordinary collection of intimate friends. The greatest orator of the period (Burke), the greatest painter (Reynolds), the greatest dramatist and poet (Goldsmith), the greatest historian (Gibbon), the greatest actor (Garrick), and the greatest wit (Johnson): such a variety of distinguished men in close communion was unexampled in history, and we may say of the chronicler that never before had one man owed so much to so many. But as in retrospect they owe as much to him, the debt was handsomely repaid. Boswell also knew that he was an adept 'feeder', never at a loss to give Johnson a lot to masticate and plenty to regurgitate. It is clear that Johnson did not always speak the exact words that Boswell put into his mouth. Short episodes and sudden repartees could be remembered with accuracy, and these are the best things in the *Life*, but the longer conversations were composed from brief notes taken at the time or just afterwards, later expanded in the journal, and much later augmented in the biography. Occasionally Boswell was seen at dinner to lay down his knife and fork, take out his tablets, and record a good anecdote. But lengthy note-taking was impracticable and would not have been tolerated by the company. He had to rely on rough notes, a retentive memory, and his mimetic skill, to reconstruct extended dialogues.

Boswell's peculiar genius, which will be fully illustrated in this book, is shown in his accounts of seemingly trivial incidents, clearly photographed on his mind because of some comic or characteristic quality, and authentically vivid. For example, the occasion when Johnson tipped the printer's apprentice, his way of talking to the lad proving the truth of his claim that he spoke to everybody in the same manner:

"Well, my boy, how do you go on?"

"Pretty well, sir; but they are afraid I an't strong enough for some parts of the business."

"Why, I shall be sorry for it; for when you consider with how little mental power and corporeal labour a printer can get a guinea a week, it is a very desirable occupation for you. Do you hear—take all the pains you can; and if this does not do, we must think of some other way of life for you. There's a guinea."

Boswell, observing the scene with relish, remarked that "the slow and sonorous solemnity with which, while he bent himself down, he addressed a little thick short-legged boy, contrasted with the boy's awkwardness and awe, could not but excite some ludicrous emotions".

His interview with George III in the royal library was doubtless conducted in the same style, but unfortunately Boswell was not there to record it. Having heard that Johnson occasionally used the library, the King took him by surprise one day, and they had a longish talk on literary matters. At one point the King hinted that Johnson should produce more works. Johnson replied that he had already done his part as a writer. "I should have thought so too if you had not written so well," said the King. When asked by a friend whether he had replied to this compliment, Johnson answered: "No, sir. When the King had said it, it was to be so. It was not for me to bandy civilities with my Sovereign." If we compare the long account of this event in Boswell's biography with the few lines devoted to the printer's apprentice, we perceive at once the difference between a reporter and an artist, the contrast being noticeable all through the monumental *Life*.

Johnson's reply to George III was perfectly serious: he had no intention of writing another book. "No man loves labour for itself," he said, and as he had as much fame and money as he wanted, he became extremely indolent, not caring for anything but talking and reading and eating. Sometimes a qualm of conscience begat a resolution. In July 1773 he attempted to learn the Low Dutch language; but his resolutions, like Boswell's, were made to be broken, though there was much less need for him to make them. While his pension induced mental idleness, it prompted physical activity, and he began to make regular visitations to the provinces, nourishing his early affections by seeing friends at Oxford, and by staying with Hector at Birmingham, with Lucy Porter at Lichfield, with Taylor at Ashbourne. Lucy was no longer gay and pretty, and he said that her good qualities were "a little discoloured by hoary virginity". She had an extremely high opinion of him, but her veneration did not prevent her from scolding him like a schoolboy if he dirtied her floor with his muddy shoes. Although short-tempered, contradictious, outspoken and rustic in manner, Lucy's intelligence, humour, honesty and kindliness made her popular in Lichfield society, and Johnson, who had once been in love with her, always treated her with deference and indulged her whims. Another Lichfield friend he always called upon was another old flame, Molly Aston; and a third was Moll Cobb, who idolised him and drove him about in her chaise and pampered him with sweets and fruit. But when someone described her as a wit, he jibbed: "How should Moll Cobb be a wit! Cobb has read nothing. Cobb knows nothing; and where nothing has been put in the brain, nothing can come out of it to any purpose of rational entertainment." Then why did he visit her so often? he was asked. "Oh, I love Cobb!" he cried: "I love Moll Cobb for her impudence."

Less cheerful were his visits to Ashbourne, where his host, the Rev. John Taylor, tried to interest him by inviting to dinner such friends as were chiefly concerned with horses and cattle and crops and local gossip. Taylor himself was mainly absorbed in his oxen. "His talk," said Johnson, quoting *Ecclesiasticus*, "is of bullocks. I do not suppose he is very fond of my company. His habits are by no means sufficiently clerical. This he knows that I see; and no man likes to live under the eye of perpetual disapprobation." But when Taylor's wife ran away from him, Johnson sided with him in the subsequent dispute with his wife's family and congratulated him when a permanent separation was arranged, adding that Taylor had nothing to regret except that the two had not parted much earlier. Johnson did his best to take an interest in country matters, writing to Mrs. Thrale from Ashbourne in July 1770: "I have seen the great Bull, and very great he is. I have seen likewise his heir apparent, who promises to inherit all the bulk and all the virtues of his Sire. I have seen the Man who offered a hundred guineas for the young Bull while he was yet little better than a calf. Matlock I am afraid I shall not see, but I purpose to visit Dovedale, and after all this seeing I hope to see You." He and Taylor were bored together but did their best to put up with one another for a few weeks every year in memory of their schoolboy friendship. Johnson defined the situation well to Mrs. Thrale, reporting in August 1771 that he had just left Taylor "in a disposition of mind not very uncommon, at once weary of my stay and grieved at my departure." No doubt Taylor had reached the limit of endurance after a month "under the eye of perpetual disapprobation".

The one place in the country where Johnson seldom felt bored was Streatham Park, the summer residence of the Thrales, about six miles from the Southwark brewery. The house itself was delightfully situated on the border of Streatham Common, the estate consisting of about a hundred acres and containing all the requisites of rural retirement: walks, shrubberies, lawns, orchards, conservatories, greenhouses, stables, a kitchen garden, a lake, cattle, poultry, horses and dogs. Here Johnson was able to enjoy what he once called "the endearing elegance of female friendship". Mrs. Thrale petted and stimulated him, and invited other women to meet him. When in the right mood he was extremely pleasant to them, treating them with an elaborate courtesy or good-naturedly teasing them. But mere beauty without brains seemed to get on his nerves, and when someone praised the face and behaviour of a pretty woman he diluted the commendation: "She says nothing, sir; a talking blackamoor were better than a white creature who adds nothing to life; and by sitting down before one thus desperately silent, takes away the confidence one should have in the company of her chair if she were once out of it." Nor did he care for too much soft soap even from attractive damsels, one of whom delivered a piece of eulogy she may have learnt by heart before their introduction and waited anxiously for his reply, which was quickly delivered: "Fiddle-de-dee, my dear!" But Mrs. Thrale knew that the way to please him was to flatter him with attentions. One way to his heart was by his belly, and his favourite dishes were constantly on the table, such as a leg of pork so well boiled that the meat almost dropped from the bone, a veal pie with plums and sugar, and the outside cut of a buttock of beef. He loved made-up dishes and soups. He poured melted butter over plum-pudding, and drowned his other victuals with sauce. He drank a lot of chocolate with quantities of butter and cream in it. He loved fruit and ate a plateful of peaches when in season every morning before breakfast.

We cannot escape the supposition that Johnson's love of comfort, good food and amusing company made him too pliant with Henry Thrale, to whom he obsequiously referred as "my master". From no one else did he endure reproof, and he could have applied to himself Macbeth's complaint: "Under him my genius is rebuked." Once, when he was enlarging on the subject of teaching, Thrale interrupted him: "There, there! now we have had enough for one lecture, Dr. Johnson; we will not be upon education any more till after dinner, if you please." In Thrale's presence Johnson would handle gently what he would otherwise have treated roughly; and the brewer even managed to effect a sartorial reformation in his distinguished guest, who changed his clothes for dinner, putting on a large worsted wig which Thrale had given him because it scarcely ever got out of curl, and a snuff-coloured coat with brass buttons. His linen at Streatham was noticeably clean, and though he continued to wear black woollen stockings his general appearance was considerably smartened. As he used to read in bed and was very near-sighted, the foretops of his wigs were burned by the candle, so that the network showed through; but at Streatham a fashionable wig was handed him by Thrale's valet at the parlour-door every day before dinner. No objection was raised by his host to the chemical experiments which he loved to make, a laboratory of sorts being fitted up for his use in the Streatham house. The fumes and stinks and explosions were permissible; but Johnson's semi-blindness made some of his investigations dangerous, and when Thrale found him one day, lost to the world and within inches of a scorching flame, the owner of the property put his foot down, and further experiments were conducted in a small brick enclosure by the kitchen-garden pump.

The Thrales passed the winter months in Southwark, their dismal house being next to the brewery in Deadman's Place (since altered to Park Street), where the reek of the polluted river competed with the smells of the filthy streets. It was a district of slums and fetid airs, the house being described by Mrs. Thrale as an "odious dungeon". Social life had to be brisk to make existence bearable, and the friendship of Johnson meant much more to Hester at Southwark than at Streatham, because he was always happiest in London, his friends frequently dined with them, and his mere presence gave distinction to their neighbourhood. Except on rare occasions, Johnson treated Mrs. Thrale with affectionate courtesy, often kissing her hand and sometimes even kneeling to kiss her foot, though his usual salutation to young attractive women was substantial, resounding, and on the face. But Mrs. Thrale was his guardian angel as well as an intimate friend, and there are mysterious allusions to fetters and padlocks with which she could confine him when a fit of acute melancholy appeared to foreshadow madness.

She had the right sort of temperament for the trials and tribulations of life. At the theatre her husband flaunted a mistress, whose likeness was enamelled on his snuff-box; but his wife sustained the travail of bearing his children. She was always either pregnant or recovering from parturition. The birth of her first child, known to us as Queeney, occurred in 1764, and she had a child or a miscarriage annually thereafter until 1778. Of her dozen children, all of them begotten by a venereally infected man for whom she did not care, eight died in infancy. Yet she remained cheerful and lively, and at one period saved her husband from certain bankruptcy and possible suicide.

A man named Humphrey Jackson conceived the original notion of making beer without malt or hops. Thrale, whose business capability was practically nil, embraced the prospect of enormous profits and provided capital for the new plant. But chemically coloured water was not to the taste of beer-drinkers, and there was no demand for Thrale's Entire. The business was ruined, though Hester did not discover what had happened until her husband, a deep sleeper and a heavy eater, became wakeful and lost his appetite. "I was big with child, as I almost always am," she noted in the summer of 1772, but she took on the job of raising capital to save the firm. She dashed down to Brighton and got a promise of £6,000 from an old friend; she rushed hither and thither, getting more here, more there; and at last the essential credit was obtained to steady the brewery. Fortunately the head clerk, Perkins, who practically ran the business, could be relied upon, while Johnson was extremely helpful with advice and sympathy. Thrale himself simply went to pieces. Whatever pride he may have had in his commercial judgment, his social position and his domestic dominion was hopelessly shattered; his credulity had wrecked the business, and if his dignity were saved he would owe it to a wife whom he had never allowed to meddle in his affairs. In despair he talked of killing himself, but he hardly had the energy to put a pistol to his head or lift a knife to his throat. Usually silent, he now became dumb, and Johnson unweariedly tried to keep him amused. It took some time to retrieve the fortunes of the house, but the situation was well in hand towards the close of 1773, and gradually the brewery again became a thriving concern, which was largely due to the exertions of Mrs. Thrale, a fact that made her husband so thoughtful that he seldom opened his mouth except to stuff it with food, though it did not incline him to lessen her labours in bed.

Boswell remained ignorant of these transactions, though he visited London in 1772 and 1773. Johnson would hardly have exposed himself or the Thrales to what he once called the "noisy benevolence" of his Scottish disciple. For at least a year after his marriage Boswell stuck to his profession and remained faithful to his wife. Their earliest address was at Chessels Buildings, Canongate, but a year or two later they moved up the hill to James's Court. Their first child, a son, died almost immediately after birth; their second, a girl, arrived on 15th March 1773, and was called Veronica. It happened that Oliver Goldsmith's successful comedy *She Stoops to Conquer* was produced at Covent Garden the same evening, a coincidence which prompted the happy father to write a congratulatory letter to the lucky author. Boswell did not like Goldsmith, but he liked cultivating the friendships of famous men, and he hoped Goldsmith would send him a witty reply which could be treasured and shown to his friends. "Write as if in repartee," he urged the now fashionable dramatist in a postscript. He also begged Garrick for a letter, for he felt cut off from the hub of life in London, longed to exercise his talents at the English Bar or in Parliament, and wished to refresh his spirit at the fountain of Johnson's wisdom. A protracted domestic life was not to his taste, and he indulged in tantrums, the petting and coaxing of his wife adding to the pleasure of yielding to them. He was fonder of Peggie than he could be of anyone except himself, and she remained fonder of him than of anyone else including herself; but the first year or two of their marriage were the happiest because he managed to confirm his affection with fidelity.

In the spring of 1772 he had to plead a case before the House of Lords, and during his stay in London he saw much of Johnson. One of their walks took them to the Pantheon in Oxford Street, and Johnson said he favoured public amusements because they kept people from vice. "You now," said he, "would have been with a wench had you not been here—O! I forgot you were married." Which shows that Johnson was well aware of Boswell's favourite occupation; and a scene between them, carefully edited in Boswell's narrative, displays Johnson's attitude to another little weakness in his biographer, who declared that liquor was excusable in a man anxious to drown care and forget what was disagreeable: "Would you not allow a man to drink for that reason?" "Yes, sir, if he sat next *you*," came the retort. But Boswell continued to praise wine. "I know no good it does," said Johnson. "Yes, it makes a man eloquent." "Sir, it makes him noisy and absurd." "But this you will allow—it makes a man speak truth." "Sir, I see no good there is in that neither, unless he is a liar when he is sober."

Early the following year Boswell again spent some weeks in London and to his great joy was asked to dinner at Johnson's house on Easter Sunday: "I supposed we should scarcely have knives and forks, and only some strange uncouth, ill-drest dish; but I found everything in very good order." Anna Williams and a female guest were the other participants, and they were treated to "a very good soup, a boiled leg of lamb and spinach, a veal pie, and a rice pudding." He saw much of Goldsmith and Paoli, but the great event of the visit was his election to The Club. That evening he dined with Johnson and Reynolds and a few other members at Beauclerk's, and after dinner he was left alone with Beauclerk's wife, Lady Di, while his fate was being decided by the rest. Some of The Club's members were not in favour of Boswell's election, but Johnson threatened that if they voted against his nominee he would in future keep out any of theirs; so a blackball was prevented by blackmail. Boswell repaid Lady Di Beauclerk's kindness in trying to alleviate his suspense during the balloting by reporting a remark of Johnson's a week later.

They were breakfasting at Thrale's house in Southwark, and when they were left alone Boswell did his best "to apologise for a lady who had been divorced from her husband by Act of Parliament", though why he should have been so officious as to apologise for someone whose behaviour required no apology he does not say. His excuse for her was that her husband had killed her affection by his brutal behaviour and that she had fallen in love with another man. The brutal husband was Lord Bolingbroke; his wife before marriage had been Lady Diana Spencer; and her lover was Johnson's friend Topham Beauclerk, to whom she was now married. With characteristic asininity, Boswell states that he "attempted to palliate what I was sensible could not be justified," and reports Johnson's even more asinine comment: "My dear sir, never accustom your mind to mingle virtue and vice. The woman's a whore, and there's an end on't." When this passage appeared in print Lady Diana Beauclerk was still alive, and from the details supplied by Boswell her many friends had no difficulty in recognising her as the 'whore' in question. Since her second marriage had also been wretched, Topham turning out to be bad-tempered, physically dirty and a drug-addict, Boswell's public reminder of her early miseries, coupled with Johnson's concise definition of her nature, cannot have raised her opinion of the masculine species.

Lady Di was not the only person whose conduct was subjected to Boswell's pique during his sojourn in London this spring. Apparently his attempts to foster a friendship with Goldsmith were rebuffed, because he exhibited no little animosity in his account of that poet's "envy and spleen"; and another member of The Club, Bennet Langton, must have read without amusement the description of himself as the object of Johnson's ridicule. The incident is related in Boswell's best manner. He and Johnson dined with General Paoli on 9th May. Johnson was not well and had to leave early, but he arranged to meet Boswell that evening at the house of an eminent lawyer, Robert Chambers, in the Temple. He was still unwell, and Chambers suggested various remedies. "Prythee, don't tease me," said Johnson. "Stay till I am well, and then you shall tell me how to cure myself." He grew better and began to talk of "the dignity and propriety of male succession, in opposition to the opinion of one of our friends, who had that day employed Mr. Chambers to draw his will, devising his estate to his three sisters, in preference to a remote male heir". Bennet Langton would have known at once that he was the anonymous friend. Having reported Johnson's description of the Miss Langtons as "three *dowdies*", Boswell continues:

I have known him at times exceedingly diverted at what seemed to others a very small sport. He now laughed immoderately, without any reason that we could perceive, at our friend's making his will; called him the *testator*, and added, "I dare say he thinks he has done a mighty thing. He won't stay till he gets home to his seat in the country, to produce this wonderful deed: he'll call up the landlord of the first inn on the road; and, after a suitable preface upon mortality and the uncertainty of life, will tell him that he should not delay making his will; and here, sir, will he say, is my will, which I have just made, with the assistance of one of the ablest lawyers in the kingdom; and he will read it to him (laughing all the time). He believes he has made this will; but he did not make it: you, Chambers, made it for him. I trust you have had more conscience than to make him say 'being of sound understanding'; ha, ha, ha! I hope he has left me a legacy. I'd have his will turned into verse, like a ballad."

His own profession being involved, Chambers did not appreciate the joke and seemed anxious to get rid of his guests. They left, but the joke went on:

Johnson could not stop his merriment, but continued it all the way till we got without the Temple-gate. He then burst into such a fit of laughter, that he appeared to be almost in a convulsion; and, in order to support himself, laid hold of one of the posts at the side of the foot pavement, and sent forth peals so loud, that in the silence of the night his voice seemed to resound from Temple-bar to Fleet-ditch.

The unimaginative Boswell could not understand the cause of this excessive hilarity, which was due to the sudden revelation of the inherent absurdity of human beings, especially when they were being grave and self-important. The silliest and most insignificant episode can remove the blinkers necessary for the imaginative man's everyday existence, disclose the panorama of life's folly, and release the spring of laughter. Bennet Langton's will was merely the starting-point, not the explanation, of Johnson's prodigious mirth.

Before his departure for the north, Boswell managed to extract a qualified promise from Johnson that later in the year he would make the journey to the Hebrides which they had often discussed; and on 14th August 1773, Johnson arrived at Edinburgh.

CHAPTER 19

Together

APART from their three months together during the Scottish tour in the autumn of 1773, Boswell did not see so much of Johnson as readers of his *Life* might suppose, and they were never again to spend more than a few successive days in each other's company. Johnson was accompanied on his way to Scotland by two friends, and wrote to Mrs. Thrale that he had seen York Minster and Durham Cathedral, his remarks on them proving that his vision for objects at a little distance was adequate, if his opinion of them was peculiar. He called the Minster "an edifice of loftiness and elegance equal to the highest hopes of architecture; I remember nothing but the dome of St. Paul's that can be compared with the middle walk", and said that the Cathedral had "a massiveness and solidity such as I have seen in no other place. It rather awes than pleases, as it strikes with a kind of gigantic dignity, and aspires to no other praise than that of rocky solidity and indeterminate duration". In a phrase, he preferred the Gothic to the Norman.

On arrival at Boyd's Inn at the head of the Canongate in Edinburgh, his fastidiousness received one of its rare shocks. The waiter took up a lump of sugar with greasy fingers and put it into the lemonade, which Johnson threw out of the window and looked as if he would like to throw the waiter after it. He and Boswell walked arm-in-arm up the High Street, Boswell wishing his companion's sense of smell were as defective as his sight, the evening stench from the gutter being an offensive introduction to the city. "I smell you in the dark," growled

Johnson. Tea was ready for him at James's Court, and Peggie Boswell had given up her bedroom for his use. His appearance shocked her; his manners displeased her; his conversation bored her; and she was scornful of her husband's subjection to such an oddity, saying "I have seen many a bear led by a man, but I never before saw a man led by a bear". But she treated him with politeness and overlooked his uncouth habits. For his part, there was little in her to arouse admiration or antagonism. Though she had "the mien and manners of a gentlewoman", she appeared to him rather colourless. It is almost certain that she took little part in the general conversation and treated him with a formality which he reciprocated.

Naturally Boswell wanted to exhibit the great man to all his Edinburgh friends, and at one supper Johnson reported that "there was such a conflux of company that I could scarcely support the tumult". He was shown the sights of the capital, but, not a sight-seer by inclination, he confided in Mrs. Thrale: "I have been taking a view of all that could be shown me, and find that all very near to nothing . . . one town, one country, is very like another. Civilised nations have the same customs, and barbarous nations have the same nature." Boswell's high spirits might have been momentarily lowered if he had read another of Johnson's communications to Mrs. Thrale: "He that wanders about the world sees new forms of human misery; and if he chances to meet an old friend, meets a face darkened with troubles." But Johnson's low spirits lifted in talk, and he sketched the character of a friend, Edmund Burke, who would some day read with mingled feelings that he was a gifted fellow but a humourless gas-bag. Another remark Johnson made at a dinner-party in Edinburgh explains his chief defect as a writer. After saying that he was unable to understand how a man could apply to one thing and not to another, he continued: "I am persuaded that, had Sir Isaac Newton applied to poetry, he would have made a very fine epic poem . . . Sir, the man who has vigour may walk to the east just as well as to the west, if he happens to turn his head that way." He should have provided a few more illustrations: *e.g.* if Shakespeare had applied himself to navigation, he could have smashed the Spanish Armada as effectively as Drake; if Marlborough had concentrated on literature, he could have written satire as well as Swift; if Garrick had studied draughtsmanship, he could have vied with Sir Joshua Reynolds as a portrait-painter. At which point it might have begun to dawn on Johnson that he was talking nonsense. In his own case, the combination of physical disability, morbid melancholy and religious bigotry impeded the flow of his natural genius and prevented him from seeing that "Genius does what it must, and Talent does what it can". Because genius embraces the whole of a man, it can only be expressed in a particular way, while talent can be displayed in a number of ways. Johnson's conversational contentiousness showed that he could not centralise his faculties. One aspect of his combativeness must have given Boswell some anxious moments during their tour, though it became a standing joke. Whenever the subject of Scotland or the Scots came up, he could not resist a crack at their expense. The natives took it in good part, glad to think that an Englishman could be funny north of the border.

The two left Edinburgh on 18th August, attended by Boswell's servant, Joseph Ritter, a tall Bohemian. Believing that he might have to fight for his life in the barbarous and warlike Highlands, Johnson had come armed with pistols, gunpowder and bullets; but he was persuaded by Boswell to leave them behind. He also left a diary of his life in a drawer, and it vexed Boswell that his wife did not take advantage of their absence and make a copy of it. But Mrs. Boswell was not a biographer, and never opened it. They crossed the Firth of Forth and started up the east coast. Boswell had with him a Bible and Samuel Ogden's *Sermons on Prayer*, which aroused his admiration so much that his constant references to them on this trip got on Johnson's nerves and provoked an explosion some years later. But on the whole Johnson found Boswell's companionship exhilarating and paid a tribute not only to his "gaiety of conversation and civility of manners" but to the fact that he was welcomed and liked wherever he went. With that queer disorientation of personality which distinguished him, Boswell once remarked that he took no pleasure in doing things for people and going out of his way to be civil and attentive to them. Three years after making this confession he noted that no one was more obliging than himself, and that his civilities and attentions were paid for the mere pleasure of making others happy, not, as with most people, for selfish reasons. Perhaps we may partly reconcile these flat contradictions by saying that what he did was usually done for a self-indulgent purpose but that he communicated to others much of his enjoyment in doing it. The companionship of Johnson in Scotland shed lustre on himself, and the more pleasant he could make the journey for Johnson the more pleasant it would be for Boswell.

Without following them in detail, we will pause only at those moments which bring their natures clearly to view. Johnson was shocked by the condition in which the reformers had left the religious buildings at St. Andrews, in the streets of which there was "the silence and solitude of inactive indigence and gloomy depopulation", and he was struck by the almost complete absence of trees along the coast, declaring that after travelling two hundred miles he had seen but one tree older than himself. At the Montrose inn he called a waiter 'rascal' for putting a lump of sugar in the lemonade with his fingers; at Cullen he was disgusted by the sight at breakfast of broiled haddocks, which had to be removed, and in his passion for fresh air he nearly broke the framework of a window in getting it open; while at Elgin he could not eat the dinner set before him. But except at occasional inns they were well fed and received with hospitality everywhere, Lord Auchinleck's name alone being a guarantee of welcome. At Aberdeen, Johnson was given the freedom of the town, but he did not bother to enquire about the trade of the place: "The manufacture which forces itself upon a stranger's eye is that of knit-stockings, on which the women of the lower class are visibly employed." For that matter he soon got tired of sight-seeing, admitting on one occasion that "love of ease surmounted our desire of knowledge", wishing on another "that our curiosity might have been gratified with less trouble and danger", and refusing to visit a second Druid's temple with the words: "To go and see one is only to see that it is nothing, for there is neither art nor power in it, and seeing one is as much as one would wish." An old acquaintance of his had become professor of medicine at King's College, Aberdeen, and Johnson shrewdly remarked: "We had no emulation, nor had either of us risen to the other's envy." Though he would not attend a Presbyterian service while in Scotland, he strictly observed every Sunday. "It should be different from another day," he said. "People may walk, but not throw stones at birds. There may be relaxation, but there should be no levity." Which suggests that throwing stones at birds was the common recreation of light-hearted pedestrians in the eighteenth century.

They spent a night at the manse of Cawdor with the minister, Kenneth Macaulay, grand-uncle of the famous Victorian writer Lord Macaulay. The minister was as dogmatic as his grand-nephew, for he talked contemptuously of the English clergy and held forth against creeds and confessions. Johnson told him that he was "a bigot to laxness", and spoke of him later in terms that would have made Lord Macaulay's strictures on Boswell more virulent than they were. But quite a few of Boswell's records were due to an engaging simplicity. At Inverness, for example, they attended the English chapel, where the preacher said that some people "connected themselves with men of distinguished talents, and since they could not equal them, tried to deck themselves with their merit by being their companions". Boswell thought that the sentiment "had an odd coincidence with what might be said of my connecting myself with Dr. Johnson". The coincidence was about as odd as that of a clergyman who, preaching before Henry VIII, happened to mention that Solomon, the wisest king in Holy Scripture, had a number of wives. Being out of the room, Boswell missed a scene at Inverness that he would have enjoyed, but it is possible that Johnson would not so have obliged the company if Boswell had been in the room. (Indulging pretty freely in liquid refreshment, Boswell's absences from any party were no doubt frequent.) On this occasion Johnson was speaking of Sir Joseph Banks's travels in New South Wales, where he had discovered an extraordinary animal called the kangaroo, the semblance and actions of which were so singular that Johnson volunteered to give an imitation of the brute. "Nothing could be more ludicrous," reported one of those present, "than the appearance of a tall, heavy, grave-looking man like Dr. Johnson, standing up to mimic the shape and motions of a kangaroo. He stood erect, put out his hands like feelers, and, gathering up the tails of his huge brown coat so as to resemble the pouch of the animal, made two or three vigorous bounds across the room."

They left Inverness on 30th August and commenced the more strenuous part of their journey on horseback, with a spare horse for the luggage and two Highlanders on foot. They rode along the southern side of Loch Ness, and Johnson observed that the waters of the lake were "beating their bank and waving their surface by a gentle agitation". At one place they passed a number of soldiers working on the road, and gave them two shillings for drink. They stayed that night at Anoch in Glenmoriston with a man named Macqueen who dwelt with his daughter in a house made of turf. Though six miles off, the soldiers came to the inn at Anoch to spend their two shillings, and Johnson felt relieved: "Having never been before in a place so wild and unfrequented, I was glad of their arrival, because I knew that we had made them friends; and to gain still more of their goodwill, we went to them, where they were

carousing in the barn, and added something to our former gift,"
with the result that, according to Boswell, they quarrelled and
fought "and left blood upon the spot, and cursed whisky next
morning." Since Macqueen had books in his house and treated
them with courtesy, it is strange that both Johnson and Boswell
should have fancied that he might cut their throats and steal
their money, the sole reason for their fear being Macqueen's
declared intention to emigrate. However, the proximity of the
soldiers gave them a sense of security, and Johnson made
friends with their landlord's daughter by giving her a book he
had bought at Inverness, *Cocker's Arithmetic*. He used to get
annoyed when people laughed at his choice of reading for a
Highland lass, but it was the only book he had with him.

Next day they passed through Glen Shiel, and Boswell
likened a mountain to a cone, but Johnson disagreed, pointing
out that one side of it was larger than the other; and when
Boswell described another mountain as immense, Johnson again
dissented: "No, it is no more than a considerable protuberance."
Johnson was repelled "by this wide extent of hopeless sterility"
and was not perhaps in the best of humours when, at the close
of a fatiguing day, they came to a mountain called Mam
Rattachan. The ascent was steep and narrow, Johnson's horse
at one point staggering on the brink of a precipice: "I called in
haste to the Highlander to hold him. This was the only
moment of my journey in which I thought myself endangered."

On reaching the summit they were met by a Captain
Macleod, presumably sent to escort them to Glenelg, from
which they were to take a boat to the island of Skye. The
descent was difficult, the weary horses stumbling a good deal.
Boswell dismounted and walked ahead, while Johnson grumbled as his horse slipped and jolted him. In the *Journal* which
he afterwards published, Boswell says that the man who was
leading Johnson's horse tried to allay the rider's displeasure by
calling his attention to the pretty goats browsing at the way-
side, and whistling to make them jump. "Little did he conceive

what Doctor Johnson was," writes Boswell. "Here now was a common ignorant Highland clown imagining that he could divert, as one does a child, *Dr. Samuel Johnson*! The ludicrousness, absurdity, and extraordinary contrast between what the fellow fancied and the reality, was truly comic." On reaching level ground, Boswell mounted his horse and rode forward to arrange for Johnson's proper reception at the Glenelg inn and to engage a boat. But a terrific bellow from his fellow-traveller stopped him. The Doctor was in a passion. Boswell explained his object in going forward but failed to pacify his companion. "Do you know, I should as soon have thought of picking a pocket, as doing so," thundered Johnson. "I am diverted with you, sir," replied Boswell, to which Johnson retorted: "Sir, I could never be diverted with incivility. Doing such a thing makes one lose confidence in him who has done it, as one cannot tell what he may do next." Boswell declares that he was so much confounded by Johnson's extraordinary warmth that he justified himself but lamely. The reader is also puzzled to account for Johnson's fury until he consults Boswell's original journal and finds that a most significant passage has been suppressed in the published version. During the episode of the goats which he thought so comical, Boswell admits that his laughter went beyond all bounds. Clearly what happened was that Johnson observed Boswell doubled up with convulsions of merriment, which must have especially riled him because their military escort and the other servant who accompanied them were silent witnesses of his humiliation. With every side-slip of the horse, every curse of the Doctor, every whistle of the Highlander, there came a howl of hilarity from Boswell, who soon suffered from Johnson's anger, made all the more violent from being bottled up at the time. Although Boswell stated that Johnson read the whole of his Hebridean journal, certain passages were no doubt concealed by the cautious journalist, and this would have been one of them, a probability strengthened by the fact that when they reached Glenelg a bottle of rum was sent them by a man whose name is given as Murchison by Boswell, as Gordon by Johnson.

The inn at Glenelg was a hovel, where nothing edible or drinkable was to be had. Their bedroom was damp, dirty and smelly, and from one of the beds "a man black as a Cyclops from the forge" darted up as they entered. Johnson's supper consisted of a lemon and a piece of bread, Boswell's of rum and sugar. Johnson slept in his riding-coat on a bundle of hay; Boswell laid sheets on the hay and covered himself with his garments.

Next morning, 2nd September, they took a boat for Armadale on the coast of Skye, where they were met by Sir Alexander Macdonald and his lady, who was a cousin of Boswell's and had once been on his list of eligible wives. Macdonald, an Old Etonian, was a miserly person and received them in a small house by the sea instead of at his inland mansion, "that he might with less reproach entertain us meanly," said Johnson. They were given such a poor dinner that Boswell wanted to leave the following morning, but Johnson thought they had better make the best of it for a few days. Several of Macdonald's clansmen were present and it soon transpired that they were equally dissatisfied with their chief; so Boswell, fortified with wine, openly criticised the parsimony of their host, who defended himself angrily. Johnson also lectured Macdonald on the proper duties of a laird, but failed to make any impression on him. They thought Lady Macdonald pretty but silly, and Johnson imitated her foolish manner of speech. After they had left the place Johnson said that she ought to be sent to St. Kilda, "that she was as bad as negative badness could be, and stood in the way of what was good; that insipid beauty would not go a great way; and that such a woman might be cut out of a cabbage, if there was a skilful artificer." His later comments on her husband were made in various places on the island. One of them ran: "*He's* frightened at sea, and his tenants are frightened on land"; and when Boswell mentioned Macdonald's claim that he left Skye with the blessings of his people, Johnson remarked: "You'll observe this was when he *left* it. It is only the back of him that they bless." Again, when informed by someone that Macdonald only visited Skye in the summer, Johnson said: "That is out of tenderness to you. Bad weather and he, at the same time, would be too much." However, they revenged themselves for their inhospitable reception at Armadale by borrowing horses from Macdonald and keeping them much longer than the stipulated period.

In his published version of the tour Boswell was not so candid as in his private journal, and he suppressed the names of the persons who called forth Johnson's comments just quoted; but he was sufficiently outspoken to be challenged by Sir Alexander to a duel. Boswell preferred a combat on paper, and in the course of their correspondence Macdonald complained of their treatment of his horses. They had, he asserted, declined to find other horses, "notwithstanding you might have been supplied at every gentleman's house upon the road; till moved, I presume, by retrospective compunction, you returned the jaded animals, lamed to the ground (without any apology) and consequently for a long time unfit for the journey which they were originally intended to perform." Boswell's attitude to the Macdonalds was partly due to panic: it was not the sort of welcome to Skye that he had envisaged for Johnson, who might easily have refused to continue the tour if such were to be his reception. Johnson's behaviour can be explained by the fun he was able to extract from a situation he had not created and so could regard with detachment.

They got away from Armadale on 6th September, and passing through Broadford stopped at a farm called Coirechatachan, where they received a hearty welcome from the Mackinnon family and where they enjoyed life for two days with a house full of jovial folk. They did not seem to think there was anything bizarre in their surroundings, though towering at the back of the farm was a reddish lava-stained coniform mountain that resembled a volcanic slag-heap, to which Johnson mildly referred: "The hill behind the house we did not climb." They next went to the island of Raasay and stayed with the laird, MacLeod, whose family danced and sang in the evenings and were so good-humoured that Johnson said "I know not how we shall get away". What he called Boswell's "perpetual cheerfulness" was reflected in the company, of which there were thirty at supper. Back on the island of Skye, Johnson became a little irritable, and at Portree vented his feelings: "I long to be again in civilised life." At Kingsburgh they met Flora Macdonald, who had helped Charles Edward Stuart to escape after the battle of Culloden, and Johnson slept in the bed which the Young Pretender had occupied during his flight, the full story of which was unfolded to them by Flora.

On reaching Dunvegan Castle they were made so comfortable by the laird MacLeod that Johnson ceased to long for civilised life. Here they stayed for eight nights, the weather being stormy, the food excellent, and Johnson having seen enough of the Highlands to feel indisposed for further travelling through the wilderness of Skye. "A walk upon ploughed land in England is a dance upon carpets compared to the toilsome drudgery of wandering in Skye," he told Mrs. Thrale, and "I am now content with knowing that by scrambling up a rock I shall only see other rocks and a wider circuit of barren desolation". He had caught a cold, which made him too deaf to take pleasure in conversation; and though he tried to make Lady MacLeod speak up, he could hardly hear what she said. His sixty-fourth birthday occurred on 18th September, and Boswell, "with some of his troublesome kindness," informed the family of it. Johnson took occasion to mourn the event in a letter to Mrs. Thrale: "I can now look back upon three score and four years, in which little has been done, and little has been enjoyed, a life diversified by misery, spent part in the sluggishness of penury, and part under the violence of pain, in gloomy discontent, or importunate distress. Perhaps I am better than

I should have been, if I had been less afflicted. With this I shall try to be content."

One afternoon, the ladies having left the table, Johnson said that wool, being an animal substance, was not so clean as linen. "I have often thought," he continued, "that if I kept a seraglio the ladies should all wear linen gowns, or cotton; I mean stuffs made of vegetable substances. I would have no silk; you cannot tell when it is clean; it will be very nasty before it is perceived to be so. Linen detects its own dirtiness." This was more than Boswell could sustain with gravity, and he repeated an offence for which he had suffered on the mountain of Mam Rattachan:

> To hear the grave Dr. Samuel Johnson, "that majestic teacher of moral and religious wisdom," while sitting solemn in an arm-chair in the Isle of Skye, talk, *ex cathedra*, of his keeping a seraglio, and acknowledge that the supposition had *often* been in his thoughts, struck me so forcibly with ludicrous contrast, that I could not but laugh immoderately. He was too proud to submit, even for a moment, to be the object of ridicule, and instantly retaliated with such keen sarcastic wit, and such a variety of degrading images, of every one of which I was the object, that, though I can bear such attacks as well as most men, I yet found myself so much the sport of all the company, that I would gladly expunge from my mind every trace of this severe retort.

This paragraph appeared in the *Journal* published by Boswell after Johnson's death, and because it stimulates the imagination it is a far more artistic evocation than the account in his original journal, where Johnson implies that a castrated Boswell would make a good eunuch in charge of a seraglio, the description here being tame and commonplace in comparison with the superb passage quoted above.

From Dunvegan they journeyed to Ullinish and Talisker, where they fell in with Donald Maclean, the young laird of

Coll, who acted as their guide for some time and proved a very pleasant companion. They revisited Coirechatachan, arriving at midnight, and Boswell celebrated the occasion with so much punch that he reeled to bed dead drunk at about five the next morning. Awaking at noon with a bad headache, he anticipated a lecture from Johnson, who had not witnessed his debauch. But Johnson was nearly always amiable when not contradicted or put to personal inconvenience, and he called Boswell "you drunken dog" in a friendly manner. When the laird proposed a dram of brandy to cure Boswell's headache, Johnson agreed: "Ay, fill him drunk again. Do it in the morning, that we may laugh at him all day. It is a poor thing for a fellow to get drunk at night, and skulk to bed, and let his friends have no sport." Having dressed, Boswell went into Johnson's room, picked up a prayer-book, opened it at random, and read: "And be not drunk with wine, wherein there is excess." Some, he thought, would have taken this as a divine interposition. But as he later reflected that little moral blame attended such excesses, which in any case were good for health, the divine interposition was evidently gratuitous.

The weather was now almost persistently bad, and they were detained by it wherever they stopped. Johnson afterwards said that they had enjoyed but one and a half days of fair weather in September and perhaps not more in October. But they whiled away the time as best they could. One evening at Coirechatachan the pretty young wife of a local doctor betted her friends that she would sit on Johnson's knee and kiss him. She won her bet. "Do it again, and let us see who will tire first," he said. She remained on his knee for some time while they drank tea together. "To me," wrote Boswell, "it was highly comic to see the grave philosopher—the Rambler—toying with a Highland beauty!" But he wisely kept his comedic sense to himself. After three days of storm they got away to Ostaig, where they stayed with the minister; and in the course of a conversation about poetry Boswell raised the subject of wearing nightcaps.

Did Johnson wear one? "No." Was it best not to wear one? Johnson did not know, but he did know his Bozzy: "Nobody before was ever foolish enough to ask whether it was best to wear a nightcap or not. This comes of being a little wrong-headed."

The storm raged, and they were kept at Ostaig for five nights. On Sunday, 3rd October, they left Skye for Mull. But the wind became unfavourable, the sea rough, and darkness descended before they could reach the island. The young laird of Coll thought that he could pilot them into one of his own harbours, and they changed direction. Johnson was sea-sick and went below to lie down. Boswell stayed on deck, but the shriek of the wind, the boom of the waves and the clatter of rain on the sails were so terrific that he had some difficulty in trusting the efficacy of prayer in such circumstances. Young Coll perceived that employment would at any rate be efficacious, and gave Boswell a rope to hold, telling him to pull it when ordered to do so; but as it was fixed to the top of a mast, the pulling could only benefit the puller. At length they managed to harbour in the island of Coll, and Boswell went down to see how Johnson had fared. "He was lying in philosophic tranquillity, with a greyhound of Coll's at his back, keeping him warm."

They could not get ashore till the following morning, and the state of the weather compelled them to remain on the island as Coll's guests for ten days. Both of them manifested signs of squeamishness while there. Johnson was repelled by the vulgar manners of a farmer's family, and said that he could not endure low life; and at a place where there was a shortage of sleeping accommodation Boswell objected to sharing a bed with Coll, not only because lying in the same bed with a member of his own sex was repugnant to him but also because many Highlanders were liable to scurvy. However, he managed to examine the young man without appearing to do so, decided that he was reasonably clean, and lay as far apart from him as possible. Another objection was the absence of a "little house" at the laird's residence. Boswell reproached Coll for this, and the two visitors discussed the subject gravely, Johnson maintaining that the brain was at its most active in a privy, Boswell considering that a man was invariably happy there.

Johnson became weary of their enforced detention, saying: "I want to be on the mainland and go on with existence. This is a waste of life." But he amused himself one evening by strutting about the room with a broadsword and target, and Boswell amused himself another evening by putting a large blue bonnet on Johnson's head. The island was duly explored and found to be much the same as other islands in those seas; and when on 14th October they sailed for Mull, the sight of a dozen vessels at anchor in the harbour of Tobermory was a pleasing reminder of civilisation. Johnson had done his best to conceal his disgust with the barren desolation of Highland scenery, but Mull made him articulate: "O, sir, a most dolorous country!" A serious loss here was his large oak stick, which he suspected had been stolen; and when Boswell tried to convince him that his suspicion was groundless and that it would be retrieved in due course, he said: "No, no, my friend, it is not to be expected that any man in Mull, who has got it, will part with it. Consider, sir, the value of such a piece of timber here." They travelled across the rocky, treeless and gloomy island on horseback, and then visited Inchkenneth, where Coll introduced them to the chief of his clan, Sir Allan Maclean, with whom they stayed. On 19th October they bade farewell to young Coll, who the following year was drowned in the waters that had so nearly engulfed themselves.

Maclean accompanied them to the island of Iona, and Johnson described their journey thither in a letter to Mrs. Thrale: "The night came upon us, the wind rose, the sea swelled, and Boswell desired to be set on dry ground. We however pursued our navigation, and passed by several little islands in the silent solemnity of faint moonshine, seeing little, and hearing only the wind and the water." Their boat could not touch land, so Maclean and Boswell were carried on men's shoulders, but Johnson stepped into the water and waded ashore. They spent the night in a barn and viewed the ruins next morning. Johnson had no inclination to visit the place, making up for his lack of enthusiasm with an imposing passage in the book he would shortly write:

> We were now treading that illustrious island, which was once the luminary of the Caledonian regions, whence savage clans and roving barbarians derived the benefits of knowledge, and the blessings of religion. To abstract the mind from all local emotion would be impossible, if it were endeavoured, and would be foolish, if it were possible. Whatever withdraws us from the power of our senses; whatever makes the past, the distant, or the future predominate over the present, advances us in the dignity of thinking beings. Far from me, and from my friends, be such frigid philosophy as may conduct us indifferent and unmoved over any ground which has been dignified by wisdom, bravery, or virtue. That man is little to be envied, whose patriotism would not gain force upon the plain of Marathon, or whose piety would not grow warmer among the ruins of Iona!

Boswell, on the other hand, had longed to see the spot, and now indulged in all the religious emotions natural to him. He went alone into the cathedral, communed with God and St. Columba, read aloud a chapter of St. James and a sermon by Ogden, and "hoped that, ever after having been in this holy place, I should maintain an exemplary conduct. One has a strange propensity to fix upon some point of time from whence a better course of life may begin". Next day they returned to Mull, and his better course of life began at Lochbuie, where he drank so much punch that he was sick; but this may partly have been a healthy reaction from his religious intoxication the previous day. He was in good form the morning after. Lady

Lochbuie proposed that Johnson should have cold sheep's head for breakfast. Her brother Sir Allan Maclean expressed displeasure at her vulgarity; but Boswell backed her up, and when Johnson entered the room she asked if he would care for some. "No, madam," he replied in a tone of angry amazement. "It is here, sir," she said, assuming he had refused in order to save trouble. For a little while they talked at cross-purposes, but he soon made it clear that cold sheep's head was not a proper dish for a gentleman's breakfast. "I sat quietly by, and enjoyed my success," wrote Boswell, without explaining why the offer was regarded as an insult by Sir Allan and Johnson.

On 22nd October they left Mull and landed on the mainland at Oban, whence they rode to Inveraray, a portion of their journey impressing Johnson more than anything he had seen in the Highlands: "The night came on while we had yet a great part of the way to go, though not so dark but that we could discern the cataracts which poured down the hills on one side and fell into one general channel that ran with great violence on the other. The wind was loud, the rain was heavy, and the whistling of the blast, the fall of the shower, the rush of the cataracts, and the roar of the torrent, made a nobler chorus of the rough music of nature than it had ever been my chance to hear before." He had little appreciation of other kinds of music, saying that he knew a drum from a trumpet, and a bagpipe from a guitar, which was about the extent of his knowledge. They found an excellent inn at Inveraray, where, as always, Johnson refused to change his wet clothes; but he broke his abstinence from fermented liquor: "Come, let me know what it is that makes a Scotchman happy," and he called for a gill of whisky, which he polished off and liked better than English malt brandy, but he did not enquire about the process of distillation, having no wish "to improve the art of making poison pleasant". Incidentally he would not let Boswell drink Mrs. Thrale's health in so rough a spirit.

Although he knew that the Duchess of Argyll disliked him

on account of his zeal in the Douglas cause, she having once been the Duchess of Hamilton and the object of displeasing comments in his novel about the case, Boswell determined to call on the Duke at Inveraray Castle. He did so, and the Duke invited him to bring Johnson to dinner the following day, though the Duchess took no notice of him. The Duke was extremely gracious, and the two travellers were shown all over the place, Johnson admiring "the grandeur and elegance of this princely seat", Boswell adoring "the ladies' maids tripping about in neat morning dresses". The Duchess was very polite to Johnson, but continued to ignore Boswell, though he had the cheek to drink her health with the appropriate salutation. An incident during their visit is described in Boswell's inimitable manner:

A gentleman in company, after dinner, was desired by the Duke to go to another room, for a specimen of curious marble, which his Grace wished to shew us. He brought a wrong piece, upon which the Duke sent him back again. He could not refuse; but, to avoid any appearance of servility, he whistled as he walked out of the room, to show his in- dependency. On my mentioning this afterwards to Dr. Johnson, he said, it was a nice trait of character.

On 28th October they arrived at the Saracen's Head Inn at Glasgow, where Johnson got the first batch of letters he had received since leaving Aberdeen. He was in excellent humour, and putting up a leg on each side of the grate he soliloquised: "Here am I, an ENGLISH man, sitting by a *coal* fire." The University professors nervously paid their respects and showed him the city, after which they proceeded to Boswell's home at Auchinleck. Dreading a furious dispute between his father, a Presbyterian Whig, and Johnson, a Church of England Tory, Boswell begged his friend to avoid religion and politics. Johnson replied that he would certainly not discuss subjects that were disagreeable to his host. All went well at first, though when another guest asked Johnson how he liked the Highlands he burst out: "How, sir, can you ask me what obliges me to speak unfavourably of a country where I have been entertained? Who *can* like the Highlands? I like the inhabitants very well." The gentleman, says Boswell, asked no more questions, and his father's presence must have checked Boswell's inclination to ask the Doctor how he liked the Lowlands.

The wonders of Auchinleck were shown to the distinguished visitor, and the five days of their stay would have passed off without friction if Lord Auchinleck had not exhibited his collection of coins, one of Oliver Cromwell's raising the subject of Charles I, Toryism, Whiggism, Presbyterianism, Episcopalianism, and cognate themes. "They became exceedingly warm and violent," reports Boswell, "and I was very much distressed by being present at such an altercation between two men, both of whom I reverenced; yet I durst not interfere." He suppressed details of the row, but many years afterwards one of his sons must have told Sir Walter Scott that when Johnson angrily demanded what good Cromwell had ever done for his country, Lord Auchinleck replied: "God! doctor, he gart kings ken that they had a *lith* in their neck" (he taught kings that they had a joint in their necks), a remark that must have thickened the atmosphere for several hours and thereafter made them austerely polite to one another. Privately Auchinleck called Johnson *Ursa Major.* Had they met frequently, Johnson would probably have invented fit names for Auchinleck.

The wanderers returned to Edinburgh on 9th November and received so many compliments that Johnson protested: "I am really ashamed of the congratulations we receive. We are addressed as if we had made a voyage to Nova Zembla, and suffered five persecutions in Japan." He soon tired of seeing so many people, of attending so many breakfasts, dinners and suppers. "Sir, we have been harassed by invitations," he complained. Boswell agreed. "But how much worse would it have been, if we had been neglected," added Johnson. He decided to leave by coach for London on Monday 22nd November, and accepted an invitation from Sir John Dalrymple to spend the week-end at his Cranston home, twelve miles south of Edinburgh, so that the coach could be caught at a later hour on Monday morning. Having heard that Dalrymple had spoken offensively about Johnson, and had "wondered how any gentleman of Scotland could keep company with him", Boswell resolved to teach the baronet a lesson. He therefore took Johnson on Saturday the 20th to see Rosslyn Castle and chapel, and then to Hawthornden, where Ben Jonson had visited the poet William Drummond; by which time they were already late for dinner at Cranston, where a sheep had been killed in their honour. On the way Johnson made merry over Dalrymple's uneasiness at their non-arrival, and when they turned up their reception was so frigid that they spent Sunday night at Blackshiels Inn, two miles further on.

Except when angry, Johnson's manners were almost invariably good, and it is difficult to believe that he was conscious of treating Dalrymple with discourtesy. We must assume that Boswell withheld something that would make credible his account of Johnson's behaviour, for in his desire to hurt Dalrymple he has libelled Johnson. But such is his ability to entertain his readers that we who have been neither hurt nor libelled are charitable enough to overlook his malice towards others.

CHAPTER 20

The Rambler Rambles

IN JANUARY 1775, Johnson's *A Journey to the Western Islands of Scotland* came from the press. Boswell says that it was received with "miserable cavillings" by the critics, but intelligent readers recognised it as an intelligent work. The one statement in the book to arouse considerable controversy was Johnson's denial of the authenticity of Macpherson's 'translations' of two epic poems said to have been written in Erse by a Gaelic bard of the third century named Ossian. James Macpherson, starting life as a bookseller's assistant, became famous with the publication in 1762 of *Fingal*, supposedly by Ossian. As the possession of a great early Gaelic poet gave pleasure to the Scots, enquiries with regard to the Erse originals were not pursued with much eagerness, and Johnson, whose credulity took another form, did not believe in their genuineness. In his opinion the poems were written by Macpherson, and he said so. If the originals were available, he asked, why had they never been seen? He thought that Macpherson had probably found names and stories and occasional phrases in the old songs, and had worked them into his own composition; but as a result of his investigations during his Scottish tour, Johnson could discover nothing to prove the existence of ancient manuscripts. "The Scots have something to plead for their easy reception of an improbable fiction," he wrote: "they are seduced by their fondness for their supposed ancestors. A Scotchman must be a very sturdy moralist who does not love Scotland better than truth: he will always love it better than enquiry; and if falsehood flatters his vanity, will not be very diligent to detect it." He considered Macpherson's *Fingal* "to be as gross an imposition as ever the world was troubled with". In the years ahead it imposed upon Goethe, Schiller, Byron and Napoleon I. But for Johnson it was a fake, and the remarks in his book brought a ferocious letter from Macpherson, who had also published a translation of Homer's *Iliad* in Ossianic prose. Johnson replied on 20th January, 1775:

Mr. James Macpherson—I received your foolish and impudent note. Whatever insult is offered me I will do my best to repel, and what I cannot do for myself the law will do for me. I will not desist from detecting what I think a cheat, from any fear of the menaces of a Ruffian.

You want me to retract. What shall I retract? I thought your book an imposture from the beginning, I think it upon yet surer reasons an imposture still. For this opinion I give the public my reasons which I here dare you to refute.

But however I may despise you, I reverence truth, and if you can prove the genuineness of the work I will confess it. Your rage I defy, your abilities since your Homer are not so formidable, and what I have heard of your morals disposes me to pay regard not to what you shall say, but to what you can prove.

You may print this if you will.

Sam: Johnson.

Having provided himself with a very large oak stick for self-defence in case Macpherson's vanity issued in action, he dismissed the subject from his mind, his opinion of the poems being so little in tune with that of the romanticists who succeeded him that he said: "Sir, a man might write such stuff for ever, if he would *abandon* his mind to it." By one of those ironic strokes of fate that help to enrich the comedy of life, Johnson and Macpherson now lie within a few feet of one another in Westminster

Abbey. Many Scots thought that Johnson's attitude to Ossian was part of his antagonism to their native country, for which he was frequently taken to task. But he could always rise to such occasions. For instance, when Thomas Barnard, Bishop of Killaloe, expressed a fear that if Johnson were to visit Ireland he might treat the natives even more severely than he had handled the Scots, he replied: "Sir, you have no reason to be afraid of me. The Irish are not in a conspiracy to cheat the world by false representations of the merits of their countrymen. No, sir: the Irish are a fair people: they never speak well of one another."

It may have been out of consideration for Mrs. Thrale that he made no comments on the Welsh, though he probably regarded them as English. A year after his ramble in Scotland he accompanied the Thrales to Hester's native country, which made no deeper impression on him than any other region would have done, from Switzerland to the Sahara. "Wales has nothing that can excite or gratify curiosity," he told John Taylor. "The mode of life is entirely English. I am glad I have seen it, though I have seen nothing, because I now know that there is nothing to be seen." Their tour lasted for about as long as the one he had undertaken to the Hebrides. It started at the beginning of July 1774 and finished at the end of September. The party travelled by coach and consisted of Thrale, his wife, their daughter Queeney, and Johnson. Putting up at the Swan Inn, Lichfield, they were taken to visit all Johnson's friends, and Mrs. Thrale was compelled to change her riding-habit before Johnson would consent to be seen in the streets with her. They stayed with Taylor at Ashbourne and viewed all the notable spots in the district, including Dovedale, which did not answer Johnson's expectations, though he thought it as picturesque as the Highlands of Scotland. They saw Chester Cathedral and stopped at the house of Sir Robert Cotton in Wales, where Johnson was not in his most agreeable mood. Mrs. Thrale praised the sweet disposition of their hostess. "True, but it is her nature, and one thanks her no more for being sweet than a honeycomb," said Johnson. Hoping for a less objective view of the food placed before them, she praised a dish of peas, asking him whether they were not charming. "Perhaps they would be so—to a *pig*," he conceded. Such invitations to commendation were usually repulsed by him, owing to his distrust of uncritical enthusiasm. On a visit to Lincolnshire one of Bennet Langton's sisters showed him a grotto, remarking that it would be a pretty cool habitation in summer. "I think it would, madam, for a *toad*," was his reply. Hester Thrale was constantly checked for her effusiveness. "Why is it," asked Johnson while they were in Wales, "that whatever you see, you are to be so indiscriminately lavish of praise?" Her answer cornered him: "Why, I'll tell you, sir. When I am with you and Mr. Thrale and Queeney, I am obliged to be civil for four!" There was some truth in this, for at one place during their journey he rudely ignored Lord Bolingbroke, the former husband of Topham Beauclerk's wife Diana, whom Johnson thought a whore. He met Thrale's expostulation over his treatment of the peer with: "Why, sir, I did not know the man. If he will put on no other mark of distinction, let us make him wear his horns."

They saw the place where Hester had been born and the parish church where she had worshipped. "The old clerk had great appearance of joy at the sight of his mistress," noted Johnson, "and foolishly said that he was now willing to die." They visited St. Asaph, Bangor, Denbigh, Conway and Beaumaris, drove round Snowdon, and rowed on the lake at Llanberis. At Carnarvon, Johnson likened their hostess to sour beer: "She could never have been a good thing, and even that thing is spoiled." In spite of his acid comments on persons and places, Hester paid tribute in her diary to his sensitiveness: "He is on every occasion so very kind, feels friendship so acutely and expresses it so delicately that it is wonderfully flattering to me to have his company."

On their way home they stopped at Shrewsbury, breakfasting

with Dr. William Adams, whom Johnson had known since his student days at Oxford and who would shortly become Master of Pembroke College. Hester thought the conversation of Adams 'cold' and was glad when they left him; but that day they experienced something more cheerless than cold conversation. It rained hard, the roads were deep in mire, "and we walked up a steep hill they called Wenlock Edge till our feet were wet and dirty." Further on, the tackle of their coach broke, the horses were tired out, and they could not reach Ombersley, where they were to stay with Lord Sandys, but had to put up at the small though excellent inn of Hartlebury. They were hospitably entertained at Ombersley, which was distinguished by Johnson as the only place, except once at Streatham, where he had a bellyful of wall-fruit. They saw the china factory at Worcester as well as the cathedral, which Johnson thought "a very fine one". But they were not so well pleased with their reception by the Lytteltons at Little Hagley, where the ladies were disagreeable to Mrs. Thrale and Johnson was asked to put his candle out when he stopped reading for a while to walk about the room.

After viewing The Leasowes at Halesowen, which had been beautified by the poet William Shenstone, they went on to Birmingham, where Mrs. Thrale made the acquaintance of Johnson's school-friend Edmund Hector and where Matthew Boulton showed them over his famous factory at Soho. They stayed at Woodstock to see Blenheim Park, at Oxford long enough to see the colleges, and finally with Edmund Burke at his Beaconsfield home, where Hester noticed that they were received "with open arms". But a General Election was pending; Edmund had to spend most of the time soliciting votes; his other guests sped the hours with the aid of liquid refreshment; and Hester made an entry in her journal: "There was an old Mr. Lowndes dined with us and got very drunk talking Politics with Will Burke and my Master after dinner. Lord Verney and Edmund came home at night very much flustered with liquor, and I thought how I had spent three months from home among dunces of all ranks and sorts, but had never seen a man drunk till I came among the Wits." Worse was to follow. She longed to spend the autumn at Streatham, but her husband informed her that they must at once start canvassing for the Southwark election: "I must be shut up in that odious dungeon, where nobody will come near me, the children are to be sick for want of air, *and I am never to see a face but Mr. Johnson's.* Oh, what a life that is! and how truly do I abhor it!" She had changed her tune. The previous year she had written to him: "I shall see you at dinner tomorrow in the Borough. Can I help rejoicing, when to see you is connected with every pleasing idea!" And quite recently she had thought it "wonderfully flattering to me to have his company." But she must suddenly have remembered that Johnson on the road was not the same person as Johnson on the hearth. While travelling he seemed indifferent to discomfort, careless of accommodation, not minding what the weather was like, whether he journeyed by day or by night, whether the food was good or bad. But when under her roof he had to be solaced with good meals and beguiled by sprightly conversation. With this doleful prospect she left Beaconsfield, and it is possible that Edmund Burke momentarily shared her gloom when Johnson shook his hand, taking leave of him in these words: "Farewell, my dear sir, and remember that I wish you all the success which ought to be wished you, which can possibly be wished you indeed, *by an honest man.*" It was not the sort of well-wishing that a politician would relish.

But Burke could honestly feel that he was right, Johnson wrong, over the American War of Independence, which broke out in 1775. Johnson was suffering from one of those pathological bursts of patriotism which are liable to afflict repressed natures at intervals. "Patriotism," he once said, "is the last refuge of a scoundrel," and the thought may have been prompted by a sense of guilt. In the early days of the colonial resistance to taxation by the British Government, he said of the Americans: "Sir, they are a race of convicts, and ought to be thankful for anything we allow them short of hanging." He therefore raised no objection when asked by the Government to write a pamphlet, *Taxation no Tyranny*, which was supposed to be an answer to the resolutions of the American Congress. He forgot his own wise remark concerning the religious reformers in the time of John Knox: "Differing from a man in doctrine was no reason why you should pull his house about his ears." He refused to hear arguments on the other side of the question, and Boswell was careful not to advance them in conversation. One visitor who dared to raise the subject was told that "had we treated the Americans as we ought, and as they deserved, we should have at once razed all their towns and let them enjoy their forests"; and in a private letter this Cromwell of the pen declared: "Our business is to pursue their main army, and disperse it by a decisive battle; and then waste the country till they sue for peace." He managed however to score one effective point: "How is it that we hear the loudest yelps for liberty among the drivers of negroes?"

He thought little of the British generals engaged in the war, but his opinion of military leaders was never high. When Boswell observed that Oliver Goldsmith had acquired more fame than the majority of officers in a recent campaign, Johnson said: "Why, sir, you will find ten thousand fit to do what they did before you find one who does what Goldsmith has done." He considered that Goldsmith was justified in feeling aggrieved when Lord Camden took no more notice of him in a mixed company than if he had been an ordinary man. "Nay, gentlemen," said Johnson, stopping the laugh with which the complaint was received, "Dr. Goldsmith is in the right. A nobleman ought to have made up to such a man as Goldsmith, and I think it is much against Lord Camden that he neglected him." Goldsmith died in 1774, and two years later Johnson wrote an epitaph in Latin for his memorial in

Westminster Abbey, containing the memorable phrase: "A Poet, Naturalist and Historian, who left scarcely any style of writing untouched, and touched nothing that he did not adorn." Unlike those inferior scribes who admire action more than reflection, Johnson never flattered soldiers and statesmen, knowing quite well that "intellectual pre-eminence is the highest superiority, and nations derive their highest reputation from the splendour and dignity of their writers".

Boswell affected to feel sorrow at the death of Goldsmith, but his real feeling was relief at the removal of a possible competitor, for it had been hinted that Goldsmith might write the Life of Johnson. A visit to London in the spring of 1775 enabled Boswell to add to his biographical material. He refers to himself as "one of the company" in an interchange with Johnson, who had recently been seen at the theatre:

"Why, sir, did you go to Mrs. Abington's benefit? Did you see?"

"No, sir."

"Did you hear?"

"No, sir."

"Why then, sir, did you go?"

"Because, sir, she is a favourite of the public; and when the public cares the thousandth part for you that it does for her, I will go to your benefit too."

Oxford University had recently conferred the degree of LL.D. on Johnson, and he received his diploma on the morning of 1st April, when Boswell tried to discover why he collected the peel of oranges; but Johnson declined to satisfy the biographer's curiosity, and we learn from another source that he used it medicinally.

One reason for Boswell's presence in London this spring was his decision to practise at the English Bar, for which he had to qualify by residence in the Temple for several terms. "I have now eat a term's commons in the Inner Temple," he announced at the conclusion of his visit. But he had also drunk more than a term's commons outside the Inner Temple, admitting "I am in that dissipated state of mind that I absolutely cannot write", and Johnson extracted a promise from him that he would read more and drink less. His other form of indulgence, held in check during the early years of marriage, was no longer restrained. "I am *too many*, as the phrase is, for one woman," he wrote to his friend Temple, "and a certain transient connection I am persuaded does not interfere with that attachment which a man has for a *wife* and which I have as much as any man that ever lived, though *some* of my qualifications are not valued by her, as they have been by other women—ay, and well-educated women too. Concubinage is almost universal. If it was *morally* wrong, why was it permitted to the most pious men under the old testament? Why did our Saviour never say a word against it?" These reflections were prompted by a pretty maid at the Grantham inn on his journey to London. But unless flushed with too much claret, he felt that he could be trusted with women, limiting himself to caresses: "There is a Miss Silverton in the fly with me, an amiable creature, who has been in France. I can unite little fondnesses with perfect conjugal love."

He still could not hit it off with his father, who thought his trip to London another proof of idleness and extravagance. When he got back, and took his wife to dine with his parents, Lord Auchinleck did not salute his daughter-in-law, "though he had not seen her for three months; nor did he so much as ask her how she did, though she is pretty big with child." Four months later their first son was born. Boswell's return to Edinburgh was accompanied by a return of melancholia. "My wife is an admirable companion for a man of my atrabilious temperament, for she has a good store of common sense and cheerfulness," he told Temple. She had to draw considerably on these resources, for after one of his wild evenings it grieved him to inform his friend that "the drunken manners of this country are very bad". The lure of London was too strong for him. How could he be satisfied to drudge in an obscure corner where the manners of the people were so disagreeable to him? he asked Temple. If only his father would give him £400 a year and let him go to the English Bar, all would be well. Instead the judge talked of cutting down his allowance from three to two hundred a year on account of a debt. In September he went to stay at Auchinleck, where his patience was severely tested. He could not bear life in the country, and he dreaded the thought that his father might disinherit him: "He has a method of treating me which makes me *feel* myself like a *timid boy*." His stepmother was narrow-minded, domineering, suspicious, "and so sourishly tempered that it requires the utmost exertion of practical philosophy to keep myself quiet. I, however, have done so all this week, to admiration; nay, I have appeared good-humoured; but it has cost me drinking a considerable quantity of strong beer to dull my faculties."

Shortly after this uncomfortable week at Auchinleck he heard that Johnson had gone to France with the Thrales. Their journey had probably been suggested by Baretti, who at that time was Queeney Thrale's Italian tutor. It seems likely that he was in love with Mrs. Thrale, who eventually repulsed him, because after living with the family at intervals for several years he left in a sudden transport of fury for no apparent reason and some years later wrote a vitriolic attack on her, calling her a "beastly mother" who had practically murdered her own children by neglect, tin pills and cold water. In 1775 however he was a popular member of the household, a favourite of Johnson's, and distinguished by a Reynolds portrait which hung with those of Johnson, Burke, Garrick and Goldsmith in the library at Streatham. He accompanied Mr. and Mrs. Thrale, their daughter Queeney, and Johnson on their holiday in France, and proved a most agreeable and useful guide.

They left Streatham on 15th September and went by Canterbury and Dover to Calais. Though a good travelling companion, because he scarcely ever complained, Johnson seldom displayed the least curiosity in the objects around him. While in Scotland he was asked whether he would like to see the room at Dunfermline wherein Charles I was born, but he showed no eagerness: "I know that he was born, no matter where." So, when Thrale spoke of the French scenery through which they were passing, Johnson gave him no encouragement: "Never heed such nonsense; a blade of grass is always a blade of grass, whether in one country or another. Let us, if we *do* talk, talk about something. Men and women are the subjects of my enquiry; let us see how these differ from those we have left behind." Throughout the trip Mrs. Thrale was mainly interested in the shops and convents, Johnson in the libraries and monasteries. His French being a little shaky, he mostly spoke in Latin, because "there is no good in letting the French have a superiority over you every word you speak."

On the journey up the Seine, between Vernon and St. Denis, there was a nasty accident. The party travelled in two carriages. The postilion of the one occupied by Thrale, his daughter and Baretti, fell off his horse at a steep descent, the traces were broken, and the carriage went downhill with a pair of runaway horses at an alarming speed. Thrale jumped out, either to save his skin or in the hope of stopping the horses, and hurt himself badly. Eventually the carriage was brought to a standstill by the efforts of their mounted servant. When they arrived at St. Germain, Thrale felt so ill that he was advised to go on at once to Paris and get himself bled. Mrs. Thrale was shocked by Johnson's apparent unconcern over the episode. He declared that accidents never happened, and that the recent event did not change his opinion, "for nothing came of it except that Mr. Thrale leaped out of the carriage into a chalkpit, and then came up again looking *as white!*" But he said that his seeming indifference was due to Mrs. Thrale's failure to give a rational answer to his enquiry as to what had taken place.

Mrs. Thrale noticed that the atmosphere of the narrowest parts of Paris was clearer than that of Hampstead Hill, the reason being that the inhabitants did not burn coal. She also thought that the populace was less rude and dangerous than in London. Fourteen years later she would have changed her mind; and Johnson, too, might have altered his opinion of the brewer Antoine-Joseph Santerre if he had known that the polite tradesman would one day be in command of the troops surrounding the scaffold at the execution of Louis XVI. As it was, he went over the brewery and heard with complacence from Santerre that he "brews with about as much malt as Mr. Thrale, and sells his beer at the same price, though he pays no duty for malt, and little more than half as much for beer. Beer is sold retail at 6d. a bottle. He brews 4,000 barrels a year."

They did all the usual things that were then done, and are still done, by all the usual people. A round of social visits left Mrs. Thrale with the impression that "self-admiration seems the grand characteristic of the country". The habits of the nation were not much to Johnson's taste: "The French have a clear air and a fruitful soil, but their mode of common life is gross, and incommodious, and disgusting." Neither did Paris attract him: "Their palaces are splendid, and their churches magnificent in their structure, and gorgeous in their ornaments, but the city in general makes a very mean appearance." Nor Fontainebleau, "a large mean town;" nor Versailles, "a mean town." But they had the pleasure of watching Louis XVI and Marie Antoinette eating their dinner at Fontainebleau, and they seem to have been impressed by the Palace, the Trianon and the Little Trianon at Versailles, where they were shown the King's theatre. Walking on to the stage, Mrs. Thrale asked: "What play shall we act? The Englishman in Paris?" "No, indeed: we will act Harry the Fifth," Johnson replied.

Wherever they went they noticed a queer mixture of dirt and finery, of slovenliness and magnificence, of stench and elegance. There was much expectoration and many cuspidors were in evidence, though some ladies spat on the floor, rubbing it in with their feet. Dining at the house of Madame du Boccage, "a literary lady of rank," they noticed busts of Shakespeare, Milton, Pope and Dryden in the drawing-room, the table of which was adorned by a spittoon. "The lady," noted Mrs. Thrale, "sat on a sofa with a fine red velvet cushion fringed with gold under her feet, and just over her head a cobweb of enormous size, and I am sure of great antiquity." After dinner "the footman took the sugar in his fingers and threw it into my coffee," Johnson complained. "I was going to put it aside; but hearing it was made on purpose for me, I e'en tasted Tom's fingers." When tea was served the mouth of the pot became choked with leaves, a difficulty Madame du Boccage easily overcame by ordering the footman to blow down the spout.

But in spite of nasty habits, dirty beds, unpleasant smells, bad cookery, and the fact that "I have seen nothing that much delighted or surprised me", Johnson's health improved in France and he thought himself growing younger. On 22nd October at Versailles he "ran a race in the rain this day and beat Baretti". As it was a Sunday, his own principles should have accused him of levity; but his rules of behaviour were subject to fluctuation, like other people's. One Sunday a guest of Thrale's noticed bird-catchers busy at their trade on Streatham Common, and inveighed against the wickedness of the times. Johnson reproved him: "While half the Christian world is permitted to dance and sing, and celebrate Sunday as a day of festivity, how comes your puritanical spirit so offended with frivolous and empty deviations from exactness? Whoever loads life with unnecessary scruples, sir, provokes the attention of others on his conduct, and incurs the censure of singularity without reaping the reward of superior virtue." No doubt Johnson was feeling high-spirited when he raced in the rain with Baretti and low-spirited when he remarked to Boswell that people should not throw stones at birds on a Sunday.

Stopping at Douai on their return journey to the coast from Paris, they witnessed High Mass, but left before the Elevation of the Host, Baretti saying that if they had stayed they would have been compelled to kneel. Mrs. Thrale admitted that she had no scruples on the point, while Johnson, now as scrupulous as the man who objected to Sabbath bird-catching, declared that he would not have knelt at such a moment for the whole city of Douai. Mrs. Thrale had already knelt on two or three of such occasions, believing that in doing so "I was not displeasing to God". But Johnson's God was made of sterner stuff.

They were back in England by the middle of November, and soon afterwards Thrale decided that the same party must visit Italy the following spring. Hearing this, Boswell made up his mind to see Johnson before he left for another continental jaunt, and arrived in London on 15th March 1776, to find that the Doctor had just moved to a house in Bolt Court, and to learn that he was about to commence his annual pilgrimage to Oxford, Birmingham, Lichfield and Ashbourne: "I shall go in a few days, and you, Boswell, shall go with me."

At Oxford, Boswell was shown many places connected with Johnson's youth and introduced to various people. In their journey thence to Stratford-on-Avon they stopped at an inn at Chapel House, and Johnson expanded on the pleasure and freedom of tavern life, closing his monologue with the oft-quoted remark: "No, sir; there is nothing which has yet been contrived by man, by which so much happiness is produced as a good tavern or inn." Little doubt that Boswell hiccupped approval. Driving along in the post-chaise after dinner, Johnson said: "Life has not many things better than this." At a later date he thought of one thing better: "If I had no duties, and no reference to futurity, I would spend my life in driving briskly in a post-chaise with a pretty woman; but she should be one who could understand me, and would add something to the conversation."

They drank tea and coffee at Stratford, spent the night at Henley-in-Arden, and went on to Birmingham, where Boswell met Hector, who took him to see Boulton's factory at Soho, then one of the wonders of England. Talking with Boswell about Hector's sister, now a widow, Johnson said that she had been his earliest love and that if he had married her it might have been as happy for him. This was a theme that attracted Boswell, who asked whether there were not fifty women in the world with any one of whom a man might be as happy as with any other. "Ay, sir, fifty thousand," said Johnson. "Then, sir, you are not of opinion with some who imagine that certain men and women are made for each other, and that they cannot be happy if they miss their counterparts?" Johnson was not of that opinion: "I believe marriages would in general be as happy, and often more so, if they were all made by the Lord Chancellor, upon a due consideration of characters and circumstances, without the parties having any choice in the matter." On another occasion he declared: "It is commonly a weak man who marries for love," and if Boswell had not been thinking of his own case he might have mildly enquired whether Johnson had married for love, with detonating effect.

At Lichfield they put up at the Three Crowns Inn, next-door to Johnson's birthplace, and Boswell was introduced to Lucy Porter, who with a fortune inherited from her brother had built an imposing house where Johnson usually stayed. Peter Garrick (David's brother), Molly Aston, Moll Cobb, Canon Seward, his daughter Anna, and several others were duly visited, and one day an old schoolfellow of Johnson's dined with them. Boswell thought him "a low man, dull and untaught", his clothing and countenance leaving much to be desired; but Johnson treated him with great kindness and listened patiently to an indistinct account of his attempts to earn a living. Breakfasting with Lucy Porter on 25th March, Johnson received a letter which upset him. "One of the most dreadful things that has happened in my time," he announced. Boswell wondered whether the King had been assassinated, or London burnt to the ground, and Johnson's next remark seemed an anti-climax: "Mr. Thrale has lost his only son." A younger son had died the previous year, and now only three out of their ten children remained alive. "This is a total extinction to their family," Johnson went on, "as much as if they were sold into captivity." Boswell thought the sentiment excessive and mentioned Thrale's daughters. "Daughters!" exclaimed Johnson: "he'll no more value his daughters than— Sir, don't you know how you yourself think? Sir, he wishes to propagate his name." Having further remarked: "I would have gone to the extremity of the earth to have preserved this boy," he calmed down, and in the evening they went to a show at the Town Hall, after which Boswell expressed regret at having felt gay and merry during the performance with the Thrales in such distress. Johnson consoled him: "I would not have you be gay in the presence of the distressed, because it would shock them; but you may be gay at a distance."

They drove on to Ashbourne, travelling in Taylor's roomy post-chaise drawn by four horses. Johnson having decided to be with the Thrales as soon as possible, they only stayed a night with Taylor, just long enough for Boswell to drop a brick. Some of Taylor's neighbours came to dinner, and in the course of conversation Johnson said that a wise man did not feel the want of anything. Boswell argued that it was better to have fine clothes than not to feel the want of them. Johnson replied that Charles XII and Frederick the Great did not require fine clothes to inspire respect or increase their dignity. "Would not *you*, sir, be the better for velvet and embroidery?" insinuated Boswell. "Sir," came the wrathful retort, "you put an end to argument when you introduce your opponent himself. Have you no better manners? There is *your want*."

Fancying that his early presence would comfort his friends, Johnson at once drove down to Streatham upon his arrival in London, but was shocked by the sight of a coach at their door and all preparations made for the departure of Hester Thrale, Queeney and Baretti for Bath. He was not in the best of tempers when Boswell called on him that same evening; and his vexation was not removed when he heard that Thrale had decided to cancel the Italian tour. It may have been due to a feeling that he was no longer indispensable to the Thrale family that on 11th April he wrote to the Lord Chamberlain, the Earl of Hertford, asking whether he could have apartments at Hampton Court Palace: "I hope that to a man who has had the honour of vindicating his Majesty's government, a retreat in one of his houses may not be improperly or unworthily allowed." The Lord Chamberlain regretted his inability to comply with the request, having already on his hands many engagements that were unsatisfied. In discussing the abandonment of his Italian trip, Boswell hinted that it would have done the Thrales good, but he did not agree: "While grief is fresh, every attempt to divert only irritates. You must wait till grief be *digested*, and then amusement will dissipate the remains of it." Nevertheless the Thrales were trying to dissipate their un-digested grief at Bath, and at the end of the month Johnson joined them. Boswell followed, and stayed at the Pelican Inn. On 29th April they visited Bristol together, where Johnson enquired into the authenticity of Chatterton's 'Rowley Poems', as he had previously investigated the genuineness of Ossian's. The sight of the chest in which Chatterton was supposed to have found the poems did not prove anything beyond the existence of the chest, and Johnson declared: "This is the most extraordinary young man that has encountered my knowledge. It is wonderful how the whelp has written such things." Their inn at Bristol disgusted them, and Johnson jokingly said it was "so bad that Boswell wished to be in Scotland".

That spring Boswell "conceived an irresistible wish" to arrange a meeting between Johnson and Wilkes. It is perhaps unnecessary to say that Johnson hated Wilkes's politics, distrusted the man, and had a horror of his atheistical opinions. In a pamphlet, *The False Alarm* (1770), Johnson justified the Ministry in repeatedly expelling Wilkes from the House of Commons and electing a Court favourite as member for

Middlesex, which county had returned Wilkes to Parliament by a vast majority of votes. After spending some time in prison on returning from the continent, Wilkes was freed, and in 1774 became Lord Mayor of London, being readmitted to Parliament, where his championship of the American colonists, his attack on rotten boroughs, and his advocacy of an extended franchise did nothing to endear him to Johnson. Carefully refraining from an open friendship with Wilkes until the connection again became creditable, Boswell then resumed their correspondence and dined twice at the Mansion House in 1775. But to arrange a meeting between the violent Tory and the irresponsible Whig, the downright believer and the cunning infidel, was a ticklish job, and Boswell knew it would be a waste of his own breath and a vast expenditure of Johnson's if he asked point-blank whether the Doctor had any objection to dining in the company of Wilkes; so he adopted a more subtle approach. On being invited by the bookseller Edward Dilly to meet Wilkes at dinner, he suggested that he should bring Johnson. Dilly demurred, but agreed when Boswell accepted full responsibility. The scene which followed is much too good to abbreviate:

"Mr. Dilly, sir, sends his respectful compliments to you, and would be happy if you would do him the honour to dine with him on Wednesday next along with me, as I must soon go to Scotland."

"Sir, I am obliged to Mr. Dilly. I will wait upon him——

"Provided, sir, I suppose, that the company which he is to have is agreeable to you."

"What do you mean, sir? What do you take me for? Do you think I am so ignorant of the world as to imagine that I am to prescribe to a gentleman what company he is to have at his table?"

"I beg your pardon, sir, for wishing to prevent you from meeting people whom you might not like. Perhaps he may have some of what he calls his patriotic friends with him."

"Well, sir, and what then? What care I for his *patriotic friends*? Poh!"

"I should not be surprised to find Jack Wilkes there."

"And if Jack Wilkes *should* be there, what is that to *me*, sir? My dear friend, let us have no more of this. I am sorry to be angry with you; but really it is treating me strangely to talk to me as if I could not meet any company whatever occasionally."

"Pray forgive me, sir: I meant well. But you shall meet whoever comes, for me."

It is easy to forget what we do not wish to remember. Johnson forgot his engagement to dine at Dilly's and arranged to have dinner at home that day with Anna Williams; so Boswell's diplomacy was again needed to persuade Anna to free him. At last she consented; Johnson bawled "Frank, a clean shirt"; and soon they were rumbling along to the city in a hackney-coach, Boswell exulting "as much as a fortune-hunter who has got an heiress into a post-chaise with him to set out for Gretna Green". There were one or two obnoxious 'patriots' at Dilly's and when Wilkes was pointed out to him Johnson had so much difficulty in maintaining his composure that he sat for some time on a window-seat pretending to read a book. Having boasted that he was equal to any sort of company, he could not very well make a scene because he had been asked to meet Wilkes. The latter placed himself next to Johnson at dinner and found a way to the Doctor's heart through his belly:

Mr. Wilkes was very assiduous in helping him to some fine veal. 'Pray give me leave, sir:—It is better here—A little of the brown—Some fat, sir—A little of the stuffing—Some gravy—Let me have the pleasure of giving you some butter—Allow me to recommend a squeeze of this orange—or the lemon, perhaps, may have more zest.'—'Sir, sir, I am obliged to you, sir,' cried Johnson, bowing, and turning his head to him with a look for some time of 'surly virtue', but, in a short while, of complacency.

After that all went well, and on the subject of Scotland both Wilkes and Johnson united in a chorus of sarcasm. When Boswell said that there was plenty of meat and drink in his native country, Johnson observed: "Why, yes, sir; meat and drink enough to give the inhabitants sufficient strength to run away from home." And when Boswell claimed the superiority of Scotland over England on one count, namely that no man could be arrested for debt there unless his creditor could swear that he was about to flee the country, Wilkes cut in: "That, I should think, may be safely sworn of all the Scotch nation."

Boswell's success in bringing the two men together was not his only achievement in the spring of 1776. He diligently made the acquaintance of Margaret Caroline Rudd, who, with two brothers named Perrau, had been tried for forgery a year earlier. The brothers were hanged, and it was commonly supposed that Mrs. Rudd's acquittal was due to her personal fascination, though she had informed against them. Her notoriety became considerable, and Boswell's instinct as a celebrity-hunter was on this occasion envied by Johnson, who said: "I should have visited her myself, sir, were it not that they have now a trick of putting everything into the newspapers." He was quite sincere about this, loving to see life in all its manifestations, and at about this time he surprised Mrs. Thrale by mentioning a female oddity he had once known.

"Bet Flint!" exclaimed Mrs. Thrale; "pray who is she?"

"Oh, a fine character, madam! She was habitually a slut and a drunkard, and occasionally a thief and a harlot."

"And, for heaven's sake, how came you to know her?"

"Why, madam, she figured in the literary world, too! Bet Flint wrote her own life, and called herself Cassandra, and it was in verse. It began:

> When Nature first ordained my birth,
> A diminutive I was born on earth,

And then I came from a dark abode,
Into a gay and gaudy world.

So Bet brought me her verses to correct; but I gave her half-a-crown and she liked it as well. Bet had a fine spirit; she advertised for a husband, but she had no success, for she told me no man aspired to her! Then she hired very handsome lodgings and a footboy; and she got a harpsichord, but Bet could not play; however, she put herself in fine attitudes, and drummed." But the drumming got on the nerves of a neighbouring 'jade', who indicted her for a nuisance; and then she stole a quilt from her landlord, who had her arrested. "But Bet Flint had a spirit not to be subdued; so when she felt herself obliged to go to jail, she ordered a sedan chair and bid her footboy walk before her. However, the footboy proved refractory, for he was ashamed, though his mistress was not. . . . When she came to her trial, the judge acquitted her. 'So now', she said to me, 'the quilt is my own, and now I'll make a petticoat of it.' Oh, I loved Bet Flint!"

When Boswell returned home his journal was filled with Johnson's sayings, two of which are not in harmony with modern democratic thought:

"It is better that some should be unhappy than that none should be happy, which would be the case in a general state of equality."

"The mode of government by one may be ill adapted to a small society, but is best for a great nation."

Another of his remarks contains the cynicism of truth:

"To act from pure benevolence is not possible for finite beings. Human benevolence is mingled with vanity, interest, or some other motive."

Concealing himself under the title of 'a gentleman', Boswell also recorded that when he was plying Robert Levett with questions, Johnson burst out: "Sir, you have but two topics, yourself and me. I am sick of both."

CHAPTER 21

Best and Worst

IT MAY PERHAPS BE SAID of most people that if religious
or political enthusiasm did not corrupt their minds and souls
they would all be more or less human. It can certainly be said
of Johnson that his mind and soul were impaired by his
religious and political feelings. His innate humanity, imaginative
sympathy, warm-hearted benevolence, exceptional intelligence
and solid sense were offset by a religious bigotry and a political
intolerance that reveal an acute internal discomfort. He longed
for absolute truth, for spiritual anchorage, for something by
which the validity of all things could be tested; yet the "obstinate
rationality" which prevented him from embracing the Roman
Catholic religion made him uncomfortable in any other. His
congenital scepticism was at war with his yearning for what was
durable, and the yells he emitted when his faith was questioned
were caused by his inner doubts. For the same reason that he
believed in what many people would have thought a diabolical
deity, he was a Tory in politics. Here again it was stability for
which he craved, something unchangeable like sunrise, and
nothing short of a cataclysm could change the Tories. His rage
against the Whigs was the counterpart of his rage against
agnostics, and the louder he shouted against both, the less
audible was the still small voice which told him that all of them
had a right to their opinions. He drowned his doubts with the
strength of his lungs.

Since there is no such striking example in history of a great
mind perverted by sectarianism, of a noble nature that could

be so ignoble, a proximate comparison of the best and worst in Johnson will illuminate his character more clearly than anything else. On the credit side, the outstanding feature of his nature was a deeply perceptive sympathy with the poor and unfortunate. "He loved the poor as I never yet saw anyone else do, with an earnest desire to make them happy," wrote Mrs. Thrale, adding that when someone questioned the use of giving halfpence to beggars, since they only spent it on gin and tobacco, Johnson gave the only civilised answer: "And why should they be denied such sweeteners of their existence? It is surely very savage to refuse them every possible avenue to pleasure, reckoned too coarse for our own acceptance. Life is a pill which none of us can bear to swallow without gilding; yet for the poor we delight in stripping it still barer, and are not ashamed to show even visible displeasure, if ever the bitter taste is taken from their mouths." He gave practical effect to his feeling by bestowing over two-thirds of his income on the needy, leaving himself about £75 a year. Innumerable poverty-stricken creatures came to his door for help, including distressed authors and bankrupt booksellers, and none were denied. Asked why he so constantly gave money to beggars, he replied: "Madam, to enable them to beg on." As he walked home in the early hours of the morning he made a habit of slipping pennies into the hands of children sleeping on stalls and doorsteps, so that on waking they could buy breakfast. He supported many who would otherwise have starved. One night he came across a woman lying in the street, too weak to walk. Taking her on his back, he carried her to his home, discovered she was a prostitute, looked after her until her health was restored, and then helped her to earn a different sort of living. When he had nothing left to give, he begged of his friends. Here is a typical letter to Bennet Langton:

I have an old Amanuensis in great distress. I have given what I think I can give, and begged till I cannot tell where to beg again. I put into his hands this morning four guineas. If you can collect three guineas more, it would clear him from his present difficulty.

The old amanuensis was probably Peyton, who had helped Johnson with the Dictionary and had been supported by him for many years. On 1st April 1776, a year after the above begging letter, Johnson announced the man's death to Mrs. Thrale in phrases that could have come from no other's pen:

> Poor Peyton expired this morning. He probably during many years, for which he sat starving by the bed of a wife, not only useless but almost motionless, condemned by poverty to personal attendance, and by the necessity of such attendance chained down to poverty—he probably thought often how lightly he should tread the path of life without his burthen. Of this thought the admission was unavoidable, and the indulgence might be forgiven to frailty and distress. His wife died at last, and before she was buried he was seized by a fever, and is now going to the grave.
>
> Such miscarriages, when they happen to those on whom many eyes are fixed, fill histories and tragedies; and tears have been shed for the sufferings, and wonder excited by the fortitude of those who neither did nor suffered more than Peyton.

Johnson's household at Bolt Court excited the surprise of his visitors. Robert Levett, Francis Barber and Anna Williams had been with him for years; but Barber now had a wife, and in addition to those four Johnson was able to give rooms to his godfather's daughter, Mrs. Desmoulins (to whom he also allowed half a guinea a week), to her daughter, and to a female known to us as Poll Carmichael. All these people were jealous of one another's position, each thinking that Johnson gave more attention to the rest, and their quarrels and complaints often made him glad to leave the house. On the other hand he got a lot of quiet fun out of their mutual hostility. "At her again, Poll! Never flinch, Poll!" he cried when Anna Williams was attacking Poll Carmichael. But he had to admit "Poll is a stupid slut; I had some hopes of her at first; but when I talked to her tightly and closely, I could make nothing of her; she was wiggle-waggle, and I could never persuade her to be categorical." Home-life in Bolt Court at the latter end of the 'seventies was full of conflict and comedy. We get glimpses of it in Johnson's letters to Mrs. Thrale:

14 Nov. '78. We have tolerable concord at home, but no love. Williams hates everybody. Levett hates Desmoulins and does not love Williams. Desmoulins hates them both. Poll loves none of them.

16 Oct. '79. Discord and discontent reign in my humble habitation as in the palaces of Monarchs.

7 Nov. '79. Discord keeps her residence in this habitation, but she has for some time been silent. We have much malice but no mischief. Levett is rather a friend to Williams, because he hates Desmoulins more; a thing that he should hate more than Desmoulins is not to be found.

16 Nov. '79. At home we do not much quarrel, but perhaps the less we quarrel the more we hate. There is as much malignity amongst us as can well subsist without any thought of daggers or poisons.

Mrs. Desmoulins, who suffered from dropsy, was in command of the kitchen; Anna Williams, who was blind, administered tea to Johnson's more favoured callers; Poll Carmichael contributed her quota of help or hindrance; and Levett bled and blistered the lot, while being disagreeable to all. Many of Johnson's other dependants have left no record of his charity, but it is known that he maintained a male cousin at Coventry and a female cousin in a lunatic asylum at Bethnal Green. He made a subsistence allowance to the inmates of his Bolt Court house, and, when at Streatham, he returned home nearly every week-end to make certain that they had three good dinners, treating them invariably with a courtesy that made them feel he was their dependant.

His consideration and tenderness were extended to the animal and piscine worlds. He once proclaimed that he would not sit at the table where a lobster that had been roasted alive was served, and he spoke with horror of the trade of butchering, though he was honest enough to add that "any one of us would kill a cow rather than not have beef". When in the Isle of Skye he borrowed a fishing-line and caught a few cuddies, each of which was instantly returned to the water; and so sensitive was he that he could not bear the sight of human bones which Boswell buried in a chapel. He was very fond of cats and always had one at home. "I once chid my wife for beating the cat before the maid," he told Mrs. Thrale because the maid might in future "treat puss with cruelty and plead her mistress's example". He used to go out and buy oysters for his cat, "lest the servants having that trouble should take a dislike to the poor creature," records Boswell, who, having an antipathy to cats, suffered much from the presence of one named Hodge:

> I recollect him one day scrambling up Dr. Johnson's breast, apparently with much satisfaction, while my friend, smiling and half-whistling, rubbed down his back, and pulled him by the tail; and when I observed he was a fine cat, saying, 'Why, yes, sir, but I have had cats whom I liked better than this;' and then as if perceiving Hodge to be out of countenance, adding, 'but he is a very fine cat, a very fine cat indeed.'

Boswell probably did not hear of an incident that had taken place in Wales, when Johnson's sentiment cost him a good dinner. While the party were staying with Colonel Middleton, the gardener caught a hare and brought it to his employer, who told him to take it to the cook. Johnson asked if he might hold the animal, which was placed in his arms. He went straight to the window, released the hare, and speeded its departure with alarming shouts. The Colonel complained that his table had been robbed of a delicacy. "So much the better, sir," said the Doctor, "for if your table is to be supplied at the expense of the laws of hospitality, I envy not the appetite of him who eats it. This, sir, is not a hare *ferae naturae*, but one which had placed itself under your protection; and savage indeed must be that man who does not make his hearth an asylum for the confiding stranger."

Johnson's feeling of kinship with all God's creatures made him hate the physiological experiments on animals that degrade surgical practice. He did not believe that the discoveries claimed by the vivisectionists had been of the least value; but even if they had conduced to the cure of illness or the alleviation of pain, he opposed them on the ground of common humanity. "It is time that universal resentment should arise against these horrid operations," he wrote in '*The Idler*', "which tend to harden the heart, extinguish those sensations which give man confidence in man, and make the physician more dreadful than the gout or stone." In Shakespeare's *Cymbeline* the Queen asks her doctor for certain drugs, which he provides:

Queen: I will try the forces
          Of these thy compounds on such creatures as
          We count not worth the hanging, but none human ...
Cornelius: Your highness
          Shall from this practice but make hard your heart.

Johnson agreed with the man of science: "There is in this passage nothing that much requires a note, yet I cannot forbear to push it forward into observation. The thought would probably have been more amplified, had our author lived to be shocked with such experiments as have been published in later times, by a race of men that have practised tortures without pity, and related them without shame, and are yet suffered to erect their heads among human beings."

From all of which it will be seen that Johnson was not the typical tough John Bull Englishman whom he has so often been supposed to represent, but a gentle, hypersensitive, compassionate, benevolent, superfine human being, with nothing of the bear but his skin, as Goldsmith perceived. While provocation and opposition ruffled him so much that his virtues vanished in rage, many of his opinions on public matters were enlightened. When Lord Kames asserted that war was occasionally a good thing because it called forth so much valour and virtue, Johnson exposed the shallowness of the argument: "A fire might as well be thought a good thing; there is the bravery and address of the firemen employed in extinguishing it; there is much humanity exerted in saving the lives and properties of the poor sufferers; yet after all this, who can say a fire is a good thing?" He dealt with the subject of war in *Rasselas*, where the inventor is made to say: "If men were all virtuous, I should with alacrity teach them all to fly. But what would be the security of the good if the bad could at pleasure invade them from the sky? Against an army sailing through the clouds, neither walls nor mountains nor seas could afford any security. A flight of northern savages might hover in the wind, and light at once with irresistible violence upon the capital of a fruitful region that was rolling under them."

Johnson's opinion of exploration was equally sane. Hearing from a correspondent in Connecticut that two ships had set sail for the Pole, he replied: "They hope to find an open ocean, but I suspect it is one mass of perpetual congelation. I do not much wish well to discoveries, for I am always afraid they will end in conquest and robbery." Sometimes he ejaculated opinions that would have been expected from John Wilkes but were unthinkable from Johnson, such as when he shocked a tableful of

Oxford dons with a toast: "Here's to the next insurrection of negroes in the West Indies!" Excusing a mob of starving rioters, he wrote: "Those who want the supports of life will seize them wherever they can be found." And the suppression of the Roman Catholics in Ireland drew this from him: "Let the authority of the English government perish, rather than be maintained by iniquity."

Such bright moments were offset by many instances of mental cloudiness, such as his belief in the divine right of property and the consequent necessity of female submission: "Consider of what importance to society the chastity of women is. Upon that all the property in the world depends. We hang a thief for stealing a sheep; but the unchastity of a woman transfers sheep and farm and all from the right owner. I have much more reverence for a common prostitute than for a woman who conceals her guilt. The prostitute is known. She cannot deceive. She cannot bring a strumpet into the arms of an honest man without his knowledge." The sacrosanctity of property was also implicit in his declaration that a woman should not marry a social inferior: "It is our duty to maintain the subordination of civilised society; and when there is a gross and shameful deviation from rank, it should be punished so as to deter others from the same perversion." It may be necessary in these days to say that Johnson was not being funny when he made such pronouncements; they expressed his dread of change, his passion for permanence. Although he admitted that "nobody at times talks more laxly than I do", he never relaxed on the theme of the American colonists. After one of his intemperate outbursts, Boswell said that he was always sorry to hear such views. Johnson bottled up his fury for a while, but he soon had an opportunity to uncork it. They were talking of a man who, unable to withstand the temptations of London, was running through his fortune there. "We must get him out of it," said Boswell. "All his friends must quarrel with him, and that will soon drive him away." The cork popped: "Nay, sir, we'll send *you* to him. If your company does not drive a man out of his house, nothing will."

We can dismiss as spasms of indignation certain of Johnson's remarks in Scotland about the religious reformers, *e.g.* that a dangerous steeple should not be demolished as "it may fall on some of the posterity of John Knox, and no great matter". But when his religion was slighted, however indirectly, he boiled over with malignant wrath. "A man who has settled his opinions does not love to have the tranquillity of his conviction disturbed," he wrote. But the tranquillity of the man who is convinced of the truth of his opinions cannot be disturbed, and Johnson's frequent rages prove that his convictions were gnawed by misgivings. His behaviour to Adam Smith is a case in point. The two men met on several occasions but were uncomfortable in each other's company. Once, when Smith was enthusiastically praising the beauty of Glasgow, Johnson cut him short with: "Pray, sir, have you ever seen Brentford?" But their temperamental divergences were insignificant compared with the cleavage in their beliefs; and when Smith stated in a published letter that David Hume had approached "as nearly to the idea of a perfectly wise and virtuous man as perhaps the nature of human frailty will permit", trouble was bound to ensue. Hume was the most notorious sceptic of his time, and not long before his death in 1776 Boswell went to see him, in the hope that on his deathbed he would renounce his infidelity and proclaim his belief in a future life. But Hume could not oblige Boswell and said that he did not fear the thought of extinction. This worried our James, who reported it to Johnson, who refused to believe in Hume's sincerity, forgetting in his heat that many ancient Greeks and Romans had died courageously without the consolations of Christianity. Nevertheless the possibility that the infidel was honest, coupled with Smith's testimony to Hume's wisdom and virtue, rankled in Johnson's mind and made it improbable that an encounter with Smith would pass off without friction. They met, and Johnson at once criticised Smith's account of Hume, to which Smith replied that he had fully vindicated its truth. "You lie!" shouted Johnson. A direct answer to such an accusation being difficult, Smith took the offensive: "You are a son of a bitch!" This closed the conversation.

We are told in the book of *Genesis* that God said "Let us make man in our own image, after our likeness." Man has reversed the procedure and made God in his own image after his likeness. The image of God which Johnson created was a reflection of his own fear, and was probably related to his ever-present dread of insanity. The subject therefore made him apprehensive, and he approached it with an awe that bordered on panic. Having mentally determined the form of faith that suited him, he disliked talking about it in public because he lived in terror of the scepticism of other people, which he had felt and fought within himself. Thus, in condemning the disbelief of others he was condemning his own, and the rage he exhibited against those who did not share his creed was rage against himself. This explains the spiritual harshness of a man whose nature was in most other respects the essence of charity. The worst recorded example of his religious rancour, and the most vivid illustration of his wrathful intolerance, was provided by Anna Seward, known as 'The Swan of Lichfield'. She was the daughter of Canon Seward and spent most of her life at the Bishop's Palace in the Cathedral Close of that city. Her poetry was much admired by a select circle of friends, and she became a figure of note in the literary world. She knew Johnson well, esteemed his genius but strongly disapproved of his prejudices in literature, his bigotry in religion and politics. Naturally courageous, she criticised his opinions and behaviour to his face, and because of her exceptional honesty he sometimes accepted her reproofs in silence.

On 15th April 1778, Johnson, Boswell, two clergymen, a well-known Quakeress named Mrs. Knowles, and Anna Seward dined with the brothers Edward and Charles Dilly at their house in the Poultry. An unpleasant scene took place between Johnson and Mrs. Knowles, a full report of which was made that same evening by Anna Seward. The notes in Boswell's journal were fragmentary, and though he admits that Johnson was in a passion and used "the severest terms of reproach", his account of the episode is relatively mild and gives the Doctor the best of the argument. As he arrived at the party in what he calls "high spirits," we may assume that his spirits became higher, his memory less reliable, as the dinner progressed. After Johnson's death Boswell spoke to Anna Seward of "the ferocious, reasonless and unchristian violence of his idol" on that occasion, and begged for her account of what had taken place, which he knew she had written down at the time. She sent it, but he neither published nor referred to it in the *Life*, unscrupulously ignoring a scene that shows his hero at his worst and gives a more lifelike description of Johnson in a violent temper than anything of the kind in his own biography.

The subject of dispute was a girl named Jenny Harry, who had forfeited her father's love together with an inheritance of a hundred thousand pounds by leaving the Church of England and becoming a Quaker. Johnson had often seen her at the house of her guardian, and had appeared to be fond of her. But when she joined the Society of Friends and resided with Mrs. Knowles, he was furious. One day she met him in the street and stopped to ask how he was. He cut her dead and marched scornfully on. She went home in tears and begged Mrs. Knowles to plead for her. Mrs. Knowles did so, at the dinner-table of the Dillys. But before the subject came up Johnson had been ruffled by several topics. One was an argument by Mrs. Knowles in favour of the equality of the sexes. Another concerned the American colonists; and having pronounced that he was "willing to love all mankind, *except an American*", Johnson whipped himself into a passion, called the Americans rascals, robbers, pirates, and said he would burn and destroy them. Anna Seward's mild comment failed to soothe him: "Sir, this is an instance that we are always most violent against those whom we have injured." He gave forth another volley of vituperation, which made him feel better, and for a while calmness prevailed. But the question of death being raised, he manifested uneasiness, and he was not in a pliable mood when Mrs. Knowles began to intercede for the youthful Quakeress, her gentle, patient, conciliatory manner, so much at variance with his own, adding fuel to his flame:

"I am to ask thy indulgence, Doctor, towards a gentle female to whom thou usest to be kind, and who is uneasy at the loss of that kindness. Jenny Harry weeps at the consciousness that thou wilt not speak to her."

"Madam, I hate the odious wench, and desire you will not talk to me about her."

"Yet what is her crime, Doctor?"

"Apostasy, madam; apostasy from the community in which she was educated."

"Surely the quitting one community for another cannot be a crime, if it is done from motives of conscience. Hadst thou been educated in the Romish church, I must suppose thou wouldst have abjured its errors, and that there would have been merit in the abjuration."

"Madam, if I had been educated in the Roman Catholic faith, I believe I should have questioned my right to quit the religion of my fathers; therefore, well may I hate the arrogance of a young wench, who sets herself up for a judge on theological points, and deserts the religion in whose bosom she was nurtured."

"She has not done so; the name and the faith of Christians are not denied to the sectaries."

"If the name is not, the common sense is."

"I will not dispute this point with thee, Doctor, at least at present; it would carry us too far. Suppose it granted that, in the mind of a young girl, the weaker arguments appeared the

253

strongest, her want of better judgment should excite thy pity, not thy resentment."

"Madam, it has my anger and my contempt, and always will have them."

"Consider, Doctor, she must be *sincere*. Consider what a noble fortune she has sacrificed."

"Madam, madam, I have never taught myself to consider that the association of folly can extenuate guilt."

"Ah, Doctor! we cannot rationally suppose that the Deity will not pardon a defect in judgment (supposing it should prove one) in that breast where the consideration of serving him, according to its idea, in spirit and truth, has been a preferable inducement to that of worldly interest."

"Madam, I pretend not to set bounds to the mercy of the Deity; but I hate the wench, and shall ever hate her. I hate all impudence; but the impudence of a chit's apostasy I *nauseate*."

"Jenny is a very gentle creature. She trembles to have offended her parent, though far removed from her presence; she grieves to have offended her guardian; and she is sorry to have offended Dr. Johnson, whom she loved, admired, and honoured."

"Why, then, madam, did she not consult the man whom she pretends to have loved, admired, and honoured, upon her new-fangled scruples? If she had looked up to that man with any degree of the respect she professes, she would have supposed his ability to judge of fit and right at least equal to that of a raw wench just out of her primer."

"Ah, Doctor! remember it was not from amongst the witty and the learned that Christ selected his disciples, and constituted the teachers of his precepts. Jenny thinks Dr. Johnson great and good; but she also thinks the gospel demands and enjoins a simpler form of worship than that of the established church; and that it is not in wit and eloquence to supersede the force of what appears to her a plain and regular system, which cancels all typical and mysterious ceremonies, as fruitless and even idolatrous; and asks only obedience to its injunctions, and the ingenuous homage of a devout heart."

"The homage of a fool's head, madam, you should say, if you will pester me about the ridiculous wench."

"If thou choosest to suppose her ridiculous, thou canst not deny that she has been religious, sincere, disinterested. Canst thou believe that the gate of Heaven will be shut to the tender and pious mind, whose *first* consideration has been that of apprehended duty?"

"Pho, pho, madam, who says it will?"

"Then if Heaven shuts not its gate, shall man shut his heart? If the Deity accept the homage of such as sincerely serve him under every form of worship, Dr. Johnson and this humble girl will, it is to be hoped, meet in a blessed eternity, whither human animosity must *not* be carried."

"Madam, I am not fond of meeting fools anywhere; they are detestable company, and while it is in my power to avoid conversing with them, I certainly shall exert that power; and so you may tell the odious wench whom you have persuaded to think herself a saint, and of whom you will, I suppose, make a preacher; but I shall take care she does not preach to *me*."

At the last thunder-clap Mrs. Knowles smiled as one who could tolerate even intolerance, and Boswell whispered to Anna Seward: "I never saw this mighty lion so chafed before."

CHAPTER 22

Tremendous Talks

WHEN Boswell said that he was in high spirits, he usually meant that he was inebriated, and this condition became more frequent as he grew older. It was always succeeded by low spirits, accompanied by remorse and resolutions to reform, followed by another burst of high spirits. From London he occasionally visited his friend Temple at Mamhead, where he solemnly vowed himself to sobriety. General Paoli made him promise not to taste fermented liquor for a year; and as he was more of a quaffer than a taster, it might be said that the promise was kept. His business as a barrister steadily declined as his temptation to drink increased, and the more he drank the more he drabbed. Quarrels with his wife became frequent. With a fatuity that would not be believed of anyone else, he showed her a portion of his journal describing several of his sordid affairs, and was shocked when she divined the import of certain cryptic passages in Greek lettering. His "high spirits" were noticeable in the courts, in the streets, on social occasions, at solemn events such as a funeral, and sometimes led him to make advances to his wife's young female relations. His father's attitude to him became more constrained, and early in 1777 he lamented that his wife and children were never invited to stay at Auchinleck. But he felt compensated for his father's coolness by Johnson's invitation that he and his wife should take up their residence in Bolt Court. For some time Johnson had been joking about Margaret Boswell's distaste for his company, but after she sent him a jar of marmalade in July 1777 the joke appeared to be over, and the moment he heard of her serious illness he asked them both to regard his home as theirs. But James could not leave Edinburgh and for a while they stayed in the country just outside the city.

Heartily sick of his company in the north, Boswell kept up a regular correspondence with his friends in the south, taking far more interest in London events than in the happenings of Edinburgh. One episode made a special appeal to him, and Johnson gave him the details at their next meeting. A famous clergyman, Dr. William Dodd, was sentenced to death for forgery. Dodd had done well for himself in the matter of preferments and had earned the name of 'Dr. Simony' in one of Foote's farces. Popular as a preacher, petted in society, and appointed a chaplain to the King, he found his income insufficient for his needs and he forged the name of his one-time pupil Lord Chesterfield on a bond of about £4,000. Chesterfield did not display the gratitude towards his former tutor that might have been expected from a lover of learning, and testified against Dodd, who had also incurred the displeasure of George III by his efforts to obtain the living of St. George's, Hanover Square. The jury recommended mercy, which was backed by a petition signed by over twenty thousand people. Although Dodd had only met Johnson once, and had thought him "the oddest and most peculiar fellow I ever saw", he got the Countess of Harrington to apply for Johnson's help. An appeal to the Doctor's humanity was seldom unsuccessful, and though it is clear he did not think much of the clergyman's character he wrote personal appeals for clemency to the Lord Chancellor and the Lord Chief Justice, as well as similar entreaties in Dodd's name to the King, in Mrs. Dodd's name to the Queen, and on behalf of the city of London to the King. He also wrote Dodd's speech to the Recorder of London before sentence of death, and a sermon by Dodd delivered "to his unhappy brethren" in the chapel of Newgate prison. In spite of all, Dodd was hanged at the end of June 1777, and his posthumous work *Thoughts in Prison* impressed everyone except Johnson, who doubted Dodd's sincerity in praying for the monarch: "Sir, do you think that a man, the night before he is to be hanged, cares for the succession of a royal family?" He thought it possible that "a man who has been canting all his life may cant to the last", but not probable: "A man who has been refused a pardon after so much petitioning would hardly be praying thus fervently for the King."

For material reasons Boswell could not visit London in 1777, but for spiritual reasons he could not let a year go by without seeing Johnson. They had talked of a journey up the Baltic, and Boswell had visions of his eminent friend's reception by the King of Sweden and the Empress of Russia, but in September 1777, Johnson announced to Mrs. Thrale that Boswell "shrinks from the Baltic expedition," and the most they could do was to meet that month at Ashbourne, where they spent ten days together at the house of John Taylor. Before leaving home on his annual excursion, Johnson sent Anna Williams into the country for her health. He reported her to be "very ill of a pituitous defluxion", and so peevish from age, sickness and pride that "I was forced to bribe the maid to stay with her, by a secret stipulation of half a crown a week over her wages". Johnson himself had not been well early in the year, and a surgeon relieved him of twelve ounces of blood. Hopeful of further relief, Johnson called Francis Barber to his assistance and reopened the orifice, but so awkwardly that he lost a total of thirty-six ounces before they stopped the flow with the help of Levett.

Nevertheless he was in excellent form at Ashbourne, where Boswell thought him "more uniformly social, cheerful, and alert, than I had almost ever seen him". Though benefiting from its occasional practice, he disapproved of phlebotomy as a regular system because it was not Nature's method of evacuation; and when Taylor confessed that he did not like taking emetics for fear of breaking some small blood-vessels,

Johnson puffed with derision: "Poh! if you have so many things that will break, you had better break your neck at once, and there's an end on't. You will break no small vessels." Life at Ashbourne was tedious because the interests of Taylor and his neighbours did not extend beyond their locality. Johnson enlivened them one evening by attacking the Hanoverian monarchy and defending the Stuarts. Taylor, a Whig, "was roused by this to a pitch of bellowing," but Johnson's lungs were in good condition and he held forth at length, the cattle of Ashbourne being temporarily forgotten in a wordy warfare on kings. One day Johnson and Boswell drove over to Derby, visiting Kedleston Hall on the way. Struck by the magnificence of the place, Boswell said: "One should think that the proprietor of all this *must* be happy." Johnson was not so sure: "Nay, sir, all this excludes but one evil—poverty." When Boswell got home and reported the saying to his wife, she observed: "It is true, all this excludes only one evil; but how much good does it let in." After being shown over the Hall, they proceeded to Derby, where they inspected the china factory. What made Boswell such good company was his delight in the pageant of human existence, which he expressed perfectly in his account of this visit:

I felt a pleasure in walking about Derby such as I always have in walking about any town to which I am not accustomed. There is an immediate sensation of novelty; and one speculates on the way in which life is passed in it, which, although there is a sameness everywhere upon the whole, is yet minutely diversified. The minute diversities in everything are wonderful.

On their drive back Johnson advised Boswell to drink water instead of wine, but Boswell never considered a dinner-table the right place for water. A day or two later he signified his discontent with Scotland, his wish to settle in London, and Johnson gave reasons both for and against the project, while admitting that "when a man is tired of London, he is tired of life, for there is in London all that life can afford". The subject of acting cropped up, and Johnson scouted the notion of paying respect to a player: "What, sir, a fellow who claps a hump on his back and a lump on his leg and cries 'I am Richard the Third'!" Boswell defended the profession: "*Who* can repeat Hamlet's soliloquy 'To be or not to be' as Garrick does it?" Johnson pointed to an eight-year-old boy, saying: "Anybody may. Jemmy there will do it in a week." Boswell had a ready reply: "No, no, sir; and as a proof of the merit of great acting, and of the value which mankind set upon it, Garrick has got a hundred thousand pounds." But Johnson was not to be beaten: "Is getting a hundred thousand pounds a proof of excellence? That has been done by a scoundrel commissary." Their sojourn with Taylor did not pass off without friction. In an unguarded moment Boswell said he wished he could see Johnson and Mrs. Macaulay together, knowing there would be a good sparring match. "No, sir," said Johnson angrily, "you would not see us quarrel to make you sport. Don't you know that it is very uncivil to *pit* two people against one another?" But on the whole Johnson was in a relaxed mood, and we are treated to a pastoral detail in what Boswell calls "the Flemish picture" of his friend:

> One morning after breakfast, when the sun shone bright, we walked out together, and 'pored' for some time with placid indolence upon an artificial water-fall, which Dr. Taylor had made by building a strong dyke of stone across the river behind the garden. It was now somewhat obstructed by branches of trees and other rubbish, which had come down the river and settled close to it. Johnson, partly from a desire to see it play more freely, and partly from that inclination to activity which will animate at times the most inert and sluggish mortal, took a long pole which was lying on a bank,

and pushed down several parcels of this wreck with painful assiduity, while I stood quietly by, wondering to behold the sage thus curiously employed, and smiling with an humorous satisfaction each time when he carried his point. He worked till he was quite put of breath; and having found a large dead cat so heavy that he could not move it after several efforts, 'Come,' he said (throwing down the pole), 'you shall take it now'; which I accordingly did, and being a fresh man, soon made the cat tumble over the cascade.

The evening before Boswell's departure was diversified with tunes played on the fiddle by several guests. Boswell told Johnson that music affected him to such a degree that at one moment he shed tears, at another he wanted to rush into the thickest part of a battle. "Sir, I should never hear it, if it made me such a fool," was the discouraging comment. Late that night, a serenely autumnal one, they stood together in the garden surveying the stars, and aware that Johnson was in a complacent mood Boswell raised the subject of a future state. Johnson thought that it would be possible to offend God, and so be punished, even in the next world, though some of the scriptural texts "may admit of a mitigated interpretation". Later still Johnson dictated his thoughts on slavery to Boswell, who then said that he was afraid he had kept the Doctor up too late. "No, sir, I don't care though I sit all night with you," replied the other; and all would have ended happily if Boswell, either maliciously or fatuously, had not spoken in favour of the American right to resist taxation. This threw Johnson into a state of violent agitation, and after a heated contest they were "very willing to separate and go to bed". But next morning Johnson was placid, and they bade one another an affectionate farewell, Boswell taking a post-chaise from the Green Man Inn, the mistress of which was "a mighty civil gentlewoman". His journal was full of Johnson's talk, from which we must extract one piece of wisdom:

"A man will please more upon the whole by negative qualities than by positive, by never offending than by giving a great deal of delight. In the first place, men hate more steadily than they love; and if I have said something to hurt a man once, I shall not get the better of this by saying many things to please him."

And one foretaste of things to come:

"Alas, sir, what a mass of confusion should we have if every bishop and every judge, every lawyer, physician and divine, were to write books."

Boswell had been brooding on his fits of melancholia, and with his usual adaptability of mind had found in this constitutional defect an excuse for his many lapses from virtue. His dipsomania, his lechery, his general infirmity of purpose, were the inevitable results of his hypochondria. It was a comforting explanation. As a rule he was able to satisfy his masochistic love of self-mortification in his journal; but now he felt the need of public disclosure, and in October 1777 he began a series of essays on 'The Hypochondriack' which continued to appear in *The London Magazine*, a periodical in which he had a financial interest, for six years. These confessions and absolutions cleansed his bosom of much perilous stuff and enabled him to regard himself as 'a case', as one whose vices were due to an affliction he could not control and whose emotions were more keenly engaged than those of less imaginative and therefore less vulnerable folk. The more sensitive the plant, the easier its pollution. The higher the growth, the lower the fall. Altogether an agreeable solution of an awkward problem.

The commencement of these essays made him feel that he was destined for bigger things, and in March 1778 he wrote a flattering letter to Edmund Burke, the sole object of which was to get himself appointed to the commission recently authorised by Parliament to discuss peace terms with the Americans: "I am to be in London this spring, and if his Majesty should ask me what I would choose, my answer will be, to assist at the compact between Britain and America." It is doubtful whether George III ever heard of the opportunity he had missed; and as Boswell spent a good deal of that spring listening to the conversation of Johnson, he was much better employed than in wasting his time as a parliamentary commissioner, though the ostensible cause of his visit was as counsel opposing a Road Bill at the bar of the House of Commons.

He arrived in London on March 18th and remained there until 19th May, during which period he stayed at General Paoli's house and reported conversations more fully than at any other time. It is the biographer's duty to select those sayings and episodes which most clearly illuminate his theme, to separate a handful of grain from a bushel of husk. Boswell found Johnson very much taken up with the Thrales but always pleased to see him either in London or at Streatham. A man who knew Johnson well once said to him: "Sir, you are like a ghost; you never speak till you are spoken to." The probability is that Johnson's conversation was so constant and remarkable that his silences were impressive and memorable. Normally he was readier to talk than most intelligent men, and his objection to John Wesley was that "he is never at leisure; he is always obliged to go at a certain hour. This is very disagreeable to a man who loves to fold his legs and have out his talk, as I do." Writing was a labour for Johnson, talking a pleasure. It surprised him that so many people had written so much when they need not have written at all, but "that people should endeavour to excel in conversation, I do not wonder, because in conversation praise is instantly reverberated". He was at the top of his form as a talker in the late 'seventies, and Boswell took full advantage of it. His exceptional sanity appears in such remarks as these:

"It is more from carelessness about truth than from intentional lying that there is so much falsehood in the world."

"From my experience I have found them (mankind) worse in commercial dealings, more disposed to cheat, than I had any notion of; but more disposed to do one another good than I had conceived."

After saying that "every man thinks meanly of himself for not having been a soldier, or not having been to sea", he went on: "Were Socrates and Charles the Twelfth of Sweden both present in any company, and Socrates to say 'Follow me and hear a lecture on philosophy', and Charles, laying his hand on his sword, to say 'Follow me and dethrone the Czar', a man would be ashamed to follow Socrates. Sir, the impression is universal; yet it is strange . . . Mankind reverence those who have got over fear, which is so general a weakness."

"Nobody has a right to put another under such a difficulty that he must either hurt the person by telling the truth or hurt himself by telling what is not true."

"All censure of a man's self is oblique praise. It is in order to show how much he can spare."

"How little does travelling supply to the conversation of any man who has travelled."

Part of Johnson's charm as a talker was his ability to give his mind to any subject that came up, however seemingly trivial. Breakfasting with Boswell one day, he said that the only "little thing" he could have done in life was to play the fiddle. Without pausing to enquire whether a young Austrian named Mozart, then aged twenty-two, would have agreed that fiddle-playing was a little thing, we will allow Johnson to continue: "Had I learnt to fiddle, I should have done nothing else."

"Pray, sir, did you ever play on any musical instrument?" enquired Boswell.

"No, sir; I once bought me a flagelet, but I never made out a tune."

"A flagelet, sir!—so small an instrument? I should have liked to hear you play on the violincello. *That* should have been *your* instrument."

"Sir, I might as well have played on the violincello as another; but I should have done nothing else. No, sir; a man would never undertake great things, could he be amused with small. I once tried knotting . . . but I could not learn it."

Boswell was now a fairly regular guest at Streatham, and was trying to wheedle Mrs. Thrale into providing him with Johnson's sayings; but she refused to be coaxed. She had read his journal of the Hebridean tour with Johnson, who had confided in her: "One would think the man had been hired to be a spy upon me," and she had no wish to assist Boswell's espionage. But while on the spot he did not need her help, and he was able to deal with a famous scene which took place in her drawing-room. He wanted Johnson's opinion on the best English sermons, and Johnson enlarged upon those of half a dozen divines. Boswell broke in with the apparently innocent comment: "I like Ogden's *Sermons on Prayer* very much, both for neatness of style and subtlety of reasoning." He had plagued Johnson with Ogden while they were together in Scotland, and the present introduction of the subject must have riled the Doctor, who dismissed it with: "I should like to read all that Ogden has written." As there were no insuperable obstacles to his reading all that Ogden had published, it seems improbable that his anxiety to do so was burdensome. Boswell continued the discussion: "What I wish to know is, what sermons afford the best specimens of English pulpit eloquence?" Johnson replied rather irritably: "We have no sermons addressed to the passions that are good for anything, if you mean that kind of eloquence." At this point a clergyman, whose name Boswell could not remember, piped up: "Were not Dodd's sermons addressed to the passions?" The combination of Dr. Dodd, whose character he disliked, with Ogden, whose very name must have rasped his nerves, caused an explosion: "They were nothing, sir, be they addressed to what they may." The stunned cleric no doubt wondered, after recovering from the shock, how he had provoked the thunderbolt.

Another clergyman, Dr. Thomas Percy, got into hot water a few days later, when Johnson and Boswell were his guests.

Though friendly over many years, Johnson did not think highly of Percy, actually allowing the parson to be misled about certain facts in his life. Percy is now remembered as the discoverer of many old songs and ballads which he published in *Reliques of Ancient English Poetry*, but in those days he was chiefly known as a lively and sociable fellow whose main concern was to establish his descent from the Earls of Northumberland and his relationship with the living Earl, whose chaplain he was. When the tiff with Johnson occurred he was about to become Dean of Carlisle. They were discussing Thomas Pennant's account of his travels in Scotland, and Johnson praised the book highly. But Pennant had written unfavourably of Alnwick Castle and its grounds, and Percy resented criticism of anything concerned with the Northumberland family; so Johnson teased him with the remark: "Pennant, in what he has said of Alnwick, has done what he intended ; he has made you very angry." Following several warm exchanges, Percy shifted the ground: "Pennant does not describe well; a carrier who goes along the side of Loch Lomond would describe it better." "I think he describes very well." "I travelled after him." "And *I* travelled after him." "But, my good friend, you are shortsighted, and do not see so well as I do." Johnson said nothing for a while, but, as Boswell said, "inflammable particles were collecting for a cloud to burst," and when Percy again disparaged Pennant the deluge descended:

"This is the resentment of a narrow mind, because he did not find everything in Northumberland."

"Sir, you may be as rude as you please."

"Hold, sir! Don't talk of rudeness; remember, sir, you told me I was short-sighted. We have done with civility. We are to be as rude as we please."

"Upon my honour, sir, I did not mean to be uncivil."

"I cannot say so, sir, for I *did* mean to be uncivil, thinking *you* had been uncivil."

Percy jumped up, hastened to Johnson, took him by the hand,

and spoke words of affectionate assuagement; upon which Johnson, completely mollified, declared: "My dear sir, I am willing you shall *hang* Pennant."

As one of those present was known to the Northumberland family, and might report Johnson's behaviour to the detriment of their host, Percy begged Boswell to mention this to Johnson, who at once wrote a highly complimentary letter about Percy, which Boswell was able to read aloud at dinner with General Paoli, among whose guests was Earl Percy.

Not all of Boswell's own contests ended so happily. Having catechised Johnson too closely one day, he received a broadside: "I will not be put to the question. Don't you consider, sir, that these are not the manners of a gentleman? I will not be baited with *what* and *why*; what is this? what is that? why is a cow's tail long? why is a fox's tail bushy?" Boswell had a weak excuse: "Why, sir, you are so good that I venture to trouble you." Johnson had a strong reproof: "Sir, my being so *good* is no reason why you should be so *ill*."

But Johnson was in a benignant frame of mind when Boswell called on Good Friday, 17th April, a day made memorable by a phrase. When they emerged from St. Clement's Church after the morning service, an old fellow-collegian named Oliver Edwards accosted Johnson, and all three walked together to Bolt Court. Edwards, now a farmer at Stevenage, had not met Johnson for close on fifty years, and they exchanged reminiscences. Johnson quoted some Latin, and Edwards said: "You are a philosopher, Dr. Johnson. I have tried too in my time to be a philosopher; but, I don't know how, cheerfulness was always breaking in." Before they separated Edwards said that he was old: sixty-five. Johnson could beat that, and cried: "Come, sir, drink water, and put in for a hundred."

The next day Boswell again called at Bolt Court and was shown the drawing-room, which he thought "very genteelly fitted up". Johnson informed him that "Mrs. Thrale sneered when I talked of my having asked you and your lady to live

at my house. I was obliged to tell her that you would be in as
respectable a situation in my house as in hers. Sir, the insolence
of wealth will creep out". Three days later the friends went in
a hackney-coach to dine with General Paoli, stopping on the
way at the corner of St. James's Place, where for the sake of his
appearance Johnson bought a pair of silver buckles at a toy-
shop. During dinner the possibility of a French army landing
in England was discussed. There had been invasion scares for
more than a year owing to the friendship between the French
and the Americans, and Johnson was utterly sick of the subject,
having forcibly expressed his feelings at Streatham: "What
signifies all this canting? The world goes on just as it did. Who
eats the less, or who sleeps the worse? or where is all this *consternation* you talk of, but in the newspapers? Nobody is thinking
or feeling about the matter, otherwise than 'tis something to
talk about." He declared that the cackle about an invasion
spoilt all his pleasure in the conversation of his friends. But as
so few people have anything interesting to say, invasion scares,
general elections, wars, earthquakes and interplanetary turmoil
give the majority something outside themselves to chatter about.
Johnson preferred to hear them on themselves; and when Mrs.
Thrale complained that she was worn out listening to a silly
woman who could talk of nothing but her personal concerns, he
rebuked her: "Madam, why do you blame the woman for the
only sensible thing she could do—talking of her family and her
affairs? For how should a woman who is as empty as a drum
talk upon any other subject? If you speak to her of the sun,
she does not know it rises in the east—if you speak to her of the
moon, she does not know it changes at the full—if you speak to
her of the Queen, she does not know she is the King's wife.
How, then, can you blame her for talking of her family and
affairs?" At General Paoli's he stopped the invasion prattle by
saying that "mutual cowardice keeps us in peace. Were one
half of mankind brave, and one half cowards, the brave would
be always beating the cowards. Were all brave, they would

lead a very uneasy life; all would be continually fighting. But being all cowards, we go on very well". Elsewhere he confessed that he had "no delight in talking of public affairs," which he said vexed no man. Boswell having expressed concern over the state of the nation, Johnson advised him to clear his mind of cant.

Early in May there was a big dinner-party at the house of Sir Joshua Reynolds. According to Boswell, less attention was paid to Johnson than usual, with the result that on some pretext he rounded on his biographer, who took it ill and kept away from him for a week. At their next meeting Boswell complained of his treatment before so many unsympathetic people, and Johnson apologised, saying: "Well, I am sorry for it. I'll make it up to you twenty different ways, as you please." Incidentally, Johnson thought himself "a very polite man", and though the description would not have struck his friends as peculiarly apt, it was true of him in tranquil mood. Unfortunately his tranquillity was easily disturbed, and not long after his apology to Boswell the midnight calm of Streatham was rudely stirred by an argument between them, Johnson maintaining that vice did not hurt a man's reputation in the world, Boswell disagreeing:

"A man is chosen Knight of the Shire, not the less for having debauched ladies," said Johnson.

"What, sir, if he debauched the ladies of gentlemen in the county, will there not be a general resentment against him?"

"No, sir. He will lose those particular gentlemen, but the rest will not trouble their heads about it."

"Well, sir, I cannot think so."

"Nay, sir, there is no talking with a man who will dispute what everybody knows."

Johnson then mentioned Lord Clive as one who had been loaded with honours and wealth, yet "had acquired his fortune by such crimes that his consciousness of them impelled him to cut his throat"; but Boswell demurred:

"You will recollect, sir, that Dr. Robertson said he cut his throat because he was weary of still life, little things not being sufficient to move his great mind."

As Johnson had a decided penchant for little things, few remarks could have fretted him more, and he blew up:

"Nay, sir, what stuff is this! You had no more this opinion after Robertson said it than before. I know nothing more offensive than repeating what one knows to be foolish things, by way of continuing a dispute, to see what a man will answer—to make him your butt!"

"My dear sir, I had no such intentions as you seem to suspect; I had not indeed. Might not this nobleman have felt everything 'weary, stale, flat, and unprofitable', as Hamlet says?"

"Nay, if you are to bring in gabble, I'll talk no more. I will not, upon my honour."

In order to floor Robertson, Boswell and Clive, he made Shakespeare take the knock.

Johnson seemed to be in martial mood just then, for soon after Boswell's departure from London he spent a week in Warley Camp with Bennet Langton, now a captain in the Lincolnshire militia. He slept in a tent, accompanied an officer on the nightly rounds, closely watched the drilling of the men, observed the musket-practice, made enquiries about ammunition, and attended a court martial. As usual the practical details interested him, the "little things" of everyday Army life; but his opinion of soldiering in peacetime had already been given in the book about his Scottish journey: "It must however be confessed that a man who places honour only in successful violence is a very troublesome and pernicious animal in time of peace, and that the martial character cannot prevail in a whole people but by the diminution of all other virtues." It is, by the way, to Bennet Langton that we are indebted for several of Johnson's hightly characteristic comments:

"Sir, among the anfractuosities of the human mind, I know not if it may not be one, that there is a superstitious reluctance to sit for a picture."

(Johnson loved the sound of long words with Latin derivations and introduced not a few into the common English speech. Boswell recalls an occasion when he said of *The Beggar's Opera*: "There is in it such a labefactation of all principles, as may be injurious to morality." His listeners suffered from suppressed laughter).

"Every man has a right to utter what he thinks truth, and every other man has a right to knock him down for it. Martyrdom is the test."

Anxious to recommend his brother to Johnson's attention, a man said: "When we have sat together some time, you'll find my brother grow very entertaining." Said Johnson: "Sir, I can wait."

Best of all, his retort to a Thames boatman who had addressed him in the sort of language that can only be used with safety on the water: "Sir, your wife, under pretence of keeping a bawdy-house, is a receiver of stolen goods."

Although Boswell's conversational methods frequently got on Johnson's nerves, the older man had much affection for the younger; indeed, we may say that Johnson was much more of a father to Boswell than Boswell's father. The chief merit of the young Scot was a liveliness of disposition in company, a virtue which made him so popular that Johnson said he "never left a house without leaving a wish for his return". But in his letters and sometimes in talk Boswell exhibited his melancholy, his lack of constancy, and it was Johnson's belief that "if a man talks of his misfortunes, there is something in them that is not disagreeable to him; for where there is nothing but pure misery, there never is any recourse to the mention of it". So in a letter he advised his young friend: "When any fit of anxiety, or gloominess, or perversion of mind, lays hold upon you, make it a rule not to publish it by complaints, but exert your whole care to hide it; by endeavouring to hide it, you will drive it away. Be always busy." Boswell having repeated that he was worried by the 'black dog' at home, Johnson told him "to get rid of all intellectual excesses, and neither to exalt your pleasures, nor aggravate your vexations, beyond their real and natural state". More whinings from Boswell brought this:

> You are always complaining of melancholy, and I conclude from these complaints that you are fond of it. No man talks of that which he is desirous to conceal, and every man desires to conceal that of which he is ashamed ... Make it an invariable and obligatory law to yourself, never to mention your own mental diseases; if you are never to speak of them, you will think on them but little, and if you think little of them, they will molest you rarely. When you talk of them, it is plain that you want either praise or pity; for praise there is no room, and pity will do you no good; therefore from this hour speak no more, think no more, about them.

If he could not be depressed naturally, Boswell was sufficiently in love with gloom to worry himself with insoluble problems, receiving a sharp rap from his monitor:

> I hoped you had got rid of all this hypocrisy of misery. What have you to do with Liberty and Necessity? Or what more than to hold your tongue about it? Do not doubt that I shall be most heartily glad to see you again, for I love every part about you but your affectation of distress.

Boswell's second son was born towards the end of 1778, three years after his first, and he now felt satisfied that the male succession of Auchinleck was secured. In March 1779 he managed to visit London, but he was "unaccountably negligent in preserving Johnson's sayings", partly perhaps because he was again suffering from ingrowing toe-nails. Late in April he was laid up with an inflamed foot, both Johnson and Reynolds calling at Paoli's house in South Audley Street to cheer him up. He retrieved one oft-quoted remark by

Johnson at a dinner-party. Speaking with contempt of claret, which he said would drown a man before it made him drunk, Johnson was persuaded to try a glass, which did not change his opinion: "Poor stuff! No, sir, claret is the liquor for boys, port for men, but he who aspires to be a hero must drink brandy."

On his way home Boswell stayed at Southill, near Bedford, the home of John Dilly, elder brother of the two publishers, whose family had owned land in that neighbourhood for two centuries. He travelled onwards by coach from Buckden, his journey made comfortable by the fact that "an agreeable young widow nursed me and supported my lame foot on her knee. Am I not fortunate in having something about me that interests most people at first sight in my favour"? The normal expression of his face being semi-comic, semi-serious, nearly everybody found something attractive in him at first sight. An exception was Edward Gibbon, the historian of Rome, now a member of The Club. "He is an ugly, affected, disgusting fellow, and poisons our literary club to me," wrote Boswell to Temple. No doubt the dislike was fully reciprocated by Gibbon, who was also antipathetic to Johnson.

Over two months passed before Boswell communicated with Johnson, who anxiously asked: "Is it a fit of humour that has disposed you to try who can hold out longest without writing? If it be, you have the victory." Boswell admitted that he had suffered in the past from long intervals of silence on Johnson's part, and had taken advantage of a fit of indolence "to try whether your affection for me would, after an unusual silence on my part, make you write first". This made Johnson peevish. "Remember that all tricks are either knavish or childish," he wrote, "and that it is as foolish to make experiments upon the constancy of a friend, as upon the chastity of a wife."

Boswell had a friend, Colonel James Stuart, who in the autumn of 1779 was recruiting a regiment in Scotland. He asked Boswell to accompany him to Leeds, London and elsewhere. As the Colonel was a convivial soul, and this would mean another instalment of Johnson within a year, Boswell leapt at the invitation. But the record he kept was scant, and little is worth our attention except Johnson's unexpected attack on Roman Catholics ("In everything in which they differ from us they are wrong") and his answer to Boswell's enquiry whether the Giant's Causeway was worth seeing: "Worth seeing? yes; but not worth going to see." He also counselled an Irishman to keep clear of the English in politics: "Do not make an union with us, sir. We should unite with you only to rob you. We should have robbed the Scotch if they had had anything of which we could have robbed them."

Boswell next accompanied Stuart to Lichfield, where they put up for a night at the George Inn. Boswell made the round of Johnson's friends and relations next morning, after which they went on to Chester, where Boswell enjoyed himself extremely. "Chester pleases my fancy more than any town I ever saw," he told Johnson, and "Had I been a bachelor, I should certainly have paid my addresses to a Chester lady," he told Temple. A religious mood overtook him at Carlisle, where he received the sacrament in the cathedral and made a discovery which he imparted to Johnson: "It is divinely cheering to me to think that there is a cathedral so near Auchinleck." Since he had passed through Carlisle on his way from Scotland to London on several occasions, Johnson must have wondered why he had not noticed the cathedral before, and drily asked: "How near is the cathedral to Auchinleck, that you are so much delighted with it? It is, I suppose, at least an hundred and fifty miles off. However, if you are pleased, it is so far well." The distance between the two being scarce a hundred miles, replied Boswell, "if I set out early on a Saturday morning, I can be at Carlisle that night, have a good sleep, rise well next morning, and attend the solemn service of a High Festival in the cathedral." So he was pleased, and all was so far well.

CHAPTER 23

Social Comforts

ALTHOUGH an essentially sedentary person, Johnson at times indulged in sudden spurts of activity, to prove to himself and others that he could be as agile as anyone else if he felt so disposed. Apart from his chemical experiments, which might necessitate rapid skips from room to corridor, he used to prune and water his vine tree at Bolt Court and he was quite capable of walking ten miles until a late period of life. One day, while strolling with him in Gunnersbury Park, a friend said that as a youth he had thought nothing of swarming up the tallest tree there. "Why, I can swarm it now!" exclaimed Johnson, then nearing his sixtieth year, and promptly began the ascent. He was begged so earnestly to come down that he abandoned his intention of climbing on to branches that might have given way and made his return to earth too expeditious. During his trip to Devonshire with Reynolds a girl in the company boasted that she could beat anyone in a race. Johnson accepted the challenge, and they were soon speeding across a large lawn. Feeling his slippers an encumbrance, he kicked them off, finished the race in his stockings, rapidly outpaced his rival, and led her back to the house in triumph. Again, while staying in the country, he proposed a race with a physically small man. Shortly after the start he picked the other up, placed him on a tree-branch, continued to run as if the competition were keen, and on his return lifted the little man down. More surprising was his behaviour on a visit to Bennet Langton, after walking with whom to the top of a hill he declared his intention of rolling down it. Efforts to dissuade him were made in vain. He said that he had not enjoyed a roll for a long time; and, having placed his keys, pencil, purse and penknife on the ground, he lay down and rolled to the bottom of the hill. Less strenuous, but quite as odd, was his conduct at Stowe Hill, Lichfield. Waiting to welcome him were many friends, who observed him standing before the tall front-gate in a state of abstraction. Rousing himself, he climbed it and went forward quickly to the house. Asked whether he had forgotten that there was a small gate for pedestrians by the side of the carriage entrance, he replied: "No, my dear lady, by no means, but I had a mind to try whether I could climb a gate now as I used to do when I was a lad."

Extended exercise, however, gave him little pleasure. While staying with the Thrales at Brighton (then spelt Brighthelmstone) he hunted the fox with as much energy as anyone, but he said that the sole enjoyment to be derived from it was that man "feels his vacuity less in action than when at rest". To show that he was not tired after a long day with the hounds, he jumped over a stool merely because Thrale had done so. The South Downs, where the sport took place, were not to his taste: "It is a country so truly desolate that if one had a mind to hang oneself for desperation at being obliged to live there, it would be difficult to find a tree on which to fasten the rope." The life of the place was as little to his liking: "You hunt in the morning, and crowd the public rooms at night, and call it *diversion*, when your heart knows it is perishing with poverty of pleasures, and your wits get blunted for want of some other mind to sharpen them upon. There is in this world no real delight (except those of sensuality) but exchange of ideas in conversation." It happened that Johnson's controversial methods once created more of a diversion than the sound of revelry. The Baths at Brighton were a social centre, and in the ante-room here one evening Johnson and the Rev. Henry Michell, vicar of the parish church of St. Nicholas, faced each other from opposite sides of the hearth. What started as a quiet discussion between the two developed into a violent altercation, and soon the disputants were emphasising their points with the assistance of the fire-irons, Johnson using the shovel to drive his argument home, Michell the poker to enforce his. The din they made rose above the clamour in the main room, where the music and dancing ceased. The ante-room was soon filled with pleasure-seekers agape, and Mr. Wade, the master of ceremonies, had to use considerable tact before he was able to calm the antagonists and persuade the revellers that they were merely listening to an exchange of ideas in conversation.

Johnson did not care for Brighton, only going there because the Thrales had a pleasant house at the foot of West Street within a stone's throw of the sea, in which he bathed. Disliking the social round, he sometimes ate more heavily than usual, and after such an occurrence he would get a servant to pump water over him in the backyard.

But he liked the Streatham home of the Thrales, which was not only luxurious but near enough to London for his friends to visit him. Here he was completely at his ease, rather too much at ease for some of the female guests, whose clothes he scrutinised and occasionally criticised. "Why, madam, this won't do! you must not go to church so," he said to one. She changed, but again he did not approve, telling her that she should not wear a black hat and cloak in the summer. After gazing at a very young woman, he suddenly said: "Nay, it's very handsome." "What, sir?" "Why, your cap. I have looked at it some time and I like it much. It has not that vile bandeau across it, which I have so often cursed." Drinking her health, he lamented: " 'Tis a terrible thing that we cannot wish young ladies well without wishing them to become old women." On the whole he was at his best in the Streatham house, tranquil, amiable, often full of fun, and capable at times of boisterous bursts of pure nonsense which "set the table on a roar". He was extremely fond of Mrs. Thrale and treated her with the freedom either of a parent or of an intimate. He pronounced judgments on her personal appearance, and on hearing that she had discarded a certain wig he wrote: "Everybody was an enemy to that wig. We will burn it and get drunk—for what is joy without drink?" As she did not have card-parties, he advised her to please the company with a profusion of sweetmeats, "for everybody loves to have things which please the palate, put in their way without trouble or preparation." Though objecting to her habit of overpraising or unduly censuring people and books, he thought her "the first woman in the world, could she but restrain that wicked tongue of hers", and to check her enthusiasms he wrote: "Horace says that *nil admirari* is the only thing that can make or keep a man happy. It is with equal truth the only thing that can make or keep a man honest." Perhaps it did not occur to him that to admire nothing is also a way to make and keep life dull.

Unlike Hester Thrale, he was extremely sceptical about everything except the Church of England. When the news of a terrible hurricane at Barbados appeared in the papers, he remained calm: "Not true, madam, depend upon't. People so delight to fill their mouths with big words and their minds with a wonder." "Did you ever believe anything reported?" "Never scarcely, and I *have* been deceived, for I did not give credit a long time to the earthquake at Lisbon." He never prophesied evil things, saying: "Whoever *does* prophesy evil, wishes it." Equally he never fancied evil of individuals. When the Irish playwright Isaac Bickerstaffe fled the country to escape arrest for homosexual practices, Thrale remarked that he had long been a suspected man, but Johnson was astonished: "By those who look close to the ground, dirt will be seen, sir; I hope I see things from a greater distance." But he was quick to ridicule pretentiousness. Speaking of a man who was said to be devoted to a friend, "Make him Prime Minister and see how long his friend will be remembered," was Johnson's comment. A young visitor to Streatham expressed regret that he had lost all his Greek. "I believe it happened at the same time, sir, that I lost all my large estate in Yorkshire," said Johnson. Hearing that someone had complained of the ingratitude of friends, Johnson suggested: "Let him do good on higher motives next time—he will then be sure of his reward." Another thing he disliked was the fuss people made about their illnesses. It was difficult, he said, for a sick man not to be a scoundrel. A regular caller at Streatham was a valetudinarian who constantly bemoaned the state of his interior. At last Johnson put a stop to it: "Do not be like the spider, man, and spin conversation thus incessantly out of thy own bowels." Bores, too, received no mercy from him. A man described in great detail how counsel upon circuit at Shrewsbury were much bitten by fleas, and he explained with care how the fleas lived in bales of cloth, moving from place to place with wonderful agility. "It is a pity, sir, that you have not seen a lion," said Johnson, "for a flea has taken you such a time that a lion must have served you a twelvemonth."

That Johnson was on very friendly terms with Henry Thrale is proved by the familiarity with which he addressed him, carefully noted by Fanny Burney: "I wish my master would say to me 'Johnson, if you will oblige me, you will call for a bottle of Toulon, and then we will set to it, glass for glass, till it is done'. And after that I will say 'Thrale, if you will oblige me, you will call for another bottle of Toulon, and then we will set to it, glass for glass, till that is done'. And by the time we should have drunk the two bottles, we should be so happy, and such good friends, that we should fly into each other's arms and both together call for the third!"

Clearly Johnson was not impressed by Thrale as a successful man of business. "Trade could not be managed by those who manage it, if it had much difficulty," he told Mrs. Thrale, and Boswell heard him say: "A merchant trader may, perhaps, be a man of an enlarged mind, but there is nothing in trade connected with an enlarged mind." Primarily Thrale won

Johnson's esteem by giving him a comfortable home and entertaining his friends. It is not always possible to exonerate Johnson from obsequiousness in his attitude to Thrale, and on one occasion a stronger word could be used.

Next to good food, for which his appetite was so persistent that his wife wrote: "I have no notion of health for a man whose mouth cannot be sewed up", Thrale was chiefly attracted to female good looks, and in the late 'seventies he met Sophy Streatfield at Brighton. She was about twenty-three years old, some thirty years younger than he and a dozen younger than his wife. She lived with her mother at Mount Ephraim, Tunbridge Wells, and was considered by both sexes the loveliest woman imaginable. In addition to her physical perfections, she had acquired a good knowledge of Greek, the ability to weep at a moment's notice for no earthly reason, just as if she had turned on a lachrymal tap, and an ingratiating manner which enslaved elderly married men. Her conquests were mainly among the upper clergy, but though deans and archdeacons fell at her feet they were not allowed to touch her lips. She seemed to think that married men were safe game, but married clergymen safer. Her soul was expressed in flirtation, and she kept her power by preserving her purity. Hand-patting was permissible, kissing disallowed. Nothing could have been easier for her than to make Thrale fall at her feet, had his physique enabled him to do so, but metaphorically he was soon prostrated. His wife said that Sophy hung about him, danced round him, cried when she parted from him, squeezed his hand shyly, and looked fondly at him with brimming eyes, pretending that it was all done for love of her dear friend Hester Thrale, who declared that "a man must not be a *man* but an *it*, to resist such artillery". Sophy reported to Hester the tender passages between Henry and herself, and behaved in what the older woman thought a wholly unaccountable manner. "Few people, however, seem disposed to take her for life," mused Hester; "everybody's admiration . . . and nobody's choice." But that perhaps was because Sophy preferred adoration to surrender. Her choice was chastity, which she preserved to the end of a very long life.

Naturally Sophy became a guest at Streatham, and an embarrassing incident occurred during a dinner-party there. Johnson and Burke were sitting on each side of Mrs. Thrale, who, in an advanced state of pregnancy, was in very low spirits. The meal having commenced, Thrale asked his wife to change places with Sophy, who might get a sore throat if she sat near the door. Hester, who had just put a spoonful of soup in her mouth, was so much upset by the callousness of the request that she burst into tears, rose from her place, said that shortly no doubt Sophy would be at the head of the table without displacing the mistress of the house, and left the room. For about two hours she struggled with her vexation in the drawing-room, and was then joined by Johnson and Burke. She described what happened:

> On seeing them, I resolved to give a *jobation* to both, but fixed on Johnson for my charge, and asked him if he had noticed what passed, what I had suffered, and whether allowing for the state of my nerves, I was much to blame? He answered, 'Why, possibly not; your feelings were out-raged.' I said, 'Yes, greatly so; and I cannot help remarking with what blandness and composure you *witnessed* the outrage. Had this transaction been told of others, your anger would have known no bounds; but, towards a man who gives good dinners &c, you are meekness itself!' Johnson coloured, and Burke, I thought, looked foolish but I had not a word of answer from either.

The great moral teacher and the world-famous humanitarian were alike incapable of a mild protest against an act of domestic barbarity done under their very noses. Thrale's dinners must have been extremely good.

It is quite likely that a mere player, David Garrick, who neither instructed the public in Christian virtues nor waxed indignant over victimised races, would have put up a better performance at this dinner-party. He would almost certainly have cracked a joke to Thrale's discomfort, and would probably have accompanied Hester to the drawing-room. But Garrick was a rare visitor to Streatham. Both before and after his farewell season in 1776 he spent most of the time at his Hampton Court villa, of which he was very proud. He showed Johnson over the place, in the grounds of which stood a temple to Shakespeare. "Well, Doctor, how do you like all this?" he asked. "Why, it is pleasant enough for the present, but all these things, David, make death very terrible." To a bibliophile like Garrick the treatment accorded his books by Johnson made life very terrible too. Having displayed his library shelves filled with rare and elegantly bound books, he was horrified by the way in which Johnson extracted various volumes, roughly opened them at the risk of splitting their spines, and flung them on the floor. "Zounds! what are you about there? You'll spoil all my books," cried the agonised owner. "No, sir, I have done nothing but treat a pack of silly plays in fops' dresses just as they deserve, but I see no *books*." On retiring from the stage Garrick made a resolution: "Now I have quitted the theatre, I will sit down and read Shakespeare." Johnson sympathised: " 'Tis time you should, for I much doubt if you ever examined one of his plays from the first scene to the last." But Johnson was very fond of Davy, whom he thought the cheerfullest man of the age, and Davy reverenced the Doctor, one word of whose praise more than compensated for all the jests he made at the actor's expense. Not long before Garrick's death the party at Streatham were discussing his appearance, and Mrs. Thrale said that he and Wilkes were the two oldest-looking men of their ages she had ever known, giving the reason that they had worn themselves out by being perpetually entertaining in company. Johnson corrected this view: "David, madam, looks much older than he is, for his face has had double the business of any other man's. It is never at rest. When he speaks one minute, he has quite a different countenance to what he assumes the next. I don't believe he ever kept the same look for half an hour together in the whole course of his life; and such an eternal, restless, fatiguing play of the muscles must certainly wear out a man's face before its real time."

But he had worn out his body too, and early in 1779, a month before reaching the age of sixty-two, he died, earning from Johnson the most famous epitaph in history: "I am disappointed by that stroke of death which has eclipsed the gaiety of nations, and impoverished the public stock of harmless pleasure." Boswell thought the eulogy too warm, but Johnson defended it: "I could not have said more or less. It is the truth: *eclipsed*, not *extinguished*; and his death *did* eclipse; it was like a storm." Boswell was not satisfied: "But why nations? Did his gaiety extend further than his own nation?" Johnson gave way, if not wholly to the other's gratification: "Why, sir, some exaggeration must be allowed. Besides, nations may be said— if we allow the Scotch to be a nation, and to have gaiety, which they have not. *You* are an exception, though. Come, gentlemen, let us candidly admit that there is one Scotchman who is cheerful." Boswell raised another objection: "Is not *harmless pleasure* very tame?" "Nay, sir, harmless pleasure is the highest praise. Pleasure is a word of dubious import; pleasure is in general dangerous and pernicious to virtue; to be able therefore to furnish pleasure that is harmless, pleasure pure and unalloyed, is as great a power as man can possess."

The famous Club which had been started by Johnson, Reynolds and others became known as the Literary Club after Garrick's death. It now embraced all sorts and conditions of men, of whom Johnson remarked: "I should be sorry if any of our Club were hanged. I will not say but some of them deserve it." Later members included Richard Brinsley Sheridan, Edward Gibbon, Charles James Fox, Adam Smith, Sir Joseph Banks,

Charles Burney and Edmund Malone; but the meetings were less gay in the absence of Garrick, and Johnson never got on sufficiently familiar terms with the younger men to abbreviate their names, as in the case of his old friends: 'Beau' for Beauclerk, 'Lanky' for Langton, 'Bozzy' for Boswell, 'Mur' for Murphy, 'Goldy' for Goldsmith, 'Davy' for Garrick, and 'Sherry' or even 'Sherry-derry' for the older Sheridan before they were estranged by a quip. A further diminution of gaiety was caused by the death in 1780 of Topham Beauclerk, who, whatever his domestic shortcomings, was a great loss to The Club, "a loss that perhaps the whole nation could not repair," grieved Johnson, whose affection moved him to write: "His wit and his folly, his acuteness and maliciousness, his merriment and reasoning, are now over. Such another will not often be found among mankind."

But there was much consolation to be found just then at Streatham, where Fanny Burney had almost become a fixture. She was the daughter of Charles Burney, the composer, teacher and historian of music, who had known Johnson for about twenty years, and whose gentle social nature made him universally liked. Fanny was the authoress of an anonymous novel called *Evelina* which was the literary sensation of 1778, even Johnson declaring that there was nothing so delicately finished in the whole of Fielding's work. There is "no character better drawn anywhere, in any book or by any author" than that of Mr. Smith in *Evelina*, he announced. He was instantaneously attracted to the authoress, a lively little person with a keen appreciation of fun, superficially modest, respectful, bashful, and solemn at the appropriate moments. He petted and fondled her, told her she was "such a darling", could not have too much of her company, and incited her to assail Mrs. Elizabeth Montagu, the famous 'blue-stocking', who was coming to dine at Streatham: "Down with her, Burney!—down with her!—spare her not!—attack her, fight her, and down with her at once! You are a rising wit, and she is at the top; and when I was beginning the world, and was nothing and nobody, the joy of my life was to fire at all the established wits! and then everybody loved to halloo me on. But there is no game now: everybody would be glad to see me conquered: but then, when I was new, to vanquish the great ones was all the delight of my poor little dear soul! So at her, Burney!—at her, and down with her!"

He gave Fanny the proof-sheets of his Life of Pope and let her read those of his other *Lives of the English Poets*, the first series of which came out in 1779, the last in 1781. He had undertaken the work in 1777 at the request of the chief London booksellers and publishers, some forty of whom wished to issue a uniform edition of the works of the English poets (or rather British poets, the Scotch and Irish being included), each to be prefaced with a brief Life by Johnson, who was approached by a committee of three and asked to name his terms. Since he defined a man who did not write for money as a blockhead, he must have thought himself one, for he suggested two hundred guineas. Edmund Malone, who knew all about the publishing trade, made this comment: "Johnson's moderation in demanding so small a sum is extraordinary. Had he asked one thousand, or even fifteen hundred guineas, the booksellers, who knew the value of his name, would doubtless have readily given it." They gave him another hundred guineas on completion of the work. Boswell was disappointed to learn that the booksellers would decide which poets were to be included in the edition, and asked Johnson if he would write the Life of any dunce they chose. "Yes, sir, and *say* he was a dunce," replied the Doctor. He was, however, responsible for the inclusion of John Pomfret, Sir Richard Blackmore, Thomas Yalden and Isaac Watts, only the last of whom is remembered today, chiefly as the author of the most famous English hymn, 'O God, our help in ages past.'

Johnson's sole objection to Watts was his nonconformity in religion, and this kind of judgment is a leading motive in the

Lives, which were inspired partly by Johnson's intense interest in human character and partly by the wish to promote piety. His favourite reading was what he called "the biographical part of literature", the only kind of history on which he set a high value being the history of manners, "and therefore I esteem biography, as giving us what comes near to ourselves, what we can turn to use." But he also wanted to show wherein his subjects had, in the words of St. Paul, "come short of the glory of God," and he was the first English biographer to deal quite honestly with his characters, not with the object of disparaging them but in the cause of morality. "If we owe regard to the dead," he had written in *The Rambler*, "there is yet more respect to be paid to knowledge, to virtue, and to truth." Yet another aspect: "If nothing but the bright side of characters should be shown, we should sit down in despondency and think it utterly impossible to imitate them in anything." Further, he must have known, though he does not mention it, that remarkable men are not made less so by the fullest recognition of their faults, that the worse their faults the greater their achievements, every defect acting as a brake on endeavour, and therefore that to ignore a man's shortcomings, the obstacles he has surmounted, is to belittle him. Against this, Johnson might have denied the strength and shaping-power of flaws in a man's nature, because he criticised Pope's theory of the "ruling passion": "This doctrine is in itself pernicious as well as false: its tendency is to produce the belief of a kind of moral predestination, or overruling principle which cannot be resisted; he that admits it is prepared to comply with every desire that caprice or opportunity shall excite, and to flatter himself that he submits only to the lawful dominion of Nature, in obeying the resistless authority of his *ruling passion*." Boswell could have studied that passage with advantage.

But whether written in the cause of truth for its own sake or for the sake of morality, Johnson's *Lives* are prototypical of all that is best in modern biography: selectiveness, brevity, impartiality, and the use of anecdotes instead of analysis for revealing character. His description of the death of Edmund Smith, giving much of the poet's nature in a short paragraph, is the finest example of his restrained humour and the best single passage in British biography. Smith had decided to write a poetic drama on Lady Jane Grey:

> Having formed his plan and collected materials, he declared that a few months would complete his design; and that he might pursue his work with less frequent avocations, he was, in June 1710, invited by Mr. George Ducket to his house at Hartham, in Wiltshire. Here he found such opportunities of indulgence as did not much forward his studies, and particularly some strong ale, too delicious to be resisted. He ate and drank till he found himself plethoric; and then, resolving to ease himself by evacuation, he wrote to an apothecary in the neighbourhood a prescription of a purge so forcible, that the apothecary thought it his duty to delay it till he had given notice of its danger. Smith, not pleased with the contradiction of a shopman, and boastful of his own knowledge, treated the notice with rude contempt, and swallowed his own medicine, which, in July 1710, brought him to the grave. He was buried at Hartham.

Johnson's original purpose was to write a brief notice of each poet, including dates and a character-sketch, but his interest in many of the subjects compelled him to expand, and some of the *Lives* are of considerable length. Apart from Savage, whose biography he had written many years earlier, Pope was his best subject. Eighteenth-century poetry was overshadowed by the muse of Pope, and Johnson was as much influenced by the fashion of his time as any other critic before or after him. While he was gathering materials for this biography, Boswell approached Lord Marchmont, who had known Pope, and canvassed his help. Marchmont said he would be pleased to call on Johnson and impart his knowledge. Boswell dashed down to Streatham, exultingly announced the successful result of his efforts, and was taken aback by Johnson's reception of the news: "I shall not be in town tomorrow. I don't care to know about Pope." Mrs. Thrale expostulated: "I suppose, sir, Mr. Boswell thought that as you are to write Pope's Life, you would wish to know about him." But Johnson was not in the vein to receive information he had not solicited: "Wish! why, yes. If it rained knowledge I'd hold out my hand; but I would not give myself the trouble to go in quest of it." About a year later, in a more pliant mood, he called on Marchmont in the company of Boswell and obtained a number of personal anecdotes. But he was too lazy to be a conscientious biographer, and did not bother to correct mistakes which were pointed out to him. "I have sat at home in Bolt Court all the summer, thinking to write the *Lives*, and a great part of the time only thinking," he told Boswell in 1780; and after finishing them he confessed that he had done the job "in my usual way, dilatorily and hastily, unwilling to work, and working with vigour and haste".

He wrote most of the *Lives* while residing with the Thrales at Streatham or Southwark. On the whole they were favourably received, though he was attacked by political opponents for his treatment of Milton, and by Cambridge professors for his depreciation of Thomas Gray. He did not mind this. The critics, he said, "tease one, but as a fly stings a horse," and he had a low opinion of their intelligence. Lucy Porter asked him whether she could trust the reviewers of new publications. "Infallibly, dear Lucy, provided you buy what they abuse and never anything they praise." In his view hostile criticism helped a writer: "I would rather be attacked than unnoticed. For the worst thing you can do to an author is to be silent as to his works. An assault upon a town is a bad thing, but starving it is still worse." Hearing someone's adverse opinion of his Life of Gray, he seemed pleased: "I hope the day will never arrive when I shall neither be the object of calumny or ridicule, for then I shall be neglected and forgotten." He disliked Gray's odes but paid a handsome tribute to the famous *Elegy*. In the case of Milton, he strongly disapproved of the man's republican principles, and could see no merit in *Lycidas*. He once told Anna Seward that he would hang a dog that read the poem twice. "What, then, must become of me, who can say it by heart, and who often repeat it to myself with a delight that grows by what it feeds upon?" Anna enquired. "Die in a surfeit of bad taste," growled Johnson, who had so little appreciation of beauty in verse that when he read it aloud, Anna tells us, "one eternal monotone frustrated the intent of the poet." Nearly thirty years before writing the Life of Milton, he had been duped by a Scot named Lauder, who had invented a lot of stuff to prove that the author of *Paradise Lost* was a plagiarist. The moment Johnson discovered the truth, he compelled Lauder to make a full confession and recantation, explaining his own deception on the ground that he thought the man "too frantic to be fraudulent". In the Life of Milton he atoned for this early error by penning a stately eulogy of *Paradise Lost*.

There were some curious omissions from the list of poets. Affection no doubt prevented him from telling the truth about Goldsmith. The imposture of Chatterton aroused Johnson's moral sense and caused his exclusion; while Churchill's profligacy was too lavishly exhibited to earn him a place in the story. But the neglected writers of one age are often esteemed by another, and nowadays we read Johnson's work not for his dated taste, but for his timeless wisdom, of which a few samples follow:

[On Cromwell and the regicides] "But combinations of wickedness would overwnelm the world by the advantage which licentious principles afford, did not those who have long practised perfidy grow faithless to each other." (*Edmund Waller*)

[On Dryden's flattering dedications] "That praise is worth nothing of which the price is known."

[On Dryden's conversion to the Romish faith] "That conversion will always be suspected that apparently concurs with interest. He that never finds his error till it hinders his progress towards wealth or honour, will not be thought to love Truth only for herself."

[On critics and professors] "But such are the conceits of speculatists, who strain their faculties to find in a mine what lies upon the surface." (*Matthew Prior*)

[On Sir Richard Blackmore] "Those whom their virtue restrains from deceiving others are often disposed by their vanity to deceive themselves."

[On George Granville, Lord Lansdowne] "The public sometimes has its favourites, whom it rewards for one species of excellence with the honours due to another. From him whom we reverence for his beneficence we do not willingly withhold the praise of genius; a man of exalted merit becomes at once an accomplished writer, as a beauty finds no great difficulty in passing for a wit."

[On Richard Savage] "The liberty of the press is a blessing when we are inclined to write against others, and a calamity when we find ourselves overborne by the multitude of our assailants."

[On the victims of Pope's *The Dunciad*] "Every man is of importance to himself, and therefore, in his own opinion, to others; and, supposing the world already acquainted with all his pleasures and his pains, is perhaps the first to publish injuries or misfortunes which had never been known unless related by himself, and at which those that hear them will only laugh, for no man sympathises with the sorrows of vanity."

[On Pope] "The man who threatens the world is always ridiculous; for the world can easily go on without him, and in a short time will cease to miss him."

[On Pope's letters] "Most hearts are pure while temptation is away. It is easy to awaken generous sentiments in privacy; to despise death when there is no danger; to glow with benevolence when there is nothing to be given. While such ideas are formed they are felt, and self-love does not suspect the gleam of virtue to be the meteor of fancy."

[On Pope] "His scorn of the Great is repeated too often to be real; no man thinks much of that which he despises; and as falsehood is always in danger of inconsistency, he makes it his boast at another time that he lives among them."

"Without Prudence Fortitude is mad; without Justice it is mischievous." (*Alexander Pope*)

[On William Collins] "He puts his words out of the common order, seeming to think, with some later candidates for fame, that not to write prose is certainly to write poetry."

[On Mark Akenside] "He certainly retained an unnecessary and outrageous zeal for what he called and thought liberty; a zeal which sometimes disguises from the world, and not rarely from the mind which it possesses, an envious desire of plundering wealth or degrading greatness, and of which the immediate tendency is innovation and anarchy, an impetuous eagerness to subvert and confound, with very little care what shall be established."

Johnson's hatred of coarseness in literature was displayed in a letter he wrote to John Nichols, printer of the edition of the English poets for which he wrote the *Lives*. A year after publication of the first series he was looking through the poetry of Nicholas Rowe, and was shocked to find an 'Epigram on a lady who shed her water at seeing the tragedy of *Cato*'. He promptly reprimanded Nichols: "In reading Rowe in your edition, which is very impudently called mine, I observed a little piece unnaturally and odiously obscene. I was offended, but still more offended when I could not find it in Rowe's genuine volumes. To admit it had been wrong, to interpolate it is surely worse. If I had known of such a piece in the whole collection I should have been angry. What can be done?" Nichols replied that the Epigram had been among Rowe's works but was transplanted into the *Miscellanies* published by Pope and Swift.

Apart from the flea-bites of critics and the printing of Rowe's Epigram, one displeasing circumstance arose from Johnson's Lives of Lord Lyttelton and William Shenstone. The former had shone brightly in the *salon* of Elizabeth Montagu, whom Johnson called 'Queen of the Blues'. The term 'blue-stocking' to designate what is now called highbrow was invented by Mrs. Elizabeth Vesey, who banned card-playing in favour of literary conversation and social gossip at her evening parties in Bath. A leading member of her circle was Benjamin Stilling-fleet, who, being unexpectedly asked to a meeting, excused himself on the ground that he was not properly dressed. "Pho, pho!" cried Mrs. Vesey, "don't mind dress! Come in your blue stockings!" That began the common use of the term, according to Fanny Burney, who was in a better position to know the facts than Boswell, who gives a different version. A *Bas Bleu* Society was then started by Mrs. Vesey in Hertford Street, Mayfair, and similar groups were soon formed by other hostesses, chief among them being Mrs. Elizabeth Montagu, who founded The Blue-Stocking Club, the meetings of which were among the chief social events of London after she had built her mansion between what later became Portman and Montagu Squares. It was Mrs. Vesey's habit to break up her parties into small groups, placing chairs back to back or anyhow except in a row. But at Mrs. Montagu's the seats were arranged in a semi-circle facing the fire throughout the evening, with herself in a seat at one end of the curve. Horace Walpole was a 'star' at her gatherings, and in the early days of the club Lord Lyttelton had been another, but he died in 1773. Mrs. Montagu made something of a reputation by replying to Voltaire's strictures on Shakespeare in an essay which Johnson thought negligible, and after her large mansion was built she added to her notoriety by giving an annual breakfast every May Day to the chimney-sweepers of London. Served on the space in front of her house, it consisted of roast beef and plum-pudding. In those days chimney-sweepers were regarded as "degraded outcasts from society", and were described as "jetty objects", as "sooty little agents to the safety of our most blessed luxury", and suchlike terms of condescending endearment. Except for this annual invasion of the lower world, Mrs. Montagu only cultivated people of consequence.

Johnson was occasionally to be seen at blue-stocking routs, and Bennet Langton once met him at Mrs. Vesey's, where the company consisted of duchesses, peers of the realm, and various heads of professions. The moment Johnson arrived and sat down "the company began to collect round him, till they became not less than four, if not five, deep; those behind standing, and listening over the heads of those that were sitting near him". Another evening, at Mrs. Montagu's, he seemed so much pleased with the attention and respect paid him by brains, birth and beauty that a friend asked if he was not highly gratified by his visit: "No, sir, not highly *gratified*; yet I do not recollect to have passed many evenings *with fewer objections*." Doubtless he aroused fear and respect more than liking in these circles, even his courtliness tending to subdue those whom he honoured. Indeed so carefully did he observe the proprieties that the ornateness of his manners sometimes impeded the traffic in the street. With the elaborate courtesy of self-consciousness he conducted his female visitors to their coaches outside Bolt Court, his strange appearance and bizarre gesticulations causing a crowd to collect and watch the performance.

But he was less polite in biography than in behaviour, and certain of his remarks about Lyttelton, between whom and Mrs. Montagu "a commerce of reciprocal compliments had long been carried on", enraged the 'blue-stockings' of that circle. A campaign of adverse tittle-tattle was launched against him, and though it did him no harm it vexed him. "Mrs. Montagu has dropped me," he reported to Boswell. "Now, sir, there are people whom one should like very well to drop, but would not wish to be dropped by." There was very little to make a fuss about. Johnson had merely said that when the poet's *Dialogues of the Dead* were commended by the reviewers, "poor Lyttelton, with humble gratitude, returned, in a note which I have read, acknowledgments which can never be proper, since they must be paid either for flattery or for justice"; further that Lyttelton's *History of Henry the Second* had been "elaborated by the searches and deliberations of twenty years, and published with such anxiety as only vanity can dictate". But what may have annoyed Mrs. Montagu more than these remarks was Johnson's account of Lyttelton's treatment of the poet William Shenstone, who had beautified his small domain, The Leasowes, making it "a place to be visited by travellers and copied by designers", none of whom took much notice of near-by Hagley, the imposing manor and grounds of the Lytteltons:

> For a while the inhabitants of Hagley affected to tell their acquaintance of the little fellow that was trying to make himself admired; but when by degrees the Leasowes forced themselves into notice, they took care to defeat the curiosity which they could not suppress by conducting their visitants perversely to inconvenient points of view, and introducing them at the wrong end of a walk to detect a deception; injuries of which Shenstone would heavily complain. Where there is emulation there will be vanity; and where there is vanity there will be folly.

For some weeks Johnson had been smouldering with grievance over the reported sneers of the Montagu faction, and in the summer of 1781 he was able to erupt at Streatham, where one of the guests was William Weller Pepys, whom Johnson called Mrs. Montagu's prime minister, a leader of the cabal against him. Pepys was extremely nervous about the encounter and before Johnson's arrival begged Fanny Burney to prevent the subject from coming up. But it was like asking a mouse to interpose in a cat-and-dog fight. Having fumed with suppressed vexation until dinner was half-finished, Johnson suddenly called out in passionate tones: "Mr. Pepys, I understand you are offended by my Life of Lord Lyttelton. Come forth, man! What have you to say to me or of me? What are your objections? If you have anything to say, let's hear it. Come forth, man, when I call you!" The red and furious face of Johnson contrasted strangely with the pale and frightened face of Pepys, who tried to avert the storm: "No, sir, not at present. I must beg leave to decline the subject. I told Miss Burney before dinner that I hoped it would not be started." But the whisperings and gibes of the clique had exasperated their subject, who trounced Pepys without mercy. The battle once joined, Pepys held his ground, and each time he was driven from it he returned to the combat. Johnson declared that it was the duty of a biographer to state all the failings of a respectable character. Pepys stood up for Lyttelton, keeping his temper so well that Johnson complimented him: "Sir, all that you say, while you are vindicating one who cannot thank you, makes me only think better of you than I ever did before. Yet still I think you do *me* wrong." During one angry passage Johnson proclaimed: "The more my Lord Lyttelton is enquired after, the worse he will appear. Mr. Seward has just heard two stories of him which corroborate all I have related." William Seward, not Anna's father, was a hypochondriac with a comfortable income from beer and a love of anecdotes. Mrs. Thrale said that he did good to everybody and spoke well of nobody. But the thought of speaking ill of somebody during such a contest scared him; and having told the stories illustrating Lyttelton's ungenerous treatment of Shenstone, he sank back in his seat and remained dumb for the rest of the meal. When the women left the men to their wine, Johnson continued the discussion, which went on after the men were summoned to the drawing-room for tea. At last Mrs. Thrale put her foot down, saying she wished to hear no more on the subject. "Well, madam," said Johnson after a pause, "you *shall* hear no more of it; yet I will defend myself in every part and in every atom!" Pepys and Johnson shook hands at parting, Pepys mentally echoing Orlando's sentiment: "I do desire we may be better strangers." The company having left, Mrs. Thrale gave Johnson a severe lecture on manners, and he promised not to quarrel again in her house; so that when, not long after, Mrs. Montagu visited Streatham, he held himself in check for a while. The Queen of the Blues was thin and of middle height. She looked unhealthy, but the expression on her face was sensible and perceptive, and she had an air of distinction which had probably been acquired. She did not curtsy to Johnson, but turned coldly from him, determined to justify her public assurance that she would never speak to him again. However he was not the sort of man to be ignored with impunity, and in a little while he addressed her roughly: "Well, madam, what's become of your fine new house? I hear no more of it." Obliged to answer, she was quickly quelled and became as civil as ever.

Johnson's position in the Thrale household was that of an autocrat, to whom everyone deferred, and if by chance a particular guest was marked down as a scapegoat the laughter of the rest was loud with relief. Boswell was once the victim. Taking a seat at the table next to Johnson, he was told that it was reserved for Miss Burney. Undismayed, he got another chair, placed it just behind Johnson, and listened, goggle-eyed, to the Doctor's conversation. On discovering his proximity, Johnson angrily dismissed him: "What do you do there, sir? Go to the table, sir!" Boswell obeyed, but rising later from his place to find something he was again scolded: "What are you thinking of, sir? Why do you get up before the cloth is removed? Come back to your place, sir! . . . Running about in the middle of meals! One would take you for a Branghton!" Boswell was out of his depth: "A Branghton, sir! What is a Branghton?" Johnson laughed: "Where have you lived, sir, and what company have you kept, not to know that?" Boswell whispered to Mrs. Thrale: "Pray, ma'am, what's a Branghton? Do me the favour to tell me. Is it some animal hereabouts?" Another guest took him aside and disclosed the identity of a character in Fanny Burney's novel *Evelina*.

But by 1781, when the Lytteltonian controversy took place, the death-knell of Johnson's literary dictatorship at Streatham and Southwark had struck, although he had not heard it, and soon he was to mourn the passing of his pleasures there:

> Condemn'd to Hope's delusive mine,
>   As on we toil from day to day,
> By sudden blast or slow decline
>   Our social comforts drop away.

Various

"PLEASURE will be paid, one time or another," and in 1779 Thrale paid the first instalment for the pleasure of gluttony with a stroke. He was dining with his widowed sister, after listening to the contents of her husband's will, from which he learnt that he would be responsible for a large sum of money, his brother-in-law having died a bankrupt. The shock of the news, coupled with his overcharged arteries, induced apoplexy, and for some time his recovery was doubtful. But a tough constitution prevailed; and though he became more lethargic than ever, his appetite returned with increased voracity. Early in 1780 he suffered another stroke, together with all the blistering and bleeding by which doctors killed their less vigorous patients in those days. Again he survived both seizure and medical attention, beginning to take notice of what was going on around him when he heard the voice of Sophy Streatfield. The doctors advised a convalescence at Bath, where the Thrale family, with Fanny Burney, stayed for some weeks in South Parade.

While they were there a General Election was held. Thrale being incapable of any considerable motion except that of mastication, his wife and Fanny departed for Southwark to solicit votes. For hours together Hester went from door to door, and being surrounded by men for long stretches of time she could not obey the calls of nature, a restriction which brought on much future pain. Johnson helped her with the canvassing; but her popularity with the constituents, whom she called "greasy rogues", did not gain their votes for the brewer, who was defeated. Johnson got the impression from something she said that her husband disliked advice on diet; so he wrote to Thrale expressing pleasure that he had not sent an exhortation to resolute abstinence and adding: "The advice that is wanted is commonly unwelcome, and that which is not wanted is evidently impertinent."

Thrale was going the whole hog at Bath, eating himself into a coma, and, when not so engaged, dreaming of delicacies that melted in the mouth. He would have remained there much longer, loading his belly with lampreys and his bladder with anything but the waters of Bath, if the Protestants of England had allowed him to continue the treatment. Parliament had recently passed an Act which relieved the Roman Catholics of certain disabilities. It was opposed by a number of Protestants, and Lord George Gordon was elected president of the association for the repeal of the Act. The mob suddenly got it into their heads that the Spanish Inquisition was about to be let loose in England, or something equally fantastic; and as the Cause opened up delightful possibilities of plunder, destruction and unlimited liquor, Lord George soon became a hero. The elevation affected his head, and he saw himself as a divinely appointed leader. On 2nd June 1780 he arrived with a petition at Westminster, backed by some sixty thousand people. To save their skins members of both Houses of Parliament were compelled to shout "No Popery!" and to wear blue cockades. The chapels attached to the Bavarian and Sardinian Embassies were then wrecked, and within two days much of London was at the mercy of the rioters, its lawful inhabitants panic-stricken.

Johnson kept the Thrales in touch with the events through which he was living. The houses of Roman Catholics and their sympathisers were burnt, including that of Lord Chief Justice Mansfield, who had supported the Act. A band of rioters would also have destroyed his country residence at Caen Wood (now Kenwood), but the landlord of the Spaniards Inn near-by diverted them with beer, and by the time the military arrived they were too besotted to think of arson. They set fire to Newgate and released the prisoners, repeating their performance at the Fleet, the Marshalsea, and other places of confinement. On 7th June, Johnson walked with a friend to see Newgate, finding it in ruins and still ablaze: "As I went by, the Protestants were plundering the Sessions-house at the Old Bailey. There were not, I believe, a hundred; but they did their work at leisure, in full security, without sentinels, without trepidation, as men lawfully employed, in full day. Such is the cowardice of a commercial place." The magistrates were frightened out of their wits and dared not do their duty for fear they would be accused of Roman Catholic sympathies. Fortunately the chief magistrate of the kingdom, George III, acted in spite of the hesitation of his Ministers, and ordered out the military on the day Johnson went for a walk. A few rattles of musketry calmed the religious fervour of the incendiaries; peace was restored in a matter of hours; and Johnson, telling Mrs. Thrale that he had no fruit, hinted that her husband "might as well give me a little, as give all to the gardener". The Thrales were then at Brighton, because the rabble had displayed their Protestant zeal by burning down the Roman Catholic chapel at Bath, and a local newspaper had announced that Thrale was a Papist. They thought there would be less chance of molestation at the seaside, and left South Parade one evening in a coach-and-four attended by two mounted guards.

That summer Johnson sat at home amusing himself with arithmetic and light verse. Mrs. Thrale says that he once computed the national debt at 180 millions, which, if converted into silver, would "serve to make a meridian of that metal, I forget how broad, for the globe of the whole earth, the *real* globe". In August he read in a newspaper that Thrale's nephew, Sir John Lade, had come of age. Knowing the young man's propensities, Johnson composed some prophetic verses and sent them to Mrs. Thrale with a note: "I have enclosed a short song of congratulation, which you must not show to anybody. It is odd that it should come into anybody's head. I hope you will read it with candour; it is, I believe, one of the author's first essays in that way of writing, and a beginner is always to be treated with tenderness." These very unJohnsonian lines have a curious foretaste of A. E. Housman's poetry:

> Long-expected one-and-twenty,
>   Ling'ring year, at length is flown;
> Pride and pleasure, pomp and plenty,
>   Great Sir John, are now your own.
>
> Loosen'd from the Minor's tether,
>   Free to mortgage or to sell,
> Wild as wind, and light as feather,
>   Bid the sons of thrift farewell.
>
> Call the Betseys, Kates, and Jennies,
>   All the names that banish care;
> Lavish of your grandsire's guineas,
>   Shew the spirit of an heir.
>
> All that prey on vice or folly
>   Joy to see their quarry fly;
> There the gamester, light and jolly,
>   There the lender, grave and sly.
>
> Wealth, my lad, was made to wander,
>   Let it wander as it will;
> Call the jockey, call the pander,
>   Bid them come and take their fill.
>
> When the bonny blade carouses,
>   Pockets full, and spirits high—
> What are acres? what are houses?
>   Only dirt, or wet or dry.

Should the guardian friend or mother
Tell the woes of wilful waste;
Scorn their counsel, scorn their pother,—
You can hang or drown at last.

Sir John Lade fully justified Johnson's prognostications by marrying what was called "a woman of the town" and by gambling his large fortune away. He became a favourite of the Prince Regent and a famous member of the Four-in-Hand Club, his ruthless, reckless driving being celebrated a century later in Conan Doyle's *Rodney Stone*. One of his notorious wagers would have appealed to his gormandising uncle, Henry Thrale. He betted the Duke of Queensberry ("Old Q") a thousand guineas that a man of his own choice would eat more at a sitting than anyone the Duke could produce. The bet was won by the Duke, whose man beat Lade's "by a pig and an apple-pie."

In January 1781 the Thrales occupied a house in Grosvenor Square, and here Hester could at last blossom out as a society hostess, while her husband passed the tedious intervals between meals in a state of torpor. It may have been his discomfort in such surroundings, or sympathy with his sluggish host, that made Johnson again drink wine, but he was observed to swallow a large quantity greedily. "Abstinence is as easy to me as temperance would be difficult," he said. He cautioned Thrale to eat less; yet when himself received the same warning from Taylor some three years later, he resented it strongly. Always ready to give good advice, he declined to take it.

Thrale's appetite increased the more he ate, and so enormous was his breakfast on 2nd April of this year that Johnson told him "such eating is little better than suicide". Next day his table-performance was on such a scale that even the servants were nervous, and the doctor said that the alternative to certain death was legal restraint. Mrs. Thrale intimated that as her husband had got the money, he had the right to spend it in his

own fashion. A large party was invited by Mrs. Thrale for
4th April, to hear a concert and to meet several travelling
Indians; but it was cancelled at the last moment because
Thrale had been struck down with apoplexy, expiring that
morning. Johnson was with him at the end, "and looked for
the last time upon the face that for fifteen years had never been
turned upon me but with respect and benignity." That
evening there was a meeting of the Literary Club, but Johnson
excused himself on account of Thrale's death, concerning
which he wrote to the widow: "No death since that of my wife
has ever oppressed me like this." He added the surprising
assertion that Thrale had "given you happiness in marriage to
a degree of which without personal knowledge I should have
thought the description fabulous". Whether he honestly believed this or was suffering from the aberration of grief it is
impossible to say. Mrs. Thrale left Grosvenor Square at once
for Streatham and Brighton, where a letter from Johnson
reached her: "I am afraid of thinking what I have lost. I never
had such a friend before. Let me have your prayers and those
of my dear Queeney."

Johnson was one of the four executors of Thrale's estate, each
of whom received £200. His friends expected to hear that
Johnson had been left an annuity, but the Doctor was probably
more pleased with the executorship than he would have been
with a larger bequest. He had always felt a desire for some
sort of administrative power, a desire that had been but partly
dissipated in talk. In 1771 he had even considered the possibility of entering Parliament, but in 1775 he drew comfort from
the reflection that "Politics are now nothing more than means
of rising in the world. With this sole view do men engage in
politics, and their whole conduct proceeds upon it". There
were few minds to which tyranny was not delightful, he once
told Mrs. Thrale: "Power is nothing but as it is felt, and the
delight of superiority is proportionate to the resistance overcome." He now proceeded to overcome the resistance of his

fellow-executors, reporting to Hester: "We met today and were told of mountainous difficulties, till I was provoked to tell them that if there were really so much to do and suffer, there would be no Executors in the world."

He was the only person concerned who did not wish to sell the brewery, and he thoroughly enjoyed what Hester called "the dirty delight" of signing bonds, leases, drafts for hundreds and thousands of pounds, and so on. Mrs. Thrale herself was soon at work in the counting-house of the brewery from nine in the morning till five in the afternoon. She was most anxious to get the business off her hands, for according to Fanny Burney they were brewing themselves into bankruptcy; so she offered John Perkins, who had been Thrale's superintendent, the Southwark house for his wife if he could find a buyer. Thus stimulated, Perkins at once got in touch with the Quaker head of a banking firm in Lombard Street, David Barclay, who bought the brewery for £135,000 and put his nephew Robert Barclay into the business with Perkins. While the arrangements for the sale were in process, Johnson was to be seen, inkhorn and pen in buttonhole, bustling about with an air of importance. Questioned as to the precise value of the property, he replied: "We are not here to sell a parcel of boilers and vats, but the potentiality of growing rich beyond the dreams of avarice." The sale was completed by June 1781, and Johnson's pleasure in the exercise of power was thenceforth confined to debate. Recovering his balance, he could again take an objective view of commerce, such as he had acutely expressed on his trip to the Hebrides: "This rage of trade will destroy itself . . . Trade is like gaming. If a whole company were gamesters, play must cease, for there is nothing to be won. When all nations are traders, there is nothing to be gained by trade, and it will stop first where it is brought to the greatest perfection."

While Johnson's ambition to be active in the world of affairs was finding scope in a brewery, Boswell's desire to take part in the management of the universe was making life less endurable in Scotland. His father remained hostile to his wife, himself and his family of two sons and three daughters, though his step-mother treated his children with some approach to kindness. Lord Auchinleck allowed his eldest son £300 a year. James would have liked £400, but his father preferred the lesser figure. Parliament, the English Bar and London were per-petually calling the younger man: "There is a fine *fame* in being distinguished in London, were it only in literary society as I am." Unable to visit the city of his dreams in 1780, he tried to persuade Johnson to travel as far as York for a meeting, but the Doctor was too indolent to stir. Boswell was luckier the following year, going to London as counsel for the member for Ayrshire in a case to be decided by a parliamentary committee. From General Paoli's house in South Audley Street he sent a note to David Garrick's widow, asking if he might call on her. She invited him, as no doubt he expected she would, to the first party she had given since the death of her husband; and on 20th April 1781 he went to her house in Adelphi Terrace, where, in a company which included Johnson, Reynolds, Burney, Percy, Barnard (Bishop of Killaloe), Hannah More, and several other ladies, he passed what he considered "one of the happiest days that I remember to have enjoyed in the whole course of my life". He did not record much conversation be-cause he was in "fine spirits", but he was able to immortalise one episode. Speaking of a certain author, Johnson said that he had married "a printer's devil". This surprised Reynolds, who said that he thought a printer's devil was a creature in rags with a black face. "Yes, sir," returned Johnson, "but I suppose he had her face washed and put clean clothes on her." Looking very serious, and speaking with much gravity, he continued: "And she did not disgrace him; the woman had a bottom of good sense." Boswell completes the scene:

The word *bottom* thus introduced, was so ludicrous when contrasted with his gravity, that most of us could not forbear tittering and laughing; though I recollect that the Bishop of Killaloe kept his countenance with perfect steadiness, while Miss Hannah More slyly hid her face behind a lady's back who sat on the same settee with her. His pride could not bear that any expression of his should excite ridicule, when he did not intend it; he therefore resolved to assume and exercise despotic power, glanced sternly around, and called out in a strong tone, "Where's the merriment?" Then collecting himself, and looking aweful, to make us feel how he could impose restraint, and as it were searching his mind for a still more ludicrous word, he slowly pronounced, "I say the *woman* was *fundamentally* sensible"; as if he had said, hear this now, and laugh if you dare. We all sat composed as at a funeral.

Johnson and Boswell left the house together, and paused by the rails overlooking the Thames. Boswell was thinking of Garrick and Beauclerk, both of whom had lived in the Terrace just behind them, and he referred to their deaths with some emotion. "Ay, sir," said Johnson tenderly, "and two such friends as cannot be supplied."

Boswell stayed in London for about ten weeks, but preserved little of Johnson's talk because he was "engaged in a variety of other matters, which required exertion and assiduity, and necessarily occupied almost all my time". One of the other matters, demanding assiduity if not much exertion, came to the notice of Hannah More, who was dining with Bishop Shipley of St. Asaph. After dinner Boswell, "much disordered with wine", joined the ladies upstairs, and addressed Hannah in a way that drew from her a sharp rebuke. Another meeting between Johnson and Wilkes took place in May, when each of them amused the other on the theme of Scotland, and Boswell recorded a significant talk with Johnson about power and wealth. Was he not dissatisfied with his small pension and why had he not a considerable office? Boswell wanted to know.

Johnson replied: "Sir, I have never complained of the world, nor do I think that I have reason to complain . . . Here, sir, was a man avowedly no friend to Government at the time, who got a pension without asking for it. I never courted the great; they sent for me; but I think they now give me up. They are satisfied; they have seen enough of me." Boswell could scarcely believe this. Were not they delighted with his conversation? "No, sir; great lords and ladies don't love to have their mouths stopped." But, protested Boswell, himself for one would always want to hear Johnson talk. "Yes, sir, but if you were Lord Chancellor, it would not be so; you would then consider your own dignity."

On 2nd June, Boswell left for Scotland. Charles Dilly and Johnson accompanied him as far as Squire John Dilly's at Southill. They stopped at Welwyn to see the house of Edward Young, whose *Night Thoughts* both of them greatly admired and whose Life had been written by Johnson. They made the acquaintance of his son, and entered the church to see his monument. At Southill they were warmly welcomed. On Sunday they attended service at the church close to Dilly's house, and Boswell, after taking the sacrament, felt himself to be a good man; but Johnson advised him not to trust to impressions. They drank tea with the family of Mr. Smith, vicar of Southill. Next day they all went to see Lord Bute's place at Luton Hooe, after which they dined at an inn in the village of Luton. On Tuesday, 5th June, they drove in Dilly's chaise to Shefford, where Johnson caught the London coach. Boswell went on with the Dilly brothers to visit friends at Bedford, where he dined with officers of the county militia, leaving for the north on the 6th.

"As a dog returneth to his vomit, so a fool returneth to his folly." Boswell returned home to suffer from the dog's vomit and the fool's folly. His hobby of wine and women had become a profession of women and wine, indulgence in either being followed by fits of melancholy, which, like drink, developed into a habit, over-indulgence leading to greater excess; and he was beginning to bore his friends, his stories of gallantry and tippling getting taller and more tedious in repetition, like those of a fisherman about the size and weight of his catch. He had tried to extract from Johnson a lenient view of his weaknesses, but with little success. On the subject of fornication Johnson's opinions were sterner, if less articulate, than Boswell's when suffering from the after-effects. "So then, sir, you would allow of no irregular intercourse whatever between the sexes?" "To be sure I would not, sir. I would punish it much more than it is done, and so restrain it." Speaking of a lady who demanded as much freedom as her husband to satisfy her sexual caprices, Boswell drew from Johnson: "This lady of yours, sir, I think, is very fit for a brothel." He would go no further than stating the property argument: that a husband's infidelity was as nothing compared with a wife's, because "the man imposes no bastards upon his wife". He was more tolerant over drink, admitting that he had drunk many a bottle of wine to raise his spirits and to escape from himself, but he had done so alone, not wishing others to witness the result. He had a steady head, being scarcely affected by three bottles of port at a sitting. But he was always pressing the advantages of sobriety on Boswell, whose promises of amendment were "as false as dicers' oaths".

Johnson himself was about to need whatever succour could be obtained from alcohol. He spent much of the summer following Thrale's death at Streatham. The greater part of the brewer's money had been left on trust to his daughters, his widow getting an income of roughly £2,000 a year, as well as the Streatham house, for life. Everybody was speculating on whether she would marry again, and the newspapers rumoured several possible husbands, including Johnson. But, as she wrote in her diary, "Love and friendship are distinct things, and I would go through fire to serve many a man, whom nothing less than fire would force me to go to bed to." She certainly had no intention of placing herself under the restraint of Johnson, whose biographer was certain that he both wished and expected to marry her; and within a few days of Thrale's death Boswell conceived an ode which was supposed to have been written by Johnson to Mrs. Thrale on their approaching nuptials. It was the sort of thing a man scribbles for the amusement of a select circle of friends, and no one but Boswell would have dreamt of publishing it even anonymously, as he did after Johnson's death. Though Johnson could give Boswell a purpose in life, he could not inoculate him with self-respect, which is the basis of all character; and there is no doubt that if he had read it the Englishman of lowly birth who first married a Mrs. Porter would never again have spoken to the Scottish gentleman who was responsible for this:

> To rich felicity thus rais'd
>   My bosom glows with amorous fire;
> Porter no longer shall be prais'd
>   'Tis I MYSELF am *Thrale's entire*! . . .
>
> Convuls'd in love's tumultous throws,
>   We feel the aphrodisian spasm;
> Tir'd nature must, at last, repose,
>   Then Wit and Wisdom fill the chasm.
>
> Nor only are our limbs entwin'd
>   And lip in rapture glued to lip;
> Lock'd in embraces of the mind,
>   Imagination's sweets we sip.

But Hester Thrale had a different object in view from that of Boswell's fancy. Although the full force of her passion had not yet been revealed to her, she loved an Italian who was engaged to give her daughter Queeney music lessons. Gabriel Piozzi was a gentle, amiable, unaffected, good-looking fellow, with a charming singing voice. An excellent pianist and teacher, his popularity in Bath and London made him partial to everything English, though he always spoke the language with a strong foreign accent. Anyone less like Samuel Johnson or Henry Thrale could scarcely be conceived. He was taken up by Charles Burney, who, anxious to convert his friends Hester Thrale and Dr. Johnson to a love of music, invited a party to his house in St. Martin's Street to hear Piozzi perform, hoping at the same time that an aristocratic guest, Fulke Greville, would be impressed by Johnson's conversation. His kindly plan was thwarted. Johnson refused to talk, and Greville stood haughtily in front of the fire until driven from that position by Johnson's surly comment: "If it were not for depriving the ladies of the fire, I should like to stand upon the hearth myself." Piozzi's singing fell on tone-deaf ears, but something in his expression impelled Hester to steal up to a place just behind him and imitate his actions, squaring and elevating her elbows, raising her eyes as if transported, and mocking all his gestures. It was a case of inverted love at first sight. About two years went by, and then, in 1780, she caught sight of him at Brighton, and asked him to teach her daughter. He was forty years of age, some months her senior, and she thought him "amazingly like" her father. Very soon she confided in her diary that he had become "a prodigious favourite with me", that he was so intelligent and so discerning that "one can't help wishing for his good opinion", that his singing surpassed everybody's, and that his hand on the pianoforte was "so soft, so sweet, so delicate, every tone goes to one's heart . . . and fills the mind with emotions one would not be without, though inconvenient enough sometimes. I made him sing yesterday, and though he says his voice is gone, I cannot somehow or other get it out of my ears—odd enough!" Clearly she had become his pupil in place of Queeney.

Though short-sighted, Johnson was a close observer of people, and nothing short of blindness could have prevented him from noticing that Hester's manner to Piozzi was somewhat warmer than that of an employer. He saw a good deal of the Italian at

Streatham after Thrale's death, quite enough for him to sense a possibility he dared not admit. That Johnson loved Hester is beyond doubt, that he looked on himself as her protector for life is hardly questionable, but whether he suggested or considered marriage is uncertain. As her late husband's friend and executor he took a proprietary interest in everything that concerned her, and as the main object of her constant care and solicitude he viewed with alarm any close relationship she might form with a member of his own sex. It was a relief to him when, in July 1781, Piozzi left for France to fulfil certain professional engagements; and it gave him no pleasure to learn in November that the fellow had returned.

That autumn he went his usual round of friends at Oxford, Birmingham, Lichfield and Ashbourne: "The motives of my journey I hardly know. I omitted it last year, and am not willing to miss it again." He communicated his own sombre feelings to the inhabitants of Lichfield, telling Mrs. Thrale: "All here is gloomy; a faint struggle with the tediousness of time; a doleful confession of present misery, and the approach seen and felt of what is most dreaded and most shunned. But such is the lot of man." His stepdaughter Lucy Porter had been ill, and was now deaf and unable to move: "I can scarcely make her understand me, and she can hardly make me understand her. So here are merry doings." The two surviving sisters of Molly Aston lived on Stowe Hill, the widowed Mrs. Gastrell in a house at the foot of the hill, Elizabeth Aston higher up. Mrs. Gastrell's husband had been the clergyman responsible for cutting down the mulberry tree in Shakespeare's garden at Stratford-on-Avon, "to vex his neighbours" said Johnson. Her sister Elizabeth had now become "a paralytic crawler", he informed Mrs. Thrale. The weather was beginning to affect him, and he found "the autumnal blast sharp and nipping, and the fading world an uncomfortable prospect."

He scarcely made it more comfortable for others. Mr. Wickins, a Lichfield draper, thought Johnson might enjoy a stroll through his garden. They entered a shrubbery, and Wickins proudly announced that what looked like an extensive labyrinth was really a deception, he hoped a pardonable one. Johnson disagreed: "Sir, don't tell me of deception; a lie, sir, is a lie, whether it be a lie to the eye or a lie to the ear." Passing an urn which he had erected to a deceased friend, Wickins asked how Johnson liked it. "Sir, I hate urns; they *are* nothing; they *mean* nothing; they convey no ideas but those of horror. Would they were beaten to pieces to pave our streets!" They came to a bathing-pool, and Wickins tried again, speaking of its salubrity. Johnson asked whether his health was good. Wickins said he felt pretty well. "Then, sir, let well enough alone, and be content. I hate immersion." On the edge of the pool stood a statue of Venus. "Throw her into the pond to hide her nakedness and to cool her lasciviousness," said Johnson. Feeling perhaps that he had not been making the best of things, he now tugged at a nail half-buried in the bark of a plum tree. Having extracted it, he cried: "There, sir! I have done *some* good today; the tree might have festered. I make it a rule, sir, to do some good every day of my life."

He certainly gave good advice on every possible occasion. From Lichfield he wrote a long letter to Queeney Thrale advising her to exterminate captiousness from her mind. To take offence easily was more destructive of friendship than open quarrelling: "The rule to be observed is, never to impute to design those negligences or omissions which can be imputed to forgetfulness, nor ever to resent as deliberate and malignant enmity such offences as may be the effect of accidental levity or hasty petulance." He confessed to Queeney's mother that the man who knew the consequence of any fault was best qualified to speak of it, and that, while offering mankind his opinion, he had never proposed his behaviour as an example.

Staying with Taylor at Ashbourne, he heard that Piozzi was shortly expected at Streatham, and wrote at once to Hester, saying that he would leave every place "as fast as I decently can, till I get back to you, whose kindness is one of my great comforts . . . Piozzi, I find, is coming . . . and when *he* comes and *I* come, you will have two about you that love you; and I question if either of us heartily care how few more you have." It may have been his present foreboding that made him try to find consolation in anxiety. "To be without hope or fear, if it were possible, would not be happiness," he told Queeney: "It is better that life should struggle with obstructions than stagnate and putrefy. Never be without something to wish and something to do." His own wish for distraction as well as cohesion was made plain in another letter to Hester: "Pray contrive a multitude of good things for us to do when we meet, something that may *hold all together*. Though if anything makes *me* love you more, it is going from you." This was followed by a cry from the heart: "Do not neglect me, nor relinquish me. Nobody will ever love you better or honour you more than . . . Sam Johnson."

While fearful of losing one friend, he lost another. Robert Levett died suddenly in January 1782. Although, as Johnson said, "in lapidary inscriptions a man is not upon oath," he must have considered himself sworn to veracity when writing a threnody, for there is no more honestly and movingly expressed poem in the language than his on the death of Levett:

> Well try'd through many a varying year,
>   See Levett to the grave descend;
> Officious, innocent, sincere,
>   Of every friendless name the friend.
>
> Yet still he fills affection's eye,
>   Obscurely wise, and coarsely kind;
> Nor, letter'd arrogance, deny
>   Thy praise to merit unrefin'd.
>
> When fainting Nature call'd for aid,
>   And hov'ring Death prepar'd the blow,

His vigorous remedy display'd
The power of art without the show.

In misery's darkest caverns known,
His ready help was ever nigh,
Where hopeless Anguish pour'd his groan,
And lonely Want retir'd to die.

No summons mock'd by chill delay,
No petty gains disdain'd by pride;
The modest wants of every day,
The toil of every day supply'd.

His virtues walk'd their narrow round,
Nor made a pause, nor left a void;
And sure the Eternal Master found
His single talent well employ'd.

Like so many poets, Johnson had begun with a blank-verse tragedy, aiming at the sun and missing it. He ended with a simple epitaph, aiming at a star and hitting it.

His provincial tour at the close of 1781 failed to improve his health, though he was glad he had undertaken it: "In age we feel again that love of our native place and our early friends, which in the bustle or amusements of middle life were overborne and suspended." From January 1782 his illnesses increased in frequency and gravity. He suffered from asthma and dropsy, and his attempted cures—mercury, opium, starvation, bleeding and blistering—lowered his resistance to disease. In this condition he had to endure the changing attitude of Mrs. Thrale, who dared not tell him of her feelings for Piozzi, and could not maintain the easy familiarity of their former relationship. Her conviction of his stern disapproval if he became aware of the position made her uncomfortable in his presence, and this caused her to avoid him, to avert her eyes in his company, to be petulant, to speak recklessly, to treat his advice with impatience, to ignore his wishes. At first he appeared to take no notice of her altered manner, and in writing from Bolt Court of his ailments begged her pathetically not to add diminution of kindness to his other distresses. Again he adjured her: "Do not let Mr. Piozzi nor anybody else put me quite out of your mind, and do not think that anybody will love you like . . . Sam Johnson." When she told him that for the sake of economy she was thinking of going to Italy, he approved; and she ascribed to indifference what was really despair. One day, as the London coach turned into Streatham Common, he pointed with a shaking finger to the mansion they were leaving, and said to Fanny Burney: "That house . . . is lost to *me* . . . for ever!" To soothe her conscience Hester tried hard in her diary to convince herself that he did not care for her; while he felt increasingly certain that she did not care for him. Allowing for their characters and the circumstances, it was an inevitable situation, and, as is the habit of human beings in such cases, each laid the blame on the other. We need not make the same error.

In June 1782 he paid a short visit to Oxford, after which he returned to Streatham, and Mrs. Thrale was able to report an improvement of his health to Boswell, who naturally replied to her letter with an assurance of his admiration and gratitude, coupled with a request for anecdotes. He could not raise the money to visit London this year, and Johnson advised him not to borrow it: "Do not accustom yourself to consider debt only as an inconvenience; you will find it a calamity. Poverty takes away so many means of doing good, and produces so much inability to resist evil, both natural and moral, that it is by all virtuous means to be avoided." Lord Auchinleck died at the end of August 1782; James became the laird; and one of the first things his wife did, no doubt at his intercession, was to ask Johnson to stay with them; but the state of his health prevented it. Although Boswell was nearly forty-two years old when he inherited Auchinleck, Johnson being close on seventy-three, the relationship between the two was the same as it had always been. Boswell continued to revere Johnson as a philosopher, to seek his counsel in all the affairs of life, and to feel a filial affection for him, tempered by awe in his presence; while Johnson took a paternal interest in Boswell, treating him now with tenderness, now with severity, occasionally with ridicule. The younger man was a convenient butt when the elder was in a satirical mood, a circumstance which contributed to the pleasure of both, for what aroused the mirth of a social circle animated the pages of the victim's journal. Above all it pleased Johnson that his company should be sought and his advice solicited by a lively young fellow, and it delighted Boswell that a great moralist should express pleasure in his company. The benefits were reciprocal, and the fondness was mutual.

The new laird of Auchinleck could now shake off the religion in which he had been brought up and proclaim himself an Anglican, fear of his father having so far restrained him. He once remarked that card-playing always made him melancholy, like a Presbyterian sermon. Politics had a similar effect on Johnson, and though he said that "it is useless and foolish, and perhaps sinful, to be gloomy", he could not suppress a passing reference to the state of the country in August 1782: "Perhaps no nation not absolutely conquered has declined so much in so short a time. We seem to be sinking." This shows that he had not meditated much on English history, which was merely following its usual pattern. When England is not rapidly going to the dogs, she is busily becoming a lion. Within Johnson's knowledge, she had risen under Elizabeth and fallen with the early Stuarts, risen under Cromwell and fallen with the later Stuarts, risen under Marlborough and fallen with Walpole, risen under Chatham and fallen with North; from all of which he might have divined that she would shortly rise again under Pitt. But he was too full of his own troubles to bother about politics.

In August 1782 Mrs. Thrale let the Streatham house for three years, and early in October Johnson ate his last dinner there, consisting of a boiled leg of lamb stuffed with raisins, a round of beef, turkey, figs, grapes and peaches, the last two unripe owing to a bad season. He also offered up a prayer to God, asking for help "that I may, with humble and sincere thankfulness, remember the comforts and conveniences which I have enjoyed at this place; and that I may resign them with holy submission, equally trusting in thy protection when thou givest, and when thou takest away". Having further commended the Thrales to the Almighty's fatherly protection, he spent some weeks with the family at Brighton, arriving there "in a state of so much weakness, that I rested four times in walking between the inn and the lodging."

His last sojourn at Brighton was made extremely uncomfortable for the household because of his illness and his rising resentment against Hester Thrale. "It is not hard to love those from whom nothing can be feared," he once wrote. Now he feared the loss of comfort and companionship at a time of life when both were more necessary than ever before, and his general behaviour gave the impression that he hated everybody. On 29th October there was a large gathering at Mrs. Thrale's house. One of the guests was William Weller Pepys, with whom Johnson had lost his temper at Streatham the previous year. The subject of wit was being discussed, and Pepys recited two lines from Pope's *Essay on Criticism* with approval:

> True wit is Nature to advantage dress'd,
> What oft was thought, but ne'er so well express'd.

"That, sir," said Johnson, "is a definition both false and foolish. Let wit be dressed how it will, it will equally be wit, and neither the more nor the less for any advantage dress can give it."

"But, sir," argued Pepys, "may not wit be so ill expressed, and so obscure, by a bad speaker, as to be lost?"

"The fault then, sir, must be with the hearer. If a man cannot distinguish wit from words, he little deserves to hear it."

"But, sir, what Pope means——"

"Sir, what Pope means, if he means what he says, is both false and foolish. In the first place, 'what oft was thought' is all the worse for being often thought, because to be wit it ought to be newly thought."

"But, sir, 'tis the expression makes it new."

"How can the expression make it new? It may make it clear, or may make it elegant; but how new? You are confounding words with things."

"But, sir, if one man says a thing very ill, may not another man say it so much better that——"

"That other man, sir, deserves but small praise for the amendment: he is but the tailor to the first man's thoughts."

"True, sir, he may be but the tailor; but then the difference is as great as between a man in a gold lace suit and a man in a blanket."

"Just so, sir, I thank you for that: the difference is precisely such, since it consists neither in the gold lace suit nor the blanket, but in the man by whom they are worn."

In reporting the scene Fanny Burney said that she only gave the summary of their argument, which was filled out with many contemptuous sarcasms from Johnson. After that, people avoided him. One man refused an invitation because of his presence; another left on hearing that he had arrived; others scuttled into corners at his approach; he was excluded from invitations to parties; those who came to Mrs. Thrale's house dared not speak to him for fear of receiving a churlish answer; and it was noticed that he was especially unpleasant to his hostess. Outside the household in West Street one person remained on cordial terms with him. This was Philip Metcalfe, who, having often met him at parties given by Joshua Reynolds, now offered his carriage whenever the Doctor wished for an airing. They drove together to see Chichester Cathedral,

Petworth and Cowdray, and occasionally Johnson dined at Metcalfe's house. Everyone else was frightened by his harshness and his wit.

The Brighton interlude lasted until 20th November 1782. At six o'clock that morning Mrs. Thrale, her daughters and Fanny Burney left their beds, plunged into the cold sea, dressed by candle-light, and as soon as Johnson could be got ready set out for London in a coach and a chaise. At dinner-time they arrived in Argyll Street, where Mrs. Thrale had taken a house for the winter. A room therein was placed at Johnson's disposal.

CHAPTER 25

Distressful Strokes

PASSION had now taken possession of Hester Thrale, and at her present age was a much more serious complaint than it would have been twenty years earlier. Broadly speaking, youth is in love with love, middle-age with a lover. The emotion in later life is therefore intensified by concentration, and the man or woman who experiences passion for the first time when past forty loses all sense of responsibility and cannot be understood by those who have never been subjected to it. Hester's case was complicated by her daughters. Her relative indifference to their father and the boredom of perpetual pregnancy had made her less maternal towards them than might have been the case if she had cared for him and spent less time in breeding. Consequently her children were not in sympathy with her, and the eldest, Queeney, now twenty, was openly hostile, the rest taking their tone from her. Parents can arouse as much contempt in children as children can provoke irritation in parents, and perhaps nothing appears more ridiculous in the eyes of the young than signs of unsatisfied desire in their seniors.

> For at your age
> The hey-day in the blood is tame, it's humble,
> And waits upon the judgment,

says Hamlet to his mother, and words to that effect were doubtless addressed by Queeney to hers. But the hey-day in the blood is far from tame between forty and fifty; it wholly

320

deprives the lover of judgment; and Hester Thrale now appeared at her least attractive before her children.

Having made a declaration of love in front of Piozzi and Queeney, she seemed to be surprised at the frigid animosity of the latter. A period of nagging followed, Queeney having taught her younger sisters to chant laments over their parent's desertion of them whenever they saw her. At length she perceived that, having married Thrale to oblige her mother, she would have to reject marriage with Piozzi to oblige her daughters. Distressing scenes took place, one of which with Queeney and two other daughters she committed to her journal: "When I was near losing my existence from the contentions of my mind, and was seized with a temporary delirium in Argyll Street, she and her two eldest sisters laughed at my distress, and observed to dear Fanny Burney that it was *monstrous droll*." In great perturbation of mind, she at length dismissed Piozzi, sacrificing her deepest feeling to the conventional view that a mother's first duty was to her children, though in this case they were rich and nothing prevented them from making a permanent home with her and their stepfather. Queeney's chief objection to her mother's second marriage was that it would provoke a scandal, which might stand in the way of a good match for herself. The scandal would be due to Piozzi's Italian origin, to his religion, and to his profession. As a foreigner he was considered a mere adventurer seeking a favourable marriage, as a Roman Catholic he was believed to be untrustworthy with sinister designs on the British polity, and as a singer he was regarded as nothing better than a conjurer or contortionist.

Piozzi left for Italy, and Hester retired to Bath in April 1783.

Fortunately Boswell was in London just then, and his company did Johnson good, but illness was making the Doctor irritable. He flew into a rage when Boswell again mentioned that he should have obtained high office and wealth in the State; and on being asked whether he had been out-of-doors on a certain day he snapped: "Don't talk so childishly. You may as well ask if I hanged myself today." Boswell raised the topic of politics, but dropped it quickly on hearing from Johnson: "Sir, I'd as soon have a man break my bones as talk to me of public affairs, internal or external." Perhaps a later comment explained his annoyance: "It is wonderful, sir, with how little real superiority of mind men can make a figure in public life." He was conscious that his own mental ascendancy had one grave drawback: "Sir, there is nothing by which a man exasperates most people more than by displaying a superior ability or brilliancy in conversation. They seem pleased at the time; but their envy makes them curse him in their hearts." His nature expressed itself in extremes. A desire for victory at whatever cost in argument, a tendency to excessive remedies for his diseases, the paring of his nails to the quick, the scraping of his finger-joints with a penknife until they looked raw: such ruthless treatment was balanced by his sensitive consideration for the feelings and interests of others, for example his advice to writers not to dedicate their works to him but to someone who could be of use to them, and his practical assistance to those in distress, like Mauritius Lowe, whose picture was rejected by the Royal Academy but admitted on Johnson's request to Reynolds. "He that has his foot firm upon dry ground may pluck another out of the water, but of those that are all afloat none has any care but for himself." So Johnson wrote to Mrs. Thrale; but it was not true of the writer, who gave a helping hand to many while he was struggling in the waves.

His biographer left for Scotland at the end of May, and he felt lonely in a house which contained "two sick and discontented women, who can hardly talk if they had anything to say, and whose hatred of each other makes one great exercise of their faculties". He kept Hester Thrale informed of his illnesses and attempted cures, and she was the first to hear of an affliction that frightened him more than all his physical disabilities put together: a paralytic stroke which temporarily deprived him of speech. But he recovered, and on 30th June wrote to Hester: "Let me have your kindness and your prayers, and think on me as on a man who for a very great portion of your life has done you all the good he could." She offered to make the journey from Bath if her presence could add to his comfort, but he replied that "What man can do for man has been done for me." In July Mrs. Desmoulins left Bolt Court, which thereafter became more peaceful, and Johnson spent a short holiday with Bennet Langton at Rochester. He returned to find Anna Williams in a very low state: "I have just been to see her, and I doubt she gave perverse answers to my enquiries, because she saw that my tenderness put it in her power to give me pain. This is hateful and despicable, and yet must not be too much hated and despised, for strongly entwisted with human nature is the desire of exercising power, however that power be gained or given. Let us pity it in others, and despise it in ourselves."

In August he stayed for some days at Heale, near Salisbury, with William Bowles, who was contemplating a political career, but reconsidered it on hearing from Johnson: "My present thoughts do not allow me to take pleasure in the expectation of seeing a mind so pure as yours exposed to the contagion of public life, and contending with the corrupt and contaminated atmosphere of the House of Commons." While at Heale the Doctor went to see Salisbury Cathedral and Stonehenge, which he described as "two eminent monuments of art and rudeness . . . the first essay and the last perfection in architecture". One of Bowles's guests happened to remark that nobody was afraid of death. "Speak for yourself, sir, for indeed I am," said Johnson. "I did not say of dying, but of death, meaning its consequences," amplified the other. "And so I mean," rejoined Johnson: "I am very seriously afraid of the consequences." At Salisbury he heard that Anna Williams had died. He returned to a quiet house. For some time Mrs.

Montagu had allowed Anna a small annuity, which Johnson wrote to say was no longer needed, receiving a very kind answer. He mentioned this to Fanny Burney, who assumed that there would now be peace between him and the 'Queen of the Blues'. Said he: "Why, I am now come to that time when I wish all bitterness and animosity to be at an end. I have never done her any serious harm—nor would I, though I could give her a bite; but she must provoke me much first. In volatile talk indeed I may have spoken of her not much to her mind, for in the tumult of conversation malice is apt to grow sprightly; and there, I hope, I am not decrepit!" (with a resounding laugh).

He was however in a miserable condition of mind and body. All his life he had dreaded the approach of mental infirmity and physical incapacity, expressing his feelings strongly about an old school friend, Charles Congreve, who had "the appearance of a man wholly sunk into that sordid self-indulgence which disease, real or imaginary, is apt to dictate" and had "put himself to nurse, a state to which an old man is naturally tempted, and which he should resolutely disdain till his powers really desert him." More people are corrupted by advancing age than by money or power, because they become increasingly self-centred with the years, and Johnson once told Mrs. Thrale that with a little more spoiling he would soon become a scoundrel. Illness augments the egotism of age, and the volubility of Johnson's complaints would in another man have aroused his contemptuous criticism. In letters to Hester he spoke of his loneliness, his boredom, his insomnia, his constant' enemies asthma and dropsy, a ferocious onslaught of gout, and a sarcocele: "I am now broken with disease, without the alleviation of familiar friends or domestic society." He played on her pity, reminding her that "a friendship of twenty years is interwoven with the texture of life" and that "You will never bestow any share of your good will on one who deserves better."

But his friends did not desert him, and he was still able to receive innumerable visitors. One caller that autumn was the famous actress Sarah Siddons. When she entered the room he looked around for a chair, failed to see one, and remarked: "Madam, you who so often occasion a want of seats to other people, will the more readily excuse the want of one yourself." The defect remedied, they had a talk about the drama, and he promised that if she again appeared as Queen Katharine in *Henry VIII* he would "once more hobble out to the theatre". He no longer enjoyed the meetings of the Literary Club, which had become "very miscellaneous and very heterogeneous; it is therefore without confidence and without pleasure. I go to it only as a kind of public dinner." To suit his present taste he started another association which was called Sam's Club because its headquarters, the Essex Head tavern in Essex Street, Strand, was kept by Samuel Greaves, an old servant of Thrale's. They were to meet for dinner three times a week, and Johnson drafted the rules, the last of which ran: "One penny shall be left by each member for the waiter." The members were of all kinds. Johnson had no great liking for the society of literary men, and once wrote: "Perhaps the best advice to authors would be, that they should keep out of the way of one another." He disrelished the tendency of authors to cultivate the society of what the world regarded as "people of importance", cared still less for those who pretended a degree of familiarity with them, and wrote of Swift: "No man, however, can pay a more servile tribute to the great than by suffering his liberty in their presence to aggrandise him in his own esteem." He had an antipathy to Swift, partly on account of the Dean's bawdy humour but primarily because he disliked worldliness in a parson. Once he was in the company of several clergymen who, anxious that he should think them jolly good fellows, interspersed their sprightly mundane chat with much laughter. Having listened gravely for a while, he turned to Beauclerk and said in a whisper that was audible enough to lower their spirits: "This merriment of parsons is mighty offensive."

It happened that the winter of 1783–4 was exceptionally

severe and prolonged, and the state of Johnson's health prevented him from enjoying the meetings of Sam's Club for the first four months of its existence. He remained indoors from 13th December 1783 till 21st April 1784, a total of 129 days, taking opium "under pressure of insupportable distress", snoozing in a chair because he could not go to sleep in bed, his days and nights passing "in morbid wakefulness, in unseasonable sleepiness, in gloomy solitude, with unwelcome visitors, or ungrateful exclusions, in variety of wretchedness." Greatly adding to his distress in the early months of 1784 was the knowledge that Piozzi had been recalled from Italy. We do not know how he became aware of it, but rumour travels fast, and, if spiced with scandal, faster. Mrs. Thrale's physical condition had at length shattered the resistance of the hitherto intractable Queeney. For almost a year she had suffered the agony of thwarted passion, and towards the end of 1783 her silent but visible torments, backed by the opinion of her physician, forced her eldest daughter to capitulate. It was a choice between the early death of Hester or the return of Piozzi, and much though Queeney detested the latter she could not face the alternative; so Piozzi's banishment was repealed.

Those who knew what had occurred were surprised that Piozzi did not come bounding over the Alps without an instant's delay; but considering the treatment he had received a year before, the insult to his natural pride, and the chilling enmity of Hester's family and friends, his delay was sensible and inevitable. No doubt he felt that sudden resolutions and changes of mind were liable to be reversed with equal rapidity; and he remained in Italy until more urgent communications removed his doubts. All that Johnson knew was that Piozzi had been asked to come back. Fanny Burney also knew it, and when she called at Bolt Court she planned to speak of other things. But Johnson's mind was obsessed with this one thing, and breathing heavily he turned towards her, ejaculating hoarsely "Piozzi!" He seemed to be convulsed with rage and indignation, but after see-sawing in his chair for a while he calmed down and became pensive. Again his feelings got the better of him as he spoke of Mrs. Thrale: "She cares for no one! You only—you, she loves still—but no one and nothing else! You she still loves, as . . . she loves her little finger!"

All the same he had heard nothing officially, and he went on writing to Hester in the pathetic hope that something of their old friendship could be salvaged from the storm of her emotions. In March 1784 he reported that, following a puncture, his sarcocele had disappeared, and that his dropsy had been relieved by the gradual evacuation of twenty pints of water. He closed the letter: "Do not reject me from your thoughts. Shall we ever exchange confidence by the fireside again?" The sensation of relief as the water drained from his body was so keen that he cried at intervals: "It is wonderful, very wonderful!" He had been preparing for death with prayer and fasting, and it seemed to him that the alleviation of his bodily distress was an answer to his petitions and "a token of the Divine mercy". Revelation can be wrought by physical as by spiritual means, and Johnson's sense of doom temporarily lifted as the water in his system subsided. "I am still very weak," he informed Hester in April, "though my appetite is keen, and my digestion potent, and I gratify myself more at table than ever I did at my own cost before. I have now an inclination to luxury which even your table did not excite, for till now my talk was more about the dishes than my thoughts." He admitted that he had only the timidity of a Christian to deter him from overeating, not the wisdom of a Stoic to prevent the indulgence. "Think of me, if you can, with tenderness", was his final appeal to her.

Arriving in London on 5th May 1784, Boswell was surprised to find him in such good health after so many bad reports, quite well enough to play his old trick of scoring off an opponent by ignoring an argument. They were fellow-guests at a dinner when Boswell contravened one of Johnson's views by quoting from his work two lines that were at variance with it. Johnson's method of reconciling his antitheses was as follows: "Sir, there is one passion I would advise you to command: when you have drunk out that glass, don't drink another." A talk they had together on Bennet Langton revealed the danger of giving advice, even when solicited. During his recent illness Johnson had begged Langton to tell him sincerely of his faults. Langton obliged with a summary on a sheet of paper. Johnson thanked him fervently, studied the paper, found that it merely contained several texts of Scripture recommending Christian charity, and angrily demanded: "What is your drift, sir?" Langton intimated that the Doctor contradicted people in conversation. There was an explosion, the criminal reprimanding the judge. Boswell heard exactly what had happened from a different source, Johnson's account being in a milder key and closing with the guileless query: "Now what harm does it do any man to be contradicted?" Boswell was diplomatic: "I suppose he meant the *manner* of doing it, roughly and harshly." "And who is the worse for that?" "It hurts people of weak nerves." "I know no such weak-nerved people."

They went by coach to Oxford on 3rd June, Johnson's conversation on the journey drawing from one of the female passengers: "How he does talk! Every sentence an essay." The dinner at an inn on the way produced an essay on the roast mutton with which the waiter could have dispensed: "It is as bad as bad can be: it is ill-fed, ill-killed, ill-kept, and ill-drest." They stayed with Dr. William Adams, Master of Pembroke College, and remained there until the 19th, though Boswell was absent for several days in order "to attend the musical meeting in honour of Handel in Westminster Abbey." Religious themes frequently came up for discussion in the Adams circle, and Johnson confessed: "I would be a Papist if I could. I have fear enough; but an obstinate rationality prevents me. I shall never be a Papist unless on the near approach of death, of which I have a very great terror." One day at breakfast Johnson was asked by Adams to compose some family prayers. He refused, but added that he had thought of compiling an anthology of the best prayers, adding a few of his own, and prefacing it with an essay on the subject. Boswell described the sequel:

> We all now gathered about him, and two or three of us at a time joined in pressing him to execute this plan. He seemed to be a little displeased at the manner of our importunity, and in great agitation called out, "Do not talk thus of what is so awful. I know not what time God will allow me in this world. There are many things which I wish to do." Some of us persisted, and Dr. Adams said, "I never was more serious about anything in my life." JOHNSON: "Let me alone, let me alone; I am overpowered." And then he put his hands before his face, and reclined for some time upon the table.

A few years earlier, at Streatham, he had shown less agitation when Sir Richard Musgrave got up from a chair and besought him to follow his *Lives of the Poets* with biographies of famous prose authors. "Sit down, sir!" shouted Johnson.

Adams lent his coach to the two friends for visits to Iffley and Wheatley, where they were pleasantly entertained by dons, and nothing but religion interfered with the tranquillity of their visit. Trouble arose when Johnson proclaimed his belief in eternal punishment. Every religion is based on some instinct or desire of mankind, and a punitive God satisfies the human passion for revenge, the condition being that the believer can fancy himself saved while those he hates are consigned to hell. Johnson's faith in a deity who is omniscient yet retributive may have been influenced by the general state of his health, inescapable disease in this world making it difficult for him to imagine anything but ineluctable torment in the next. At any rate, when he said: "I am afraid I may be one of those who shall be damned," and Adams asked what he meant by damned, he cried out loudly: "Sent to hell, sir, and punished ever-lastingly." Adams disagreed with this doctrine, which started an argument, which Johnson closed abruptly and dictatorially with "I'll have no more on't." Another day, in a more placid humour, he dealt with books of travel, one of which, about the inhabitants of the South Sea islands, had just been published.

"There can be little entertainment in such books; one set of savages is like another," he pronounced.

"I do not think the people of Otaheite can be reckoned savages," dissented Boswell.

"Don't cant in defence of savages!"

"They have the art of navigation."

"A dog or a cat can swim."

"They carve very ingeniously."

"A cat can scratch, and a child with a nail can scratch."

Boswell gave it up.

On their return to London, Boswell stayed with General Paoli, who had moved from South Audley Street to a mansion at the corner of Portman Square and Upper Seymour (now Wigmore) Street. Probably "high spirits" interfered with note-taking on a lavish scale during the last ten days of June 1784, Boswell's final chance of seeing and hearing Johnson, but he made up for the lacuna in his journal by preserving one or two good things he had heard, such as Johnson's comment after listening to a magistrate's tediously long description of a case that resulted in his sentencing four convicts to transportation: "I heartily wish, sir, that I were a fifth." And a first-rate example of Johnson's two conversational styles. Having said that Buckingham's comedy *The Rehearsal* "has not wit enough to keep it sweet," he pulled himself together and spoke *ex cathedra*: "It has not vitality enough to preserve it from putrefaction."

They dined at the Literary Club, Johnson's last appearance in what Boswell calls "that respectable society", on 22nd June, and soon afterwards it was agreed among certain of the Doctor's

friends that something ought to be done for the sake of his
health. They thought he should spend the coming winter in
Italy, which could only be managed if his income were augmented. Reynolds and Boswell put their heads together, and
the latter wrote to the Lord Chancellor, Thurlow, suggesting
that the King might extend "the royal bounty". Johnson was
in complete ignorance of this, and knew nothing about it until
Thurlow, signifying his willingness to urge the petition, replied
that "It would be a reflection on us all if such a man should
perish for want of the means to take care of his health."
Boswell then broke the news to Johnson, who was much moved.
"This is taking prodigious pains about a man," he said. "O!
sir, your friends would do everything for you," exclaimed
Boswell in tones that brought tears to the Doctor's eyes. "God
bless you all!" he said with deep emotion. Boswell, too, shed
tears, and for a time they were unable to speak. Overpowered
by his feelings, Johnson left the room.

But the King was not in a melting mood, and the Lord
Chancellor had to report failure. Thurlow, however, offered
to lend Johnson five or six hundred pounds, and to spare him a
feeling of obligation said that his pension could be mortgaged.
Johnson was grateful but declined the offer, making the excuse
that if he got better the journey to Italy would be unnecessary,
if worse he would be unable to travel.

Boswell heard of this after his return to Scotland. But before
the two friends separated for ever they dined together at Dilly's
and at Paoli's, where Johnson's appetite showed no sign of
abatement. Nor was there any diminution of Boswell's appetite
for horrors: one morning he witnessed the execution of fifteen
men in front of Newgate prison, and edified himself by morali-
sing on the spectacle. On 30th June they dined quietly with
Joshua Reynolds, no one else being present, and hopefully
discussed the measure of the royal bounty. Johnson said that
he would rather have his pension doubled than receive a grant
of a thousand pounds, because with £600 a year he could

pass the rest of his life "in splendour". Talking of a rural existence, Johnson summed up his feelings: "They who are content to live in the country are fit for the country." Boswell argued that a refined taste was not an advantage, since those who had it were less satisfied with things than those without it. "Nay, sir, that is a paltry notion," said Johnson. "Endeavour to be as perfect as you can in every respect." They drove in Sir Joshua's coach to the entry of Bolt Court, and Johnson, who hated being left with long hours of sleepless solitude before him, asked Boswell to stay for a while. Boswell, afraid that it would make him melancholy, refused:

We bade adieu to each other affectionately in the carriage. When he had got down upon the foot-pavement, he called out "Fare you well"; and without looking back, sprung away with a kind of pathetic briskness, if I may use that expression, which seemed to indicate a struggle to conceal uneasiness, and impressed me with a foreboding of our long, long separation.

The following day Johnson heard from Queeney Thrale that she and her sisters had left their mother, who intended to marry Piozzi. He replied in two notes: "I read your letter with anguish and astonishment, such as I never felt before. I had fondly flattered myself that time had produced better thoughts. . . . What I think of your mother's conduct I cannot express, but by words which I cannot prevail upon myself to use." On 1st July, Piozzi arrived in Bath, and on the next day Johnson received a circular letter addressed by Mrs. Thrale to the executors of her late husband's will, informing them that her daughters had left for Brighton and intimating that she would shortly be marrying Piozzi. This circular letter was enclosed in another to Johnson personally, begging his pardon "for concealing from you a connection which you must have heard of by many, but I suppose never believed. Indeed, my dear sir, it was concealed only to save us both needless pain; I could not have borne to reject that counsel it would have killed me to take, and I only tell it you now because all is irrevocably settled, and out of your power to prevent. I will say, however, that the dread of your disapprobation has given me some anxious moments, and though, perhaps, I am become by many privations the most independent woman in the world, I feel as if acting without a parent's consent till you write kindly . . ."

Johnson lost control of himself. The long-gathering resentment due to her growing indifference, the rage caused by her concealment, the indignation springing from a sense of impotence, the jealousy evoked by a foreign supplanter, and the pricking of his vanity as an intimate friend by her reference to him as a parent made him for the first and last time in his life write a letter that was as ill-considered as the most outrageous of his conversational imprecations:

Madam,—

If I interpret your letter right, you are ignominiously married; if it is yet undone, let us once more talk together. If you have abandoned your children and your religion, God forgive your wickedness: if you have forfeited your fame and your country, may your folly do no further mischief. If the last act is yet to do, I who have loved you, esteemed you, reverenced you, and served you, I who long thought you the first of humankind, entreat that, before your fate is irrevocable, I may once more see you.

I was, I once was,—

Madam, most truly yours,

Sam: Johnson.

I will come down, if you permit it.

Hester did not permit it. On the contrary she desired "the conclusion of a correspondence which I can bear to continue no longer". She praised the qualities of Piozzi and said that his religion would "teach him to forgive insults he has not deserved". She sent her best wishes and concluded: "You have always commanded my esteem, and long enjoyed the fruits of a friendship never infringed by one harsh expression on my part during twenty years of familiar talk. Never did I oppose your will, or control your wish; nor can your unmerited severity itself lessen my regard; but till you have changed your opinion of Mr. Piozzi let us converse no more. God bless you."

Meditation in the interval had made Johnson aware of the intolerance and ingratitude displayed in his letter, and the style of his next indicated contrition:

Dear Madam,—

What you have done, however I may lament it, I have no pretence to resent, as it has not been injurious to me: I therefore breathe out one sigh more of tenderness, perhaps useless, but at least sincere.

I wish that God may grant you every blessing, that you may be happy in this world for its short continuance, and eternally happy in a better state; and whatever I can contribute to your happiness I am very ready to repay, for that kindness which soothed twenty years of a life radically wretched.

After advising them to settle in England instead of Italy, he wrote: "The tears stand in my eyes." Hester thanked him for his "sweetly kind" letter, again spoke highly of Piozzi, and closed with the assurance of her true affection; but by that time Johnson's rage was again uppermost, and he violently erased her signature. In his heart he never forgave her for preferring her own happiness to his comfort, and some five months later, on being asked by Fanny Burney whether he ever heard from her, "No, nor write to her," he savagely answered. "I drive her quite from my mind. If I meet with one of her letters, I burn it instantly. I have burnt all I can find. I never speak of her, and I desire never to hear of her more. I drive her, as I said, wholly from my mind." Which shows, of course, that she remained insistently in his mind. He was not a very competent incendiary, because over a hundred of her letters survived his ravages.

Late in July, Hester and Gabriel were married in London by the Roman Catholic chaplain of the Spanish Embassy, and two days afterwards they went through the Protestant ceremony of marriage at Bath. "The outcry of surprise and censure raised throughout the metropolis by these unexpected nuptials," wrote Fanny Burney, "was almost stunning in its jarring noise of general reprobation; resounding through madrigals, parodies, declamation, epigrams and irony." Fanny herself described the union as a "grievous catastrophe". The anger of Hester's friends and critics would no doubt have been increased had they known that the marriage was to be an exceptionally happy one. But the periodical outbursts of moral indignation by sections of the community, against those who are supposed to have affronted the fashionable standard of taste or violated the momentary social code, provide material for the historian and pathologist, not the biographer. Johnson is our present subject, and we must now accompany him on the final stages of his earthly pilgrimage.

The Race with Death

FOUR DAYS after his last letter to Mrs. Thrale, a note was despatched by Johnson to the rector of Bromley asking permission to lay a stone on the grave of his wife and sending the inscription for it. At the same time he requested the man who would be responsible for the work "to let the whole be done with privacy, that I may elude the vigilance of the papers". Over thirty years had passed since the death of Tetty, whom he now described in lapidary Latin as "a woman of beauty, elegance, ingenuity and piety". That was how she appeared to him in comparison with the treacherous Hester; and his somewhat belated action was caused by a sudden renewal of loyalty to one who had never let him down and a pang of conscience due to his forgetfulness of her amid the luxuries of Streatham and Southwark.

The woman who for twenty years had soothed a radically wretched life was now beyond the pale: "I thought that either her virtue or her vice would have restrained her from such a marriage. She is now become a subject for her enemies to exult over, and for her friends, if she has any left, to forget or pity." He wrote to Queeney: "I love you, I loved your father, and I loved your mother as long as I could." And he gave her the sort of advice we should expect from a typical time-server: "In matters of human judgment and prudential consideration, consider the public voice of general opinion as always worthy of your attention; remember that such practices can seldom be right which all the world has concluded to be wrong." Had his

own life been governed by this axiom, his biography would not
be worth writing; but that part of him which found in conven-
tion and orthodoxy a refuge from mental scepticism was also
disclosed in his Life of Pope: "Of things that terminate in
human life, the world is the proper judge; to despise its sentence,
if it were possible, is not just; and if it were just, is not possible."
The Johnson who wrote this would have risen to high office in
the Church.

In July he began his last provincial tour, starting at Oxford,
going on to Lichfield, and staying with Taylor at Ashbourne for
the months of August and September. He provided his doctor
and his friends with bulletins of his health. He took opiates
regularly, and in the middle of August his asthma "perceptibly
remitted", his dropsy almost disappeared, his appetite was keen,
and he developed "a voracious delight in raw summer fruit".
Taylor, who was on a milk diet, took him for drives: "My
friend's chariot is always ready. We have run this morning
twenty-four miles, and could run forty-eight more. *But who can
run the race with death?*" Receiving letters from friends was his
main pleasure. His conversation with Taylor consisted of complaints and groans over their respective ailments, Johnson's
irritation being increased by the fact that Taylor was enlarging
and rebuilding his house, which made it look uncomfortable:
"That a man worn with diseases, in his seventy-second or third
year, should condemn part of his remaining life to pass among
ruins and rubbish, and that no inconsiderable part, appears to
me very strange." Johnson visited Chatsworth, where he was
welcomed by the Duke and Duchess of Devonshire and pressed
to stay, but his poor health made him decline the offer.
"Though I am now in the neighbourhood of the Peak," he
wrote to a friend, "you must expect no account of its wonders,
of its hills, its waters, its caverns, or its mines; but I will tell you,
dear sir, what I hope you will not hear with less satisfaction,
that for about a week past my asthma has been less afflictive."

The first balloon ascent in England was made from Moorfields on 15th September 1784, by an Italian, Vincenzo Lunardi. It remained two and a half hours in the air and came down at Ware. Johnson was interested in the experiment, but soon became bored with a subject that filled the correspondence of his friends to the exclusion of human and personal affairs. He declared that balloons were useless unless they could be guided; and that until they were able to rise above the clouds, nothing could be learnt of the state of the air beyond the mountain-tops. "The first experiment, however, was bold and deserved applause and reward," he wrote. "But since it has been performed and its event is known, I had rather now find a medicine that can ease an asthma." He begged Reynolds for news, but qualified the request: "I have three letters this day, all about the balloon; I could have been content with one. Do not write about the balloon, whatever else you may think proper to say."

He was back at Lichfield in October, his diseases once more gaining upon him. "My limbs are very weak," he reported; "my legs would not carry me far if my breath would last, and my breath would not last if my legs would carry me." He told another friend: "My diseases are an asthma and a dropsy, and, what is less curable, seventy-five." Even when relatively healthy he had shrunk from death, admitting that "However unhappy any man's existence may be, he yet would rather have it than not exist at all." And in his book on the Scottish tour he wrote: "To be told that any man has attained a hundred years, gives hope and comfort to him who stands trembling on the brink of his own climacteric." The reward of those who believe in a future hell is that they create a present hell within themselves; and Arthur Murphy noted that, when not taking part in a conversation, Johnson could often be heard by those who sat near him repeating Claudio's speech in *Measure for Measure*:

> Ay, but to die, and go we know not where;
> To lie in cold obstruction and to rot;

This sensible warm motion to become
A kneaded clod; and the delighted spirit
To bathe in fiery floods, or to reside
In thrilling region of thick-ribbed ice;
To be imprison'd in the viewless winds,
And blown with restless violence round about
The pendent world; or to be worse than worst
Of those that lawless and incertain thought
Imagine howling:—'tis too horrible!
The weariest and most loathed worldly life
That age, ache, penury, and imprisonment
Can lay on nature is a paradise
To what we fear of death.

Solitude vivified such ideas, and while at Lichfield the Doctor asked Anna Seward to call often, though he did not relish her strong disapproval of his literary, religious and political opinions. One day she told him that she had seen a pig capable of doing all the tricks normally exhibited by dogs and horses. A young clergyman present remarked that great torture must have been applied to make the pig submissive. Johnson asked: "How old is your pig?" Three years, said Anna. "Then the pig has no cause to complain," decided the Doctor; "he would have been killed the first year if he had not been *educated*, and protracted existence is a good recompense for very considerable degrees of torture." Another day Anna called at Lucy Porter's house and found Johnson "in deep but agitated slumber in an arm-chair". More callers arriving, he awoke "with convulsive starts", got up with surprising alacrity, and accompanied Anna to the study, where he sat astride a chair, his face to its back, kept up "a trotting motion as if on horseback", and spoke eloquently and amusingly to his visitors about all sorts of things, including the well-taught pig.

Early in November he wrote: "I am relapsing into the dropsy very fast and shall make haste to town," but his illness did not prevent him from staying a few days with Hector at Birmingham on the way, and a few more with Adams at Oxford. He reached London on November 16th, and at once sent for his friend and doctor, Richard Brocklesby, who perceived the gravity of his condition but would not give straight answers to direct questions. Yet his sufferings from asthma and dropsy were soon considerable, and he knew the end was not far off. His nights were tedious because he could neither sleep nor read, but he kept his mind exercised by translating Greek epigrams into Latin verse, and he wrote an epitaph on his mother, father and brother, for a stone in the centre aisle of St. Michael's Church, Lichfield. Bennet Langton was often with him, and one day read him a letter from an admirer praising his work. "The applause of a single human being is of great consequence," said Johnson in an earnest manner. He believed that all his works had helped the cause of religion. They had certainly not been written with the main object of making money, nor of gaining popularity, unlike those of Dryden, who had, said Johnson, placed his happiness in the claps of multitudes, and "let it be remembered that minds are not levelled in their powers but when they are first levelled in their desires". Though untroubled by the tendency of his literary productions, he was seriously concerned over personal shortcomings, warning a friend to lead a better life than he had done. "A better life than you, my dear sir!" was the incredulous response. "Don't compliment now!" frowned the Doctor.

Towards the end of November he received a visit from Fanny Burney, who, perceiving him to be in pain, soon took her leave. Pressing her hands affectionately in his own, he spoke with emotion: "Be not longer in coming again for my letting you go now." As she was leaving the room, he called her back and said: "Remember me in your prayers." Reynolds and Langton were constant callers, and Burke too was seen with several others in his room. "I am afraid, sir, such a number of us may be oppressive to you," said Burke. "No, sir, it is not so, and I must be in a wretched state indeed when your company would not be a delight to me." Burke spoke through his tears: "My dear sir, you have always been too good to me," and left at once. Several doctors attended Johnson regularly, to one of whom he said: "You cannot conceive with what acceleration I advance towards death." Brocklesby called every morning, and Johnson made it clear that he was more anxious about his spiritual than his physical state by asking Macbeth's question:

> Canst thou not minister to a mind diseas'd,
> Pluck from the memory a rooted sorrow,
> Raze out the written troubles of the brain,
> And with some sweet oblivious antidote
> Cleanse the stuff'd bosom of that perilous stuff
> Which weighs upon the heart?

Brocklesby replied:

> Therein the patient
> Must minister to himself.

Two friends, John Hoole and an Italian master named Sastres, sat with him for hours on end, speaking rarely. Occasionally he broke the silence, but soon relapsed, muttering "I am now like Macbeth—question enrages me." When a pillow was readjusted to make him more comfortable, he said: "That will do—all that a pillow can do." A man was employed to remain with him the whole of one night, but failed to give satisfaction: "The fellow's an idiot! Instead of watching, he sleeps like a dormouse, and when he helps me to bed he is as awkward as a turnspit dog the first time he is put into the wheel." He exhorted his friends to read the Bible regularly, not to work on Sundays, and not to neglect their prayers.

On 8th December 1784 he made his will, adding a codicil on the 9th, wherein small sums of money were left to certain needy people, his books to various friends, and the rest of his estate, about £1,500, to Francis Barber. One of the executors, Sir John Hawkins, objected to this "ostentatious bounty and favour to negroes", but would perhaps have substituted the phrase "modest bequest in favour of an old friend" had himself been the legatee.

Johnson dictated his last letter on 10th December. It was addressed to the publisher, William Strahan: "I am very unwilling to take the pains of writing, and therefore make use of another hand to desire that I may have whatever portion of my pension you can spare me with prudence and propriety." He signed a receipt for £75, one quarter's pension, three days later.

On the 11th, Charles Burney found him seated in a large chair, propped up by pillows, and tranquil in mood. They sat mostly in silence, broken only with scraps of conversation, for half an hour. After praying for himself, Johnson brightened up and said to Burney: "Tell Fanny, I think I shall yet throw the ball at her again." At such moments he still hoped for life, and when the surgeon used the lancet gently he cried out: "Deeper, deeper; I want length of life and you fear giving me pain, which I care not for." Once the surgeon declined to repeat the operation, and Johnson said to those in the room: "You all pretend to love me, but you do not love me so well as I do myself." At length Brocklesby was compelled to admit that only a miracle could save him. "Then I will take no more physic, not even my opiates," he said, "for I have prayed that I may render up my soul to God unclouded." Apart from cider and water, he thereafter refused all sustenance, though begged to take some: " 'Tis all very childish; let us hear no more of it." He received the sacrament and composed a prayer.

But during the night of 12th December his desire for life returned with its former intensity; he seemed to feel that even an hour of existence was a respite snatched from an uncertain eternity; and early in the morning of the 13th he ordered Francis Barber to give him the lancet, using abuse and threats when the fellow hesitated. He had also managed to conceal a pair of scissors in his bed; and with one or other of these instruments he gashed himself in three places, drawing no water but losing much blood. Then he lay still, and spent the greater part of the day in a doze, conscious enough at intervals to take a little warm milk, to bestow a blessing on a girl who besought it, and to utter the words "*Jam moriturus!*" in a tone of lament to Sastres. At about seven o'clock that evening he quietly expired, his terror of the Last Judgment vanishing with his last breath.

A week later his body passed through "the full tide of human existence" at Charing Cross into the cloistral calm of Westminster Abbey.

CHAPTER 27

The Laird and the Lord

"BOSWELL, *lend* me sixpence—*not to be repaid*," said Johnson one day; which suggests that on previous occasions he had not been allowed to forget his debts. It also shows that in money affairs as in everything else Boswell's behaviour was incalculable. He could be as generous one moment as he was penurious at another; now kind, now cold. His conduct as a laird surprised those who did not understand his personality: he was efficient, just, discriminating and beneficent. Pride in his ancestry brought out all that was best in him; he could draw strength from the achievements of his forefathers but not from his own nature. His disposition made him dependent upon someone or something outside himself, and nothing was so fixed and permanent as his pedigree. Though he might cry to God in vain, though Johnson might treat him harshly, though Paoli might be aloof, though his wife might be unsympathetic and Temple censorious, he could always cling to the family tree. His constantly expressed belief in rank and position, in a state of feudalism, in government by heritable distinction, in what he called the grand scheme of subordination, was due to the necessity of buttressing Boswell in his own esteem and in the eyes of the world. Johnson supported him in this belief, but the Doctor's views were based on reflection, Boswell's on inclination.

When, therefore, he succeeded his father as laird, he obeyed Johnson's precepts about the duty of landlords, expressed his own good-nature, and above all pleased himself with an exhibition of patriarchal importance and responsibility. He

344

acquainted Johnson with one of his first actions, "my having brought an old man of eighty-eight from a lonely cottage to a comfortable habitation within my enclosures, where he had good neighbours near him". The one function of a laird that he found it impossible to perform was to reside on his estate. Country-life bored him, and, like town-life, drove him to drink; but apart from that his ambitions put it out of the question. The English courts and Parliament, to say nothing of London, enticed him. Johnson had approved his wish to practice as a barrister in the south, and in 1786 he was called to the English Bar, spending a considerable part of his time thereafter in London. He appointed an agent for his Scottish estate, telling him "to act without partiality or love of popularity, except what you may acquire by being just between man and man", warning him not to be "elated by the trust I give you, for its continuance will depend entirely upon your good behaviour", and recommending "great moderation". When the agent wrote a letter beginning "Good Sir", Boswell informed him that the proper way to address a master was "Sir". None of his tenants had any reason to fear that he would be a hard landlord, he declared, and he frequently sent presents of money and food to the poorer ones: "I am sure I wish well to my tenants, and to the best of my knowledge would let them have reasonable bargains." He was "very unwilling to proceed to extremities" against any of them, charging his agent to tell one man that he must not work too hard, to deal easily with another who had suffered losses, to make a gift of his rent to a third. Though he dealt firmly with those who tried to evade their responsibilities, he was considerate and benevolent with the rest, and hoped his descendants would be the same. In his will he granted leases to eight families for their lives and besought all his heirs to be kind to their tenants "and not to turn out old possessors to get a little more rent". If he could have endured the drudgery as he enjoyed the pride of being a landlord, he would have been happier; but he was not the sort of man to sacrifice a love of notoriety for a sense of obligation.

Ambition "has ever raged in my veins like a fever", he wrote, and his main desire in life had been the achievement of wealth and eminence in the world of affairs, in place of which he had been compelled to assuage his sense of failure with the celebrity of an author. He would have suffered less disappointment if he had acted in accordance with Johnson's wise maxim: "Nature sets her gifts on the right hand and on the left." Human beings must take their choice. If they refuse, they will receive nothing. If they snatch at both, each will elude them. Had he known anything about himself, Boswell would have recognised that he was a born writer. Instead he thought that he could make a better thing of politics than his one-time college acquaintance Henry Dundas, who became in effect the dictator of Scotland. Boswell's nature totally unfitted him for the life of a politician, which largely consists of leaping prudently from tuft to tuft in the quagmire of affairs. Boswell's eye was too uncertain for this class of activity. Misjudging the distance between the tufts, he would soon have been sucked into the bog, a creditable but uncomfortable conclusion. Yet he yearned to be a leading figure in Parliament; and when Fox brought in a Bill imposing restrictions on the East India Company, Boswell fancied it would undermine the prestige of the Crown, and in 1784 published an absurd *Letter to the People of Scotland*, which was merely an excuse to parade his own patriotism. He sent a copy to Pitt, who acknowledged it in handsome terms. In 1785 he published another *Letter* to his countrymen, criticising the proposed decrease in the number of Scottish law lords, and dragging in the names of his more notable friends. His next letter appeared in a newspaper, the readers of which were informed that Boswell had the situation well in hand. "Be not afraid," he comforted his fellow-Scots, "I am *upon the spot*. I am *upon the watch*. The bill *shall not pass* . . . Collect your minds. Be calm; but be firm. You shall hear from me at large a few days hence."

For a while it looked as if Dundas would help him to a seat in Parliament, but nothing came of it, and some years afterwards Boswell pardoned the man who had by then become the Lord Advocate in words that would scarcely have softened the heart of a politician: "I was fortunate enough to become convinced that politics was the strongest poison in the human mind, and would insensibly instigate excellent men to do very wrong things. I excused your Lordship's ardent ambitious conduct. I upon my honour forgave you . . . " On a later occasion, under the benign influence of claret, Dundas promised his support and even said that he would speak to Pitt about an appointment; but when Boswell reminded him of this, he hinted that the promise only existed in the other's whimsical mind; upon which his assistance was again uselessly invoked by the implied criticism in a passage of Boswell's reply: "As to your compliment on my lively fancy, it has never yet exerted itself in inventing facts; nor am I one of those who are blessed with an accommodating memory which can recollect or invent facts as it may suit self-interest for a time." It is not surprising that Dundas declined to aid a man who mixed such punches with his appeals; and Boswell's tireless efforts to represent his county in Parliament were unsuccessful. As we know, Boswell was not of a piece. Independence and servility, like all the other opposites, were equally mixed in him, and he could never be depended upon to do or say the right thing at the right moment.

The death of Johnson gave him something to think about besides politics and the English Bar. The news of the Doctor's decease did not melt him with grief; it stupefied him, leaving him torpid and tearless. He had arranged a supper-party that evening, did not put it off, and behaved as if nothing had happened. It would be absurd to say that any death could drive him to drink, because life did that without any extraneous assistance, but now he began more frequently to drink himself blind, or, more exactly, unconscious, and the periods when he felt frigidly indifferent to all spiritual and religious emotion increased in number and length. Apart from his wife, Johnson was his chief prop, his rod and his staff, and he experienced the momentary stupefaction of one whose hand searches vainly for a support that has been removed, not the sorrow of one who has lost an intimate friend. But he quickly perceived that there were compensations. He would be able to publish his account of the tour to the Hebrides, and he could begin to arrange the material he had collected for the *Life* he had so long determined to write. Posterity was about to reap the reward of his social irresponsibility. Had he possessed a fairly consistent character instead of a wholly freakish nature, had he been a dependable and presentable human being, his gregarious virtues of gaiety and amiability would have earned him some sort of public position from the patrons of office. It is no exaggeration to say that we owe his best works not only to his unintegrated mentality but to the consequent deterioration of his morale. At this moment of his life Pitt or Dundas might have given him a job that would have prevented the composition of his books on Johnson and left his memorials of the Doctor in his journals, which, but for his reputation as a biographer, would almost certainly have been destroyed by his family. When a writer takes to politics, it is worse than taking to drink, so far as his literary output goes. Fortunately for us, Boswell remained faithful to the bottle, and though in his heart he longed for worldly distinction it is doubtful whether he could have remained sober even to become an ambassador.

Though he still hoped for a legal or political appointment, he started to collect Johnsoniana from all who had known his subject, and in the spring of 1785 went to London, expecting to get some legal work and intending to polish off his Hebridean *Tour*, in which he was greatly helped by Edmund Malone, an Irishman of independent means who was slowly preparing an edition of Shakespeare for the press, and who delighted in Boswell's high spirits and good humour. On 20th May Boswell attended a Court levée in a scarlet suit and had a short talk with the King about Johnson. He was much concerned over the correct description of Charles Edward Stuart in the account of the Young Pretender to be given in his book, and wrote to ask the King's advice. On 15th June he again appeared at Court, and put the question to George III, saying that he thought the word 'Pretender' ungentlemanly, wondering whether he should refer to him as 'Prince Charles' or as 'the grandson of King James II', and incidentally mentioning that he was Charles Edward's distant cousin, leaving the King to conclude that he and Boswell were related. His Majesty replied that it was immaterial to him, as the Hanoverian House had the right of sovereignty in view of James the Second's abdication, the Protestant succession, and so on. While in London Boswell witnessed several public hangings, drank much wine, enjoyed intercourse with several women, sat for his portrait to Sir Joshua Reynolds, and finished the book on his Scottish trip with Johnson.

Its publication brought a furious letter from Sir Alexander Macdonald, whose hospitality to the travellers at Skye was criticised, and who had no difficulty in identifying himself as the Scottish chieftain who inspired several caustic comments by the travellers. He accused Boswell of outraging the laws of hospitality, of behaviour without precedent in the records of civilisation. Many phrases in his letter were so insulting that Boswell felt his honour demanded a duel. But he hated the thought of shooting anyone, still more the thought of being shot, and he got his friends to act as intermediaries, sent a written apology for the opprobrious passages in his book, and gave Macdonald permission to publish it on condition that no use whatever was made of the insulting sentences in the letter which the other had written. At first Macdonald shilly-shallied, but when Boswell, shaking inwardly, sent a challenge to a duel at the ring in Hyde Park, the Highland chieftain weakened and agreed to suppress the objectionable remarks in his letter, Boswell at the same time undertaking to omit certain strictures from the second edition of his work. On both sides honour was satisfied, and dishonour dissatisfied.

In 1786, Boswell decided to transport his family to London. During the spring he was alone in the house he had taken for them at 56 Great Queen Street, and as he had just ended his liaison with Caroline Rudd, an intimacy that had lasted with intermissions for ten years, he felt at a loose end. He attended the courts at Westminster Hall, worked with Malone on his *Life of Johnson*, and could not make up his mind whether it was wise to leave the Scottish for the English Bar. He was elated when in July he received a card from Lord Lonsdale asking him to dine off a turtle one day the following week. Here at last was the opportunity for which he had been waiting, not to say baiting, since a page in his second *Letter* to the Scots was devoted to a sustained eulogy of Lonsdale as the hope of the nation.

Sir James Lowther, first Earl of Lonsdale, having inherited various estates, was the largest and most influential landowner in the north of England. Four years older than Boswell, he had turned politics to his own use, and had nine parliamentary seats at his disposal, the members representing them being known as his "Ninepins". To gain his patronage it was necessary to lick his boots; to keep it, the licking had to be continuous; and the slightest hint of independence resulted in the perpetual banishment of the offender. Only a natural parasite could put up with his tyranny and his tantrums. He was known throughout Cumberland and Westmorland as "the bad Earl", and had the reputation of being "more detested than any man alive". Those who knew him well considered him mad, though he was too rich to be locked up. He fought duels against inoffensive antagonists because they refused to do as he wished, being dreaded by his opponents as much as he was loathed by his dependants. When not engaged in the business of politics for his own ends, he backed Lord George Gordon, no doubt feeling sympathy with a fellow-lunatic, opposed the war with America, probably for the purpose of annoying the Ministry conducting it, and forced the electors of Appleby to make William Pitt their Member of Parliament, certainly with the intention of giving him orders, a design thwarted by Pitt's adoption three years later by the University of Cambridge.

Altogether Lonsdale was the type of man that anyone but a born sycophant would have avoided like the plague; but the bare chance of securing the patronage of the powerful owner of Lowther Castle made Boswell feel that his ambitions were about to be realised. The possibility that the invitation was a stratagem made him cautiously plead a prior engagement; but he was soon informed that his published praise of Lonsdale had caught the eye of that nobleman, who saw the likelihood of capturing a willing slave with a ready pen and a glib tongue, and gave him employment as counsel at the forthcoming Carlisle election. At the end of 1787 Boswell applied to Lonsdale for the Recordership of Carlisle, received the appointment in January of the following year, and his servitude commenced.

Margaret Boswell hated London and begged her husband to live at Auchinleck. She was the victim of consumption, and experienced the variations of that complaint, sometimes feeling quite well, sometimes being prostrated by weakness. As usual Boswell halted between two opinions. He felt it was cruel to keep his wife in London, but thought it advisable for him to stay there. At last the state of her health necessitated her return to Auchinleck, and he began to spend as much time there as he could, though he was frequently absent on the Northern Circuit, or acting as Recorder at Carlisle, or running round after Lonsdale, or collaborating with Malone on the Johnson biography in London. Disliking the rats which scampered about the house in Great Queen Street, he moved to a pleasanter residence in Queen Anne Street West. His two boys went to a school in Soho Square, his daughter Veronica remained with him, while the other girls lived with their mother at Auchinleck. Though constantly agitated by the condition of his wife, he continued to appear at Westminster Hall in the hope of work that never came, to dance attendance on Lonsdale in the expectation of a seat in Parliament which never materialised, to go on circuit as a briefless barrister, to labour with Malone, to make vows of temperance, and to drink himself silly. He sometimes felt remorseful over the long periods of absence from his wife, but consoled himself with the thought that "tenderness should yield to the active engagements of ambitious enterprise".

Such was the progress of his life until the spring of 1789, when, hearing that his wife was extremely ill, he went north with Veronica. Before leaving he described his appearance at Court in a letter to Temple: "I was the *great man* (as we used to say) at the late drawing-room in a suit of imperial blue lined with rose-coloured silk, and ornamented with rich gold-wrought buttons. What a motley scene is life." He found his wife's health worse than he had expected, with no hope of recovery, and he was in despair, accusing himself of having treated her badly in the past, of having stayed out late at night drinking when she was ill, of having wakened her needlessly when he got back. Even now, when she was at death's door, he spent many hours of conviviality away from home, and once, riding back in the dark, fell off his horse and hurt his shoulder. While laid up as a result of this accident he heard that Lonsdale wished for his company from Lowther to London, where he would have to appear as Recorder for the Corporation of Carlisle in a case brought against them at Westminster Hall. His wife encouraged him to go, and in pain he went, still expecting that his patron would give him a seat in Parliament. Soon after he reached London he heard that his wife was dying. With his two sons he left on 4th June. They travelled by post-chaise day and night, reaching Auchinleck in just over sixty-four hours, only to find that Margaret Boswell had died early in the morning of the day they set out. "I cried bitterly and upbraided myself for leaving her, for she would not have left me," he wrote to Temple. " . . . I could hardly bring myself to agree that the body should be removed, for it was still a consolation to me to go and kneel by it, and talk to my dear dear Peggie." He found relief in reading the funeral service over her coffin in the presence of his two boys, and was gratified to observe that nineteen carriages, together with a large body of horsemen and tenants, followed the hearse. He wrote a short description of her character, which was orally delivered by the minister at the next Sunday service.

No woman could have been a better wife for the man he was. Though she had sometimes hotly reproached him for infidelity and insobriety, she had recognised his mental and physical flabbiness and treated him as a child whose naughtiness was the obverse of his winsomeness. Moreover he appealed to her maternal instinct, just as he appealed to Johnson's paternal instinct, and both were gratified by his dependence on their protectiveness. Margaret never ceased to love him, despite his total lack of consideration for her in several important respects, because of his agreeable qualities as a companion, his fondness, his kindness, his cheerfulness, and his complete reliance on her. His misery when she died partly reflected his consciousness of the unhappiness he had caused her in life, but was chiefly due to the loss of the mainstay of his existence, the only person in whom he could confide all his successes and failures, all his joys and griefs, and from whom he had never failed to receive stimulation or consolation. In a sense he went to pieces after her death; in a deeper sense he had always been in pieces; but thenceforth there would be no one to put them together and give his life some sort of shape, however momentary and insubstantial.

He remained at Auchinleck for nine or ten weeks, during which he stood for Parliament as a candidate for his own county, but was defeated by Dundas's nominee. He left home to join the Northern Circuit at Carlisle, but he told Temple that his mind "was so sore from my late severe loss that I shrunk from the *rough* scene of the roaring, bantering society of lawyers", and Lonsdale allowed him to stay at Lowther Castle. There was a large house-party and he had to share a bedroom with two other guests. The next morning he could not find his wig, and a prolonged search failed to discover it. In those days a man without a wig on his head was as queer an object as he would be today if he wore one, and Boswell, in a nightcap, could not join a party that picnicked on the banks of a lake, nor take part in the dance that night. "I was in a ludicrous situation," he wrote to Temple. "I suspected a wanton trick, which some people think witty, but I thought it very ill-timed to one in my situation." Finding himself an object of mirth, he rode twenty-five miles to Carlisle, where he got a wig fitted in a few hours. Then he went to stay for two nights at Rose Castle, the residence of his friend John Douglas, Bishop of Carlisle, before returning to Lowther "to show that I am not at all in a pet". Lonsdale, who called himself "Your friend" in a letter to Boswell, must have felt that ridiculing a bereaved man was an act of friendship. After enjoying his joke for some weeks, the Lowther corridors ceased to ring with laughter, and the wig was handed back to its owner.

Boswell was now indulging in the luxury of grief. Everything in the world seemed "stale, flat and unprofitable", and he wanted to die. He knew that he was constitutionally unfit for any employment and that only the *Life of Johnson* kept him going: "I cannot express to you, Temple, what I suffer from the loss of my valuable wife and the mother of my children. While she lived, I had no occasion almost to think concerning my family. Every particular was thought of by her, better than I could. I am the most helpless of human beings. I am in a state very much that of one in despair", which of course called for alcoholic sustenance. His eldest daughter Veronica was placed with a widow in London, and eventually ran his house. His second daughter Euphemia went to an Edinburgh boarding-school. His youngest Betsy boarded at a Chelsea school; and a friend of hers, aged fourteen, was once upset because Boswell's bibulous demonstrations of fondness while she was enjoying his hospitality went beyond the limits of adult decorum. His elder son Sandie (Alexander) soon left the Soho Academy for Eton, which he detested at first, but eventually became reconciled to his lot. Boswell was delighted with his own reception by the headmaster, who asked him to dine at the Fellows' table. With his prandial bonhomie and classical quotations, he made what he thought "a creditable figure". His younger son James entered Westminster School, loathing it at the start but gradually adjusting himself to the conditions then universal in public schools, of magisterial flogging, adolescent bullying, galley-slave wretchedness, and general viciousness.

Boswell's children were not estranged by his tipsy habits, because of his sympathy and affection when sober, but they could scarcely be expected to revere a parent who sometimes had to be steered from one place to another, making more noise than all of them put together, and they were liable to oppose his will and ignore his instructions, which provoked him all the more since he knew that their attitude was due to his example. He perceived that he had no authority over them, and that such influence as he possessed came from their affection.

Another matter that troubled him and discouraged sobriety was the state of his finances. He frequently borrowed money, and as frequently lent it. His estate brought him in about £1,600 a year, of which something like £750 went in annuities, expenses of upkeep, and interest on debts. This left £850; and as his five children cost him about £500, he could only count on £350 himself. But when not in the depths of melancholy his gaiety broke forth in all sorts of ways; once by loudly calling the hours in the streets at night-time, his excuse being, when committed to the watch-house by a constable, that he had done so as a corrective to the watchman, who only called the half-hours.

The autumn of 1789 found him in London working hard on the Johnson book with the invaluable assistance of Malone, his efforts being frequently interrupted by Lonsdale's demands on his time. So complex and difficult were his labours on the biography that he confessed to Temple: "Many a time have I thought of giving it up." Meditation on Johnson brought to mind the revolution that had recently broken out in France, and he gave Temple the benefit of his views, calling the stormers of the Bastille "the ruffians in France who are attempting to destroy all order ecclesiastical and civil. The present state of that country is an intellectual earthquake, a whirlwind, a mad insurrection without any immediate cause, and therefore we see to what a horrible anarchy it tends. I do not mean that the French ought not to have a *Habeas Corpus* Act. But I know nothing more they wanted." He must have travelled through France with his eyes shut, possibly owing to his ingrowing toe-nails, for Goldsmith, who had seen the country at an earlier date, noted the starving peasants in the midst of aristocratic plenty, and would not have agreed that Utopia could be established with a *Habeas Corpus* Act. But Boswell was inclined to optimism when his liver was in good running order, and soon after writing his reflections on the French Revolution he was dining out nearly every day in different company and describing London as "a heaven upon earth—*comparatively*". He was offered "a cool thousand" for Johnson's *Life* and was tempted to take it, as he had purchased some land contiguous to his estate at Auchinleck; but he resisted the lure.

In May 1790, Temple was his guest in London, but they had scarcely enjoyed a good talk together before Boswell's presence was commanded by Lonsdale, then residing at Laleham on the Thames. Leaving Temple to look after himself, Boswell went to Laleham, where he was grossly insulted by Lonsdale, who accused him of keeping low company, instancing Reynolds. Announcing his pride in the eminent painter's friendship, Boswell inwardly determined to break away from Lonsdale; but within a few days he was glad to find himself again in the Earl's company. In June he was ordered to accompany the autocrat to Carlisle. He remonstrated on the ground that his greatest friend Temple was staying with him, but without success. Describing himself as utterly dislocated, he said that he would resign the Recordership.

Before they started for the north, Lonsdale cursed him in the presence of servants for not wanting to go, asked him what he did for his salary (£20 a year), said that if he fancied people enjoyed his company he deluded himself and that if he hoped for a seat in Parliament he had better abandon it, as Lonsdale never had the slightest intention of giving him one; and finally reminded him that he had solicited the office of Recorder and could not resign it until a successor was found. They then walked from the Earl's house in Grosvenor Square to his coach in Hanover Square, and as they went Boswell hinted that if he were in Parliament his independent views might not harmonise with those of his patron. Lonsdale was annoyed; but the worm had now turned and inside the coach Boswell persisted with his theme, which infuriated the Earl, who threatened a duel and asked the Recorder what sort of person he imagined himself to be. Boswell's reply that he was a gentleman and would prove himself to be a man of honour drove the other frantic, and there was a harrowing moment when Lonsdale implied that Boswell would soon appear to better advantage as a corpse. The duel would have taken place when they stopped at Barnet if Boswell had been able to borrow pistols, Lonsdale refusing to lend a brace; but after eating dinner they ate their words, and the rest of the journey to Lancaster passed without joviality.

A General Election was pending, and Boswell had to fulfil his duties at Carlisle in a despondent frame of mind, made less endurable by the return of a physical complaint to which custom had not immunised him, recently incurred perhaps in the London streets. At the end of June he sent in his resignation of the Recordership to the Mayor and aldermen of Carlisle, and, having withstood more abuse from his noble patron, cut himself free from the Lonsdale thraldom in the middle of July.

But he made one more bid for parliamentary distinction. On 9th November 1790 he sang a ballad of his own composition at the Lord Mayor's banquet in London. William Pitt, an honorary member of the Grocers' Company, had just managed to avoid a war with Spain over trade rights, and Boswell seized the opportunity to celebrate the achievement in verse, the chorus refrain running:

> There's a Grocer of London who watches our trade
> And takes care of th'Estate of JOHN BULL.

The song went well, and the singer received five encores. Pitt was present, and according to one account listened with gravity at the outset but joined in the general laughter as the chorus became more hilarious. Yet he felt no desire to reward such zeal, and he remained "reservèd and austere", or, as Boswell thought him, arrogant and ungrateful.

All the same, Boswell was "in great spirits" that month. He dined with Wilkes, who was cultivating his garden at Kensington Gore, where he occupied a pleasant house with his latest mistress and their daughter. Boswell had promised a friend to remain practically a teetotaller until 1st March, and he was limiting himself to four good glasses of wine during dinner and a pint after it. In spite of this severe regimen he managed to enjoy himself at the London Tavern, at dinner with Warren Hastings, and at various other places. A meeting of the Literary Club was spoilt because Burke monopolised the conversation with anathemas against the French Revolution. Boswell had once asked Burke to visit Auchinleck in order to view the caves and rocks. Burke had suggested that his friend's real desire was to show him the wine-vaults. But Boswell's wine was less intoxicating than political partisanship. The French Revolution had gone to Burke's head and made him drunk with passion.

A bad year ended badly. On 14th December, Boswell

presided at the Literary Club, and was "sadly mortified" because his nominee, General John Burgoyne, was blackballed. The success of the General's play *The Heiress* had not wiped out the memory of his failure as a soldier in the American War of Independence.

CHAPTER 28

The End of the Story

1791 WAS THE YEAR made memorable by the publication of a work that immortalised Johnson and Boswell. Three books had already appeared on the Doctor, causing his biographer considerable uneasiness: a *Life* by Sir John Hawkins, a collection of *Anecdotes* by Mrs. Piozzi, and the latter's correspondence with him. The work of Hawkins is remembered solely on account of an anecdote. It contained a single reference to "Mr. Boswell, a native of Scotland", who accompanied Johnson to the Hebrides. The said native called on Hawkins to remonstrate: "Surely, surely, Mr. *James* Boswell." Hawkins saw the point: "You would have had me say that Johnson undertook this tour with *The* Boswell." The reminiscences of the former Mrs. Thrale, if carefully sifted and checked with her original diary contain the best Johnsoniana outside Boswell and, taken in conjunction with the records of Fanny Burney, Anna Seward, Arthur Murphy and the sister of Sir Joshua Reynolds, give us a more informal and endearing portrait of Johnson than that of his chief biographer. Like Hawkins's book, Mrs. Piozzi's *Anecdotes* contain but one reference to "Mr. B——", who is reported as calling forth a severe remark by the Doctor about drinking. Boswell took full revenge for these slighting allusions by Hawkins and Hester in his book on Johnson. Mcreover he had staked a claim in the property of Johnson, and no one could be allowed to trespass on his preserves with impunity.

Fanny Burney saved herself from his malice by keeping quiet. He saw her at Windsor in 1790, when she was Queen Charlotte's

maid of honour, and rallied her: "I was told you were lost!—
closed in the unscalable walls of a royal convent. But let me
tell you, madam, it won't do. You must come forth, madam!
You must abscond from your princely monastery and come
forth. You were not born to be immured, like a tabby cat, in
yon august cell! We want you for the world! . . . You must
resign!—we can put up with it no longer." Having made it
clear that she was wasting her life, he next explained how she
could make reparation: "You must give me some of your
choice little notes of the Doctor's. We have seen him long
enough upon stilts; I want to show him in a new light. Grave
Sam, and great Sam, and solemn Sam, and learned Sam—all
these he has appeared over and over. Now I want to entwine
a wreath of the graces across his brow; I want to show him as
gay Sam, agreeable Sam, pleasant Sam; so you must help me
with some of his beautiful billets to yourself." He then pulled
out proofs of his book, and standing at the gate of the Queen's
Lodge began to read extracts of Johnson's conversation,
imitating the Doctor's voice and manner. The passers-by
paused to listen, and Fanny felt embarrassed. The approach
of the King and Queen drove her in panic from the spot. Like
so many others, Fanny found it difficult to resist Boswell's
comical manner, his oddity of speech and appearance, which
made people laugh with him and at him simultaneously; but
she was determined not to appear in his book, and reserved her
memorials of Johnson for herself.

All his friends helped and encouraged him with the work,
but early in 1790 he was deprived of one great source of comfort.
The National Assembly in Paris had granted complete freedom
to the Corsicans as citizens of France, and General Paoli had
been persuaded to return as Governor of the island. With his
departure another of Boswell's supports vanished, and no one
now remained on whose strength he could lean with the assurance that he would never be let down. Ultimately Paoli came
into collision with the French republicans, fought and beat

them with the aid of British troops, and the crown of Corsica was handed to George III. He returned to London in 1795, after Boswell's death, and a year later the British evacuated the island. Paoli lived, a pensioner of England, until 1807. He and Boswell never met again.

So far as the book on Johnson was concerned Boswell depended on the unremitting assiduity of Malone, whose temporary absence from London was described by his friend as "a severe stroke to me" and "a woeful want in all respects". Early in 1791 Boswell moved to 47 Great Portland Street, where melancholy again marked him for her own, and he was full of complaints. "Not only have I had a total distaste of life, but have been perpetually gnawed by a kind of mental fever. It is really shocking that human nature is liable to such inexplicable distress. O my friend!" he apostrophised Temple, "what can I do?" One thing he did was to buy a ticket in the English State Lottery, which enabled him to live in hopes, quickly blighted, of winning enough money to pay his debts. Another thing was to write and publish a silly piece in rhyme called *No Abolition of Slavery, or The Universal Empire of Love*, which he dedicated to "Miss B——", a lady named Miss Bagnall whom he thought of marrying, her income being six or seven hundred pounds a year. The doggerel dealt with the physical slavery of negroes and the spiritual slavery of passion, and he deplored the abolition of either. The collocation of the two in the same set of verses may explain why Burke, Pitt and Dundas remained unconvinced of Boswell's suitability for a responsible post.

A month after the printing of this drivel his *Life of Samuel Johnson* came out (16th May 1791). While the work was in progress he felt convinced that "my mode of biography . . . is the most perfect that can be conceived, and will be *more* of a *Life* than any work that has ever yet appeared", that "it will exhibit him more completely than any person ancient or modern has yet been preserved", and that "it will be the most

entertaining book that ever appeared". As the date of publication approached, he suffered qualms about its sale and still
wondered whether he had done well to refuse the "cool
thousand". He described his mental condition six weeks before
its issue in a letter to Temple: "I get bad rest in the night, and
then I brood over all my complaints—the *sickly mind* which I
have had from my early years—the disappointment of my
hopes of success in life—the irrevocable separation between me
and that excellent woman who was my cousin, my friend, and
my wife—the embarrassment of my affairs—the disadvantage
to my children in having so wretched a father—nay, the want
of *absolute certainty* of being happy after death, the *sure prospect*
of which is *frightful*. No more of this." Then he spoke of the
biography: "I am at present in such bad spirits that I have
every fear concerning it—that I may get no profit, nay, may
lose—that the public may be disappointed and think that I
have done it poorly—that I may make many enemies, and even
have quarrels. Yet perhaps the very reverse of all this may
happen." Next a mood of excitement possessed him at the
thought of meeting Miss Bagnall: "Here now, my Temple, I
am my fluttering self.—A scheme—an adventure seizes my
fancy." There were several more matrimonial projects in the
next two or three years, but none of them matured.

He need not have worried about the biography. It was well
received by both critics and public, and earned him about two
thousand pounds on a sale of as many copies. An author has to
run the gauntlet of posterity, and Boswell has survived the
ordeal with less damage than any other writer in English since
Shakespeare. But many of his contemporaries felt that he had
done a shocking thing in printing Johnson's remarks on living
people, and in taking down the conversation of fellow-guests at
dinner-parties, of fellow-members at a club. We have it on the
authority of Fanny Burney, Bishop Percy and others that he
was shunned by many previous acquaintances and excluded
from a number of respectable circles, because people were

frightened that he might report their unguarded talk. When he heard of one nervous case, he wrote to his informant "that the conversations of people in general are by no means of that nature as to bear being registered and that the task of doing it would be exceedingly irksome to me." On the larger issue he had Johnson on his side: "Sir, it is of so much more consequence that the truth should be told, than that individuals should not be made uneasy, that it is much better that the law does not restrain writing freely concerning the characters of the dead." However, the real complaint was not so much the truth that Boswell had written about Johnson as the retailing of the Doctor's unconsidered comments on those who were still alive to read them. A person with a less wayward and disconnected mind would have been more discreet, but indiscretion was an essential part of Boswell's equipment as man and writer: without it he would not have been the biographer to whom we are so much indebted. Yet it is easy to sympathise with some of his victims. Lady Diana Beauclerk must have learnt with some discomfort that Johnson considered her a whore; Reynolds probably winced on reading that Johnson thought he drank too much; Langton cannot have enjoyed being exhibited as a figure of derision; Hannah More may have resented the suggestion that Johnson's use of the word 'bottom' caused her to blush; Burke would have forgotten Johnson's praise of him and remembered that the Doctor questioned his political honesty, said he had never made a good joke in his life, and believed him capable of picking up a prostitute; while it is doubtful whether Wilkes laughed heartily over Johnson's view of him as an abusive scoundrel who ought to be "well ducked" by menials. No one minded Goldsmith being used as a target for Boswell's malice, but Oliver's old fellow-clubmen were more touchy about themselves.

It has been observed that Malone passed these indiscretions; but apart from the fact that Boswell may have fought and over-ruled him on some points, it is asking too much of human nature to expect a man to be as much concerned over his friend's reputation as his own. Besides, the effort of preparing such a work for the press was enough to excuse Malone from using a hawk's eye on every passage.

So many people objected to the manner in which they appeared in the *Life* that Boswell could have claimed one of the chief virtues of a biographer, commonly called 'bad taste'. His interest in human nature was so keen that he eagerly reported things that dismayed those who read them in print, for he believed that others were equally interested, and was quite as ready to expose his own oddities as theirs. His only serious departure from the truth was the quite unfounded suggestion that Johnson in his early London days had behaved like Boswell, who put it in this way:

> He owned to many of his friends, that he used to take women of the town to taverns, and hear them relate their history. In short, it must not be concealed, that, like many other good and pious men, among whom we may place the Apostle Paul upon his own authority, Johnson was not free from propensities which were ever "warring against the law of his mind",—and that in his combats with them, he was sometimes overcome.

According to himself Boswell's "sacred love of truth" compelled him to this disclosure on his subject's weakness, which he excused by quoting Johnson's remark to someone in Scotland: "Sir, are you so grossly ignorant of human nature as not to know that a man may be very sincere in good principles, without having good practice?" An explanation of Boswell's sanctity in this instance is simply that he wished to excuse his own conduct by showing that even so great and good a man as Johnson shared his frailty, though it is quite possible that he was unable to believe in a vigorous man's chastity. All knowledge of human nature derives from self-knowledge; and as Boswell's understanding of himself was restricted to the fact that he could not withstand temptation, his insight into the nature of others was unreliable.

Boswell, in fact, had little critical or selective sense, and this is his chief fault as a biographer. Believing that everything about his hero was interesting, he included many dull and unrevealing letters, many conversational repetitions, and many of Johnson's dictations about matters of no interest, interspersed with lengthy comments by the author, mostly of an infantile order; and the book is about twice as long as it ought to be, which may explain why it is almost unknown in foreign countries. Yet half of it is so fascinating that readers have been hypnotised into believing the whole is good. Boswell is really a great diarist, and whenever he is not personally on the scene the narrative lacks animation. The discourses and episodes for which he alone is responsible are unique in biographical literature, the longer conversations owing much to his ability to recreate the style of the speakers. Johnson once tested his method of shorthand to see how closely he could reproduce a passage read aloud at a rate much slower than that of ordinary talk. His copy was very imperfect; and we now know that many of his dialogues were largely helped by his excellent memory and mimicry, which, added to his remarkable gift of vivifying incidents and the nature of his subject, resulted in a great book, whatever its faults as a biography.

Still avid for renown in the law courts, he went "the full round of the Home Circuit" after the publication of his work, "and though I did not get a single brief, do not repent of the expence, as I am shewing myself desireous (*sic*) of business, and imbibing legal knowledge." Reynolds had obtained for him the honorary post of Secretary for Foreign Correspondence in the Royal Academy, which solaced him, but a visit to Auchinleck in the autumn of 1791 plunged him deeper than ever into "languour and gloom". His depression continued on returning to London, where he attended the courts at Westminster Hall without "the least prospect of my having business". In

February 1792 Sir Joshua Reynolds died, and his sense of desolation increased. More than ever he wanted the support of friendship, and he arranged to visit his friend Temple, now vicar of St. Gluvias, near Falmouth, in Cornwall. His reputation being considerable among literate folk, he decided to make a carefully planned progress through the western shires as "the Great Biographer", and advised several notabilities of his coming.

On 17th August 1792 he left London with his daughters Veronica and Euphemia, and on Saturday the 18th arrived at Salisbury in time for four o'clock dinner at the Bishop's Palace. He stayed two nights with the Bishop, John Douglas, recently of Carlisle, and went to see the cathedral as well as other ancient buildings. On Monday the 20th they breakfasted at Wilton with Lord Pembroke, who urged them to stay for dinner, which they did, spending that night at the Angel Inn, Shaftesbury. They received more hospitality at Exeter, and then proceeded via Bodmin and Truro to St. Gluvias, which in those days was separated from Penryn by an arm of the sea. Temple had four sons and two daughters. His wife Ann disliked Boswell, who reciprocated the feeling, thinking her drab, peevish and unsociable; but she may have been familiar with the sort of confidences he reposed in Temple, and a lot of women are averse to such interchanges between their husbands and other married men.

The Boswells stayed at St. Gluvias from 24th August to 11th September, being entertained by the neighbouring gentry. It rained almost continuously, and Boswell and Temple spent one wet day going through all the letters the former had written to his friend. Another time Boswell accompanied Temple's sons to the play at Falmouth. The theatre consisted of two rooms in a commonplace inn. Boswell's interest was not aroused by the performance but by the sight of a French girl he had known in London, sitting in a box with three foreigners. Since he thought her contemptible and avaricious, the nature of his previous dealings with her is sufficiently indicated. He took his daughters to see Land's End, staying the night at Penzance both going and returning. They visited St. Michael's Mount, and called on a friend at Redruth on their way back. On the whole he was fairly abstemious throughout their stay in Cornwall, though during the journey home they stopped at Lord Falmouth's place, Tregothnan, where both he and his host got tight, causing him to fear that his hostess might have considered his conduct rowdy.

They reached home at the beginning of October, and it soon became clear that his daughters had not been impressed by his general behaviour. In some way they slighted him, making him nag at them. Unable to exercise parental authority, he concluded that he should never have been married. It may have been due to them that he became far more cautious about his amatory experiences in his later journal. Girls are liable to pry. A few brief references suggest that his sexual potency was diminishing and that he made experiments on his domestic staff; but the prospect of discovery intimidated him, and he soon resolved to remain chaste under his own roof.

Having no professional work with which to occupy his time, he laboured philanthropically. Rochefoucauld and Johnson agree that there is no such thing as pure benevolence, that acts of apparent disinterest are performed with an admixture of selfish motives. The alloy in Boswell's altruism is easily defined. He wished to vindicate himself, to be of importance to someone else. Since he relied so much on the support of stronger natures, he liked to think that he was strong enough to support others; and his natural kindliness was reinforced by the spasmodic assertiveness of a weak man. There are several records of his beneficence. The case of the sheep-stealer John Reid, at the beginning of his career as a barrister, has already been mentioned; and two more instances at the close of his life claim attention. One day he came across a boy named John Constantin, who was sitting on some steps sobbing his heart out.

368

The lad was an apprentice to a tailor, who treated him cruelly. Boswell took a great deal of trouble to get him released from his master and part of the money paid for his indentures returned to his mother. The second case called for more sustained application and displays Boswell's impulsive generosity along with his craving to justify himself both in his own esteem and in the eyes of those he succoured.

Mary Broad, aged twenty-two, was sentenced to transportation for stealing a coat, and sailed with a gang of convicts for Botany Bay in 1787. She married another convict, William Bryant, who had resisted the attempts of revenue officers to appropriate smuggled property. After she had given birth to two children, they escaped from the penal settlement of Port Jackson in an open boat with seven other convicts, and after a series of terrifying experiences reached the Dutch island of Timor in ten weeks. The Governor at first believed their story that they were the survivors of a shipwreck, but clapped them in prison when a drunken member of their party gave the game away. They were handed over to an English naval captain, who put them in irons and sailed for home. On the journey two of the convicts died, one jumped overboard, and Mary's husband and children succumbed to the hardships. She was twenty-seven years of age when she arrived in England and again stood in the dock.

Boswell championed the cause of the convicts, and at once made an appeal to the Secretary of State, Dundas. He also approached the Under-Secretary and the Chief Clerk of that office. Considering the sufferings they had undergone, the Government did not intend to treat the escaped convicts harshly; but they were kept in Newgate prison, which they described as paradise after all they had endured. Boswell's efforts no doubt expedited their release. Mary was pardoned and freed in ten months, the rest of them six months later. Mary occupied a room in Little Titchfield Street, and Boswell collected subscriptions for her maintenance. Among others he called on Thurlow, the Lord Chancellor, who showed no sympathy at first but, moved by his eloquence, promised a donation and invited him to bring his daughters to dinner. But Boswell, sternly moral on the subject of legitimacy, would not let his daughters dine with the Lord Chancellor's bastards, and managed to sidetrack the invitation. Mary's parents wanted her to return home, and Boswell made all the arrangements for her sea-journey to Fowey in Cornwall. He took her by hackney-coach to Beale's Wharf, Southwark, where they had a bowl of punch in a public-house, and then accompanied her on board, paid for her passage and subsistence on the boat, gave her some money, and assured her that she could count on an annual allowance of ten pounds. He kept his promise and paid the sum out of his own pocket till the end of his life.

In November 1792 he gave a dinner to celebrate the success of the Johnson biography, but he did not feel elated. The after-effect of drink now plunged him into deeper gloom, and the more depressed he became the more he drank. The unvarying gaiety of an atheistical rake like Wilkes perplexed him. It never crossed his mind that a man, convinced that he would not have to answer for one life in another, and paying no attention to the laws ascribed by human beings to their Creator, could enjoy himself with an easy conscience as much as he pleased, acting solely in accord with his instinctive moral sense. Boswell's beliefs continually wavered with the fluctuations of his nature. Socially he remained the cheerful, amusing, adaptable man whose company had usually delighted Johnson, but the darker intervals were becoming longer and more frequent. Most of his old friends were dead; his later acquaintances were fickle; and the younger generation regarded him as a joke. Even his interest in life, which in the past had made him so agreeable, had become intermittent, and the one means of escaping from his thoughts was the bottle. But he was still able to dramatise himself. In February 1793 he announced to his oldest friend that he was off to Auchinleck, as the minister, his old tutor, the Rev. John Dun, had just died, and he had to approve the congregation's choice of a successor: "Only think, Temple, how serious a duty I am about to discharge. *I James Boswell Esq*! You know what vanity that name includes. I have promised to come down on purpose, and *his Honour's* goodness is gratefully acknowledged."

His Honour's need of seeing himself as an important figure in the drama of life, of receiving the sympathy of others with his defeats and their salutations for his victories, led him always to overact both misery and joy. His was the fancy of a child, not the imagination of a man, and in nothing else is the difference between himself and Johnson so clearly marked. Boswell's fancy turned molehills into mountains, and he wallowed in self-pity just as he revelled in self-aggrandisement. Johnson's melancholy was too deep and real to be indulged or dramatised. It was due to constant ill-health, and a vivid imagination which, warped at the source by his belief in a retributive deity, recognised the chasm between his genius and his achievement, and the constitutional sloth that prevented him from bridging it.

One night in June 1793, a few months after his journey north on ecclesiastical business, Boswell was attacked in Titchfield Street, knocked down, stunned, robbed, and left lying in the roadway. A passing stranger helped him home with the aid of a watchman. He had a nasty cut on the back of his head, both his arms were badly bruised, and he was laid up with a fever for two or three weeks. Temple read of the incident and took occasion to warn him of the risk of death whilst under the influence of drink. "This, however, shall be a *crisis* in my life," he replied. "I trust I shall henceforth be a sober, regular man. Indeed my indulgence in wine has, of late years especially, been excessive . . . Your suggestion as to my being carried off in a state of intoxication is awful. I thank you for it, dear friend. It impressed me much, I assure you." But the impression soon wore off.

He wished to visit Holland and Flanders that summer, and

stay at Valenciennes, the headquarters of the British army. The Allied forces were doing well against the French Republic, and he was anxious to inspect them. But first he went on the Home Circuit, and then visited Bennet Langton, who was on duty as a major in the militia at Warley Camp, where Johnson too had stayed. As he had not properly recovered from his misadventure, the noise in the camp got on Boswell's nerves; he could not sleep and he caught a cold. Leaving sooner than he had intended, he returned home, explaining why his departure had been so abrupt in a letter to Langton: "O London! London! there let me be; there let me see my friends; there a fair chance is given for pleasing and being pleased."

The second edition of his *Life of Johnson* had just appeared, and he took several copies to Eton for presentation to the headmaster and others, all of whom enjoyed his company and entertained him liberally. No doubt his experience at Warley Camp decided him not to visit Valenciennes; and in September 1793 Temple came to stay with him. Early in December he dined in a tavern with the members of the Royal Academy Club, returning home in a condition that impelled him almost at once to go out again, when he came a cropper in the street. Shortly discovering that he had lost £50 in notes, he went back to the tavern, where he fancied he had dropped them; but eventually they were found in his cabinet, where he must have placed them in the short interval between his arrival home and his exit therefrom. Another time he attended a city dinner, towards the close of which he passed out, and awoke the following morning without knowing how he had got home or to bed.

Still in hopes of picking up a wife with a steady income, his habits were against his chances. Though normally "his eyes were set at three i' the morning", they were sufficiently alert some hours later to spot a pretty girl. He noted one at the chapel of the Spanish Embassy, and followed her to see where she lived; but his courage and desire were diminishing, and he pushed the investigation no further. The year 1793 closed for him with a banquet on the twenty-fifth anniversary of the Royal Academy's foundation. He took part in the discussions, and would have enjoyed the whole evening if music had not interfered with talk.

A final chance of distinction presented itself in March 1794. British forces having defeated the French republicans in Corsica, it became clear that Great Britain would have to be represented by a Minister. In view of his friendship with Paoli, who would welcome him wholeheartedly, and the fact that he had made the island known to his countrymen, Boswell applied to Dundas for the post, saying that it would be agreeable to Paoli and the Corsicans if he were chosen, asserting that his qualifications were such "as almost to preclude competition", and mentioning that Sir John Dick, who for many years had been British Consul at Leghorn, supported his petition. But Dundas would not have become Viscount Melville if he had been the sort of man who acted on an impulse of generosity or gratitude. He replied in formal terms that Boswell's services were not required, and appointed Sir Gilbert Elliot as Commissary Plenipotentiary. Although he felt the slight keenly, Boswell was relieved, as he did not wish to quit the comparative paradise of London, the only place where a man had a fair chance of pleasing and being pleased.

His fitful interest in the human scene caused him to dine with all sorts and conditions of men. A session with Wilkes was followed by a decorous meal with the Bishop of London at Lambeth Palace, which was succeeded by a dinner at the Freemasons' Tavern, where the wine flowed more freely than at the episcopal table. In the spring of 1794 Temple again advised him to be more sober. "I *do* resolve *anew* to be upon my guard," came the customary response; "as I am sensible how very pernicious as well as disreputable such a habit is. How miserably have I yielded to it in various years." July saw him at Auchinleck, where he stayed until January 1795 and was as usual unhappy. "How hard it is that I do not enjoy this fine place," he lamented to his brother David, who wanted him to settle there. His daughters were with him, and for their sakes as well as his own he entertained as many people as possible. He also contrived to employ himself by sampling various liquors in his cellar and making notes of their several conditions.

Returning to London at the beginning of 1795, he asked some friends to dinner, at which a psychic phenomenon, then the subject of controversy, was discussed. No doubt he dined out frequently, but he had stopped making entries in his journal by this time. In the middle of April he went to a meeting of the Literary Club, but before it broke up he felt so ill that he had to be taken home and put to bed. When able to do so he started to write a letter to Temple, but after the first sentence he was too weak to continue and he dictated the rest to his son James, who thenceforth kept Temple apprised of his father's condition.

Boswell was in great pain owing to a tumour in the bladder, and from the first his recovery seemed improbable. Some days later the pain left him and he felt much better. Then came an attack of fever, severe shivering, a violent headache, and much sickness. On 24th April he was well enough to dictate a letter to Warren Hastings on his acquittal. His physician, he said, had now given him the pleasing assurance that his sufferings were nearly at an end—as indeed they were, though not perhaps in the sense the doctor had intended; and Boswell promised himself the pleasure, the moment he could leave the house, of flying to Hastings and expanding his "soul in the purest satisfaction". But it was not to be. He grew steadily weaker, could take no nourishment, and when lifted out of bed he fainted. Early on 19th May 1795 he died, in the presence of his brother David, his two sons and his two elder daughters.

His body was taken to Auchinleck, where his spirit had never been at rest.

Bibliography

JOHNSON

The Life of Samuel Johnson, LL.D., by JAMES BOSWELL.

The Journal of a Tour to the Hebrides with Samuel Johnson, by JAMES BOSWELL.

A Journey to the Western Islands of Scotland, by SAMUEL JOHNSON.

The Letters of Samuel Johnson, collected and edited by R. W. CHAPMAN, 3 vols., 1952.

Thraliana: The Diary of Mrs. Hester Lynch Thrale (later Mrs. Piozzi), 1776–1809, 2 vols., edited by KATHARINE C. BALDERSTON, 1942.

Johnsonian Miscellanies (including Mrs. Piozzi's Anecdotes, Arthur Murphy's biography, and much else), 2 vols., edited by GEORGE BIRKBECK HILL, 1897.

Diary and Letters of Madame D'Arblay (Fanny Burney), 6 vols., 1904.

Memoirs of Dr. Burney, by MADAME D'ARBLAY, 3 vols., 1832.

The French Journals of Mrs. Thrale and Dr. Johnson, edited by MOSES TYSON and HENRY GUPPY, 1932.

Letters of Anna Seward, 1784–1807, edited by A. CONSTABLE, 6 vols., 1811.

Dr. Johnson and Mrs. Thrale, by A. M. BROADLEY, 1910.

Young Samuel Johnson, by JAMES L. CLIFFORD, 1955.

Samuel Johnson, by HUGH KINGSMILL, 1933.

Samuel Johnson, by JOSEPH WOOD KRUTCH, 1945.

Mrs. Thrale of Streatham, by C. E. VULLIAMY, 1936.

BOSWELL

The Private Papers of James Boswell from Malahide Castle, edited by GEOFFREY SCOTT and FREDERICK POTTLE, 18 vols., 1928–34.

Letters of James Boswell, collected and edited by CHAUNCEY BREWSTER TINKER, 2 vols., 1924.

Boswell's London Journal, 1762–3, edited by FREDERICK A. POTTLE, 1950.

Boswell in Holland, 1763–4, edited by FREDERICK A. POTTLE, 1952.

Boswell on the Grand Tour (Germany and Switzerland), 1764, edited by FREDERICK A. POTTLE, 1953.

Boswell on the Grand Tour (Italy, Corsica and France), 1765–6, edited by FRANK BRADY and FREDERICK A. POTTLE, 1955.

Boswell in Search of a Wife, 1766–9, edited by FRANK BRADY and FREDERICK A. POTTLE, 1957.

Young Boswell, by C. B. TINKER, 1922.

The Journal of a Tour to Corsica and Memoirs of Pascal Paoli, by James Boswell, edited by MORCHARD BISHOP, 1951.

Who's Who in Boswell, by J. L. SMITH-DAMPIER, 1935.

Boswell and the Girl from Botany Bay, by FREDERICK A. POTTLE, 1938.

James Boswell, by C. E. VULLIAMY, 1932.

The Hooded Hawk, or the Case of Mr. Boswell, by D. B. WYNDHAM LEWIS, 1946.

Index

[NOTE.—*To avoid overloading the entries on* Johnson, Samuel *and* Boswell, James (*referred to respectively as* J. *and* B. *throughout the index, except under the titles of their published works*), *wherever a sensible alternative heading is equally applicable it has been preferred. E.g. references to their dealings with their friends, etc., will be found under those friends' names only, Boswell's Corsican activities only under* Corsica; *and even certain abstract characteristics applicable to both persons, such as* Melancholia *and* Religious beliefs, *are indexed under the abstract, not the personal, heading.*]

377